THE ROAD TO WEALTH

Paul Clitheroe is a founding director of ipac securities, one of Australia and New Zealand's best-known research and investment houses, and has been involved in the investment industry since he graduated from the University of New South Wales in the late 1970s. He has completed the two-year postgraduate course offered by the Securities Institute and in 1999 was made a Fellow of that professional body. He was a board member of the Financial Planning Association of Australia between 1992 and 1994; in 1993 he was elected the Vice President and in 1994, the President. He has completed the FPA's two-year diploma course and holds the Association's highest professional designation of CFP (Certified Financial Planner).

Since 1993 he has been hosting the prime-time Channel 9 program 'Money' and he is the Chairman and Chief Commentator of *Money Magazine*. He has been a media commentator and conference speaker for over fifteen years and is the author of the best-selling *Making Money*.

THE ROAD TO
WEALTH

PAUL CLITHEROE

Securing your financial future

VIKING

Viking
Penguin Books Australia Ltd
487 Maroondah Highway, PO Box 257
Ringwood, Victoria 3134, Australia
Penguin Books Ltd
Harmondsworth, Middlesex, England
Penguin Putnam Inc.
375 Hudson Street, New York, New York 10014, USA
Penguin Books Canada Limited
10 Alcorn Avenue, Toronto, Ontario, Canada M4V 3B2
Penguin Books (NZ) Ltd
Cnr Rosedale and Airborne Roads, Albany, Auckland, New Zealand
Penguin Books (South Africa) (Pty) Ltd
5 Watkins Street, Denver Ext 4, 2094, South Africa
11, Community Centre, Panchsheel Park, New Delhi 110 017, India

First published by Penguin Books Australia Ltd 2001

10 9 8 7 6 5 4 3 2 1

Designed by Melissa Fraser, Penguin Design Studio
Typeset in 12.5/15 Apollo by Midland Typesetters, Maryborough, Victoria
Printed and bound in Australia by Australian Print Group
Maryborough, Victoria

National Library of Australia
Cataloguing-in-Publication data:

Clitheroe, Paul.
The road to wealth: securing your financial future.

Includes index.
ISBN 0 670 87543 0.

1. Finance, Personal – Australia. I. Title.

332.02400994

www.penguin.com.au

contents

acknowledgements

While my books are driven by my commonsense views on money, many people helped out with their expertise in specialist areas. But before I acknowledge them, I would like to thank Anthony O'Brien who spent eighteen months checking out facts and figures, finding new sources of information, contributing a large number of ideas for this book and excerpts from some of his articles for *Money Magazine*, and then working with my editor Heather Cam to pull the entire book together. Prior to working on this book Anthony held a range of communication roles for companies such as IBM, BT Australia and Link Telecommunications. He has also worked in government and as a PR consultant. Anthony has a BA in history, an MA in Political Economy from Macquarie University, and has undertaken postgraduate courses in marketing, economics and public affairs.

My company ipac securities and its technical team supplied much advice and assistance, as did ASSIRT, APRA, ASX, the Australian Taxation Office, the Australian Bureau of Statistics, ASIC, Pam Walkley, Harold Bodinnar, Peter Bobbin, David Wood, Diana Olsberg, Martin Schoeddert, David

Wesney, David Welfare, Vince Kernahan and Jim Kilkenny. Special thanks is due to Chris Walker, in particular for his substantial contribution to Chapter 4. Also my thanks to my personal assistant at ipac, Jodie Williamson, who coordinated the typescript.

I would also like to acknowledge Glyn Davies whose work, *History of Money from Ancient Times to the Present Day* (University of Wales Press, 1996), served as a source for a number of the 'Money in History' boxes.

Special thanks
This book would not have been possible without my wife Vicki and my children: Marcus, Jordi and Ellie. Money is important, but the love and support of my family are invaluable.

introduction

I have wanted to write this book for a long time.

It is about the new world. No, not the world of dot com companies, most of which had collapsed by the start of 2001, but the real world. Experts can prattle on about money and economic theory all they want, but let's face it, *we* are the economy. How we feel and what we do determines the direction of our economy. Our confidence (or lack of it) drives the booms and busts.

What fascinates me is that for the first time in human history, the vast percentage of us no longer thinks that life is simply about working and dying. We are spending more time at school or university, having fewer children, investing earlier, focussing on lifestyle and planning to stop work earlier. Because of improvements in medicine and our attention to our health, we are living longer and retiring at a time when we are still active and enthusiastic.

This is very exciting. But what concerns me is how important our dreams and acting on them are to achieving success in life. I hear terrific stories about how we hope to live in the future, but of course, we want it all today as well.

My best-selling book, *Making Money*, is about the mechanics of investment. If you have already read it, *The Road to Wealth* provides an excellent extension. But while you certainly don't have to read *Making Money* to easily follow what will be said in these pages, you should know that *The Road to Wealth* takes a more philosophical view. I feel more strongly than ever that people all too often fail to achieve their financial goals not because they don't understand the basics of money (though many don't!), but because they simply won't build their finances as they would build a house: from the foundations up. And those foundations rest on an examination of what we value in life and what kind of life we would like to lead in the future.

I hope this book encourages you to think more about what is important to you, to have a clear vision of what you want your life to be like, and to allow you to develop a solid financial foundation.

It is very obvious to me that financially successful people are not those who earn the highest incomes. In fact many successful people earn relatively low incomes. A common theme in those who succeed is knowing what's happening and changing in the world around them, what they want to achieve, and having a solid plan which enables them to do so.

If you are after miracle solutions my best advice to you is not to buy this book. But if you want to put in a bit of effort to be financially successful, *The Road to Wealth* will go a long way to helping you to achieve your goals.

chapter 1

CHANGING TIMES

We've changed. And our world has changed.

Sure, change is inevitable, but today the speed of change can be quite frightening and exciting. Prior to the Industrial Revolution in the late 1700s, the world still changed, but at a relatively slow rate. Financial security came from owning land and having lots of children. The land provided an income and your children took care of you in your declining years.

The Industrial Revolution brought vast changes as people left the land and crowded into cities and towns to work in mills and factories. The jobs created were many – but they were often tough, dirty and repetitive. By the late 1800s many people had determined to save and escape the factory jobs by opening a corner store, or taking up a trade to service the growing middle classes.

In more recent times, we've developed the idea of saving so that we can enjoy some leisure in our later years and one day stop working altogether. Over thousands of years of human history, this dream has only been possible for the chosen few – the very rich top 1% of the population. But suddenly, the vast majority of the population (me included) decided that working forever was a pretty silly idea.

The ability to make this choice was driven by a number of factors. First, there was the fact that high inflation in the late 1970s and 80s drove up property values, meaning that a mortgage taken out in the late 1950s or 60s was basically irrelevant, even if not paid off.

Secondly, there was the safety net supplied by the age-pension system which had been introduced after World War I. While it has never provided a champagne lifestyle, until the introduction of the income test and then the assets test in the early 1980s, it provided a very handy 'top up' to males aged 65 and over and to females aged 60 and over, regardless of their wealth or income. Today, even after restricting it to those more in need, the age pension on its own still provides a modest standard of living to people who have accumulated limited or no savings or assets during their working lives. If you own a home, you are able to live reasonably well – so long as owning a car, travelling or eating out on a regular basis are not included in your list of activities.

Money in History

3000–2000 BC

Banking originates in Babylonia out of the activities of temples and palaces that provided safe places for the storage of valuables. Initially deposits of grain are accepted and later other goods including cattle, agricultural implements, and precious metals were used as a medium of exchange.

Let's pause and take a look at some facts about our population. If you are not yet retired and are counting on living on just the pension with no additional savings, I've got some bad news for you.

If current trends continue, two decades from now we can all expect to spend far less of our lives in the work force than out of it. According to the Australian Bureau of Statistics (ABS), those older than 65 years (the traditional age for retirement) are increasing both in number and as a proportion of the total population. Current life expectancy according to the ABS is 75.9 years for males and 81.5 years for females.

In Australia, the current age-pension age of 65 years for males was set in 1909, when it was above the average life expectancy at birth (just under 60 years of age). In essence, early this century people were expected to work until they died and only a very small proportion of individuals lived long enough to obtain government support in their old age. The age pension was meant to be a safety net for the very old, not a long-term lifestyle support system for the masses. How things have changed!

Although today life expectancy is considerably higher (75 years or more), the age at which we are eligible for the age pension remains unchanged. With more and more people retiring at 55, modern-day Australians can expect to be out of the work force for some 15 to 40 years, and on average for 20-plus years!

The baby boomers were born between 1946 and 1964.

In 1998, older people (those over 65 years of age) comprised 12% of the population, whilst ABS projections indicate that this figure will increase to almost a quarter of the population (21.3%) by 2031, when the youngest of the baby boomer generation will have already turned 65.

So what does this mean? Well, the implication is that we

Population Trends in Australia (1989 to 2051)

Statistics	1989	1994	1998	2011#	2031#	2051#
Total population (000's)	16,814	17,855	18,751	21,017	23,720	24,945
% of population aged 0–14	22.2	21.6	20.9	18.3	16.5	15.6
% of population aged 15–64	66.9	66.6	66.9	67.7	62.2	60.2
% of population aged 65–80	11	11.8	12.2	14	21.3	24.2
% of population aged 80+	2.1	2.5	2.8	3.7	5.8	8.4
Median age (years)*	31.8	33.4	34.6	38.3	42.2	44.1

\# Projections
* Median age represents the age at which half the population is younger and half is older
Source: ABS, 'Australian Social Trends 1999'

aren't going to be able to depend on the government to fund our retirement in the future – and certainly not to the standard we dream about.

As the population that is aged 65 and over increases in size over the next 30 years, the Australian labour force is projected to grow at a slower rate. The ABS projects that by 2016 the annual labour force growth could slow to as little as 0.4%.

Traditionally, the taxes paid by Australia's work force have supplied the funding for the aged pension. However, according to the Centre on Ageing and Retirement at the University of New South Wales, by 2011, when the first of the baby boomers turn 65, they will need to provide for the majority of their own retirement funding and won't be able to depend on significant government support.

So, the point of all this is something you probably already knew. If you want a decent standard of living, you're going to need to provide the funds for it yourself.

Australia's population is projected to grow to between 23.5 million and 26.4 million by the year 2051, a potential rise of 7.9 million or 42% from the 1997 population of 18.5 million. Although the rate of growth varies at different times during the projection period, there is a clear long-term trend declining from 1.2% in 1996–97 to between 0.0% and 0.3% by 2051.

The United Nations' projections show the world's population increasing by 72% between 1995 and 2050 and present prospects of a widening gap in terms of population size between South-East Asian countries and Australia. Indonesia, already 10 times Australia's population could increase to nearly 319 million or 12 times Australia's population.

Source: ABS Population Projections, 1997 to 2051

It's easy to get gloomy about money, but what this information tells me is:

- I am likely to live to a ripe old age.
- Chances are, I'll be in good health.
- There are millions of people like me who feel that work is just one part of life, not your entire life, so, if I want to be semi-retired by age 55, I'll have plenty of people with whom I can travel, do courses, have over for a drink, and meet to play a game of tennis or golf.

Now you'll get no argument from me that there's not much point in living in retirement or semi-retirement for 20 or 30 years if you've got no money. I'd rather keep on working. But let's face it, living longer and working longer sounds like a more flexible option than being dead.

The current generation of retirees, thanks to the inflation-inspired boost to the value of their homes and access to an age pension, are travelling reasonably well. But most are certainly not living a life of luxury, in fact a 'snapshot' of their income is rather stark, despite all the positive noises made about inflation and superannuation.

Older people (65 and over) live independent, active, healthy lives and are involved in a wide range of social, leisure and community activities. Compared with other age groups they have more free time and in 1997 spent about 6.5 hours per day on leisure activities ranging from reading and watching TV to sport. In 1995, over 100,000 older people provided 24 million hours of voluntary work to the community. Older people play an important role as carers, often looking after grandchildren, people with disabilities and other older people.

Older people are generally healthy with 2 in 3 rating their health as good to excellent and they are keen to maintain their health with over half exercising regularly.

Projections also show that the ageing of Australia will continue. This is the inevitable result of fertility remaining at low levels over a long period. As growth slows, the population ages progressively with the median age of 34 years in 1997 rising to 40 to 41 years in 2021 and to 44 to 46 years in 2051.

By 2051, between 24% and 26% of Australia's population is projected to be aged 65 years or over, compared with 12% in 1997. The highest annual rates of growth for this age group occur between 2011 and 2021 when the peak of the baby boom generation enters it.

Source: ABS, 'NSW Older Population – Their Story', (Cat. No. 4108.1)

RETIREE INCOME

Apply a bit of basic maths to the following table and it shows that 3.4% of the 1.9 million or so Australians aged over 65, have $36,349 and above a year to spend. This would represent a comfortable retirement. Quite frankly, to live on $15,548 or less a year looks pretty tough to me, yet this is what 82.1% of retirees are doing, leaving the 14.5% on $15,549 to $36,348, as those somewhere in the middle.

Income of Retired Australians Aged Over 65

Annual income	Percentage
Less than $6,188*	7.3
$6,189–$10,348	53.7
$10,349–$15,548	21.1
$15,549–$36,348	14.5
$36,349–$51,948	1.9
$51,949–$77,948	0.8
More than $77,949	0.7

* The pension is $394.10 per fortnight or $10,246 p.a. The reason older people are living on less than the pension is because it appears some are misreporting their actual income by not treating things like rent or cash payments from family trusts as income. There is also anecdotal evidence that suggests many retirees are living off their capital to fund their retirement.

Source: ABS

LET'S TALK ABOUT YOU

So how much money do you need to be financially free?

Well, now we need to look at you. One of the great joys of our society is that we are free to choose our own life. Some may be happy to live in a small country town, where it is possible in many parts of Australia to buy a home for under $50,000, grow vegetables and live peacefully on little income. If you choose not to own a car, you could live comfortably on under $15,000 a year.

At the other extreme you could have the goal of owning a private jet to shoot around the world visiting your luxury yacht. The cost of this depends on the size of the jet and the yacht, but I doubt you'd see much change out of $5 million a year.

So back to my original question, how much do you need?

When I ask people this, the answers I get are often

downright ridiculous. We seem to have little idea about the cost of things and how we want to live. So let's look at a comfortable, but not exotic lifestyle, and see what it will cost. I'll assume it is for a couple, who wish to maintain two cars and keep the house they own in good order. They like to eat out twice a week, entertain friends once a week, play golf and take a long Australian holiday each year, and go overseas every three years. They love to spoil their five grandchildren and one of their kids periodically lives at home.

Costing Our Dreams

Item	Annual estimated cost ($)	
Two cars	15,000	(including depreciation)
Maintain house	5,000	(based on 1.25% of house value of $400,000)
Run house	2,500	(rates, insurance, electricity, gas, telephone)
Eat at home	5,000	
Entertainment (out)	6,000	
Entertainment (at home)	2,000	
Children/Grandchildren	2,000	
Sporting	1,500	
Australian travel	2,500	
International travel	4,000	($12,000 over 3 years)
Health	2,000	
Total	47,500	

Yes, this could be reduced easily by selling one car ($7,500) and not maintaining the house ($5,000), but even so the annual cost is still $35,000.

So what's the point? Well, I'd really like you to sit down (I find a glass of red helps here) and think about what you'd like your life some way down the track to be. Don't worry too much about how you get there at this stage, just jot down your thoughts about how you would like to live one day if you were financially free.

To help you with this let's turn to the next chapter and take a look at us – and believe me, as I said right at the start, we've changed and our world has changed.

chapter 2

NEW AGE

This is not an understatement or a sweeping generalisation. It really is a new age. Economists and sociologists will fill millions of pages, web sites and CD-ROMs with facts, figures and opinions about what is going on, but, as I see it, two main factors are driving change.

1 THE INFORMATION AGE

This is the biggest thing to hit us since the Industrial Revolution of the late 1700s. Back then we went from a rural society to an industrial society in the space of a century. Things happened that our predecessors must have struggled to accept. Some of those were not complex, for example, all but the very wealthy made their own clothes and furniture. The idea of buying such things would have been ridiculed, as would the thought of living in cities. Even as recent as the late 1800s and early 1900s, early technology breakthroughs such as electricity and the telephone were seen as novelties, and initial views on the car included the conviction that it would never catch on as, at a speed of above 30mph, humans would be unable to breathe!

The lesson to remember here is that we don't really like change, but change is inevitable. In the 1700s and 1800s much of the world's wealth and opportunities shifted from the rural society to the industrial society. So today the industrial society is transforming into the information society. (Incidentally, it does not have much to do with short-term share prices. Some people suspected that falling technology share prices throughout the year 2000 meant at least a slowing of the Information Age, but falling prices did not mean an end to change, it just reflected the too-rapid rise of prices in the exuberant late 1990s.)

Money in History

1813

In 1813 Governor Lachlan Macquarie introduced the first Australian currency – the Holey Dollar and the Dump. Few coins in history have had such a colourful background of debauchery, greed, drama and intrigue. Here's how they came about.

When Governor Macquarie was appointed to the penal settlement of New South Wales in 1810, he saw immediately that John Macarthur and his cohorts from the New South Wales Corp – the so-called 'Rum Corp' – held a Mafia-type grip on the new colony. The conservative Macquarie also noticed that rum had replaced the official British coinage as currency and had become the symbol of the New South Wales Corp's power.

Macquarie decided that one way to break the power of the Corp was to introduce an official currency to replace rum. But due to the scarcity of British coins, he bought 40,000 Spanish coins and had the centre of each coin punched out to make two coins from every original. The outer ring, which came to be known as the 'Holey Dollar', because of the hole in the middle, was given a face value of five shillings. To the centrepiece, known as the 'Dump',

Macquarie gave a face value of fifteen pence. The Dump would buy nearly three loaves of bread in 1813.

When they were released in 1813, the coins solved the colony's immediate monetary problems and provided a tidy profit in the process. A nice footnote to this tale is that the man enlisted for the job of minting these historic coins was a convict named Henshall. Henshall had been transported for forgery!

According to the University of Western Australia's Economic History Department, the banks and merchants hoarded the Holey Dollars as soon as they were released. The reason being that they were tradeable with the British Treasury and could be used to fund imports.

The Holey Dollars were eventually melted down by the banks for their silver content, and few have survived. The Dump was more commonly circulated and so there are more of them. The Perth Mint values the Holey Dollar at $15,000 to $60,000, depending on the coin's condition, and the Dump at $2,000 to $22,000, again depending on its condition.

The Information Age will help us to live longer, be better informed, alter the way we live at home, and how we buy things. It will make our lives easier and entertain us in ways we did not think possible.

One of the most obvious signs of the Information Age is the rapidly growing use of the Internet. It is sliding into our lives, as the radio, TV and dishwasher did scores of years before.

According to Sinewave Interactive (www.top100.com.au), in January 2000, Australia ranked fifth in the world with 36.1% of the population using the Internet. The USA was first with 44.7%, followed by Iceland and Canada.

A report issued by Roy Morgan Research found that the majority of Australians aged fourteen and over have now accessed the Internet, with the trend continuing. Australian professionals, business owners and managers continue to lead the way with regard to having ever accessed the Internet and accessing the Internet at least monthly. 80% of Australian professionals, business owners and managers had accessed the Internet at least once, with almost three-quarters (73%) of professionals, business owners and managers accessing the Internet at least monthly (compared to 31% in April–June 1997).

Everything is changing – even gifts!

Forget about china and linens. The 24 million couples getting married in the USA in 2000 can register for what they really want – stocks, funds and real estate via a company called stockgift.com (www.stockgift.com). Fund managers and stockbrokers are generally ill equipped to accept gifts on behalf of customers. Minimum-balance requirements and security concerns often present insurmountable hurdles.

But with stockgift.com, couples choose as many as four securities. Family members and friends go to the site, navigate to the couple's personal wedding page and learn what stocks and mutual funds the duo has picked . . .

Source: *Fortune*, © 2000 Time Inc.

When Australians who have ever accessed the Internet were asked by Roy Morgan Research what they mainly use the Internet for, the top ten responses were:
- e-mail (55%)
- academic research (20%)
- general browsing/surfing (20%)
- business research (12%)
- searching for personal information (11%)
- chat rooms (9%)

The rise and fall of a publishing giant

In 1768, three Scottish printers began publishing the earliest and most famous encyclopaedia, the *Encyclopaedia Britannica*. By 1990, sales of *Britannica* had reached a peak of $650 million. Dominant market share, steady if unspectacular growth, generous margins and a 200-year history all testified to an extraordinarily compelling stable brand. Since 1990, sales for *Britannica* and all printed encyclopaedias have collapsed by over 80% – blown away by the CD-ROM. Whereas *Britannica* sells for $US1500+, a CD-ROM-based encyclopaedia lists for $US50–70. But hardly anyone pays that with many given away to promote the sale of computers, etc. The publishers tried many responses like ignoring the threat and producing their own CD-ROM version which failed.

The decline of *Britannica* is more than a parable about the dangers of complacency. It illustrates the new economics of information: how the evolving technological capabilities for sharing and using information can transform business definitions and competitive advantage. It illustrates how the most stable of industries, the most focused of business models and the strongest of brands can be blown to bits by new information technology.

Source: Excerpts from Philip Evans and Thomas S. Wurster, *Blown to Bits: How the New Economics of Information Transforms Strategy*, Harvard Business School Press, 1999.

- downloading software (9%)
- general entertainment (8%)
- sports information (7%)
- news information (6%).

Only 0.5% said they used the Internet for grocery shopping, 1.5% for other shopping and 2% for paying bills, while 5.5% said they used the Internet for games and recreation, 3.5% for banking transactions and 2% for share trading.

I find the Internet too clumsy, too slow and it has too

much information. But while it is certainly not the only representative of the Information Age, I do accept that it is part of the process of change we are going through.

2 US

I cannot believe how much we have changed in just a couple of decades. Consider these points, and then I'll tell you a story about us and our money. Today:

- We retire, on average at age 57 (65 in 1970).
- Two-thirds of school-leavers go onto a tertiary degree or diploma (18% in 1970).
- We change jobs frequently.
- Redundancy is a common term (over three million redundancies in the 1990s).
- Over half of us own shares (barely 5% in 1970).
- We marry much later.
- We have fewer children and many couples will choose never to do so.
- In a relationship, both couples work and do so after children are born.
- Travel is a habit, not a luxury.
- Barely anyone works 9 to 5.
- Workers do not believe the government will pay for their retirement.
- Our children rarely leave home to live elsewhere. If they do, they come back.
- We are health-, food- and lifestyle-conscious.
- We increasingly outsource tasks from housecleaning to ironing, gardening to walking the dog or minding the pre-schooler.
- Work is something we do, and many of us enjoy it, but it is a part of our lives, not our life.

A demonstration of our aspirations was captured by the

AMP TV ads during and after the 2000 Olympics. After seeing them hundreds of times, they started to drive me nuts, but the point they made about us was revealing. The ads looked at us in the future. A young woman on a beach meets herself in 20 years time and it turns out she owns a beautiful home on the beach. A young man meets himself and he is no longer a salesman, he's become a successful artist. The answer to how they achieved their dreams, of course, is that they invested with AMP. Putting this aside, what really interests me is that AMP didn't run those ads during the Olympics (at vast cost) without doing stacks of research. Clearly that research must have told them that we no longer dream just about getting by. We dream of career change and lifestyle assets – such as a house by the beach and a creative, fulfilling career.

Money Tip

The world is changing rapidly. Many people see this as a threat to their jobs and their money, but change brings opportunity. People who embrace change and use it to their advantage will have more money-making opportunities than ever before.

You will also remember that the ABC TV program 'Sea-Change', about a city lawyer moving to a coastal village, was one of the hit series of 1999 and 2000.

This fascinates me. Our changing habits will change our economy dramatically, so throughout this book I'll try to link change to a successful investment strategy, but at the most basic level. You don't need to be Albert Einstein to see that if we change how and where we live, work, retire and invest, then a successful wealth-creation strategy must take account of and incorporate these changes.

FINANCIAL FREEDOM

Above all, I sense that we don't want to be fenced in – at least not forever. And a lack of money can be one of the most claustrophobic fences of all. It can really push in on you. However, a lack of money is a fence that we can remove, or at least push back. We all have constraints. These are placed on us by society, our peers and our families. Some are for our safety, some for the safety of others, and some to allow our democracy to function. Most of these we need, but they can restrict what we do. Money though can be an absolute tyrant.

One way to avoid a problem with money is to adjust your goals. At one extreme you could become a missionary, or live in a cave in the bush. Money becomes pretty much irrelevant, providing you maintain a non-materialistic lifestyle. Another option is to 'downsize' your lifestyle: buy or rent a smaller home; drive a cheaper car; move to a lower-cost area. These are all perfectly valid options, but for many of us the best way to remove the 'money fence' that places constraints on a great part of life is to develop a sensible financial plan. The next chapter, 'Planning to be Free', will demonstrate how to do this, but let's first look at us in a bit more detail.

The baby boomers are the dominant portion of our population and have had, and will have, a major impact on all aspects of our society. Born after World War II, the baby boomers grew up on rock and roll, flexed their political muscles over the Vietnam War, acquired a university education in a period when it was as accessible and as affordable as it had ever been in history, and enjoyed the job opportunities and prosperity of the 1970s and 1980s. By the 1990s they were settling down. Whilst life expectancy for their generation is 75 years plus for men and 80 years plus for women, the reality is that many are going to live much longer than that. In fact, according to the book *Living to 100* by

19

Harvard Medical School researchers Thomas Perls and Margery Silver, many baby boomers are planning to reach 100 and beyond supported by a blend of miracle herbs, hormones and the teaching of gurus. Whether this is possible or not isn't a topic for this book. But if you are planning to live for an extra 20 years beyond the current life expectancy, then you better start thinking about what you are going to do with these years and how you will fund them.

According to the National Centre for Social and Economic Modelling (NATSEM) at the University of Canberra, it is estimated that of the four million baby boomers in Australia in 1993 each had, on average, assets of $120,000. But this masks tremendous inequalities. The top 20% held assets of almost $320,000, while the bottom 20% held less than $10,000 of assets on average. Housing continues to be the major asset of the overwhelming majority of baby boomers, whilst a further 25% was invested in superannuation and 10% held assets in family-owned businesses. However, according to the ASX Share Ownership 2000 survey, the level of share ownership is highest amongst baby boomers (that is, those aged 35 to 54) than any other age group.

The baby-boomer generation is significantly larger than preceding generations and represents the first generation that will need to provide for itself in retirement. By 2011 the first of the baby boomers will reach the age of 65, the traditional age for retirement. Many baby boomers are now in the midst of the prime years for setting aside long-term savings as their loan repayments are under control and their children are becoming self-sufficient.

And setting aside savings for the future is what baby boomers would be well advised to do, because with retirement inevitably comes reduced income. According to the ABS, in 1997—98 the average weekly income for couples aged 65 years and over was $460 and $248 for singles. More than

'Back in the old days, things were cheaper'

This is a common catchcry of the older generation. But were they? *Choice* magazine has come up with the answer in a survey that looked at how many minutes, days or weeks it took to earn enough to buy various household goods in 1962, compared with today.

Back in 1962 it took:

- Only 31 days to earn the equivalent of the annual average income tax bill. These days it takes more than twice that at 65 days.
- A house cost the equivalent of 212 weeks of earnings, now it takes 353.
- Private girls' school fees took 25 days to earn while private boys' school fees took 41 days to earn. Now it is 65 and 67 days respectively.
- The cost of newspapers has gone from 2.5 minutes to 2.7 minutes.

But, we are in front in some instances:

- The basic Holden takes 38 weeks of earnings compared with 47 weeks in 1962.
- A Sydney to London economy airfare took 131 days to earn in 1962 but now takes only 13 days.
- A 350-litre fridge would have taken 57 days of earnings but only takes 5 days today.
- Similarly a washing machine took 49 days of earnings back in 1962, but takes only 3.5 days now. A TV set took 44 days, but now takes only 2.5 days.
- A local telephone call used to take 1.7 minutes of earnings, but now takes 0.7 minutes.
- Milk has reduced from 5.1 minutes to 2.2, whilst bread has dropped from 8.6 minutes to 4.9 minutes.

Source: Reprinted from *Choice* – with the permission of the Australian Consumers' Association, www.choice.com.au

two-thirds of older couples were dependent on government cash pensions, and the remainder depended on superannuation and property incomes as their main source of income.

A most important point is that self-funded retirees will enjoy a very different retirement from those dependent on the age pension. Research from NATSEM estimates that there are almost twice as many pensioner retirees in Australia today as there are self-funded retirees, but that self-funded retirees have $23 billion a year to spend in total, while age pensioners have only $20 billion a year to spend. According to the ABS, it appears likely that many, though not all, baby boomers will be in a better financial position than the current older generation to provide for a financially secure retirement without relying on the age pension for most of their income. Self-funded retirees aged 65 to 74 years in 2010 are expected to receive almost twice as much income as pensioner households of the same age. They are expected to devote almost 20% of their weekly spending to entertainment and recreation, compared with only 13% for pensioner retirees.

NATSEM tells us that, in contrast, pensioner households will have to spend more of their money on the necessities of life. While food is expected to absorb 22% of the weekly spending of pensioner households, for self-funded retirees the comparable figure is only 18%. Self-funded retirees are forecast to spend twice as much each week on eating out at restaurants and clubs as pensioners do. Sounds like fun to me!

DO WE HAVE TO WAIT FOR 65 TO ENJOY LIFE?

For many, retirement is the 'pot of gold' at the end of a long and, at times, difficult working life. Retirement is when we can sit back, relax and enjoy the fruits of our labour. But do we really need to wait for retirement to enjoy these benefits, shouldn't we begin to take control now?

For many baby boomers *now* is the important time to examine their lifestyles and to plan for the free time ahead. Life-skills experts are emphasising the need to use the next decade to develop new skills in preparation for the years of retirement. Until recently, work has often provided the main focus of identity and support for the primary income earner, and the thought of that being removed at retirement often upsets retirees.

Reasons people want to be financially free

- I want to spend more time with my family.
- I want to spend more time bushwalking, gardening, enjoying nature.
- I want to lower my golf handicap, learn a language, develop musical/artistic/literary/dramatic skills, volunteer my time and expertise.
- Work interferes with what I really want to do with my life.
- I'm not interested in working nights and weekends.
- Once I'm financially free, every day will feel like Saturday.
- I'm sick of the corporate grind.

For most of us, life revolves around our work. For many of us, it involves getting dressed in work clothes, driving to work in a car that we are still paying for to get to the job that we need to pay for the clothes, the car and the house that we leave empty all day so that we can afford to live in it. It can be a vicious circle. Not surprisingly, many people are frustrated with their lives. They spend a startling amount of time worrying about their job, their financial situation, and the lack of time they have to spend with their family, whilst wishing they had more time and money to do what would truly make them happy.

TAKE CONTROL NOW

If some of these reasons for wanting to be financially free strike a chord with your own longings and dreams, then maybe it's time to reassess the direction your life is taking. Remember if you are unhappy with your life, you are the only one with the power to make a meaningful change. In most cases it's not up to your boss, your co-workers, your spouse, or your company to make your life better or provide you with 'job and life satisfaction'. If you don't first connect with who you are, what talents you have and what you are passionate about, then it's going to be difficult to truly enjoy your life, despite how well paid or successful you currently are.

If, on the other hand, you can find a way to connect with those special talents and then use them to the best of your ability, you can be assured of looking back on your life with a sense of satisfaction! But this means that now is the time to focus on the things that are really important.

When I sit down with my clients to discuss their retirement plans, before we look at the wide range of investment tools that can help them to become financially free, I first ask them what is important to them in their lives. Much to my pleasure, these discussions generally have little to do with a new car or other material items. I generally get a few anxious initial questions about investment returns and tax, but then we get onto the really important stuff. Things like:

- the life we want to lead
- dreams and aspirations
- children and grandchildren
- sport and clubs
- where to live
- travel
- health
- elderly parents
- amount of money required.

LifeSkills Coaching at www.lifecoaching.com.au tells us that the things we want are not aligned with the things we spend most of our time chasing. Have a look and see if these lists match your desires and ambitions.

Top 10 things people want (in descending order)

- Love
- Connection
- Fun
- Peace
- Freedom
- Security
- Growth
- Self-expression (i.e. be yourself)
- Adventure
- To contribute

The things we spend most of our time chasing

- Money
- Fame
- Sex
- Recognition
- Power
- Responsibility
- Achievement
- Big house
- New car
- Swimming pool

So what do you do about these discrepancies between what you want and what you actually aim for in life?

LifeSkills says that if your current wants are fully aligned with what you spend most of your time doing, then you probably feel contented and fulfilled. However, if your priorities are not aligned with what's really important to you, you are probably very busy, constantly rushing, a little stressed, and when you get what you are chasing – it's never enough! You turn around and think 'What's next?' (Unfortunately, this sounds like me!)

To get what you really want on the first list, you need to take control of your life. LifeSkills Coaching recommends you take the following three steps.

Steps to gain more control over your life

Step 1

Ask yourself: 'What's one thing I want more of in my life?'

- Power?
- Fame?
- Love?
- Adventure?
- Peace?
- Full self-expression?

Step 2

What do you spend your time chasing? If you value intimacy or strong friendships most, do you work on actively building and strengthening your friendships, or do you spend your time instead working to buy the second car?

Step 3

If you're aligned, congratulations! If not, now's the time to write down how you are going to find more time to spend on those things that are important to you. What are you willing to give up to do this? Specifically, what is the action you will take?

You define the life you want for yourself. You are the only person who can truly make it happen. Not your boss, your business partner, your financial planner, your spouse or life-partner. Just you.

Success on any level begins when you accept responsibility for creating the life you want. It starts when you stop looking outside of yourself for all the answers, and find the courage to look within.

In 1979, my first year in the investment industry, I would have said that this personal goals stuff was nonsense. My view was that if you do well with money, everything else will sort itself out. I was certainly right that money helps, but, unless you have goals and objectives to aim for, financial success alone is pretty sterile!

So, in conclusion, in the new age that we live in information rules. We're living longer, retiring earlier and spending buckets of cash on our lifestyle. Sensibly, we are lifestyle-oriented, but how on earth can we enjoy life today, yet plan for the future? Well, from here on I'll be showing you how it is possible to live life today, yet save for tomorrow. The next chapter is about planning, and how personal objectives are a key part in that process.

chapter 3

PLANNING TO BE FREE

Freedom. What a wonderful word. But what exactly does it mean? To each individual it will mean something different. In some countries to have freedom of speech and travel would be a major victory. In more liberal/democratic societies such as ours, these basic rights are set in concrete. Funnily enough, this actually makes freedom even more of an individual issue. We don't really have to worry about the foundations of freedom, so to us freedom is more likely to relate to our work, money and family.

I've asked many people what freedom means to them. The answers I get are incredibly different and include:
- not to have to travel several hours a day to and from work
- not to have to work
- to be out of debt
- to own a house
- to run my own business
- to be free of financial responsibilities to my children (i.e. see them grow up and leave home)
- to escape to a tropical island.

Since this is a book about money, I'll stay clear of what freedom means to you in terms of your relationships and your philosophy, and stick with the simpler stuff – money.

I know that some of you love your work, some of you hate it, and others just want to do something different, but in all of these cases, planning to be financially free is a worthwhile goal. If you love your work, believe me, you'll love it even more if you do it for pleasure and the money you earn is irrelevant. If you hate work, financial freedom means you don't have to work, and, if you want to change what you do, financial freedom gives you this opportunity.

Sounds great, but how do we get there?

Well, as I outlined in Chapters 1 and 2, you have got to decide at an emotional and financial level what financial freedom means to you. You have to have a vision of what freedom looks like to you and then, the nasty bit, you have to be totally practical and put a price on it. At the end of Chapter 1, I looked at freedom for one comfortably-off couple and arrived at a cost of $47,500 a year. One way to generate this is for them to work, but if they work they won't have the time to do what they want to do, a classic Catch-22. Clearly, it would be preferable to have assets that generate the $47,500 a year. But what level of income and what assets do you need to achieve this income, and how do you achieve your goals?

FAILURE

The main reason most people fail to ever become free is that they have no idea where they are going. You need to work out:
- what your vision of freedom encompasses, and
- what this lifestyle will cost on an annual basis.

> You must know where you want to be, how much income you
> need, and the capital required to generate that income.

Once you know how much you will need, I can give you
a simple formula that allows you to set genuine goals because
you will know something few people have the first clue
about: your capital target. In other words you will know
where you want to be, what it will cost, and how much
capital you will need. By applying some basic mathematics
you will be given some clear goals. The simple formula, or
rule of thumb, I have used for many years is to take the
amount you need, in this case $47,500 for a couple and mul-
tiply it by 17 if you want to be financially free at 55, 15 for
age 60, and 13 for age 65. Let's look at this:

How Much Do I Need To Be Financially Free?

Age you want to be free	Annual income required	Factor	Capital needed
55	$47,500	17	$807,500
60	$47,500	15	$712,500
65	$47,500	13	$617,500

As you can see, freedom does not come cheaply. And a word
of warning, this is worked out assuming that you will own
a home and you will die at the average life expectancy. Die
early and you'll have money left over. Die later and you'll
run out!

LIFE EXPECTANCY

I strongly suggest that you don't do your planning on the basis of living to 120. Not many of us will get to 100 at this point in history, and anyway I think that if I can live very well until I'm 80, then I'll worry about it then. But, I do expect at age 80 that my cost of living should be less, and if necessary I'll fall back on the value of my home if my investment capital is depleted. If you plan to have enough capital to fund your lifestyle until 120, most of us will be working until we are about 90, which seems a bit pointless.

Money Tip

Don't plan to retire on an age pension in the 21st century.
Nearly five million of us will be retired by 2025. We just won't have the number of taxpayers to support us all in the comfort we desire.

HOW MUCH DO YOU NEED TO BE FREE?

'How much do I need to be free?' is one of the most common questions for the baby-boomer generation. And no wonder. In just two decades, we've managed to decide that we want to retire ten years earlier, greatly expand on our desire for material possessions, develop grand lifestyle plans and develop the ability to spend, and build up personal debt like there was no tomorrow. Compound this with the fact that we're living longer and you have a somewhat daunting scenario.

Over the next 30 years Australia's population of people over 65 will expand from 1.9 million to 5 million. Meanwhile our retirement dreams have changed dramatically. We've gone from planning a basic three Gs retirement (the grand world trip, grandchildren and gardens) to what in the vernacular of the day can be aptly described as a chardonnay retirement. And this is hardly surprising. In the past the average male had a span of around seven years in retirement. (Retiring at 65, dying at 72). For a female this was much longer, on average eighteen years (retiring at 60, dying at 78). But as we retire younger and healthier, we plan an active retirement. This is terrific, but the bad news is that most of the activities we are planning are not exactly low-cost gardening and strolling on the beach. My work over the last twenty years with seminar programs for over 50,000 Australians aged between 18 and 80, points to the fact that being mentally and physically active is a primary goal in most people's retirement plans, and this is a good thing! But what is alarming is that the majority of people have absolutely no idea how much an active retirement will cost and even less of an idea about how much capital they will need to provide the required CPI-linked after-tax income stream to pay for the dream.

This is where the application of some basic business planning principles comes in very handy. A business will have a mission statement. This is generally a succinct statement that captures the essence of what the business is trying to do. Their very simplicity makes things crystal clear. An individual could have a mission statement that says: 'I plan to be financially independent by age 55. This will allow me to lead my life without financial reliance on anyone else and give me the choice of whether to work or not.'

Sounds good. But now we need to have a vision of what you want your future to look like, a strategy to get there, and a business plan. This should incorporate those nasty little disciplines we like to avoid (but that are essential to a successful business) like cash-flow management and a budget.

Strategy

Your strategy does not need to be that complex. Certainly, it will vary depending upon your personality and goals. A conservative person may well have a strategy of saving 15% of what they earn, using that to build a deposit, buy and pay off a home, top up their super, and build a share portfolio. Someone with a vision of a mega bucks retirement may have a strategy that involves much more risk, such as borrowing to start a business or businesses and borrowing to invest.

Vision

So your vision of your future life and your goals will to a great extent determine your strategy. If you want a comfortable but certain future, by saving around 15% to 17% of your salary from the day you start work and investing it sensibly over your working life, providing you don't fall into one of life's financial black holes (long-term unemployment, illness, divorce and so on), you should end up with about 75% of your final salary. This won't give you mega bucks, but it's the closest thing to guaranteed financial success.

How much do you need?

Now this is all very well, but it hasn't helped you with the key question. How much capital is needed to give a couple that level of income? In my experience, when asked how much they need to retire, couples most commonly respond 'Around $25,000 a year'. When asked why this amount, they say that the kids will have left home, the house will be paid off and, anyway, $25,000 is a lot more than an age pension for a single person (which is a bit over $10,000) or, indeed, for a couple (which is a bit over $15,000).

This may be true. But what does our $25,000 really buy? Running and maintaining a house will cost on average $5,000 a year. The NRMA says running and replacing even a modest car will set you back around $7,500 a year. So if you have two cars, there goes 60% of the $25,000! Food is also pretty important. And it wouldn't be too hard to spend $100 a week, leaving you with around $7,500 to pay for health, restaurants, theatre, presents for the grandkids and maybe some of the interesting courses you always wanted to do, not to mention holidays and travel and health costs.

Only you can work out the amount of income you will need. Please note that if you grossly underestimate the amount you need, your strategy is flawed. Your business plan may well deliver you the results you planned – but not the result you really wanted.

On that cautionary note, let's now take a look at a couple of scenarios. To highlight the important issues means I won't get bogged down in details, so tax is ignored in these examples. Anyway, with annuities, allocated pensions, franked dividends, income-splitting and so on, tax should not be a big issue for retirees.

Let's look at John, aged 55 with a lump sum of $300,000. He needs $30,000 a year. Assuming he nominates a conservative fixed-interest strategy and that inflation averages around 3% per annum, his money will run out when he is 67.

Now this is pretty crook. John runs out of money far too soon. So what can he do? He could cut spending down to $25,000 a year, but even then it runs out by age 69. He could retire at 65 in which case at $25,000 a year his money will last to his life expectancy. Or he could move his investments up the risk curve.

Options with a $300,000 Lump Sum

Income required	Investment strategy	Age when the money runs out		
		Retire at 55	At 60	At 65
$25,000	Fixed interest	69	74	79
	Growth	73	78	83
$30,000	Fixed interest	67	72	77
	Growth	70	75	80

What on earth does 'moving up the risk curve' mean? Well, it means investing in riskier areas. By investing in a diversified-growth portfolio of shares, listed property trusts and fixed interest over a ten-year-plus period, he could realistically assume an 8% per annum return. This gives John a decision-making matrix as can be seen in the table above. John may not like the look of this, but at least he knows where he stands.

But what about a more luxurious retirement lifestyle? You'd reckon that a lump sum of $500,000 would do quite a bit of damage. But would it?

$500,000 is ample money if John wants $30,000 a year and is happy to invest in growth assets, but if he wants to retire at age 55 on $50,000 a year, and is only willing to invest in fixed interest, his money runs out at age 67.

Are you beginning to see why it is estimated that 78% of Australians require a pension or part pension by age 65 and 90% by age 70? The amount of money needed to fund a lengthy, comfortable retirement is scary.

Options with a $500,000 Lump Sum

Income required	Investment strategy	Retire at 55	At 60	At 65
		Age when the money runs out		
$30,000	Fixed interest	76	81	86
	Growth	90	95	100
$40,000	Fixed interest	70	75	80
	Growth	76	81	86
$50,000	Fixed interest	67	72	77
	Growth	70	75	80

Obviously these numbers would look much better if we utilised the good old investment salesperson trick and cranked up the projected returns, but, sadly, a return of 8% per annum on a growth portfolio in excess of inflation is historically about right, as is 5% per annum on fixed interest.

Baby boomers

It is a frightening task facing the baby-boomer generation, if they are to have any hope of leading a comfortable life in retirement early in the twenty-first century. Early retirement combined with increasing life expectancy, plus plans for a chardonnay retirement, are a major challenge. As you have seen, a lump sum of $300,000, even if invested primarily in growth assets, would fund only a $30,000 a year CPI-linked retirement for 15 years. Even the quite grand sum of $500,000 would pay for only a $40,000 CPI-linked retirement for 21 years. Put your money into low-risk fixed-interest investments, and your chances of a comfortable lifestyle that keeps pace with inflation over 20 or more years in retirement is negligible.

Given the quite overwhelming sum required to fund a long-term retirement, one thought is to give up altogether. We could enjoy life to the full today, expect a major lifestyle reduction upon retirement, and draw an age pension. This is one of the arguments put forward as a disadvantage of a highly developed welfare system. The 'safety net' provisions take away the incentive to save, in particular if the benefits of saving seem hardly worthwhile. Certainly it can be argued that saving, say, $200,000 over a lifetime of work, makes it difficult to get a pension and the investment returns hardly replace the amount of pension you lose. Consider the quite dramatic attempts made by retirees to obtain a full pension, or at least to qualify for fringe benefits by obtaining the minimum pension payment. While under the 'deprivation' provisions, pensioners can no longer gift large amounts to family and friends to qualify for a pension, you would be quite amazed at the number of people who have quite legit-imately upgraded or renovated their home or taken a trip in order to shed assets and qualify for a pension or part pension. These are perfectly reasonable decisions to make if they are required to maintain or improve an individual's or couple's standard of living. But if made simply to gain a pension, they are a poor use of capital from the perspective of both the community and the individual.

Since it is projected that there will be 5 million Australians over 65 years old in 2031, this debate may well be altogether beside the point, as exactly how our current tax system will be able to fund an age pension at even today's modest level is beyond my comprehension.

Start saving now

It seems to me, unless you are absolutely sure that you'll drop dead at or prior to retirement, in order to live your dreams of financial freedom in the future, you are going to have to get your financial act together, and the earlier the better. David Knox, Professor of Actuarial Studies at the University of Melbourne, has done much work on the subject of whether we can actually afford to pay for our dreams. To achieve a CPI-linked retirement at age 65 which is equivalent to two-thirds of his final salary, a 20-year-old male would need to save 14.4% of his salary. His female equivalent would need to save 18% since, on average, women live around six years longer than their biologically weaker brothers. If he plans to retire at 60, our 20-year-old male needs to save around 21% of his salary (25% for a female). An age 55 retirement means he needs to save 30% and she will need to save 36%.

Now this is bad enough. But what about a spot of reality. Today some 27% of all jobs are part time, and many people, in particular women, still have breaks in their career to have a family. Professor Knox points out that if a female works full time to age 30, then part time until age 40, then full time to 65, she will need to save 21% of her salary. If full time to age 25, then no income-generating work until 35, part-time work until 45, then full time to 65, a savings target of 30% is required.

Will we save this much? Well, as my children would say so eloquently 'yeah right'. These are very tough targets indeed and won't be met by many.

So what is the solution?

Is it all too hard and should we just give up after all? My view is that we shouldn't, but we have to be more realistic. Professor Knox says that something will have to give, and that our typical planned retirement date of 55 is just not realistic for most people. And he is absolutely correct. Not only will most of us not be able to afford to retire at the level of income we want to at age 55, even retiring at age 65 looks dodgy.

This will hardly make your day, but let's face it, in a few thousand years of human history, our plans for 20-plus years of comfortable retirement is an historical anomaly. At a time when our birth rate is low, thereby generating proportionally fewer taxpayers of the future, the proposal to support millions of young retirees who live longer than ever is not exactly an advisable scenario.

A few things are likely to happen. Firstly, a very small percentage of people will retire at their target date with enough to sustain an independent, inflation-linked lifestyle. Secondly, quite a few will retire young, but either reduce their lifestyle expectations or supplement their income with part-time work. This is likely to come from working in the booming household services sector. Thirdly, the largest group will extend (that is, delay) their retirement date.

This may not be what you want to hear, but let's not forget that there are solutions. The good old-fashioned basic savings strategy is still very powerful. As the table on the next page shows, regular savings and compound returns are a powerful combination.

Over this century, based on 20-year rolling periods, Australian shares have shown an average real return of over 6% per annum. Today there are plenty of share funds around where you can invest $100 a month and achieve this type of return. Over 20 years you'll create $59,000. Once the mortgage is paid off, by investing this amount on a regular basis, compounded returns can turn this into a very handsome sum. Again, invest $1,000 a month for 20 years and based on 6% per annum, it will grow into $590,000.

It won't be easy to accumulate the amount of wealth needed to fund a long-term, active retirement. But it is far from impossible. The real trick is to take control of your cash flow now, and to direct surplus income in a disciplined fashion into quality investments.

Regular Savings and Compound Returns

Investment period	$100 a month at 6%	$400 a month at 6%	$1,000 a month at 6%
10 years	$18,600	$74,400	$186,000
20 years	$59,000	$236,000	$590,000
45 years	$419,000	$1,676,000	$4,190,000

Source: ipac securities

Key steps in planning to be free

So what are the key steps in planning to be free? Much can be learned about this important issue from high achievers, such as sports stars. They are an excellent example of how having goals and a plan to achieve those goals is fundamental to success. Listen to Cathy Freeman, John Eales, Ian Thorpe or Susie O'Neill talk about their career and it becomes pretty obvious that they didn't get where they are by accident – or quickly and easily.

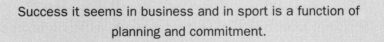

Success it seems in business and in sport is a function of planning and commitment.

When I speak with senior executives of Australia and the world's leading companies, I always ask 'What is the primary cause of your company's success?'. It is hardly surprising to find that each points to a very similar range of factors: having a vision for the organisation; setting goals; commitment to a budget; discipline; attention to detail; a strategic plan and an operating plan to achieve the strategy.

It's painfully obvious that these are exactly the principles that we need to apply to be financially successful, yet it is plain that few people, regardless of education, income or career, can clearly articulate any realistic goals and objectives for the future. Even those who can, struggle when asked what amount of capital is required to meet their lifestyle goals, let alone whether their current savings habits and investments will allow them to accumulate the amount required.

By now it is clear to all of us that we need to have some money put aside to be able to live as we choose. Saving or investing with no real purpose other than 'everyone says I'll be destitute if I don't' is about as effective and sustainable as a fad diet. Rather than being motivated purely by fear, it would be better to be driven by a positive view of what we can achieve.

Have you ever found yourself suddenly becoming a very effective saver when you have a clear-cut goal? I know I have on many occasions, but only when my goal was worthwhile and it appeared to be achievable. So the first step to financial freedom, as I see it, is very simple. Have a plan.

> Want to get rich? Have a plan.

This sounds pretty simple, but exactly what should be in your plan? (And be careful you don't get too carried away with planning your life down to the last detail. This is clearly not going to work, and the younger you are the more impossible it is to predict your career path, marriage and divorce prospects, children and so on.) You may have read my views on planning in my book *Making Money*, or in *Money*

Magazine, but let me repeat these since having a plan, at any age, is not as complex as you might think.

The young

I would like to think that a young person in the work force might have things like this in their plan:

- I will complete a relevant part-time course in the next three years that will enhance my career, and improve my skill set and my prospects for a better income.
- Over the medium term (three years) I will live at home and save $150 a week. During this time I will use part of my savings to travel overseas, but also to build a deposit with which to purchase an investment property or shares.
- My compulsory employer contributions will start to add up, and I'll make it my business to understand more about superannuation.

The middle-aged

Here we can get a bit more serious as our lives are now set in more of a routine. Your plan might contain any or all of the following:

- By switching from monthly to fortnightly repayments, adding my annual tax refund and another $20 a week, I will clear my mortgage in nine years rather than 20 years. By then investing my repayment, I can add up to an additional $500,000 to my wealth in 20 years.
- Each time I get a pay rise, I will 'salary sacrifice' half of my increase into my super fund.
- I want to be financially independent at age 60. This means I will need $30,000 a year – or a capital target of $500,000 (for this calculation go to the table on page 36).

The retired

You may wonder if it is too late to plan once you are already retired. It isn't. Issues in a retiree's plan could be:

- Our children are going well financially, so we plan to use all of our wealth to live comfortably.
- We don't want to leave our home, but we are happy to use part of its value, so we will consider a reverse mortgage. (This is when you get a monthly amount which is eventually taken from your estate or the proceeds of the sale of your property.)
- We wish to manage our investments in a way that will allow us to draw an age pension if possible.
- Our estate planning is in place, and our wills are up to date.

OK, I'm sure you get the point, but the more detailed your plans and the clearer your objectives, the better the chance you have of achieving them. Once you have done a bit of basic thinking, your plan should contain the following details.

Money Tip

Financial independence should be the goal of all Australians. To see how much you need to be independent work out how much income you need to live on at, say, age 60. Then multiply this amount by 15. This becomes your retirement lump sum target.

To retire at age 55, multiply your desired income by 17.

To retire at age 65, multiply by 13.

YOUR PLAN

Your objectives

This includes your broad objectives, as above, but it really does need to have your short-term (one year), medium-term (one to five years) and long-term (beyond five years) objectives.

Examples of this could be a short-term goal to clear all credit-card debt and a medium-term goal of saving a home deposit. Your long-term goal should be to achieve financial freedom. This is highly personal, as we all have a different view of what financial freedom means.

Your budget

I've got some bad news here. The budget is not an optional item, it's a must-do. The good news is that it isn't too hard to do. Write down everything you spend. If necessary, collect bills, receipts, credit-card statements for three months and you'll see exactly where your money goes. Add it up, take it away from your after-tax income and you have a budget. It may terrify you, but at least you know where you are. You've got to have a go – and be realistic. Most budgets are completely useless because we don't put in the things we enjoy: a few beers or a bottle of wine; a dinner out or a movie.

Your budget should be realistic and typical, not that of a monk who has taken an oath of poverty.

Your current position

This is basically your balance sheet. List and add up all of your assets, then subtract from this sum the total of your liabilities. This will leave you with your net wealth today.

List all important assets

Here you should list your insurance cover, your income, your partner's income, house, car and other assets. Your thoughts on estate planning and the fact that you have a valid will are also important.

SUMMARY: WHERE ARE WE?

Let's now pause and sum up where we have got to. At this stage of your planning you should have a much better understanding of:

- where you are now and where you want to be
- your assets and liabilities
- a realistic income requirement, if and when you stop work
- an effective budget that is a reflection of how you really live, or want to live
- your estate planning and insurance.

And at a minimum, you will have the ability to articulate how you see your long-term goals.

Please don't think that your plan can't change. Mine does almost on a yearly basis as I get older and, I hope, a bit smarter. Change is no excuse not to plan, change is inevitable and your plan should evolve as you do. By getting a firm grip on where you are now and where you want to be, your plan sets the strategy that most effectively gets you from one point to the other.

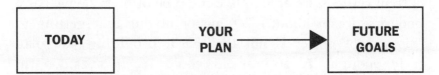

This is where a good financial adviser can offer real value. Any decent planner will have some form of computer model that will take your position today, look at your current wealth-creation initiatives (super, paying off your mortgage, saving plans, etc.) and project these forward in time so you can see exactly what you will have at age 55, 60, 65 or whenever you choose. These models will also allow you to build in what-if scenarios. For example, what happens if you increase your super contributions when your children finish school, your partner takes a part-time job, you get an inheritance, and so on? Your planner can also run a sensitivity analysis showing what happens if you retire five years earlier, or work five years longer, or borrow to invest, and a myriad of other issues relevant to you.

By thinking about your future goals and lifestyle aspirations, you should have been able to come up with a realistic cost of living that reflects the way you want to live. This is an important issue, because it allows you to set a capital target. As I said earlier, take your projected annual living costs and multiply by 17 if you want to retire at age 55, by 15 for age 60 and by 13 for age 65. Sure, you can run a far more sophisticated analysis than this, but you'll find that this basic system is pretty accurate. So if you want to retire at age 60 and you think that your lifestyle will cost you $35,000 a year, you'll need to multiply $35,000 by 15, giving you a target of $525,000.

Once you've recovered from the state of panic this has put you into (now you can probably see why under 4% of current retirees are able to live the type of lifestyle we baby boomers dream about!), let me point out that getting to this sort of target is not that hard, providing you plan early enough. A 20-year-old could reach $525,000 (in today's dollars) by saving around $125 a month until age 65. A 45-year-old who had paid off their mortgage could reach $525,000 just by directing their mortgage repayment (the Australian average is around $1000 a month) into a sensible investment such as a managed share fund, until they were 63.

Don't forget, many people have a very low capacity to save until they are into their late 40s or early 50s. At this stage the mortgage is often paid off and the kids have grown up. I know of couples with very limited assets at age 50, who find that due to them both working, having no mortgage to pay off and with their children now in the work force, they can save up to two-thirds of their after-tax income.

Now this all seems sensible for people still at work, but what if you have already retired?

TIPS FOR RETIREES

Before looking at some practical ideas for retirees to maximise their financial fitness, let me touch on a rather sensitive issue. The majority of retirees live on an age pension of a bit over $15,000 a year for a couple. This is above the starvation level, but luxuries are few and far between. Some have no asset base at all and don't own a home, but it greatly saddens me to see retirees living highly restricted lives when they own a home. In our large cities there are tens of thousands of retirees struggling to get by, yet living in a home worth hundreds of thousands of dollars. If living in your home is the most important thing to you, then it makes sense to me, but, if it is being done solely to maximise the kids' inheritance, I believe a major rethink is required. Even if you hate the thought of retirement accommodation, a shift to a town-house or unit in your own area can free up tens (or hundreds) of thousands of dollars.

Another option is reverse mortgages which enable retirees to receive a monthly payment which is taken, with interest, from your estate or when your home is sold. Reverse mortgages are very popular in the USA, England and other parts of Europe, but are not so popular in Australia. Such products would be of great assistance to many retirees here as well.

Retirees need growth too

Too many retirees leave their money in the bank because it is nice and safe, and it is, in the short term anyway.

However, ten or twenty years later this strategy starts to look pretty silly. I often reflect on the real-life example of two retirees who came to see me in 1983, each with nearly exactly $100,000. Neither of them took my advice to set up a balanced portfolio with a spread of shares, property, fixed interest and cash. One of the retirees told me he couldn't sleep at night with money in shares, so we popped the whole lot into term deposits, where it still sits today. This year he will earn around $5,400 from his investments and his capital is still worth $100,000. The other retiree listened to me intently, did some of his own research and proudly announced that he would put the whole lot in shares. I could feel my heart skip a beat – 100% in shares was not exactly what I had in mind. Anyway he would not be deterred. In the following years his wealth rose and fell like a yoyo, but he stuck with his strategy, and today his $100,000 is worth over $1 million, and this year will give him $45,000 in mainly fully franked dividends. Guess who is living the better lifestyle?

Saving for retirement

The beauty and simplicity of regular savings over a lifetime of work was highlighted in the December 2000 issue of *Money Magazine*, based on a story I did on 'Money' in 1998:

> *After more than 40 years on Sydney's rail network, 58-year-old Arthur McLean had no intention of missing out on life's little pleasures. By contributing to a compulsory saving scheme from the start of his working life, he guaranteed a comfortable retirement.*
>
> *'It was called a ten and a penny scheme, which is ten shillings and a penny,' Arthur explains. 'Looking back at it now, if I hadn't done that in those days, I wouldn't be where I am today.' Arthur's ten shillings and a penny grew*

to around $380,000. 'I have reinvested $310,000 of it and elected to receive a monthly annuity,' Arthur says. 'It's practically the same wage as I was getting from work, without the mortgage repayments.'

Arthur took the advice of the 'Money' TV show two years ago and decided to keep the bulk of his money within the super system. An allocated annuity lets you invest any of your accessible superannuation and provides you with a regular and flexible income. It is possible to structure an annuity with various risk exposures to shares, property, cash and fixed interest. The steady allowance is one of the most popular ways to generate an income stream in retirement and allows the option to vary repayments and withdraw lump sums if required.

Arthur pays no tax on the investment earnings of the annuity. He has also nominated a certain minimum period of 20 years. If he dies before that time, the balance of the account can be used to pay an income to his wife until the money runs out, or paid as a lump sum to the beneficiaries of his estate.

Arthur was always certain he wouldn't retire a millionaire, but he wanted to ensure he didn't have to rely on the age pension either. After the $310,000 ends, he estimates that there will be $100,000 left over.

'I've always said that you have to take some responsibility for your retirement, you can't just rely on the government,' he says.

The money taken from Arthur's pay was about 20% of his wage. That may seem a lot, but he had enough left over to pay off the mortgage and car, and enjoy life along the way. 'It was a good idea because you never got it in your hand, so you never really missed it,' he says.

Without any gimmicks or get-rich-quick schemes, Arthur will enjoy his golden years, all thanks to simple *saving. 'I'm glad I was forced into saving and it has ensured that we won't have to change our lifestyle.'*

Arthur's wife, Rosalie, is considering retirement at the end of the year. 'In retirement I plan to play more bowls,' says Arthur. 'And there's a lot of places in Australia that we haven't seen and there are things to fix up around the house. Or we can drive each other mad for the next 20 years!'

Retirees should not pay tax

This is a practical statement, not a political one. By using allocated annuities, allocated pensions, income splitting and franked dividends, most retirees, regardless of how much capital they have, really should not be paying tax.

If you are, go and get a financial planner to show you how to construct a decent portfolio that maximises your returns and minimises your tax.

Avoid scams

The shonks in our society know retirees are hurting. While I want you to generate better returns, I don't want you to lose all your capital to a scamster. At the end of the day, you can get higher returns by sensible investment and taking a reasonable level of risk, but it just isn't possible to earn the 12% to 14% per annum returns being promised in 'risk-free' investments.

> Risk does equal return.

The legacy of the Pyramid Building Society, Estate Mortgage, the Wattle Group and a small number of mainly Queensland solicitors offering 'safe' 13% plus per annum mortgages should not be forgotten.

Pensions

Even a small part pension can extend the life of your capital and improve your lifestyle. I strongly recommend that retirees plan their affairs in order to maximise their pension entitlement. But don't be silly about it. Blowing more money on a holiday than you would normally just to get rid of some assets is downright silly, as is putting in a new kitchen that you don't really need.

Maximise your investment returns as much as you can, but always try to do this with the pension, either now or in the future, clearly in mind.

10 STEPS TOWARDS FINANCIAL FREEDOM

Anyway, regardless of your age and situation, my common-sense approach will work. Let's look at ten valuable steps that I reckon will help you to achieve your goals.

1 Work out a realistic budget

How often do I hear 'My budget doesn't work'? It doesn't work because your budget didn't reflect the reality of your lifestyle in the first place. As I mentioned before, most people put together a budget that reflects the life of a Buddhist monk. Once you've done a realistic budget, and find you are still spending more than you earn, you have two choices. You could economise on your lifestyle, or increase your earnings – and doing both is even better!

Personally, I tend to worry about what I save, not what I spend. My budget is a document that tells me what my expenses are and what my capacity to save is. Let's say I target a savings of 20% of my income. My employer is already investing 8% of my salary into super (will go up to 9% in 2002–2003), so I need to target 12%. This I arrange to have taken out of my salary (in the form of top-up super, increased mortgage repayments, etc.) and then I must live on the rest. This strategy is known as 'pay yourself first'.

2 Save little, save often

I hope I've made this point strongly by now, but just to remind you, that a twice weekly $7 punt on Lotto, if invested sensibly, would have turned into a little under $500,000 over the space of your working life.

3 Don't plan to save cash

Let me guess. Your budget said you should have saved $2,000 last year. But where is it? Look, unless you have your savings put somewhere you can't get your hands on them, you'll spend them. Commit your savings to a specific account or a specific purpose (the mortgage or superannuation), otherwise you are just kidding yourself.

4 Plan to own a home, debt-free

Yes, I know the average share portfolio has been performing consistently better than the average Australian property. But if you are living in one place for the long haul, property ownership forces you to save and it provides lifestyle benefits.

5 Investment property

One way to get started in property, in particular if you are living at home or in low-rent accommodation, is to use rent and tax deductions to get you started.

I am also comfortable with existing home owners buying an investment property providing that they buy in a location that suits the new century, or in other words it appeals to young working couples and the millions of younger-than-ever retirees. It must be in a job-growth area and near public transport, recreational facilities, nightlife and restaurants.

A big back yard is not high on my list of twenty-first-century features.

6 Borrowing to buy shares

This is fine providing you understand the risk and the fees involved. As an under-five-year strategy, I reckon you'd need to be a lunatic, but give me over five years, preferably ten, then I think this is a realistic wealth-creation strategy.

7 Super is good

'No it's not' is probably what you are thinking. It's too confusing and the rules keep on changing. That's true, but if you are earning, say, $45,000, you're paying 31.5% (including the Medicare levy of 1.5%) tax on the part of your income above $20,000. Direct, say, $5,000 into super via salary sacrifice and you'll pay 15% tax, leaving you with $4,250. Take the $5,000 home in your pay and you'll have $3,425 to play with. Who do you think will be richer: the person investing $4,250 each year or the person investing $3,425?

8 Minimise tax

My basic strategy is to avoid like the plague any tax schemes involving rural products. There is absolutely nothing wrong with angora goats, ostriches, emus, boars and so on, but there really is no established market for the by-products of these creatures, so once a few breed up, their value collapses, leaving the middle men the only ones laughing.

However, fully franked dividends, income splitting and super are legitimate and effective ways to reduce tax, as is negative gearing.

9 Go for growth

In the short term, cash is your safest investment, followed by fixed interest. Property and then shares are your most risky. But over the longer term, shares and property are far more effective wealth-creation assets.

Back in 1983, mainly thanks to my parents putting a small amount into shares each year, I had enough money to put down a deposit on a small semi-detached home and to start my business with four partners. These were two key decisions, but I often think back to what would have happened had I left the money in a back account. After tax and inflation, today I'd have just enough to buy a basic car.

10 Take advice if you need it

Clearly as a financial adviser, I have a bias towards recommending you take expert advice, but I do recognise that many people like to do the research themselves. This is fair enough if you have the time and expertise, but few people really have the depth of knowledge to handle all aspects of local and international investment, of superannuation legislation and our very complex tax system. I'm OK in the investment area, but when it comes to tax, I find having an accountant absolutely essential.

Follow the ten steps, give them time and your financial freedom should follow.

Remember, you must plan in order to be financially free.

chapter 4

CAREERS

If you are in permanent retirement this chapter may be of limited interest to you, but if you are interested in working and are aged between about 15 and 65, this chapter is one of the most important in this book.

But what's a chapter on careers doing in a money book? Well, it's pretty simple. Your career will be your main source of money. Too many people spend time hoping to win the lottery, inherit a fortune, pick a share-market winner or a property investment that triples in value in a year. Dream on.

People like me prattle on about how we can help you to make good investment choices. My track record in this area is very public – my thoughts have been aired on radio since 1982, in magazines since 1985, on TV since 1985 (the 'Money' show since 1993) and in my books. It's clear my commonsense approach works and I think I can help you to make better investment choices. But people like me don't make you money. *You* make the money from your career, whether it's working for someone else, or in business. What people like me do is work with your income and any assets you have, to maximise your returns for the level of risk you want to take.

Yes, I've made some terrific investments in shares and property, but 99.99% of my wealth comes from:

- choosing the right career
- working hard at it
- once I had experience, opening a business in my chosen career area (managing money).

> Your career is the engine of your wealth.

I chose the investment field because it interests me and I knew it had vast growth potential. Sure, I started as a junior researcher on $13,500 a year in 1979, but I quickly completed relevant post-graduate qualifications from the Securities Institute of Australia and the Financial Planning Association, took a writing and speaking course, showed enthusiasm and off I went – and so did my salary.

In 1983, with four partners I turned my career into my business, ipac securities. At the end of 2000, we had $5 billion under management and owned similar businesses in Taiwan, South Africa and Europe.

The wealth I have is modest compared to Kerry Packer's, but I made it, and it allows me and my family to make terrific lifestyle choices. Yes, I've done well in property and shares, but the ability to invest was created by my choice of career, not to mention the value of my shares in ipac.

Frankly, the best investment anyone in the work force can make is very simple. It's not in shares or property – it's in you and your skills.

> Invest in yourself.

If you want to be on the BRW's rich list, then you are going to need to come up with a winning business strategy, make some tough decisions and take some risks to make it work. Even then there's no guarantee you will end up wealthy. For those at the other end of the scale, who have less ambitious career goals, a good solid job can provide you with the sort of income you need to live a good life. And in between there are any number of combinations that can help you to achieve the lifestyle you want. But whatever course you take, you need to make sure that you have got your money working for you and not the other way around.

For most of us, the ability to earn an income is easily our most valuable asset and its absence would make life look very different indeed. So whether you take the career path or the own-a-business path, you need to be aware that the market is always changing and that you need to be prepared for any new trends that affect the way you earn your income.

AGEING POPULATION

Throughout *The Road to Wealth*, I talk about the opportunities that an ageing population provides for all of us from an investment viewpoint. But on the debit side there are some implications that we also need to consider. It's a fact that more people will retire over the next ten to twenty years than at any time in Australia's short history. Obviously this is a great time to invest your money in the grey dollar, but what are some of the big issues facing this group?

According to the Australian Bureau of Statistics (ABS) it appears more and more of us are going to have to rely on a job to sustain our lifestyle. In 1997 alone, there were 2.9 million men aged 45 and over and, of these, 1.3 million (48%) had retired from full-time work, and nearly all of these had left the labour force entirely – many being put out of the work force earlier than expected. According to research from the University of New South Wales's Centre on Ageing and Retirement, 40% of recently retired academics across Australia were forced into retirement earlier than they had planned.

My concern is that I doubt they have enough money set aside for their retirement, given that our average life expectancy is almost 80 years of age and is continuing to increase. So if you're forced to retire at 45 years of age and find you live another 35 years, how do you find the money to fund such a long retirement? Well, it's got to be another job, a new career or a small business.

If there is one characteristic that really marks the current employment landscape, it would have to be ever-accelerating change, driven primarily by developments in high-tech communications. Look at the mega takeover in 2000 of Time Warner – the world's biggest and arguably most venerable media company, with roots reaching back to the early part of last century – by America Online (AOL), an Internet provider that 20 years ago didn't even exist. In a time when change is the only constant, employees are ceaselessly reminded of the need to be forever upgrading skills, to carefully plan where careers are heading, and to question whether there are, in fact, any more jobs for life.

GROWTH AREAS OF EMPLOYMENT

As Chris Walker wrote in the February 2000 edition of *Money Magazine*, whether you're trying to land a new job or fast-track your career, I strongly recommend that you take the time to research the job market to pinpoint the 'growth industries'. The work landscape is constantly changing and it's really important that you get the qualifications, skills and experience to position yourself so that you can make yourself more employable and take advantage of careers that offer solid opportunities in the future. The latest Department of

Employment, Workplace Relations and Small Business 'Job Futures' report (DJF) (find it on the Internet at www.dewrsb.gov.au) forecasts that the strongest potential for job growth is in 'professional' occupations including computing, business/information, sales/marketing and advertising, health, social welfare and accountancy/auditing. These generally require you to have a degree or higher qualification. Some less skilled jobs (such as carers/aides) also have strong growth prospects.

Money Tip

Education is your best investment.
The more you know, the more you grow.

Information technology

Industry experts have identified the number one growth area as being 'technology and communications', with the 'service' industries (particularly finance and banking) ranking a close second. Chris Adams, Managing Director of Michael Page International has nominated Information Technology (IT) as the leading area of executive-level job growth in Australia. He reports 'aggressive growth within the areas of IT, the Internet and telecommunications. We're living in a fast-paced environment, with dynamic companies participating in a new economy driven by the Internet'.

However, due to the speed at which technology is changing, workers in the IT area face the risk of uncertain conditions as a result of the dynamic environment. Another thing to keep in mind for those of you contemplating a career in the IT industry is the relative 'newness' of many companies operating in this field. Many of these companies, especially start-up dot com businesses have not returned the expected profits. Only time will tell how many will survive in the short term, and then go on to become viable in the long term. The current assessment of the IT industry indicates rapid change, with continuous evolution because of new developments, leading to growing employment opportunities. Some time down the track, the fairly unstructured environment of the IT industry will probably settle down as more rigid organisational structures are put in place.

The services sector

The 'services sector' has been earmarked as another future growth industry and it already accounts for 70% of the Australian labour market. This broad term covers community services, wholesale and retail trades, public administration and defence, finance, property and business services, and recreational services. Extremely high employment growth has been recorded in the sales area; and industry forecasts suggest that a steady rate of growth will carry on into the future.

The good news for people looking to enter the sales area is that a lot of people can match their skills and experience to this line of work. This area also experiences a high employee turnover and, according to the DJF, projection figures for future job growth exceed the national average. The specific areas of telemarketing and call centres have experienced enormous growth and this trend is predicted to continue as demand for these types of services continues to expand. Consequently, skilful sales representatives and telemarketers are unlikely to find themselves out of work for any extended period of time. Finally, a job in the area of sales is a real possibility for most people because it requires a skill that can be learnt without ongoing formal education.

Companies in the services sector are now leaning towards providing more flexible staffing arrangements and working conditions. Contract, part-time and casual jobs are becoming more common and, along with outsourcing, they are changing the traditional face of work. In the past people grew their own vegetables and kept chickens to provide eggs, now we simply throw our groceries into a supermarket trolley, or even order them online. The next step could see us outsourcing all of those mundane domestic tasks that never seem to get done!

DECLINING INDUSTRIES

While the outlook for growth in the IT and services sectors is really positive, more reliance on outsourcing could have a negative impact on job creation. Outsourcing is all about 'economy of scale' and consolidating work functions, which can lead to fewer overall positions. An example of this is in the operations area or 'back office' of stockbroking. In the past, every broker ran their own back office to process (settle) their clients' trades. Now, this service is increasingly outsourced to operators specialising in this function, meaning that fewer people are required to do the same job in a centralised environment.

The DJF report paints a less than positive picture for the agricultural, mining and manufacturing industries, these areas are shedding jobs rapidly. The future job opportunities for labourers, product packagers, process workers, textile machine operators and tradespeople, road and rail transport drivers, and base-level clerks are also considered to be unpromising. While tertiary qualifications are an asset, some graduates with degrees in the visual and performing arts, psychology, social and life sciences, and languages face more obstacles in landing full-time jobs. However, the higher percentage of graduates from these disciplines not participating in the paid work force could be due to a greater number of these same students seeking postgraduate qualifications.

JOBS AND THE AGEING POPULATION

As I mentioned earlier, Australia's ageing population will have a major impact on emerging employment trends. Job opportunities in health-related services are expected to increase to meet the demand for carers in retirement villages and for domestic-help providers for older people still living in their own homes. Likewise, an increase in the demand for medical support in the form of nursing services has been predicted. The disposable income of the baby-boomer generation could trigger some growth in the tourism industry, as this segment of our population will probably have the time and the money for travel in their retirement.

GET AN EDUCATION

The importance of a good education can't be overstated. In fact, I have seen research from overseas that indicates that not only does an education help you find a job, but it also assists you in earning more money. Research from the US Department of Labour shows that the average American university graduate earned 71% more than the average American high-school graduate. Whilst this statistic is quite staggering, it probably wouldn't surprise many of us here in Australia.

This is not to say, however, that everyone has to go to university. Many people can't go, either because of their academic record or, increasingly, because of cost, while many simply don't want to go because university doesn't teach them what they need to know, or give them the piece of paper they need for their chosen career path. Encouragingly, more people are going into apprenticeships than ever before, with numbers increasing by 100,000 in the past four years.

If you're intent on pursuing a professional career (such as medicine, law or accounting), where the growth prospects are best, a degree is a basic requirement. Getting a degree gives you a headstart if you are aiming for a successful career.

TAKE TIME TO PLAN YOUR CAREER

I know it might be stating the obvious, but it's really important that you plan your career carefully. Because such a large chunk of your life is spent at work, making sure that you end up in the job that's right for you should be a major priority. Remember, it also makes sense to find a job in an area where there is growth potential, and with a progressive company that has a commitment to training and education. As the labour market becomes increasingly competitive, it's critical that you meet the key job requirements so that you can position yourself to take advantage of opportunities in your chosen field.

CHANGING TO A PREDICTED GROWTH INDUSTRY

If you are considering a career change, the key is being aware of your strengths and being flexible. Even if you are made redundant, there are steps you can take to safeguard your chances of remaining employable.

The attitude of employers towards variety in a candidate's employment history is generally positive. Some diversity demonstrates flexibility and the capacity to adjust to a new position and company ethos. Holding jobs in several areas also carries the added benefit of having been exposed to diverse management practices. Occasional job changes aren't equivalent to committing career suicide. Being proactive in managing your career by taking the occasional risk and branching out into new areas can add to your value as an employee. Likewise, seizing the opportunity of working overseas, or making lifestyle changes can reveal a candidate's enthusiasm for embracing challenges and the ability to take decisive action

Other areas that you might wish to consider are freelancing, working from home or subcontracting your skills. A word of advice, think carefully before jumping headfirst into the unknown (such as embarking on a total career change) and never take too lightly the value of experience. Experience is the key for establishing and maintaining useful contacts and industry-specific knowledge. Potential employees that can move straight into a job and don't face a steep learning curve because they already have the necessary skills and information are valuable. An alternative to a wholesale career change is that of moving into an area that shares some common ground with your existing occupation. This is a lower-risk option that exposes you to new career possibilities by allowing you to marry your current skills with recently acquired ones.

You don't have to be a rocket scientist to realise that a great way of increasing your chances of earning good money is to invest time and energy in your own education. The reason for this is pretty simple. A certificate or degree shows employers that you have been trained to think and find solutions to problems. And best of all you have a piece of paper to prove it – which also helps your bargaining power with future employers.

But don't despair if you're not qualified. You can get qualified by doing a course at university or TAFE. Talk to a career adviser about a course that can help you.

However, if this sounds daunting and you feel you lack education, training and/or experience, probably the best place to begin developing your skills is in IT. It is becoming increasingly obvious that it doesn't matter what career you choose, you'll need to know something about computers. Computers are a key component of how we work, so it is important that you stay abreast of new technology. If nothing else, computers are a great way to find a job.

Steps to boost your employment chances

- Professional presentation and punctuality are critical for creating the best possible first impression at a job interview.
- Construct a professional, concise, easy-to-read resumé focusing on your achievements rather than a laundry list of all the jobs you've held in the past. Adapt your resumé to match individual job descriptions and keep it brief, no more than three pages. Be sure to explicitly deal with all selection criteria covered in the advertisement.
- Conduct a fact-finding mission. Research the company and the people with whom you are interviewing.
- Be technology savvy and send online job applications when email addresses are provided.
- Recognise the possibility of having to sit for a psychological test. Prepare yourself by researching the standard tests on the Internet or at your local library.
- Be prepared to sell your strengths. An interview provides the perfect opportunity to showcase your skills, so market yourself effectively without lapsing into shameless self-promotion.
- Persistence brings rewards when job hunting. But remember, there is a fine line between persistence and annoyance, so tread carefully.
- Rehearse for interviews. Pre-empt questions and formulate responses, try to use practical examples to display your skills as you've applied them in real-life job situations.
- Be proactive and ask questions about the job. This shows

that you've done your homework and are genuinely interested in the position.

- Be confident and personable. Make eye contact with the interviewer, offer a firm handshake, smile and speak clearly. Consider using an icebreaker by commenting on something in the room at the start of an interview; avoid the urge to crack a lame joke. Speak confidently, don't babble, listen closely and resist the impulse to interject. Remember to breathe, and present a self-assured and relaxed image.

Job searching

When hunting for a job, your first port of call will probably be the 'Classifieds' section of the major metropolitan newspapers. Local papers also carry employment classifieds – usually on Wednesdays. If you are open to the possibility of relocating, you might like to consult regional classifieds or those covering other States.

Another great way to hunt for jobs is via the Internet. Some handy web sites to start searching are:

- **Australian Careers Directory** –
  www.detya.gov.au
  This is a good starting point featuring a comprehensive list of links to other sites which you can also use to search for jobs. There are also links to overseas job sites.
- **Seek Communications** – www.seek.com.au
  This site will email jobs to you according to the type of position you specify, and enable you to create a resumé online.
- **The Monster Board** – www.monster.com.au
  Abiding by the principle that practice makes perfect, this site features a virtual interview page which asks some questions that are sure to test the most experienced of

interviewees. You can also search for jobs overseas via Monster Board.

- **Job Network** – www.jobnetwork.gov.au
  If you are a job seeker, you can also call 13 62 68 for access to Job Network's services.
- **New Apprenticeships Centres** –
  www.newapprenticeships.gov.au or phone them on 1800 639 629.

If looking to 'upskill' or find out about vocational training, a phone call to your local TAFE college will set you straight about what sort of courses are on offer and when they commence (TAFE course info line: 13 16 01).

Look in the Yellow Pages under 'Business Colleges' for courses in fields such as travel, technology, business studies, personnel consulting, hospitality, marketing, secretarial or public relations.

Did you know?

For more than two decades, dentistry and medicine have offered the highest graduate starting salaries at figures of $43,000 and $40,000 respectively. Close behind are the earth sciences, optometry, engineering and computer science.

If you refer to the 'University and Tertiary Education Colleges' listings, you'll find contact details for a wide range of institutions offering university-accredited courses, as well as advanced diplomas, certificates or Masters degrees in everything from computing, management, marketing, commerce, engineering and IT, through to the more traditional university subjects. You can find this information by visiting the Universities and Admissions Centre (UAC) web site at www.uac.edu.au and following the links to the tertiary admission centre in your State.

Finally, don't overlook the value of word of mouth. Be open to suggestions and well-grounded advice, ask questions, and remember that sometimes having a strategically located contact can open career doors.

Out of the cold

According to Julia Ross, even though there are plenty of available positions, it is hardest to place people for jobs during the months of May, June and July because there is a distinct lack of applicants. She believes this can be put down to the fact that there are less overseas workers here in the winter months, and because people tend to coincide changing to a new job with the new year. Hence, mid-year may be a more constructive time to reassess career plans or seek an alternative position.

A LIFE AND A LIFESTYLE

Above all, choosing the right career for you is important because it is where you will spend a huge amount of your most precious resource – your time or, in other words, your life. The ideal career is one which engages your interests and your particular talents, provides a service to others, and a good lifestyle to you and your family.

chapter 5

FINANCIAL PLANNING

AN INSIDER'S GUIDE TO CHOOSING AN ADVISER

Just about everyone I bump into wants to know if I can recommend a really good financial adviser. And it's a question worth asking. In this section I'll give you insiders' insights from four advisers: three senior longstanding advisers and myself. These will help you to identify what to look for when choosing a financial planner.

Let's face it, it's a complex world. It is bad enough having to manage your money, choose the right mortgage and the best low-interest car loan and work out the most tax-effective salary package, let alone having to think about which investment to make and whether to borrow or not, which superannuation fund to choose and whether to salary sacrifice into super. We need to know whether we are saving enough to meet our long-term goals. Being able to work out how much money we need in order to retire would also be a big help.

In a perfect world we would be assigned a financial angel who would be available 24 hours a day and able to help us for free in a completely unbiased fashion, not corrupted by high levels of commission on crappy products. What happens in the real world? What exactly can or can't an adviser do for you?

One of the unpleasant realities of life is that advisers simply can't afford to help the great majority of people. An adviser running an office with secretarial and technological support is also required to maintain quite high levels of ongoing training. The overall cost of rent, wages, technology and training is not insignificant and few advisers could afford to charge less than $150 to $200 per hour for advice, or they would go broke.

I know many of my 'Money' show viewers and *Money Magazine* readers would benefit greatly from an adviser spending half a day with them to sort out everything from investments to mortgages, cash flow and credit cards. But to do this the adviser would need to charge $600 to $800, which is where we come to the problem. Those who would most benefit from such advice often simply can't afford to pay for it.

As a result, some advisers tend to focus on people to whom they can sell enough product to cover their costs and make a profit. In the past this has led to some dreadful abuses, such as some truly appalling insurance company savings plans, where you or I were convinced by a salesperson to sign up $10, $20 or more a week to a long-term plan. The salesperson pocketed a very handsome commission cheque, and typically after three years the investor had an account balance of zero. It had all gone in fees and charges.

Paul's advice on choosing an adviser

I reckon that you need to take a realistic view when it comes to choosing an adviser. These are my thoughts on the subject.

- *There is no such thing as free advice.*
  Commission disclosure, consumer knowledge and increasing regulations have forced most of the rogues out of business. However, remember that if you use the services of an adviser, at some stage they must have some hope of getting paid – or of selling you something that pays them a commission.

- *A competent honest adviser will make it clear how they are paid and happily tell you in detail how this happens.*
  Somewhere, somehow, people need to be paid. If it is not clear to you how your adviser is paid, keep on asking. You must understand how they are paid, so you can understand their bias.

- *At your first meeting, or over the phone, get straight to the point about your position and what you want.*
  Professional advisers who are successful have good technical skills, but they also have strong people skills. Advice is a personal business and few advisers will be willing to offend people by saying early in a meeting that you are just not the sort of client they want to look after, so it really is up to you to be able to succinctly say, 'Look, this is my situation, am I the sort of client you serve?'

- *The best advisers want to give you ongoing advice and will charge you an annual fee for this.*
  It is important to have an ongoing relationship with your adviser. You want someone who will understand your needs and help you solve your investment problems now and in the future. You don't want someone who sells you a product, takes the commission and then forgets you. Be very cautious about an adviser who only earns a commission when you buy something. They will only wish to see you on an ongoing basis if you want to buy something or

they can sell you something. Frankly, if the 'advice' is always free and the adviser only makes money when you buy product, it is very hard to see how you are ever going to get unbiased advice.

• *A good adviser should be giving you quality advice that suits your needs – not using you to help fund his or her personal deals.*

One of the great traps in financial advice is buying deals from the adviser when the adviser is personally involved in the deals. You might recall Margaret Fulton's story reported in *Money Magazine* and elsewhere in the media. She nearly lost her home when her accountant involved her in his deal to construct a retirement village. A professional adviser needs to keep a critical eye on your investments. This means that they should not be personally involved. If they have lots of their money tied up in the deal, this may sound like a good thing to you, but it may also cause the adviser to become too emotionally tied to the investment, leading to poor decisions on your behalf.

• *Don't expect a professional adviser to waste valuable time trying to work out things that really only you know. Approaching an adviser in a logical, prepared fashion will pay big dividends.*

The biggest obstacle to finding a professional adviser is not being clear about what you want. So, before you find an adviser, sit down with a pencil and piece of paper somewhere quiet and pour a glass of wine if it helps. Write down all of your assets and liabilities, your income and spending habits. Think about your aspirations for your career, relationships, any dependents and estate planning. List your insurance and your long-term goals. Consider when you want to stop work, how much income you would like to have and where you would like to live. Imagine if you went to your doctor and couldn't say what was wrong with you, nor describe any symptoms. The appointment would not be very useful.

Money Tip

Be careful of financial advice from well-meaning family and friends.

Gwen Fletcher

Gwen Fletcher is joint managing director and a principal of Fletcher Green Financial Services, and the founder and co-principal of the Investment Training College. Gwen is a pioneer of financial planning in Australia, and in 1987 the Financial Planning Association (FPA) awarded her its first life membership.

Like our other two experts, Gwen's response to the question 'What's the key thing you should look for in a financial planner?' was 'being on the same wavelength'. Does the adviser understand what you want and are you confident you can work together? Having cleared this hurdle, you should check their qualifications.

In the case of married couples, Gwen says partners should choose an adviser together and the decision should be unanimous. Both must be comfortable with their financial planner to get the best results, and in the event of one partner dying, the relationship with the adviser ideally should be ongoing for the one remaining.

Gwen says much of financial planning is counselling, so life experience is vital in an adviser. In this regard, she thinks younger advisers are at a disadvantage compared to their older counterparts.

Then there is the matter of formal qualifications. As financial planning firms (licensed securities dealers) actually authorise those within them to act as financial planners, the calibre of a firm becomes something you need to think about. The financial planners within any given firm will probably reflect how good or bad it is overall, and how likely it is going to continue in business for as long as you need it.

An important question Gwen urges you to ask a prospective adviser is 'If you are not here next time I come in, who will look after me?' She would like the answer to be something like 'I work here with my colleagues, and one of them (and here a name may be given) would look after you'. In other words, continuity of service is important, and reflects on how solid the company the adviser works for is. Of course, if you're happy with your planner and he or she moves to another securities dealership, should you follow them to their new firm? Gwen says that's really a personal decision, but do check the calibre of the new firm, probably letting that be the main determining factor.

What about fees? These can be levied on a fee-for-service basis (at say, an hourly rate for the adviser's time) with all commissions rebated to you; conversely there may be no service fee charged with all commissions being retained by the adviser; or a combination of these. Gwen says it does not really matter which fee basis you proceed under, as long as it is declared up front, that it is well understood by you, and that you're happy with the arrangement. If you're not happy with the way a particular planner charges, it's simple: take your business elsewhere.

Finally, there is the dicey matter of trying to determine the integrity of an adviser you've only just met or hardly know. How can you tell what they are really like? This is where referrals come in. Gwen is a great believer in asking people you trust if they could recommend a financial planner. It makes the search for a good adviser that much easier, though, in the end, the choice is yours and the adviser has to be able to cut the mustard.

Laura Menschik

Laura Menschik is the managing director of Millennium Financial Services. She has many years experience in the financial planning industry and is a past board member and chairman of the FPA.

When asked what is the most important thing you should look for in a financial planner, Laura replied, 'A good line of communication. Only through good communication can you convey to the planner exactly what you want and can they convey to you the best way to achieve your goals'. Laura says personality also comes into play, 'Some clients want a straight-to-the-point, no-nonsense-type adviser, others want a more chatty, soft and cuddly one'. Laura says she has won and lost clients on her personality and sees nothing wrong with that.

Next, Laura says you must ensure your prospective adviser has the right credentials. By this she means having a suitable level of formal qualifications, such as being a CFP (Certified Financial Planner) and being a member of an appropriate professional body like the FPA.

Then there is experience. Laura considers good experience in the industry to be essential in your adviser. This does not mean that you should automatically choose an older person. She knows some very good young advisers who have been in the financial planning industry for many years, as distinct from some older, presumably more life-experienced advisers, who have actually just joined the industry. Asking your prospective planner how long they have been a financial planner is a vital question.

When asked should the adviser be a similar age or sex to the client, Laura replied, 'Only if it makes the client feel more comfortable'. Perhaps it's all to do with the fact that a good adviser should be able to ask, indeed ought to ask, some very personal questions.

This leads to the issue of being judgemental about clients' goals and lifestyles, which Laura says a good adviser must definitely not be. Take, for example, two clients, a lesbian couple, who wanted to have a child. To be effective, Laura had to be able to discuss freely and frankly with them how the baby was going to be conceived and by whom, whether there was going to be a known father playing some sort of rearing role or an anonymous sperm donor, and other questions. All the answers have distinct, long-term financial implications. Laura thinks an older, more conservative male financial planner may have had difficulty asking some of these questions, and for that matter the two women may have been reluctant discussing them with him – to everyone's detriment.

In the end, it all comes down to the client's trust in the adviser, which the adviser must earn. Laura equates a good financial planner–client relationship to a good doctor-patient relationship. If finding the right person means going through a few financial planners along the way, so be it. Laura is all for shopping around to find fair value and the right person.

Bob Hawley

Bob Hawley is a senior financial planner with Deutsche Bank Financial Planning. He has a Bachelor of Commerce degree, is an FPA senior associate, and has been in the industry since 1981. Bob has three children, two of whom have followed their father into financial planning. He is also a longstanding mate of mine with whom I have enjoyed many rounds of golf.

He agrees with Gwen and Laura that, above all else, there should be good communication between you and your financial planner. It's like choosing a doctor – you want someone you can talk to, can confide in and from whom you can expect to get the best. 'There must be rapport between the client and the adviser, and it must be there from the start,' he says. 'If it's not there at the outset, it will never be there and actually the relationship will just get worse to the point of becoming useless.'

Bob reckons it shouldn't matter whether you deal with a male or female adviser – either should be able to help you. What does matter though, he says, is the adviser's experience – and not textbook experience so much as life experience. Bob says you need someone who has been around a bit and seen the bad times and things like share-market crashes, high-interest rates, property-trust collapses, residential-property slumps and so on. You need someone who 'can take you by the hand and lead you through the good and the bad times, because they have lived through the bad times themselves and know what to expect'.

Bob also recommends you look for an adviser who is an investor themselves, particularly a direct investor in the share market. Again his rationale is one of practical experience versus theory. You will benefit from an adviser who is in the markets, who is effectively 'getting their hands dirty', who is giving advice partly based on what they are experiencing in the markets themselves.

In terms of the adviser's attitude, Bob says look for one who is positive, proactive and inclined to provide direction, coming to you off their own bat and saying, 'Look, this is where you ought to be heading and I think you should be doing this and that', rather than an adviser who waits for you to make all the moves.

What about when you've found a few advisers you think may be OK, but you would like someone else's opinion about them? Bob says your prospective adviser should give you the opportunity to talk to some clients to get their feedback.

If the adviser is reluctant or refuses to allow you to, say, phone some of his or her clients for a testimonial, Bob says to 'think twice about them'.

According to Bob, the three most important things you should look for in an adviser are:

- rapport and good communication
- experience/credibility
- good all-round management skills, such as providing good service and being on the ball.

FINANCIAL PLANNING BENEFITS AND KEY QUESTIONS

Having looked at how to choose an adviser, let's consider the reasons to use an adviser, and how to find one.

1 The benefit of financial advice

I am forever meeting people who say to me 'Paul, I work hard and try to budget and save, but can't seem to get ahead'. And how true it can be! So many of us pour our time and energy into our regular jobs and may even supplement our income with part-time work and overtime. Often it's not a case of how much money we are earning, but what we are doing with it. It's not that we're frittering it away on expensive clothes, rare paintings, fancy restaurants or overnight stays in the best hotels either. If only! In many cases the money we earn is being spent on everyday expenses like food, mortgage or rent payments, utility bills, school fees, vehicle expenses and childcare.

So it's little wonder that many of us feel that it's a case of one step forward and two steps back. We work more, we earn more, yet often don't seem to have much more to show for it. My advice to people in this situation is to sit down as soon as you can and work out what your goals are. Once you've done this, finding a financial adviser who can help you choose the best investments and strategies to assist you achieve those goals is a good idea. But let's be realistic.

2 How a financial adviser can help

A good financial adviser is not dissimilar to a good doctor. Both are professionals trained to help us. A doctor watches over our physical health, while a financial adviser focuses on our financial health. To provide us with the best treatment, a doctor will review our medical history, whereas the adviser learns about our financial history from which they will develop a 'financial plan'. This plan focuses on where we want to go with our lives and, like a road map, should show us how to get there.

A financial adviser can generally help us:
- develop a sound financial plan
- make informed decisions about our money
- maximise our savings
- choose investment products that suit our needs
- plan for retirement
- understand risk and return.

3 Choosing the right financial adviser

As we've seen, it's important that you choose an adviser with whom you feel comfortable and that they are trustworthy, credible and effective. Start by getting recommendations from friends, relatives, colleagues and people in similar situations to you.

You can also save a lot of time by contacting the Financial Planning Association who will refer you to qualified financial advisers. The main advantage of contacting the FPA is that the advisers it recommends are certified. This means they've met a combination of the following criteria: a degree in either economics or finance; a Diploma in Financial Planning from the Securities Institute of Australia (SIA); and at least two years financial planning experience. Advisers certified by the FPA have the letters CFP (Certified Financial Planner) after their name.

Once you have a list from the FPA, telephone a few advisers and ask them to send you a copy of their *Advisory Services Guide* (ASG). This will outline what services the adviser offers and the costs involved. If an adviser says they don't have a guide, cross them off your list immediately. Also ask them about professional indemnity insurance. Since the *Financial Services Reform Act 2000* passed through Parliament, it has become a legal requirement that all financial advisers are covered by indemnity insurance. Indemnity insurance helps you receive compensation if your adviser gives you poor advice. To find out more, contact the FPA on 1800 626 393 or visit their web site at www.fpa.asn.au.

4 Be prepared for the initial interview

Once you have selected some advisers from the list, you need to make an appointment to meet with them. Advisers will either come to you or you can visit them at their office. Don't expect instant solutions at the first interview. Often the initial meeting is free and will be brief. Remember this is an opportunity for both you and the adviser to see if you can work together. It's only at the second interview that you will start to get into the nuts and bolts of developing a financial plan. By asking the following questions, you should be able to make up your mind if this person is the right adviser for you.

*   *How long have you been giving advice?*
    Remember you can't beat experience. It is important that your advisor has experienced the bad times as well as the boom times. This experience will be vital during the slow times.

- *What are your qualifications?*
  A degree in economics or finance is a good start, but also keep an eye out for professional qualifications such as ASIA (Associate of the Securities Institute of Australia) or DFP (Diploma of Financial Planning). Remember, the best-qualified advisers are likely to have the letters CFP (Certified Financial Planner) after their name. You'll be able to double-check this when you meet them.

- *Tell me about your company. Do you have equity in it, and who are the shareholders?*
  Find out how long the company has been in business and what its background is. A financial adviser representing a bigger firm will generally be able to call on the best research and latest technology to help them provide you with the best investment advice. Be aware that it's generally more difficult for a sole operator to compete with this level of expertise.

- *What type of clients do you specialise in?*
  Whilst in theory it might seem to be a good idea to meet with the top financial advisers, the reality is that you may not be the type of client they want and as such will not be well looked after. The reality is that many of us wouldn't be able to afford them anyway. But this is no reason to despair, there are still plenty of good advisers around who can provide you with the level of expertise you need.

- *Do you give independent advice?*
  Ask the adviser whether a large financial institution such as a life insurance office owns the company they represent. If it does, find out whether the adviser can still provide you with advice about investments managed by its competitors.

- *Will I get my advice in writing?*
  If you don't, leave straight away. A plan in writing will make it easier for you to monitor the progress of your investments. Also in the event that something goes wrong with your investments, you may need to produce a copy of the financial plan for legal purposes.

- *What ongoing services do you provide?*
  Once we have a financial plan, most of us probably need ongoing advice. The reasons for this might include fluctuations in the financial markets (such as a share-market slump that affects the way our investments are performing), or a change in our own financial situation (such as receiving an inheritance or retiring). Find out how the adviser provides this ongoing advice. You also need to know that if you want more advice and your adviser is not available there is somebody else you can comfortably speak to. For this reason it might be worth meeting the back-up person, so you get to know them too.

- *Do you provide copies of previous plans and testimonials?*
  You can ask the adviser for copies of plans compiled for other people with similar goals and objectives to your own. You could also ask to speak to these people. This will help you get a better feel for the way the adviser operates and how good they are at their job.

- *How are you paid for your services?*
  In the world of money, there's no such thing as 'free advice'. If something looks free, you need to be aware that this is probably not the case. An understanding of an adviser's fee structure will put you in a better position to evaluate their investment advice. Some advisers charge a fee, some a commission, whilst others charge a combination of both.

When you consult a fee-for-service adviser, you will usually find that there is either a basic flat fee for a financial plan or a time-based fee (where the time charged includes the time it takes to assess your needs and then prepare a plan). On the other hand, a commission-only adviser won't charge you a fee, but will earn a commission from the financial institution whose investment products he sells you. Almost two-thirds of advisers will offer you a choice of fees or commissions or a combination of both. Both methods are acceptable. What is most important is that you are given an explanation of how these costs are structured, so that you are aware of how much you are likely to pay for the financial advice. This information should be disclosed in the institution's *Advisory Services Guide* (ASG).

Generally speaking you can expect to receive independent advice from the 'fee for service' adviser, as their advice is not connected to commissions in any way. Usually they will give you a rebate on all or part of any commissions paid to them by the financial institutions from whom you buy the investment product.

5 Commissions, trailers and other benefits

There are a number of commissions of which you should be aware:

- The *upfront commission* is paid by the financial institutions to the adviser when you first put your money into their investments. These commissions can generally range from 0% to 5%.
- The *trailing commission* or *trailer* is an ongoing commission paid by financial institutions to the adviser for as long as their client holds the investment. Trailers range from 0.25% to as high as 1%.
- *Soft-dollar benefits* are non-cash incentives (subsidised office space, computers, access to research, client databases

and advertising rebates and subsidies) paid by the financial institutions to the advisers on an ongoing basis to encourage them to sell their products.

• *Cumulative awards* are incentives paid by the institutions to advisers who sell a certain amount of their investments. These awards generally include prizes such as overseas trips or cash.

It's also useful to be aware that it is common for advisers to sign contracts with companies to recommend their products and research. Advisers will specify with which financial institutions they have signed these agreements and this information will also be disclosed in the *Advisory Services Guide*.

6 The second meeting

After the initial meeting, your new financial adviser now needs to obtain more in-depth information from you that will help in the preparation of a financial plan. They will want to know basic details such as your age, how healthy you are, your income, your current disposable income, how much superannuation and insurance you have and your everyday expenses. Don't worry if you don't know all these details, as your adviser will work through them with you. However, you will find the meeting far more fruitful if you have done some thinking about these issues in advance and brought along as much detail about your personal finances as you can – preparation really does help.

Your adviser will talk to you about your attitude to risk. As discussed in Chapter 6, 'Savings and Investment', risk is a vital issue and is not of itself something to be feared – it is something to be managed.

And you will be asked about your financial and lifestyle goals. These could include anything from an overseas holiday, to a new car, home renovations, a holiday home or a caravan. The adviser will need to know about any financial or personal issues you might have, such as whether or not you are secure in your current employment, have any dependents (invalid children or parents, a sick spouse, etc.), or whether you are expecting any financial windfalls, such as an inheritance.

7 The financial plan

Armed with this information, your adviser will go away and develop a financial plan for you. It is a bit like a road map that indicates where you want to go and the best way to get there. The plan should contain investment advice and information about the level of risk involved with the investments your adviser has recommended. A good plan will also address issues such as what insurance you should consider, your taxation position and finally any retirement and estate-planning issues.

8 Checking your plan

- Check that the plan agrees with the financial and lifestyle goals you set with your adviser and if you don't understand something, don't be afraid to ask. They are there to help you and it is only natural that you'll have questions. Also if something seems strange and somewhat at odds with the strategies you discussed earlier, ask about it. An example could be if your adviser has recommended only one company's products. You could also ask him/her whether this strategy spreads the investment risk widely enough.
- If you are investing a larger sum of money and your plan seems to be weighted towards one type of investment over another, ask your adviser for an explanation. If, for example, you have told your adviser that you'll need money in twelve months yet your plan suggests investing

in shares, an investment that typically does well over the medium to longer term (three to five years), you need to establish the reason for this.

- If you are planning your retirement, it may not be appropriate to primarily tailor the financial plan so that you get social security benefits. Often people try so hard to get the pension that they put an absurd investment scheme in place that actually costs them money.

- Think carefully about any plan that recommends borrowing money to invest. Done sensibly, it's OK. Borrowing money to invest can provide bigger returns, but can also work against you. You could end up paying back a loan, paying interest, and wearing a significant loss as well.

- Does your plan explain what happens if you withdraw your money from an investment early? Are there any exit fees?

- Does the plan recommend you invest all your money without keeping any cash for an emergency? Emergencies happen and you may need cash in a hurry. A plan that leaves you with nothing tucked away may not be very helpful in such a situation.

- What ongoing service is being recommended and what does it cost?

9 Working with a financial adviser

It's important to remember that you shouldn't expect the adviser to take full responsibility for your finances. It's the same as a professional footballer visiting a doctor with an injured back. The doctor will present a diagnosis and perhaps even prescribe some medication to ease the pain. But according to the doctor the best medicine is four weeks' rest and definitely no football. However, if the footballer ignores the advice and goes out and plays after only a week and injures his back again forcing him out for the rest of the season, it's not the doctor's fault. The footballer didn't follow his advice. At the end of the day the footballer is responsible for his own injuries. Think of your financial adviser in the same way. Your adviser can only advise you. I have spoken to dozens of people who have taken the plunge and had a financial plan developed only for it to sit in a filing cabinet gathering dust until their next financial crisis. It's important that you constantly refer to your financial plan and seek the ongoing advice of your financial adviser.

10 *You don't have to live with the wrong adviser*

If you do actually identify an issue that you need clarified, your first step should be to approach your financial adviser directly with your problem. If this doesn't deliver a satisfactory outcome, then you can contact the complaints person within your adviser's organisation. If you are still unhappy, you can then lodge an official complaint with the Financial Services Complaints Resolution Scheme on free call 1800 670 040.

You should be aware that even if you have followed all the advice in this book, things could still go awry when it comes to the competence or integrity of the adviser you choose. If suddenly your adviser suggests concentrating too much of your money in one investment or does something else that strikes you as unusual, it's worth asking a few questions to make sure that the new recommendation is right for you. Remember – and this really needs to be stressed – if you aren't comfortable with any piece of advice, don't feel pressured into accepting it.

Key Points

- There is no such thing as free advice.
- Understand how your adviser is paid so you understand their bias.
- Professional advisers do not hide how they are paid.
- Be able to clearly state what you want at the first meeting.
- If an adviser only makes money through the products sold, can they give unbiased advice?
- Does the advice suit your needs or the adviser's personal deals?
- Good preparation generally yields better results.

chapter 6

SAVINGS AND INVESTMENT

I have already pointed out how important and powerful regular saving can be. But, I'm absolutely certain that most people miss this basic fact, so let me remind you that $100 a month (around $23 a week or $3.30 a day), invested at 6% will turn into $59,000 in 20 years and $419,000 in 45 years. Let's imagine you pay off your mortgage at age 40 and then invest your $1,000 a month repayment until age 60, again at 6%. This results in $590,000 – a huge amount of money.

My industry seems to love using jargon to make investment even more complicated than it already is. In Chapter 3 I listed the ten steps towards financial freedom and, of these, three form the basics of saving and investing. So if you want to get wealthy, slowly, use these three basic ideas and thoughts.

1 It's not what you earn, it's what you save

I know people earning $500,000 a year who are broke, and people earning $35,000 who are well off. Wealth has nothing to do with income, but it has everything to do with saving. If you can save, you can pay off your mortgage, you can top up super, or negatively gear investments.

> No savings equals no wealth.

2 Save on a regular basis

Frankly, I don't really care whether you buy decent property, buy shares, top up super, pay off your home or add to a managed fund. What is important is that you do *something* on a regular basis.

> Do something – regularly.

3 Invest in growth assets

Do not, I repeat, do not leave money in the bank year after year. Sure, the bank is a terrific place for your everyday spending money, but it's no good for your investment money. If you really want to stick with the bank, don't leave money in it, buy shares in it.

> $1,000 in a Commonwealth Bank Savings Account five
> years ago would be worth around $1,200 today.
> If you had bought shares in the bank at the same time,
> you'd have nearly $3,000!

INVESTING IS NOT THAT HARD

Personally, I don't think investment is that hard. It's doing the simple things on a regular basis. Yet it seems that just about every time I switch on the radio these days, a bookie from one of the online betting firms is talking about the latest odds for the next big event on the Australian or international sporting calender. When I was a kid, people placing a (legal) bet had the simple choice of horses or greyhounds, but now the online bookies offer us the chance to bet on football, cricket, car racing, golf, swimming, athletics, boxing and any other sport you can name.

No matter which way you look at it, this new age of punting only serves to provide us with more chances to lose our hard-earned money, while the bookies who understand the mathematics and set the odds sit back and get rich. And why is it that over time the bookies prosper? Well, while they seem to be experts on every sport across the globe, what they really do is spread their risk, while punters concentrate theirs – and, over time, it's clear which is the better strategy.

> *Take the example of the US Masters Golf Championship, which is a little closer to my area of expertise and interest than horse racing. A bookie spreads their risk by continually changing the odds in such a way as to encourage punters to back as many of the golfers as possible – ideally, every golfer in the championship will have a bet placed against his name. And, if for example, Greg Norman or Tiger Woods are heavily backed, some of the bookies might consider minimising some of their exposure by occasionally placing a bet with other bookmakers. This way, no matter which golfer wins, the bookie will have a mix of wins and losses. If they spread their risk well, their wins should generally outweigh their losses.*
>
> *The punter, on the other hand, doesn't work this way. What the punter does is concentrate all their money on one or two golfers out of a possible field of 120. If they do well, they are rewarded handsomely, if not, they lose the lot. Not only that, but the more times you punt, the greater your chances of losing become.*

This is not what I call investing. In my book, investing means putting your money on something that has a good chance of winning in the short to medium term, and an even better, if not dead-certain, chance of winning in the long term. Fortunately, there are money-making vehicles that can do this for us, and they are the classic assets of quality shares, well-located property, fixed-interest securities and cash deposits.

To strengthen your returns, you should consider investing a little in all of these categories, not a lot in one. Investors call this 'diversification'; bookies call it 'hedging their bets'. They both mean the same thing: namely, not putting all your eggs in the one basket. By doing this, over time you will have a better chance of minimising the risk that your investments won't perform in the way you want them to.

RISK

A dictionary definition of 'risk' is 'the possibility of incurring a misfortune or loss'.

In fact, it's fair to say that every time we make a choice, there is the risk that something we didn't intend could happen or we could lose.

> *Take the example of a friend of mine, who decided to buy a second-hand, six-month-old computer from a private sale. The private vendor offered a price that was too good to refuse, but, as it turned out, after a couple of months a number of mechanical problems occurred that weren't apparent at the time of purchase. The computer ended up costing my friend more to fix than if he had purchased it new from a retailer.*

In an investment context, risk should be thought about in similar terms. Risk is the likelihood that the investment returns we anticipate are not met.

Investors should be aware that there are a number of risks to consider when making the decision to invest in an asset class. These include:

- the risk that your investment won't return what you expected or needed
- the loss of some of your original capital (original investment)
- the possibility that another investment performed better than the one you chose
- you sold the investment at a time when it was not performing well
- your investment failed to beat inflation.

But don't for a moment think that I am against taking sensible risks. Taking higher risks, such as borrowing to invest or investing in shares rather than interest-bearing securities (provided you have a clear understanding of the risk involved), should, over time, magnify your returns.

RETURN

More than ever, investors are faced with a confusing choice of investments. The only way that investors can compare the different investment choices is to understand what factors make up their returns. The return is the money that we earn from our investments. Depending on the asset we choose to invest in, return can take the form of:

- income, such as an interest payment or dividend (income is important to investors because it provides them with a regular stream of money to live on)
- an increase in the value of the asset, which is called a 'capital gain' (a capital gain is realised only when the asset is sold or cashed in).

A trade-off usually exists between the risk and return for

a particular asset. Generally speaking, the lower the level of risk associated with an asset, the lower its expected return. On the flip side, the greater the risk, the greater is the expected return. The risk and return for the major asset classes are shown in the table following. Please note that a 'real' return is the return in excess of inflation.

Risk and Return for Major Asset Classes

Major asset classes	Risk	Projected real annual long-term returns
Cash in the bank	Very low	0% to 1%
Term deposits (1 to 3 years)	Low	0% to 2%
Long-term fixed interest and bonds (3 to 10 years)	Medium	0% to 3%
Residential property	Medium	1% to 3%
Commercial property	Medium-High	3% to 5%
Australian shares	High	5% to 8%
International shares	High	6% to 9%
Emerging markets (e.g. South-East Asia, Latin America)	Extremely high	10% to 25%

Source: ipac securities

Money Tip

Save on a regular basis.
People forget that by saving just $3 a day and investing it sensibly over a working life, you'll end up with around $1 million.

VOLATILITY: THE RELATIONSHIP BETWEEN RISK AND RETURN

'Volatility' is a word that is often used in relation to risk. Volatility measures how much the value of the investment moves up and down. Generally, riskier investments like shares and property which produce strong long-term returns can be quite volatile in the short term. On the other hand, investments with lower risk usually produce less volatile returns.

The chart below highlights the relationship between volatility and return for various types of investments between 1993 and 2000. You can see that investments with lower volatility, such as cash and fixed interest, are likely to produce lower returns.

Volatility Versus Return for Major Asset Classes (December 1993–December 2000)

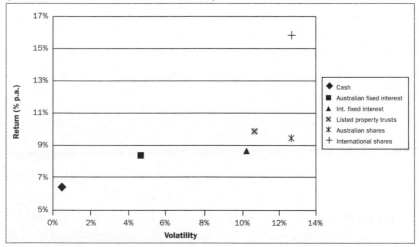

Source: ASSIRT

In the chart, volatility has been measured as the amount by which returns have varied during the period. For example, international shares have produced a return of 15.8% p.a. over 7 years, but in any given year the majority of returns could fall either 12.71% above or below 15.8% p.a.

How do we measure risk?

Everyone has his or her own concept of risk. Some asset classes seem to be more or less secure than others. For example, cash in the bank is viewed as a very low-risk investment, whereas many people would view shares as a more risky investment.

Arun Abey and Ean Higgins in their book *Fortune Strategy* (Allen & Unwin, 1995) make the observation that plenty of people tend to associate risk with losing money, without considering that they could just as easily make money.

As a result of the concern about risk, the investment industry developed a way of measuring both the upside and downside risk of an investment, or what we call its 'standard deviation'. Standard deviation measures the probability that the expected return from an investment will actually be achieved. To work out the standard deviation, investment experts first work out the average return from an asset. They then try and find the range between which 68% of all returns for that investment are to be found.

I know this is all a bit technical, but it can be a useful tool in understanding the risk associated with your investment. Let's look at an example.

Suppose Investment A has returned an average of 14% over the past 20 years and its standard deviation has been measured at 8%. This means that 68% of the twenty annual returns have fallen between 6% (8 percentage points below the average) and 22% (8 percentage points above the average). Australian and international shares have high standard deviations and are therefore viewed as riskier investments than cash and bonds, which generally have a lower standard deviation.

Dealing effectively with risk

Is the best-performing investment the best to have? It all depends on when you have it. Many of today's best performers are tomorrow's duds. The best of 1999 and 2000 – the period of the dot com boom – was a classic example of this.

All investments involve an element of risk and, typically, the higher the risk, the higher the return, but also the higher the chance of a loss. There are two important principles to keep in mind:

1 Most investors have an aversion to risk. However, investors need to understand that if they take no risk, they'll get a low return. Therefore, you shouldn't be afraid of risk: it's a fundamental part of the investment equation.

2 The secret of successful investment is not avoiding risk, because by doing so you'll also avoid a reasonable return. Rather the secret is to sensibly manage the risk. This goes right to the heart of the question 'What's the best investment to have?' The answer is: an investment where your returns are maximised for the level of risk you take.

Good-quality risk versus bad-quality risk

Now, there's also the concept of good-quality versus bad-quality risk. What you should try to do is increase the good and reduce the bad as much as possible.

Wide, diversified exposure to an investment class, say shares, over an extended period is good-quality risk. However, trying to pick highs and lows by rapidly moving in and out of the market is low-quality, speculative risk which is best left to stock-market traders.

The research of University of California behavioural finance expert, Terence Odean, has show that investors who trade shares frequently actually reduce their returns. He also found that the shares the investors had sold on average outperformed those that they bought to replace them. In other words, it would have been in their interests to have left their share portfolio alone!

High, long-term exposure to growth assets such as shares and property can be good-quality risk, provided you spread your investments across many industries and countries. But focussing on a couple of shares increases your risk.

It may sound easy getting the benefits of good-quality risk through the holding of a well-diversified portfolio over the long term, but, in reality, it means hanging on to your investments when they fall in value and watching other people do better in the short term. This can hurt, but by sticking with this strategy through thick and thin, you'll come out on top in the long term.

Remember, you shouldn't avoid risk, because you need it to get a reasonable return. The secret is to manage it in such a way that you improve the quality of your investment portfolio. This means that you effectively reduce the danger of losses and increase the chances of better returns.

TIME

The other key aspect of successful investing is time. In the short term, investment performance can be highly volatile – just look at how the share-market changes every day. If you could pick these movements in advance (and, in my experience, many so-called 'hot tips' turned out to be duds), you'd be a genius (a very rich genius). Clearly this is nigh on impossible – unless you are an inside trader, which carries stiff penalties, including jail, if you get caught.

However, over the long term (at least five to ten years) it's a different story. The investments that are most risky in the short term, such as shares and property, become less risky over time, and historically generate the highest long-term returns.

According to our research at ipac securities, over a

twenty-year period, historic after-inflation, average annual returns have been:

- from cash around 1%
- from fixed interest around 1.5%
- from investment property around 4%
- from Australian shares between 5% and 8%
- from international shares between 6% and 9%.

However, investing in higher risk assets such as shares for a week, a month or even a year is about as sensible as driving a car too fast with no brakes. An accident is a certainty.

To minimise risk and get the lifestyle you want by utilising a car means purchasing and maintaining a safe car, using the seat belts and driving safely. To get the lifestyle benefits (more money) from investing in growth assets, such as shares and property, time is the equivalent of a safety belt.

> With quality assets time minimises risk.

PORTFOLIO DESIGN

An 'investment portfolio' is the term we use to describe a carefully planned selection of assets that will meet an investor's financial and lifestyle objectives. This selection process will generally involve a trade-off between risk and return over a certain period of time to ensure that the investor meets their objectives. But before you can work out which are the best investments for you, you really need to think about what your objectives are and how much risk you are prepared to take to achieve them.

Investor profile

I have lost count of the number of people that I run into who ask me for some advice on what assets they should invest their money in. While, elsewhere in this book, I have spoken about the relative merits of the different asset classes: shares, fixed interest, cash and property, it can be hard to provide investment advice to people without first knowing something about them. This information gives financial advisers what is called an 'investor profile'.

Some investors (such as retirees or those nearing retirement) may need short-term access to their money and, therefore, may not be able to tolerate short-term price fluctuations. Younger people, conversely, might be looking for ways to build a nest egg for their distant retirement and are therefore prepared to wear these short-term price fluctuations if it means that their wealth will grow.

Financial planners also need to find out about the assets that the investor already owns. Very few investors are starting from scratch, if nothing else they will have a bank account (cash), a house (property), money in a superannuation fund and, perhaps, a few shares.

As I've stressed throughout this book, you must establish your lifestyle goals and objectives. These may include providing security for yourself in retirement, preserving the buying power of your money against inflation, supplementing present income or leaving a large inheritance for children.

Money Tip

Spending less than you earn is the simplest strategy to get rich.

Needs *(what we must have)*

Financial advisers also look at how much money the investor is spending on essentials, such as food, rent or mortgage, school fees, clothes, petrol (I won't list them all – unfortunately, we are all too well aware of them!).

Wants (what we dream about)

Many of us have dreams and aspirations. We call these wants. Mine is to play golf on all the major courses around the world with my mates. Whether it be a dream holiday home, bungy jumping in the Grand Canyon, or visiting the world's best art galleries, you are going to have to finance your dreams somehow and this might mean considering investments that pay you a higher return, but also involve a higher level of risk.

Investors need to rank their goals in order of priority and determine how much of their money is likely to be required in the short term and how much is available for long-term investment (at least three to five years).

Tax

Tax is an important issue in developing an investor's profile. It is best for investors in the high-tax brackets to decide on their asset allocation in terms of after-tax returns. Because of the tax advantages (such as dividend imputation and capital gains) relating to shares and property, taxpayers in the higher-income brackets will tend to lean towards these assets. For investors who pay little tax or no tax, the gross (before-tax) returns are more important. For these investors, tax issues only arise if the returns from an investment push them into a new tax bracket.

Risk

After we have evaluated all these other considerations, we need to work out how much risk an investor is prepared to take. The technical issues here include income security, age, underlying assets and commitments (such as family, job, and so on). The emotional issues – which are just as valid – relate to the temperament of the investor. Some people may prefer life in the fast lane and will accept a higher level of risk in the hope of gaining a better return, while others aren't comfortable with the prospect that they could lose money. This is where an understanding of standard deviation is useful. As we have already discussed, it can be used to compare the chance that an investment will record an expected return. Once you know the standard deviation of this investment, you can compare it to the standard deviation of other investments over the same time horizon.

> **Remember**
> The lower the standard deviation, the lower the risk;
> the higher the standard deviation, the greater the risk.

Time horizon

Although it is important to develop a list of financial and personal objectives, it is also essential to fit all the issues mentioned above into a loose time frame called the 'time horizon'. The time horizon will show roughly when you can expect:

- to receive certain sources of income (pensions)
- to stop receiving others (wages or salaries)
- significant needs and wants to occur and be fulfilled
- major milestones (such as retirement) to be reached.

ASSET SELECTION

When the broad framework of your investment strategy is worked out, it's then time to select the right assets. Don't choose investments based on tips you pick up around town, like the ones you get over the back fence from a neighbour or over the front seat from a taxi driver. Be aware too that even where recommendations come from investment professionals and are quite reasoned, they still might not be suited to your preferred risk level.

Risk–return characteristics of the asset classes
Cash

Cash is the safest asset class. It covers such investments as savings accounts, cash management trusts, and similar short-term, interest-bearing investments. Traditionally, cash carries the lowest risk of the major asset groups, but also generates the lowest returns. It's a great short-term investment for someone looking for total safety and accessibility to their money.

Bonds/fixed interest

These are also interest-bearing investments, but involve a longer period of maturity than does cash. The good thing about bonds and other fixed-interest securities is that you know what your return will be and how long your investment term is. You also know that you will get all your money back at the end of the term providing you hold the investment for its full period. While this locked-in interest rate may seem safer, it actually exposes the investor to more risk, because if inflation or short-term interest rates go up during this period to maturity, the investor loses out. Bonds are a low-to-medium risk–return asset class.

Property

Property covers the whole range of real-estate investments, from rural estates to office blocks. Property is a medium-to-high-risk asset class. While good over the long term, returns can fluctuate over the short term. This factor, plus the capital gains tax considerations, makes it best suited to long-term investment where it can be a tax-advantaged asset class. Property is a good candidate for geared investment strategies.

Shares

This is the highest risk asset class that in the long run generally produces the best returns. An investment in shares means a direct share in the profit and losses of companies and, as a result, in the economy itself. There are potential tax advantages to be had by buying shares with franked dividends (see Chapter 7, 'Shares – Get Rich Slow'), as well as the benefits of geared strategies (see Chapter 11, 'Borrowing to Invest'). Because of the short- and medium-term volatility of shares, along with the tax considerations, this asset class best lends itself to long-term investment.

Key Principle

An important principle in examining the asset classes is the time horizon and inflation. Although in the short term cash and bonds are safer, in the longer term they provide less protection against inflation. On the flip side, property and shares provide investors with better protection against inflation in the long term.

Some tips on asset allocation

The most important decision an investor will make is how to invest available funds among the four asset classes. A number of studies have shown that this is the overwhelming factor in the performance of a portfolio and is more important than market timing or stock selection.

In his book, *Fortune Strategy*, my ipac colleague Arun Abey mentions the findings of a US study. This research found that 91.5% of the variations in a portfolio's performance were explained by the pension fund's asset allocation, while stock selection accounted for 4.6% and market timing only 1.7%.

Some advisers tell clients to diversify their portfolios to decrease risk by spreading their money evenly across the four asset classes to get the best mix of risk and return – but this doesn't necessarily work.

Comparison of Australian Portfolios, Arbitrary and Optimised, 1985–1994

% of portfolio in	Portfolio A	Portfolio B	Portfolio C	Portfolio D
Cash	25	19	14	11
Bonds	25	50	50	50
Property	25	10	10	10
Shares	25	21	26	29
9-year return (%)	11.7	11.7	12	12.2
Risk (%)	8.6	7.0	8	8.6

Source: Abey and Higgins, *Fortune Strategy*, Allen & Unwin, 1995

What this shows is the potential for superior asset class allocation (rather than a randomly diversified portfolio, such as Portfolio A) to produce better overall results for investors. This could mean decreasing risk (Portfolio B), increasing return (Portfolio D), or both (Portfolio C).

Financial advisers use asset allocation models, which calculate the best portfolios for investors based on their risk and return profile. What the computer does is sift through all the possible combinations of assets and selects the best combinations.

However, if you want to do this yourself, you can use the knowledge about the risk/return characteristics of the asset classes against the three main criteria of the investor's profile (risk, tax, time horizon) to develop an asset allocation strategy.

Money Tip

Don't be trapped by investments promising high returns with low risk.

High return will inevitably mean high risk.

As the old saying goes, a fool and their money are soon parted.

LET'S RECAP

Tax: It is best for high-income earners to develop their portfolio in terms of after-tax returns. Because shares and property offer high-income earners tax advantages (such as dividend imputation and capital gains) they should include more of these asset classes in their portfolio than cash and bonds. For investors in the lower income groups, tax only becomes an issue if the returns from their investments push them into the next tax bracket.

Risk: The investor who is looking for higher returns and is prepared to wear more risk will generally allocate more of their portfolio to shares, property and international investments. Those whose profile would indicate that they are more comfortable with less risk will generally allocate more to cash and bonds, while the medium-risk investor will go for a more balanced approach with some money invested in each class.

Time horizon: How much time the investor has should impact on his or her view of the relative risk of the asset classes. For example, the investor who wants to invest for the long term will find property and shares to be relatively safe investments.

Portfolio Optimisation and Construction for Five Investment Profiles

	Defensive (%)	Low growth (%)	Balanced (%)	Growth (%)	High growth (%)
Asset sector					
Domestic property	12	20	17	15	10
Domestic equities	11	15	28	32	40
Domestic bonds	45	30	15	9	Nil
Domestic cash	15	10	6	Nil	Nil
Overseas property	2	3	10	12	15
Overseas equity	5	12	20	32	35
Overseas bonds	10	10	4	Nil	Nil
Total	**100**	**100**	**100**	**100**	**100**
Minimum investment term	1 year	2 years	3 years	5 years	7 years
Real return over term	0% p.a.	2% p.a.	4% p.a.	6% p.a.	7.5% p.a.
Likelihood of negative return	1 year in 12	1 year in 9	1 year in 7	1 year in 6	1 year in 5
Investor objectives and suitability					
Secure short-term income	High	Moderate	Low	N/A	N/A
Capital stability	High	Moderate	Low	Very low	N/A
Steady growth	Moderate	High	Moderate	Low	N/A
Wealth accumulation	N/A	Low	Moderate	High	Very high

Source: ipac securities

For the long-term investor, the problem of short-term volatility is less of a worry. Subsequently, they will go for the high returns that growth investments like property and shares generally offer. On the other hand, investors with a short timeframe will require less volatile assets in their portfolio, and will tend to be attracted to bonds and cash.

Sounds good, but what do you do about building a portfolio? Well, here I will turn to ipac's broad strategy for five types of portfolio targeting 0% above inflation (very conservative) to 7.5% above inflation (aggressive). The table on the previous page shows how an investor's money is split across asset classes.

BUT WHAT ABOUT MY OTHER ASSETS?

I recommend you have a plan to create three pools of wealth: your home; superannuation; and other investments. This is based on a simple view about diversification. This strategy gives you exposure to property (your home), shares and fixed interest (through your super) and other investments you buy yourself. These might be shares, money in the bank or an investment property.

It also gives you protection from a tax and legislation perspective. Super is a highly regulated area, and the main reason I would not rely solely on super is because it is another type of risk – the risk of changing legislation. Over the past decade and a half, there have been thousands of changes to legislation, so it has become quite confusing.

How you diversify depends upon your age, income, family and so on. The younger you are, the less diversification you are likely to have, but as you get older you will diversify more as your wealth grows and you want to reduce the amount of risk you are taking on.

For my kids, for example, I'm concentrating their small amounts of money in one high-risk investment area – international equities and emerging markets. My retired clients, on the other hand, have a very diversified portfolio, because they are trying to minimise risks. My children

Money Tip

Teach your children about money as early as you can.
Saving habits, even learnt with part of their pocket money, tend
to stick with them for life.

are trying to create wealth, my retired clients to preserve wealth.

There are three important principles to follow:

- *Principle 1:* Spread risk by investing in the different asset classes, such as shares, bonds, property and cash. By doing this you can minimise the impact of price fluctuations in any one class. History indicates that the asset classes tend to compensate for each other: when share prices are high, cash rates are down, and so on.
- *Principle 2:* We can also spread risk across countries and industries, and this can minimise the impact of major events like a regional economic crisis, a change of government, or the downturn in a particular industry.
- *Principle 3:* You can also take diversification into a narrower context. For example, with a share portfolio you should diversify by choosing different sectors within a market, such as banking and finance, building and construction, media, telecommunications and IT and resources. Within the telecommunications sector, you might further diversify by choosing several shares like Telstra, Optus, and even one of the smaller, aggressive players.

GROWTH VERSUS INCOME INVESTMENTS

With mainstream investments you have two broad areas to select from.

- Income investments (cash and fixed interest) are lower risk and usually generate a modest, secure and regular income. For most investors there is no capital growth and the returns are fully taxable.

- Growth investments (property and shares) are higher risk, and in the early days may generate little or even negative income. On the other hand, these investments generate capital growth over the longer term and returns may be taxed favourably.

Retirees or those approaching retirement are particularly drawn to income investments rather than growth investments, since they feel they have a need for a regular and secure income and don't want to risk losing their capital. But this traditional investment focus may not be the way to go in the long term.

For starters, as we have seen we are generally planning to retire earlier than past generations and, due to better health care, we are living longer. Modern-day Australians retiring at age 55 can expect to be out of the work force for anywhere from fifteen to forty years. It's a long time for your capital (which should provide the bulk of your retirement income) to last, and therefore it will need to be managed wisely.

Let's say you're a retiree with a $200,000 nest egg and you decide to put it in a bank account. Let's also assume that you can earn 6% on your cash, that your average rate of tax is 17% and that inflation averages 4%. Now while this may well be a (virtually) risk-free income investment, your long-term financial prospects aren't that great.

In this example, the 6% you earn, is 5% after tax. In other words, you are generating an after-tax return of 1% above inflation. And even if you can live off the 5% and not touch the capital, inflation will start to eat away at it. Indeed, after twenty years, 4% inflation will reduce the buying power of your $200,000 to just $91,277.39. Equally *depressing is the thought that even the interest income you earn each year from your bank deposit buys you increasingly less.*

This is the basis of the argument for investing in the growth investments of shares and property. Not only will your money grow in value over the long term, but so will the income you receive. This is because both rents and share dividends, unlike interest returns grow over time.

If you made a $10,000 investment in the local share market – a 'growth' investment on 1 January 1983, by 31 December 2000, it would have grown in capital value to $137,449, and the dividend income it produced in 2000 would have been around $5,000 (and partly tax-free due to dividend imputation).

Compare this to a fixed-term deposit of $10,000, also made on 1 January 1983, and rolled over every 12 months. By 31 December 2000, its capital value would still be only $10,000 and the interest income it generated in 2000 would have been just over $600 (and would be fully taxable).

The difference in the annual incomes produced by these two investments after almost twenty years is massive, dramatically demonstrating how the income produced by riskier growth investments over the long term is less of a financial and lifestyle risk. This is a lesson retirees, particularly those who hope to live for many years, need to note.

INVESTING INTERNATIONALLY

One of the truly historic changes over the past twenty years, has been the fact that when it comes to investment, the world is truly a global village.

Money can now flow at the touch of a computer key from a bank in Sydney to a bank in Zurich or Tokyo – all in the blink of an eye. This has meant that we can now quickly and easily buy assets such as shares, fixed interest or even property in practically any country.

Global implications

This has important implications for all of us because our long-term standard of living depends on how competitive we are as a nation internationally. If we are underproductive and allow foreign debt to grow, we can send the value of our dollar into a tailspin. This happened at the beginning of 2001. If our dollar falls, imports become more expensive, and no matter how hard we try, it will be difficult to buy only Australian products if this scenario eventuates.

When the Aussie dollar is weaker against the American dollar, we can expect, for example, to pay relatively more for imports from the USA, such as cars, electrical equipment, clothes and some foods. To counteract the risk that the Australian dollar might fall against overseas currencies, many investors put some of their money into overseas investments. Just as there is no reward for investing in a single share, there is no reward for investing in a single currency – even our own – when diversification can help protect against the risks.

The chart that follows looks at the performance of various investments over the past fifteen years to 2000. You'll see that international shares have performed better than the other asset classes during this period.

Now in two of those fifteen years (1990 and 1994), international shares showed a loss (-15% and -8%, respectively). Compare this to the performance of the local share market. With an annualised return of 12.5% the Australian market had four negative years over the same period.

Returns from Major Assets Classes, 1985 to 2000

Date	Local shares	Local fixed interest	Overseas shares	Overseas fixed interest	Australian property	Cash	CPI
1986	<u>55.22</u>	18.92	45.62	25.13	35.42	18.12	9.77
1987	**-7.86**	<u>*18.60*</u>	7.01	13.78	5.75	15.33	7.14
1988	<u>*17.88*</u>	9.36	**4.14**	13.34	16.06	12.84	7.60
1989	17.40	14.40	<u>*26.15*</u>	18.83	2.35	18.37	7.83
1990	**-17.52**	<u>*19.10*</u>	-15.09	13.51	8.70	16.24	6.85
1991	<u>*34.24*</u>	24.75	19.96	18.14	20.08	11.20	1.51
1992	**-2.31**	<u>*10.41*</u>	4.58	9.62	6.99	6.92	0.28
1993	<u>*45.36*</u>	16.32	24.21	14.31	30.12	5.39	1.95
1994	**-8.67**	-4.69	-8.04	-3.02	-5.57	<u>*5.34*</u>	2.55
1995	20.19	18.64	<u>*26.05*</u>	19.89	12.74	**8.06**	5.05
1996	<u>*14.60*</u>	11.90	**6.24**	10.67	14.49	7.57	1.52
1997	12.23	12.23	<u>*41.64*</u>	10.65	20.31	5.63	-0.25
1998	11.63	9.54	<u>*32.34*</u>	10.80	17.95	5.14	1.58
1999	16.10	-1.22	<u>*17.19*</u>	0.30	**-4.97**	5.01	1.8
2000	4.80	12.08	**2.19**	10.36	<u>*17.92*</u>	6.27	5.8
Average return	12.50	12.43	14.36	12.21	12.68	9.72	4.42

Year's worst returns
Year's best returns
Source: ipac securities

All of this suggests that it makes a lot of sense to hold at least part of a portfolio in international shares. In fact, I think it makes sense to hold around 40% of your investment assets in offshore assets. But don't forget that some Aussie companies such as AMP, NAB and Westfield Holdings do a lot of their business offshore, effectively giving you some international exposure.

But even buying 'global' Aussie shares won't do the trick. We are a tiny economy and to get genuine exposure to the major growth areas of the global economy, you need to invest in these markets directly, or a more effective way to go is to invest in an international share fund.

I am really positive about Australia and its economy. It's a great place to live, work and raise a family. But there are a number of issues that affect our ability to compete with our foreign trading partners. Issues such as a high level of foreign debt, some poor workplace practices and our reliance on commodities continues to hold back the productivity of Australian companies. With this is mind, investing overseas begins to make a lot of sense.

Investing overseas will work in exactly the same way that diversifying across industries and companies does for a port-folio in Australian shares. Different national economies move in different ways because they display a different blend of natural and human resources, industrial, political and economic characteristics.

For instance, the Australian economy is quite different to Japan's. The Australian economy is very dependent on the production and export of commodities such as coal, wheat and wool. Japan, on the other hand, devotes much energy to adding value to the commodities that it imports from countries like Australia. When commodity prices are high, Australia thrives, whereas the Japanese economy will thrive when commodity prices are low.

Although this shows that investing overseas is a great way of managing risk, there are also plenty of other good reasons why buying international assets will help an investor grow their wealth.

The Australian share market represents less than 2% of the global share market. This means that there is a whole world of investment opportunities to which we aren't exposed if we don't invest overseas.

Investment performance broadly reflects the economic

conditions and these vary from country to country and year to year as the following table shows. Note that the highest performer was Asia in 1993 with a return of 83.2% and compare that with the returns from other countries in the same year and other years.

Comparative International Share-Market Performance

Year	Australia	Japan	Europe	Asia	UK	USA
1989	17.4	9.5	39.5	25.3	27.3	37.2
1990	-17.5	-35.0	-1.1	-8.1	8.4	-3.4
1991	34.2	10.0	15.5	38.8	13.4	29.2
1992	-2.3	-14.1	5.5	17.9	2.3	14.8
1993	45.4	26.5	31.8	83.2	22.4	8.7
1994	-8.8	5.6	-10.2	-24.7	-16.6	-13.2
1995	20.7	4.3	27.3	18.2	22.3	40.5
1996	14.3	-21.3	13.8	13.3	15.4	13.6
1997	11.4	-7.5	51.4	-15.6	45.2	60.6
1998	8.5	10.8	36.9	-0.4	22.0	36.8
1999	19.3	50.5	8.9	34.2	2.9	13.3
2000	5.8	-15.8	8.1	-0.1	1.8	1.8

Source: ASSIRT

Australia: 1989–1993 Old All Ords. 1994–2000 S&P/ASX 500 Acc (New All Ords)
Japan: MSCI Japan $A Index
Europe: MSCI Europe Acc $A Index
Asia: MSCI Pacific Ex-Japan Acc $A Index
UK: MSCI UK $A Index
USA: MSCI USA $A Index

These figures provide further evidence that a mix of international investments will expose you to the benefits of better performing economies, while minimising the effects of poorer performing ones.

By buying shares we can become part-owners in some of the biggest companies, in some of the biggest economies (e.g. Japan, the USA and Germany) in the world. Share ownership also allows us to participate in the rebuilding of Eastern Europe or to take a stake in emerging markets in South-East Asia and Latin America.

At the time of writing, the emerging markets, in particular, were showing record levels of economic growth and I would therefore recommend owning shares in companies in these economies. Be warned though that over the longer term, investors should also expect some major short-term fluctuations in the value of shares in these markets – in spite of them being classified as 'growth' investments.

If you don't know which shares to buy, you can invest in the emerging markets through managed share funds. These funds typically invest in dozens of economies and hold hundreds of different shares, mostly in Asia and Latin America. You can talk to your financial adviser or contact a fund manager directly for more information.

HOW DO WE MEASURE DIVERSIFICATION?

We have spoken about how we measure risk, but there is also a very useful way of measuring the benefits of diversification across a portfolio. We call this 'correlation'.

Fortune Strategy discusses studies that have shown how some investments may all go up at the same time, others will move in the opposite direction, and others will react in a completely unrelated way to an 'investment theme'. An investment theme is something that underpins the performance of an industry or individual asset, for instance, a hike in oil prices or a drop in consumer confidence as a result of an economic crisis caused by a recession or a war.

As *Fortune Strategy* explains, correlation is measured on a scale of -1 to 1. Two investments that move in the same direction are said to have 'perfect correlation'. Those that move in the opposite direction, are said to have a 'perfect negative correlation of -1'.

Most investments sit between the two extremes of -1 and 1. If you refer to the table below, you'll see that transport and building have a high correlation of 0.68 and will generally react to an issue in a similar fashion.

However, oil and transport have a lower correlation of 0.39 and usually react differently to an issue such as an oil crisis, thus providing greater diversification benefits within a portfolio. The reason for this is that when oil prices are down, the cost of transport is generally cheaper. Theoretically, the overall impact on the investor will be that while the value of his oil shares will generally fall, his transport shares will continue to perform, thus protecting the overall performance of the portfolio.

Risk, Return and Correlation for Major Indices on the ASX, July 1983–December 2000

Index	Return (%)	Risk (%)	Building	Gold	Oil and gas	Retail	Transport
Building	12.9	19.5	1				
Gold	1.2	38.8	0.39	1			
Oil and gas	8.9	23.7	0.57	0.47	1		
Retail	16.4	20.0	0.65	0.34	0.44	1	
Transport	17.5	23.6	0.68	0.31	0.39	0.68	1

Source: ipac securities

Let's look at a fictitious example of low correlation, where an investor has shares in a shipping company, Acme Liners, as well as Astro Oil, a fictional oil company. Because of the low correlation (0.39) between oil and transport as the table above indicates, a fall in the share price of one will generally be offset by an increase in the share price of the other, to maintain the overall return of the portfolio.

> *Let's assume that an oil crisis occurs in the Middle East. The initial crisis and the resulting recovery runs over the medium term (three to five years). The following table reflects the time frame for the crisis. Year 1 represents the first year of the crisis. Oil prices are at all-time highs, and Astro Oil's share price is showing record returns. On the other hand, Acme Liners, which relies on oil to do business, will feel the pinch as the soaring cost of oil pushes up its operating costs.*
>
> *However, when the oil crisis is resolved at the start of Year 2, and the price of oil begins its return to pre-crisis levels, Acme Liners' operating costs will also begin to fall making it more profitable for it to do business.*
>
> *Alternatively, there will be a squeeze on Astro Oil's profits as oil prices return to pre-crisis levels over the five-year period its share price will generally reflect this.*
>
> *However, the good news for the investor, is that during this five-year period, the average return from the portfolio has maintained an average annualised return of between 11.65% and 12.8%, despite the fact that the assets within the portfolio have shown both record lows and highs.*

Portfolio Returns on Astro Oil and Acme Liners

	Year 1 return	Year 2 return	Year 3 return	Year 4 return	Year 5 return	Average
Astro Oil	31.0%	17.4%	4.3%	-8.8%	-21.9%	4.4%
Acme Liners	-7.7%	6.1%	19.9%	33.7%	47.5%	19.9%
Average	11.65%	11.75%	12.1%	12.45%	12.8%	12.15%

Source: Adapted from *Fortune Strategy*

Now this stuff is a little scientific, but I want to cover it in detail because exactly how investors go about spreading risk never ceases to amuse me.

It seems that diversification in property is to own a home and an investment property – often in the same suburb! Managed fund diversification often comprises investment in several fund managers, who upon closer examination have a similar investment philosophy and hold similar assets. A share portfolio is deemed by its owner to be diversified due to the inclusion of three or four stocks. Clearly, if we've got the general idea of what the word 'diversification' means, these instances fail dismally in implementation.

Before we dive into the do's and don'ts, let's get back to basics and mull over why diversification is seen to be such a vital component in investment strategy. When it comes down to it, we can really only invest on a passive basis in a limited number of broad asset classes: namely Australian shares; property; fixed interest and cash; plus international shares; and fixed interest. If your crystal ball worked better than mine, you wouldn't have to bother with diversification at all. You'd just place all your investment money into the asset class that you believe will do best in the next year or so. Equally and about as intelligently, you could punt the whole lot on the nag you think will win the Melbourne Cup.

The best argument for not diversifying came from a gentleman at a seminar I was speaking at in the mid 1980s. During question time, he stated that my views were a load of crap (the joys of free speech!). Further inquiry caused him to state that he put everything into property, and has made a fortune out of purchasing property and land about to be rezoned. I commented that he must have a terrific research facility, but he responded that even better than research, he had a close relative on his local council!

Putting aside a few minor issues including ethics, morality

and corruption, this was a difficult argument to counter. However, for the rest of us mere mortals to whom insider trading is an unlikely temptation, diversification will remain a way of managing the risks of an uncertain world.

Returns from the major asset classes

Let's take a look at the returns from the major asset classes in 1990.

1990 Returns	
Australian shares	−17%
International shares	−15%
Australian fixed interest	+19%
International fixed interest	+13%
Listed property trusts	+8%
Cash	+16%

Share investors did terribly. Fixed-interest investors did well. Investors diversified equally across all those areas earned around 3%. Not great, but at least it was a positive return.

Now let's look at another year, say 1993.

1993 Returns	
Australian shares	+45%
International shares	+24%
Australian fixed interest	+16%
International fixed interest	+14%
Listed property trusts	+30%
Cash	+5%

Clearly, we would have liked to have been in shares. But

even the average return to a fully diversified investor was around 18%.

So diversification is an imperfect tool, because while it dulls the downside, it also minimises the chance of an investment bonanza, because not all investments boom at the same time and in the same amount.

Indeed, there are times in your life when you shouldn't be fully diversified. For a wealth preserver (usually a retiree or near retiree), true diversification is essential. It's a matter of tailoring your asset allocation (your diversification strategy) to suit your risk profile. If you weigh your portfolio towards shares and property, your long-term returns will be higher, but there will be more short-term volatility. Invest too conservatively and you may run out of money before you die.

But what about younger investors and baby boomers? We're conscious of the need to build up real wealth to preserve our lifestyle. Should we diversify?

Frankly, I don't think wealth creators should diversify across all the major asset classes. A long-term holding in cash and fixed interest should play no part in our plans. We should hold growth assets – in the main Australian and international shares.

But within these asset classes we must take quality risks. Holding a few shares is a downright stupid risk. There is enough risk in the market without destroying our future plans by taking on management risk. Hold just a few shares and your main risk is not the market, it's the people running your companies. Imagine a portfolio consisting of just the two blue chip icons, BHP and Burns Philp, in the late 1990s. If you gave up and sold them late in 1999, what a flogging you would have taken.

The market will not reward you for stupidity. And it is truly idiotic to hold just a few companies when it is so simple and relatively cheap to diversify your holdings. Larger investors can simply buy a broader spread of shares, or use a good managed share fund. Even small investors with $1,000 have no excuse. A managed share fund will expose you to typically 40 to 60 stocks, effectively eliminating management risk.

Yes, global share markets are reasonably correlated, but not completely. So diversifying Australian share market risk by adding international markets to your portfolio is absolutely essential. Quality international share funds abound, and for around $2,000 global diversification becomes simple and cost-effective.

So before you glibly say 'Yes, I am diversified', pause and consider whether you should be diversified, if you *really* are diversified, and if your risk management strategy is in line with your goals. Above all, don't shrug off diversification by seeing yourself as a big risk-taker. Because risks that could be easily diversified and aren't are simply stupid risks – and the markets rarely reward idiots.

Money Tip

'If it looks too good to be true, it will be.'
When it comes to investment this is the single best thing to remember!

REBALANCE YOUR INVESTMENTS REGULARLY

Knowing when to transfer funds from one asset class to another is crucial to managing a portfolio. This is called 'rebalancing' your portfolio.

We have looked at how and why asset classes move in different ways, and it is quite surprising how quickly market movements can change the balance of your portfolio. An example will help to make this clear.

Let's say that you had constructed a diversified portfolio of investments that looked like this.

Australian shares	30%	(in value)
International shares	22%	
Australian fixed interest	25%	
International fixed interest	15%	
Australian property	8%	
Total	**100%**	

If the share market roared ahead (as was the case from 1995 to 2000) and, if you as an investor did nothing, sometime later your portfolio could look something like this.

Australian shares	37%	(in value)
International shares	32%	
Australian fixed interest	13%	
International fixed interest	9%	
Australian property	9%	
Total	**100%**	

The share weighting (the value that your shares proportionally comprise of a portfolio) has increased dramatically without the investor having done anything to it. It's all been due to the strong performance of shares. But, the higher share weighting means that the overall portfolio risk is now higher, because shares are the riskiest of the major investment classes.

Now you may decide that you are happy with this and you may decide that this higher risk weighting is OK for you, but unless your attitude to risk has changed, you should rebalance back to the correct portfolio mix at least twice a year. This may incur switching fees in some cases and the payment of capital gains tax on profits, but if you don't rebalance, this could cause bigger losses than you are prepared for.

Rebalancing also has the added attraction of enforced discipline. It forces the investor to sell when assets are expensive and buy when they are cheap.

How? Well, if you always keep the original 30% value of your portfolio in Australian shares and rebalance this when it falls or rises by 2% (at 32% you sell some shares, at 28% you buy some shares) by definition an investor must sell when expensive and buy when cheap. It's a simple discipline, but it works.

And remember, one thing we do know is that buying the best-performing asset class over the last twelve months is consistently a worse strategy than buying the worst-performing asset class.

DON'T TRY TO TIME THE MARKET

Now it's pretty obvious that you should buy when things are cheap and sell when they are expensive. It's so delightfully simple, but guess what most investors do? When the news is good and investments are expensive, they buy. When the news is bad and investments are cheap, they sell. And as I said earlier, chasing the 'best' performer is a poor idea.

My company conducted research during the period 1986 to 2000 that showed how difficult it is to pick the best-performing market each year. If you were good enough to pick the highest performers during that fifteen-year period, your average annual return would have been a healthy 25.47%. But if you had been unlucky enough to pick the worst performers in each of the fifteen years in this survey, your average annual return would have been 1.81%.

Another excellent example of the benefits of long-term investing in the share market was demonstrated by a study of the US share market between 1980 and 1993. It is a classic piece of research, though now somewhat dated, but I have included it because the results are revealing. The study found that if an investor kept their money in the market during this period, they would have averaged a 15% return per annum. However, if they missed just ten of the best trading days during this period, their return was reduced to 11.9%. If you missed the forty biggest days, this reduced your return to 5.5%. This is further proof to support the value of not trying to pick the market.

Time, Not Timing: Returns on the US Share Market, 1980 to 1993

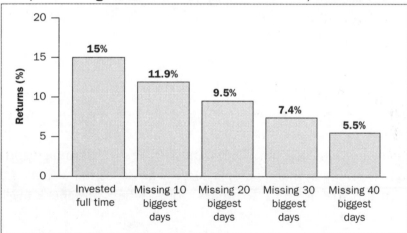

DOLLAR-COST AVERAGING

Dollar-cost averaging is a principle that means that investors can actually benefit from the fluctuations in the price of an asset. This is because when the market is up, an investor's units or shares are worth more, but when the market is down, they are cheaper to buy.

This is a really important concept, simply because it works so well. It helps us pick the right time to buy an asset. All you have to do is decide how much and how often you are going to invest. You may decide to invest on a monthly, six-monthly or yearly basis – it really doesn't matter – it's entirely up to you and what you can afford. Let's look at an example:

Dollar-Cost Averaging (Investing $1000 Every Six Months)

	Share price	Number of shares you get
1 January 2000	$1.00	1,000
1 July 2000	$1.20	833
1 January 2001	$0.80	1,250
1 July 2001	$1.00	1,000
1 January 2002	$1.40	714
1 July 2002	$1.30	769
Total shares		5,566

Look at when you bought the most shares – in January 2001 when our imaginary share's price was 80 cents. When did you buy the least? In January 2002, when the share price was $1.40.

Better still, at the end of the period, your $6,000 invest-ment (not including dividends and tax) is worth $7,235.80 based on the share price on 1 July 2002.

Human nature tends to lead us to sell when things are cheap (times are bad) and buy when they are expensive (times are good). Dollar-cost averaging forces you to buy most shares when they are cheapest, and buy the least when they are most expensive. This is a discipline worth using.

STAYING AHEAD OF INFLATION

Inflation refers to the rise in consumer prices as measured by the Consumer Price Index (CPI).

Back in the 1970s, the re-emergence of high inflation after almost thirty years was the precursor to the private investment industry. Inflation created an awareness of the need for investment products that stayed ahead of it. These products aimed at giving people more 'bang for their buck' in terms of what they did with their savings. But it took the pain of an entire generation to create this awareness.

The generation that lived through the high inflation of the 1920s, the Great Depression of the 1930s and finally World War II were particularly security conscious. They put the bulk of their savings in banks – mostly in bank accounts at 3.75% interest.

During the low inflation of the 1950s and 1960s, this proved to be a satisfactory strategy, that is until inflationary pressures hit the Australian economy in a big way following the fuel crisis in the Middle East at the end of 1973.

According to the ABS, by December 1973 inflation had risen to 13% from 5% in 1970. It stood at more than 14% by the end of 1975 and remained a big issue for the Australian Government for the best part of the next ten years.

Inflation eats away at the buying power of your money. For instance, ABS figures reveal that if an investor had saved $100,000 in 1970, by 1980 its buying power would have been equivalent to a mere $37,000 and a paltry $14,000 by 2000.

On the other hand, Real Estate Institute of New South Wales figures tell us that an investor could have paid $18,000 for an average three-bedroom home in Sydney in 1970, but would have needed $68,900 by 1980 (and a whopping $310,000 by September 2000) to buy the same house. These examples show how inflation can really hurt savings and buying power.

COMPOUNDING

Compounding is one of the key elements of successful investment over the medium to long term. Understanding compounding also helps us better understand investment returns. Let's look at an example based on interest rates.

> An investor, let's call him Bill invests $10,000 for three years in a savings deposit account, that pays 10% each year or $1,000. If, at the end of Year 1, Bill decides to spend the $1,000, he is then back to square one with $10,000 sitting in his bank account. If he earns 10% for the next two years, but spends it on a holiday, he will still have $10,000 in the bank. This is in an example of simple interest.
>
> However, if the annual inflation rate is 4%, at the end of the three-year period his $10,000 will buy the equivalent of around $8,890 worth of goods based on today's pricing, because of inflation.
>
> Bill's friend Liz decides at the end of Year 1 to reinvest the interest earned back into the bank account, so she now has $11,000. In the second year, she again earns 10% interest or $1,100, which she again reinvests. She now has $12,100 invested and earns $1,210 worth of interest during Year 3, which at the end of that year will be worth $13,310. At the compound interest rate of 10%, the investment has yielded $3,310 over three years, in contrast to Bill's $3,000 simple interest.

While the concept of compounding is easy, the implications for investors when applied to the long term are quite dramatic. The difference in just a couple of percentage points can also have quite a substantial impact on the growth of your portfolio as the following table indicates.

Impact of Different Interest Rates on the Future Value of $10,000

Period of investment	5%	8%	10%	12%	15%
Now	$10,000	$10,000	$10,000	$10,000	$10,000
5 years	$12,760	$14,690	$16,110	$17,620	$20,110
10 years	$16,290	$21,560	$25,940	$31,060	$40,460
15 years	$20,790	$31,720	$41,770	$54,730	$81,370
20 years	$26,530	$46,610	$67,280	$96,460	$163,670
30 years	$43,220	$100,630	$174,490	$299,590	$662,110

Source: ipac securities

The lesson here is that it is worth investing for the long term. If, for example, a financial adviser offers you an investment package whereby you invest $10,000 and in 30 years it is worth $100,000, this might sound pretty good, but it represents a compound interest rate of about 8%. If we invest in an asset class that is returning, say, an extra 2% (10%), we could walk away with more than $174,000 for the same $10,000 investment.

> With investing the old dictum holds: 'Time is money'.

CONCLUSION

So, after all that the point I want to make is that investing is not as hard as it seems. If you spread your risk by investing in a range of asset classes, across a number of countries, and hang on to these assets for the long term, then you should grow your wealth.

Finally, I wouldn't be doing my job if I didn't point out

that nobody ever got rich by doing nothing. I know that diversification is the best investment strategy, even if you only invest in one asset class, this is still better than not investing at all. So my advice to you is to start *now* and don't wait.

chapter 7

SHARES – GET RICH SLOW

Since I started in the investment industry back in 1979, I have been encouraging people to seriously consider jumping into the market, and it is really pleasing to see that today millions of Australians have realised the benefits of share ownership. In fact, it is estimated that over half of adult Australians now own shares. This is partly due to the fact that our knowledge about shares increased dramatically during the 1990s and we have become more comfortable with them. But the greatest number of new shareholders has come from the sale of government assets such as the Commonwealth Bank, Telstra and the TAB, not to forget the demutualisation of AMP, which meant that its policyholders were given shares in the newly listed company.

But not only have a large proportion of the Australian population become shareholders, many have also become very happy shareholders (until Telstra 2 disappointed the high hopes held for it in the wake of the previous Telstra success). The new floats have generally soared in value, as have many other favourite shares such as Lend Lease, Coles, Woolworths and News Corp PBL (Publishing and Broadcasting Ltd) – the owners of the TV station Channel 9, which has been running my 'Money' program since 1993 – has also done very well for shareholders.

On the other hand one famous blue chip stock, Burns Philp, has had a very tough time, giving its shareholders a very rough trip, from which it is just emerging. Telstra 2 was also a shot of reality for investors as its first instalment of $4.50 dropped to under $3.00 at one stage.

Generally though the news has been consistently good for shares. The chart on the next page shows the returns you would have earned each year for the fifteen-year period up until the end of 2000 for Australian and international shares. The return given each year is a combination of both the growth in value of the major companies in Australia and the dividends they pay, or, in the case of the international figures, the major companies listed on international share markets. If you're wondering how to work out these returns, I'll let you in on a secret that makes it easy. All you need to do is look at the 'Accumulation Index' for the Australian market or the 'Morgan Stanley Capital Index – World Accumulation Index', and all the work is done for you. You can get this information from a stockbroker.

Anyway, as you can see, simply by buying a selection of decent quality shares and hanging onto them for fifteen years, you would have done very well. ipac research reveals that $10,000 invested in Aussie shares in 1986 (with dividends reinvested) would be worth $58,520 in 2000, and $10,000 in international shares would be an even healthier $74,870.

Now all of this sounds pretty good. But how realistic is it? Most people can remember the crash of October 1987 when the Aussie market fell by more than 40%. Some lost all of their money by investing in companies run or owned by

Returns for Australian and International Shares, 1986–2000

Date	Australian shares	International shares
1986	52.22%	45.62%
1987	-7.86%	7.01%
1988	17.88%	4.14%
1989	17.40%	26.15%
1990	-17.52%	-15.09%
1991	34.24%	19.96%
1992	-2.31%	4.58%
1993	45.36%	24.12%
1994	-8.67%	-8.04%
1995	20.19%	26.05%
1996	14.60%	6.24%
1997	12.23%	41.64%
1998	11.63%	32.34%
1999	16.10%	17.19%
2000	4.80%	2.19%
Annualised 15-year return	12.50%	14.36%

Source: ipac securities

Alan Bond, or our seemingly permanent overseas holiday-maker, Christopher Skase. So are shares just another sucker's game?

Well, to answer this, let's take a step back into history. Not just one year or fifteen, but a few centuries.

THE FIRST SHARE MARKET

One of the earliest known share markets was pretty informal. Dutch businessmen would meet under a tree in Amsterdam back in 1602, and buy and sell certificates (effectively

What does a share market do?

Since 1828, when Matthew Gregson, Australia's first share broker, was given permission to deal in Bank of New South Wales shares, share markets across Australia and more recently the Australian Stock Exchange (ASX) have provided two distinct functions. Firstly, the share market assists companies to raise long-term capital (money). No matter how big or small a business is, there may come a time in the development of that business when its owners decide they need more money to buy extra stock, employ more staff, purchase more machinery or bigger premises. The secondary role is to provide investors with a way of buying shares at current prices as determined by other investors wanting to sell.

shares) in what was to become the Dutch East Indies Company. To my amusement, an early version of 'insider trading' (people buying or selling because they have knowledge of a company's activities not known to people outside the company) started as canny Dutch shareholders sent out fast vessels to see if the Dutch East Indies ships had survived pirates and the weather and were nearing Holland. Naturally, the arrival of a ship loaded with goods boosted the share price, so those 'in the know' bought before the ship's safe arrival was generally known – or sold if a ship was running so late it was thought to have been captured or sunk.

By the 1700s share markets were open in most European capitals, and one of the better documented boom-and-bust cycles took place in London in the 1720s: the so-called 'South Sea Bubble'.

A similar boom and bust took place in the 1880s, which led to a great depression, and readers will be well aware of the events of 1929, when markets plummeted generally by over 75% and depression reigned.

In fact, if you looked at the major plunges in share prices

Money in History

1719–1720

The Mississippi Bubble was a classic incident of financial mania. It began with the scheme of John Law, a Scotsman in Paris, to establish a national bank to issue paper money backed by (potential) revenues of the Mississippi Company.

Set up to exploit the wealth of French colonies, especially in Louisiana, this company was given a monopoly on trade with the East Indies and China in 1719. A speculative boom in the value of its shares ensued. The boom, combined with the over-issue of notes by the Banque Royale, led to a drain of precious metals from France to London. Law's enemies persuaded the Regent to dismiss him from his post as Minister of Finance, the bank stopped payment and the boom collapsed. This debacle set back the development of banking in France by about a century.

over the centuries, you wouldn't go near shares with a barge pole. The really important point here is that just as the sun and tides rise and fall, so will the share market. 1987 was a disaster for short-term share investors – but an opportunity for long-term investors. 1994 was a poor year, but overall the 1990s were marvellous for shares. In 1999, the news was all excellent: low inflation and high growth. But in early 2001 the market fell and the result was low growth, but with low inflation. But as you can see from the table on the next page, even in low inflation times, markets are volatile. Let's look below at the period from 1929 to 1970.

As you can see, it's not exactly smooth sailing! Equally, don't forget that share markets like the low-inflation, high-growth environment, and when this is threatened by the fear of inflation once again rearing its ugly head (as is the case in the USA) and the prospect of rising interest rates (to control inflation), then the markets can get volatile.

The Ups

Period	Length (months)	Rise
June 1932–February 1934	20	137.38%
March 1935–February 1937	23	115.3%
April 1938–October 1939	18	30.4%
April 1942–May 1946	49	138.5%
June 1949–January 1953	43	87.4%
September 1953–July 1956	34	109.6%
December 1957–July 1959	19	48.1%
October 1960–December 1961	14	33.5%
October 1962–January 1966	39	66.1%
October 1966–December 1968	26	38.1%

The Downs

Period	Length (months)	Drop
September 1929–June 1932	33	-84.8%
February 1934–March 1935	13	-27.7%
February 1937–April 1938	14	-45.3%
October 1939–April 1942	30	-39.2%
May 1946–June 1949	37	-25.3%
January 1953–September 1953	8	-11.1%
July 1956–December 1957	17	-17.5%
July 1959–October 1960	15	-10.1%
December 1961–October 1962	10	-21.7%
January 1966–October 1966	9	-17.3%
December 1968–May 1970	17	-28.6%

But to finish my brief share history lesson, let's take a look at the returns from the Australian share market this century. The table on the next page looks at the total return (growth and income) from Australian shares in each year from January 1900 to December 1999. This shows the total return on shares (growth and income) for each calendar year since 1900.

The Historical Performance of Australian Shares, January 1900–December 1999

-30–-20	-20–-10	-10–0	0–10	10–20	20–30	30–40	40–50	50–60	60–70
				1999					
				1998					
				1997					
				1996					
				1989					
				1988					
				1977					
				1961					
				1958					
				1955					
				1948					
				1947					
				1941	1995				
				1936	1978				
			1976	1934	1972				
			1966	1929	1963				
			1964	1928	1957				
			1962	1927	1954				
		1994	1956	1926	1946				
		1992	1953	1925	1943				
		1987	1945	1924	1937				
		1984	1944	1919	1935				
		1971	1939	1918	1932				
		1965	1921	1913	1923		1993		
		1960	1917	1911	1922		1985		
1974		1949	1915	1910	1920	1991	1980		
1973	1990	1942	1912	1909	1914	1969	1979		
1970	1982	1940	1907	1906	1908	1951	1968		
1952	1981	1938	1902	1905	1904	1950	1967	1986	
1930	1931	1916	1901	1900	1903	1933	1959	1975	1983

Note: Calendar year return based on the accumulation index.

Source: ipac securities

As you can see, the most common return on the Australian share market has been between 10% and 20% per annum, but there are also some fantastic years such as 1983 and pretty sad ones such as 1930, 1952, 1970, 1973 and 1974.

But on balance, the news is good. The market rose in 79 years and fell in 21. Historically this is pretty normal. In fact, research we've done at ipac shows that share markets generally fall one year out of four. Now, I know your next question, and the answer is: no, I never know which year it is going to fall before it happens. If I did, do you really think I'd be running a business, doing a TV show, and writing books and magazines – I'd be playing golf!

Shares have done well for centuries

However, what history does tell me is that shares have consistently returned around 10% per annum over the centuries. This doesn't allow for inflation, but shares have reliably returned 6% to 8% above inflation over 20-year-plus periods. From 1930 to 1950 shares averaged 9.7% (inflation was barely 1% per annum). From 1951 to 1970 returns increased to 10% per annum (inflation was slightly higher), and then from 1971 to 1990 average returns jumped to 13.6% per annum with inflation averaging around 5%. The figure you often see me quoting, that shares have historically returned 6% to 8% above inflation over the long term, is based on share history over many, many decades. Now I accept that as the typical share advertisement says 'past returns quoted cannot be guaranteed', and my 6% to 8% fits into the same category, but unlike many of the silly returns you see in advertisements, at least my numbers relate to centuries, not months or a year – so I reckon they are pretty robust.

Shares are not a mystery

Let me wrap up this historical segment by summarising why I feel comfortable about shares as we look forward into this new century. Shares are not a mystery. A share is just a part-ownership of a business. Business, not property (as some people seem to think), is the central plank of the global economy. Business provides jobs and rewards shareholders with a share in the profits of the business. Those employed by businesses may use their salary to borrow, in order to buy property. Shareholders may use their dividends to buy property, but if business fails globally, the impact would be equally disastrous for both share and property values. However, as our global population continues to grow and former communist countries move towards a capitalist model, the demand for goods and services will keep on growing – and businesses supply goods and services.

In most parts of the world our standard of living is improving. At the same time we are living longer, retiring earlier, and planning a more active retirement. This causes hundreds of millions of people to save on a compulsory basis (generally in the form of superannuation) or on a voluntary basis. This money needs to be invested, and a significant proportion ends up in shares.

The global economic outlook is surprisingly positive. Yes, Japan is struggling and South-East Asia is politically and economically volatile, and its economies still have fundamental issues to resolve. Russia is, to put it politely, in a difficult situation, but, taking a long-term view, the situation in Europe and America is reasonably positive, despite the USA experiencing some difficulties at the start of 2001, after a long period of growth.

Now, I really can't see any reason why shares won't continue to generate significant above-inflation returns in this new century. But don't let my history lesson lull you into a sense of comfort about the limited potential for significant downturns. Every couple of decades we have had a major fall in prices, and one thing I am sure of is that if I survive to my life expectancy of around 76 years, then over the next 30 years as a share investor I'm nearly *guaranteed* to have my share portfolio drop by 70% or even more, and no doubt I won't see it coming. But what history does show is that the market always recovers. This has certainly been the case with overseas markets, and indeed ever since 1900 the Australian share market has never failed following a fall to rise above the previous high point, as you can see from the chart on the following page.

TIPS TO REMEMBER
1 Share-market timing

One of the most common questions I'm asked is: 'When is the best time to invest in the market?' It's a good question and I just wish I knew the answer, because unless we're able to jump into a time machine like Michael J. Fox in the movie *Back to the Future*, it's almost impossible to tell where the share market will go. Even the experts often don't get it right.

The current bull run of the US market that began in 1982, is a great case in point. (A bull run describes a share market that experiences consistent gains.) Some leading fund managers predicted an end to the current American bull market as far back as August 1982. At that time, some experts predicted an impending crash, but within nine months the Dow Jones had risen by 80%. In the early 1990s I wrote an article saying that the Dow Jones looked expensive at 4000. Thank heavens I stuck to my discipline and didn't sell out.

Another example of the benefits of long-term investing in the share market, which I have already mentioned in the

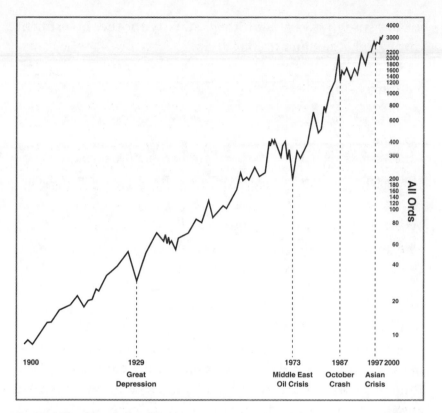

Source: ASX and Standard and Poor's

previous chapter, was in a study of the US share market between 1980 and 1993. The study found that if an investor kept their money in the market during this period, they would have averaged a 15% return per annum. However, if they missed just ten of the best trading days during this period, their return was reduced to 11.9%. If you missed the forty biggest days this reduced your return to 5.5% – further proof to support the value of long-term investing. (Refer back to the 'Time, Not Timing' chart on page 125 for a graphic representation of this.)

My advice is to get started now as nobody really knows for sure when the market will fall and when it will rise. People who make money aren't afraid to make decisions and invest straightaway, and then stay with the investment through the medium to long term.

> ## Money Tip
>
> Don't leave money lying around in low-interest bank accounts. $1,000 left in a typical bank savings account since the early 1990s today is not worth a lot more. However, if you'd put it into bank shares, today your money would have quadrupled in value.

When is the right time to buy?

The answer to this question is very simple – when you have the money. If you wait for the market or a particular share to bottom (the best time to buy), you could be waiting forever, because there is no way of knowing when a share or the market has bottomed.

There is no doubt you can make tons of money by good market timing, but there is also no doubt that good market timing involves a lot of skill and probably an even greater amount of luck.

When is the right time to sell?

The answer to this question is also very simple – generally when you need the money. If you don't need the money, don't sell. It's not a good strategy to turn your shares over too often. If you do:
- you will only stack up unnecessarily high brokerage fees
- you may miss out on the payment of dividends
- you may be out of the market during 'hot' periods.

In fact, about the only other sensible time to sell is if one share in your portfolio grows very strongly and represents too large a part of your overall assets. One example of this is News Corp. I first recommended this on 'Money' in 1997, when it's shares were selling for $5.60. By October 2000, the shares had risen to over $26. At this time I said on 'Money', 'If News Corp now represents a significant part of your portfolio, you should consider selling part of your holding, and using the money to buy other shares to better diversify your portfolio'. This was much easier to say after the *Ralph Report* led to capital gains tax changes that have made share investment an even more attractive proposition.

2 Take a long-term view

This rule is essential. If we aren't prepared to take a long-term view, we may as well consider taking our savings down to the TAB for a bet. Returns on share investments are impossible to predict over one, two or even three years. We must look to the long term, meaning at least five years. The average long-term return from shares is 5% to 8% per year above inflation, but returns from year to year can be very volatile.

ipac conducted an analysis of the returns from the share market in Australia from 1900 to 2000 and discovered that the average return since 1900 was 13.3% (this is without taking out inflation). So if your great-grandfather had invested just £5,000 (call this $10,000) back in 1900 for his family, it would now be worth a cool $2.6 million.

According to other research by ipac, if investors ignored the advice of the experts who predicted that the US market would crash at the start of August 1982, and invested US$10,000 in the Dow Jones Index at that time, the investment would have been worth US$113,547 by December 1998.

3 Values recover

On two occasions this century, shares have fallen by around 75% of their value. It happened in 1930–31 during the Great Depression and many of us will remember the crash of 1973–74 created by the Middle East oil barons' cartels. The cartels hiked up oil prices, after Saudi Arabia cut supplies to the USA in the wake of the Nixon administration's support for Israel in the October 1973 war. At some point in the future share prices will collapse again, and it could even happen while you are reading this book, but values will recover. Historically, the share markets have always bounced back. It took around five years for shares to bounce back in the 1930s and after the early 1970s crunch, things were on the up again by 1976.

4 Invest regularly

I have referred to the concept of dollar-cost averaging in Chapter 6, but it's worth talking about again. Dollar-cost averaging is a buying strategy which involves investing the same amount say, every month, into the share market. This strategy allows us to get more shares when prices are low, and buy less when prices are higher. This way we build up our portfolios, slowly but surely, getting good value for our money along the way.

The logic behind this strategy is simple and compelling. Firstly, it is a disciplined investment move. Secondly, it acts to average out the cost of the shares you buy, even if the share price fluctuates. This process frees you up from having to worry about getting your market timing right. Take the following example:

Let's say you invest $150 ($450 a quarter) a month into Bonzer Ltd, which has a share price of $1.00 when you begin:

Quarter 1 invest $450 and acquire 450 shares at $1.00.
Quarter 2 invest $450 and acquire 563 shares at $0.80.
Quarter 3 invest $450 and acquire 643 shares at $0.70.
Quarter 4 invest $450 and acquire 750 shares at $0.60.
Quarter 5 invest $450 and acquire 900 shares at $0.50.

By now you own 3,306 shares with a current market value of $1,653 (3,306 × $.50) and have invested $2,250. What many investors might be tempted to do at this stage is sell out their holding of Bonzer, but let's see what happens if you decide, after reviewing Bonzer's future earning capabilities in the annual report, to hold onto the shares:

Quarter 6 invest $450 and acquire 750 shares at $0.60.
Quarter 7 invest $450 and acquire 643 shares at $0.70.
Quarter 8 invest $450 and acquire 563 shares at $0.80.
Quarter 9 invest $450 and acquire 500 shares at $0.90.
Quarter 10 invest $450 and acquire 450 shares at $1.00.

The share price has recovered to $1.00 and you now own 6,212 Bonzer shares with a current market value of $6,212. Your total investment is $4,500. This is a return of $1,712 or 38.04% on the money you have invested – and this does not include any dividends you might have earned along the way.

Key thoughts

- Take a long-term view.
- Values recover after a downturn.
- Invest regularly.

5 Managing risk by diversification

(See also Chapter 6, 'Savings and Investment'.)

Owning shares in just one or two companies isn't really investing, it's punting. In most cases, it is normally accepted that the more risk you take, the higher the return you can expect. Remember that investment risk depends entircly on your general attitude to risk, your age, income, dependents and so on. Now, if you're really into risk, you might like to know that risk can be divided into four categories.

- Portfolio risk
- investor risk
- company-specific risk
- market risk.

  Let's have a look at each of these risk categories:
- Portfolio risk is the risk that your portfolio of stocks underperforms the market. This could be due to poor share selection or not owning enough shares. Studies have shown that a selection of about 30 shares can provide you with a portfolio that largely reflects the market, and this helps you manage risk and maximise return.
- Investor risk is the risk that we as investors take if we don't diversify our share portfolio or are forced to sell our shares at the wrong time due to illness, divorce or losing our job — the 'us' factor.
- Company-specific risk is the risk that one or more of the companies in our portfolio fails to perform up to expectation. In the extreme case, a company could go into liquidation or a serious decline, which may impact on the return of your overall portfolio. Ongoing monitoring of available research could help alert you to any company-specific risk, but holding many companies is the safest way to manage this.
- Market risk is the risk that the overall market is in decline. As I said earlier, ipac conducted some research on annual returns from the Australian share markets during the period 1900 to 1999, and found that roughly one year out of every four saw a falling share market. But also remember that the share market will bounce back.

Look, you can't get rid of all the risks. Let's face it, just living is risky. But you can easily avoid silly risks, such as holding one or two companies by buying a few more. Yes, taking sensible, riskier investments can improve your returns, but the market is unlikely to reward you for stupid risks such as holding only one company, when a trained chimpanzee could avoid the risk by diversification.

6 Rules

As you probably know by now I'm pretty keen on investment rules – mainly because they work – so here are my thoughts on how to become a successful share investor.

Rule 1 Long-term view
This really is essential. If you're not prepared to take a long-term view, you'd be better off at the racetrack. Returns on share investments are impossible to predict over one, two or even three years. You must look longer. And by long term, I mean at least five years.

Rule 2 Time is your friend
Historically, share values have fallen on average one year in four. Be aware of this. When it happens – not if, but when it happens – don't panic and sell. When it comes to shares, time is your friend.

Rule 3 Values recover
On two occasions this century, shares have fallen by around 75% of their value. It happened in 1930–31 and again in 1972–73. At some point in history this will happen again – but values will recover. It took around five years for shares to bounce back in the 1930s – in the 1970s things were on the up again by 1976.

Rule 4 Diversify
Don't own shares in one or two companies. That isn't investing, it's punting. Diversify across both local and overseas markets. If you've got limited capital, $1,000 in a managed fund will do this for you.

Rule 5 Invest regularly
Regular investment into shares is your best strategy. Investing the same amount every month, every quarter or every six months

means that you can buy more shares when they are cheap and less when they are expensive.

Rule 6   Get started now
Excuses are easy. 'I'll start next month, the market is too high'. 'The market is falling and will fall even further.' People who make money are not afraid to make decisions.

SHARE TIPS RETROSPECTIVE

I print share tips each year in *Money Magazine* and show you them on the 'Money' program, but as it is such an important issue, let me show you how they have gone as at 31 December 2000. (One of the problems with giving extremely public tips on shares, is that it is all too easy to see how hopeless I am!)

Since 'Money' started in 1993 I have given 22 share tips. These have had good and bad moments, but the absolute doozey has been Holyman. When I tipped this in July 1996, its prospects as a transport company looked pretty good, but its $3.64 share price then declined 90% to $0.34. Very impressive! Fortunately, in September 1999 Plzen Pty Ltd, a subsidiary of Lang Corporation, made an offer to shareholders of $0.93 for each of the ordinary shares in Holyman Ltd as part of their takeover of the company.

Other pretty ordinary tips included Western Mining ($8.38 to $2.81) and North Broken Hill ($3.90 to $2.81). However, as I said in my rules, time is your friend. For example, as at 31 December 2000 Western Mining had recovered to $7.66, while North Broken Hill (which changed its name to North Limited) shareholders were offered $4.75 per share as part of a takeover package by Rio Tinto.

But, given my very public statements that picking one share is about as silly as hoping to win Lotto next week, when you look at all the tips we've given, they've actually been okay. Highlights were News Corp ($5.85 to $14.00 at 31 December 2000), Commonwealth Bank ($10.45 to $30.90 at 31 December 2000), Woolworths ($2.45 to $8.42 at 31 December 2000). In fact, if you'd bought all of my tips, you'd have earned 14.1% per annum.

This is a very nice return, and ridiculously in front of my target with shares of 6% to 8% above inflation, but let's not forget that luck was on my side with the float of such quality government assets as the Commonwealth Bank and Telstra. We won't see many more of these!

Equally, in the words of the billionaire investor Warren Buffett 'all boats float in a rising tide' – and since 'Money' started in 1993, the Australian market has risen around 12.95% at year end 2000, but here is a list of some of my tips.

Some of Paul's Share Tips

Share tip	Date given	Price then	Price at 31/12/00	Annualised return
Woolworths	30 June 1993	$2.45	$8.42	25.4%
Boral$^\Diamond$	1 June 1994	$3.50	$2.05	2.1%
Santos	1 June 1994	$3.80	$6.02	17.1%
CBA (two instalments)	19 May 1996	$10.45	$30.90	38.3%
AAPC$^\alpha$	17 July 1996	$0.78	$0.75	-0.9%
Aust Vintage$^\#$	17 July 1996	$2.00	$2.98	9.4%
BHP	17 July 1996	$16.15	$18.96	9.4%
Holyman$^@$	17 July 1996	$3.64	$0.97	-25.4%
NAB	17 July 1996	$11.26	$28.81	32.7%
Western Mining	17 July 1996	$8.38	$7.66	1.7%
National Mutual	23 August 1996	$1.75	$3.00	19.1%
CSR	21 May 1997	$4.51	$4.68	7.1%
News Corp	21 May 1997	$5.85	$14.00	27.6%
Telstra$^\theta$	27 May 1998	$5.75	$6.43	8.8%

Colonial Mutual*	27 May 1998	$16.86	$30.90	26.4%
North Limited⁺	27 May 1998	$3.90	$4.84	8.6%
Mayne Nickless^Ω	27 May 1998	$6.85	$5.84	6.7%
AMP	17 June 1998	$16.00	$22.22	12.7%
NSW TAB	10 June 1998	$2.05	$3.16	23.7%
James Hardie	11 July 2000	$4.23	$3.60	−24.6%
CSL	11 July 2000	$33.91	$39.06	36.7%
Westfield	11 July 2000	$11.30	$13.45	46.9%
Average return				14.1%

φ 2 for 1 stock split in 3/00. Now trades as Origin Energy. Close $2.05.

α Takeover by Cobefin – $0.65 per share (reinvest @ 5.6%).

Takeover by Simeon (SWS). $3.60 + 4 SWS for 5 Australian Vintage.

@ Takeover by Plzen 1/00. $0.93 per share (reinvest @ 5.6%).

θ $4.35 adjusted to $5.75.

* Commonwealth Bank takeover: 3 CBA shares for 1 CGH. Assume no dividends.

+ Takeover by RIO 8/00 $4.75 per share (reinvest @ 5.6%).

Ω $6.85 adjusted to $5.84 for return of capital 30/12/98.

Notes:

• Where cash has been received from a takeover, it is assumed to be reinvested at 5.6% p.a. to 31/12/00.

• Total returns are calculated using Bloomberg standard 'Total Return' allowing for all stock splits and reinvesting dividends in the same stock.

• No dividend calculations are included for takeover stocks.

• Annualised returns are compound interest equivalents.

• Averages assume equal amounts invested in each stock.

• Transaction costs are not included in calculations.

Now over the years my strategy has been to buy and hold, but, as I have mentioned, I did recommend that investors with a large exposure to News Corp sell part of their holdings in September 2000, when the share price was over $26. This thought was more of a technical rebalancing recommendation rather than any gloomy thoughts about News Corp.

Over the years, I've also recommended a number of managed funds. Managed funds are one of my favourite ways to own shares – you get professional management and, with a relatively small amount of money, you can have part ownership of typically 40 or more shares in an Australian share fund, and dozens of global share markets and hundreds of shares in an international share fund. In May 1998, I recommended three funds, Colonial First State, Perpetual, and Advance Fund Management. The following table shows how they have performed.

Share Fund Performance

Name of fund	Performance to date (Three years to 31/12/2000)
Australian share funds	
Perpetual Industrial Share Fund	20.10%
Advance Imputation Share Fund	14.58%
Colonial First State Imputation Fund	20.90%
International share funds	
Fidelity Perpetual International Fund	21.50%
Advance International Share Fund	20.97%
Colonial First State International Share Fund	22.21% (9/1997 to 31/12/2000)

Source: ASSIRT

I also recommended managed funds on 12 June 1996. Their performance has been:

Managed Fund Performance

Name of fund	Performance to date (Three years)
BT Lifetime Fund	15.8% (to 3 May 1999)
MLC Australian Share Fund	11.9% (to 30 April 1999)
CBA Growth Fund	14.1% (to 28 Feb. 1999)
Rothschild Balance Fund	12.2% (to 30 April 1999)
County Share Fund	11.9% (to 30 April 1999)

Source: ASSIRT

The reason I want you to see my tips is to demonstrate the difficulties in creating wealth based on buying a couple of shares. Some of my tips have been complete dogs, some pretty good, but the trick with shares is to buy a decent number (a minimum of 18 to 20) across many industries. That way you are investing and not gambling!

Given the time it takes to publish a book, giving you share tips is downright dangerous. My TV show is a better vehicle for these, but let me show you the areas that interest me most in this 21st century.

SHARES FOR THE 21ST CENTURY

A quick look at the tables in the business section of any major newspaper would be just about enough to cause a new investor interested in shares to give up and return to the easily understood bank account. Statistical information often sprawls over ten pages. Daily information is available on over 1600 individual shares, options and convertible notes, not to mention warrants, call options, put options, currency values, commodity prices, futures and just about every market index known to humanity. (We will discuss share tables in more detail on pages 169–72.) Given this vast quantity of information, many readers may well be wondering how you choose which share or shares to invest in today, let alone worrying about what to buy for the 21st century.

Improving lifestyle is good for shares

Most people want to get ahead. We want to live a comfortable life surrounded by our family and friends and to be able to take advantage of the quite remarkable range of goods and services available to us to make our lives better, or, at least, more comfortable. At 46 years of age, I'm plenty old enough to remember when houses didn't have appliances such as dishwashers, but the look on my three children's' faces when we recently holidayed in a flat without a dishwasher was just classic, not to mention having to share a single toilet and one bathroom. You'd have thought I'd asked them to sleep in a cave!

This constant quest for a better life and a seemingly endless supply of material items is certainly good for business. And all that a share is, is part ownership of a business (a share of that business). Choose the right business to invest in (either one you buy yourself or a share that you buy in that business) and as the business grows in size and improves its profitability, so the value of your share grows.

Shares are volatile

But don't ever forget that the economy goes through cycles, so business earnings – and hence share prices – can and will rise and fall quite dramatically at times. While it's certainly reassuring to look at long-term share-market returns (such as the Australian market, which has averaged around 10% per annum for this century), it should be remembered that on average, shares fall around one year in four. In the previous century, Australian shares rose in 79 years and fell in 21. Some of these falls were very spectacular, such as the nearly 80% drop in the 1929 Depression and the 42% drop in October 1987. Will we see a fall like these again? Yes. When will it happen? Who knows? But centuries of share-market history tell us that sooner or later it will. This certainly shouldn't stop us from buying shares, and it is well summed up by the BT advertisement that you may have seen: 'Had you been unlucky enough to invest $10,000 in the BT Split Growth Fund the day before the 1987 crash . . . you'd now have $57,884'. As the old saying goes, when it comes to share investment, it's time in the market, not timing that makes you money.

> It's time in the market, not timing that
> makes you money.

Index funds

Quite frankly, probably the easiest and cheapest way to follow a philosophy of buying a wide range of shares and hanging on is to simply invest in an indexed fund. An indexed fund is nice and easy to understand. Take the Australian All Ordinaries Index, this is made up of our largest companies and an indexed fund would simply buy the companies in the index, so if a particular company represented 2% of the index, the fund would invest 2% of its investors' money in that company and so on. The big plus is that you get a broadly diversified portfolio of shares for around $2,000, and the management fees for an indexed fund are typically half that of an active manager, who will employ a large research team to select shares they believe will perform better than average.

This is one approach, but, if you own shares, it still pays to understand something about how the share market works.

WHY YOU SHOULD INVEST IN SHARES

As I have shown you, the share market has generally performed very well in relation to the other major asset classes (such as cash, bonds and property) and above inflation over the long term. Australian shares have generally returned between 5% to 8% above inflation, while international shares have returned between 6% and 9%. Compare this to cash in the bank, which has returned little more than 1% above inflation, or commercial property which has returned on average 5% over inflation and you can begin to see what an attractive long-term investment shares can be. ipac securities conducted research that showed if you had invested $100,000 in Australian shares in January 1983, by December 2000 it would have been worth $1,374,490, while the same investment in international shares would have been an even healthier $1,933,540.

Economic growth

There are a number of fundamental reasons why shares will continue to perform well over the long term. Over the last decade economic growth worldwide was running at record levels due to increased demand for goods and services – not only in the West, but also in emerging markets such as Eastern Europe, South-East Asia and Latin America. Companies (both big and small) will continue to supply this demand, and investment in these companies will continue to make very good sense to most investors. With the collapse of communism in the 1990s, there are now an extra billion or so people with high material expectations.

Baby boomers

More importantly, the share market will benefit from the ageing population. We baby boomers are determined to maintain our grand style of living and we are investing as much as we can. Equally, retirees are now living in retirement for 20, 30 or more years, meaning that growth investments, like shares, have become more appropriate for at least part of your portfolio than simply holding fixed interest.

Shares and superannuation

Another reason why share ownership will continue to be an attractive option is the link between shares and superannuation. Across the globe, hundreds of millions of people are saving on a compulsory basis (generally in the form of superannuation) or on a voluntary basis. Although this money is invested across the other asset classes (property, fixed interest and cash), a significant proportion is invested in shares. This trend is set to continue because people are living longer, retiring earlier, and planning a more active retirement.

Okay, so that's a broad look at the world of shares, but let's get into some specifics.

HOW WE MAKE MONEY FROM SHARES
Capital growth

We make money from shares in a number of ways. The first and perhaps most obvious way is through capital growth. Capital growth occurs when the price of a share in a given company rises on the share market. This could be the result of a news report outlining the company's positive financial performance, a favourable economic environment, and good business prospects.

The success of the deluge of Internet and technology shares (Solution 6, Melbourne IT, Dav Net and LibertyOne, amongst others) in 1999 and early 2000 caused many to feel that instant wealth was with us. But as was the case in other share booms, enthusiasm overtook reality and, by the end of the year 2000, some companies collapsed completely and others had fallen substantially. The reality is that successful share investment generally involves a long-term commitment to a diversified quality portfolio, and that only through holding shares for the long term can worthwhile capital growth generally be assured. As an investor, it's worth understanding some of the key factors that influence share-price movement, as it will help you manage your share portfolio more effectively over the long term. I will discuss this in the next section, 'Fundamentals of investing in shares'.

Income

It's not surprising that with the focus on the share price many of us forget about the benefits of dividends. Dividends are regular payments to shareholders out of the after-tax profits of the company. If you invest in blue chip companies, for example, you can expect to receive dividend payments of 3% or 4% of the share price (or substantially higher in some cases). But there is more to dividends than the half-yearly or annual cheque you receive as your portion of the profits made by a company in which you have invested. To fully understand the benefits of dividends, you should be aware of the power of dividend imputation, also covered later in this chapter.

FUNDAMENTALS OF INVESTING IN SHARES

Many people I meet tell me that the share market is a bit of a mystery to them. To a certain extent this mystique has been fuelled by images on the nightly news of stockbrokers in brightly coloured jackets, wildly swinging their arms around, looking alarmingly stressed and on the verge of collective nervous breakdowns. However, in most cases these are images of highly professional traders reacting to a new piece of economic or financial information. They are playing a high-risk game, that if done correctly can result in some very significant short-term gains, but on the flip side, if things go awry, there are potentially serious losses too.

There are many reasons that explain why share markets exhibit such regular short-term volatility. ('Volatility' is a word used to describe the ups and downs in the price of a share. All it means is risk.) Some major causes of volatility include unexpected announcements by governments in relation to the economy, interest-rate fluctuations, wars, or trade embargoes. Volatility can also be attributed to announcements by specific companies in relation to takeovers, mergers or profit announcements. In many cases, just the threat of any of these announcements will send share prices sky high or plummeting back to earth in a matter of minutes.

But as a long-term investor, it is generally more useful to look at the broader picture in which the share market, the industry sectors, and the individual companies we are interested in operate. An understanding of the broader picture helps us to make better decisions about what shares to invest in. Three sectors that I recommend you keep an eye on have already been mentioned earlier in this chapter, but let's now look at some of the broader issues that have an impact on shares and will help you to understand the market better:

- future earnings
- information
- supply and demand
- management
- government policy.

Future earnings

As my colleague Arun Abey suggests in *Fortune Strategy*, what ultimately makes share prices move is the changing perceptions within the market about a company's future earnings capability. While actions like takeovers and mergers also affect the share price, those who launch these actions and those who respond are generally reacting to what they reckon a company or its assets can earn in the future.

If an oil company discovers a new oil deposit, its share price will generally go up, as the market perceives a higher earnings capacity. While all this is happening, its major competitor is developing a new drilling process, the results of which may not be known for a few years. As such the share price of the competitor will move more slowly in the short term, but speed up as information about the success of the new drilling process and the impact on its earning capacity reaches the market.

Information

It could have been a stockbroker who coined the term 'information is power', because information is one of the significant drivers of the share market. The question facing many investors like us is which bits of information are useful and which bits should we ignore? The best advice I can offer here is to take a long-term view and diversify your portfolio of stocks so that it roughly represents the market. Diversification is discussed at length in Chapter 6, 'Savings and Investment'. But broadly speaking, diversification is an investment strategy whereby investors manage risk by putting their money into a number of different assets like Australian shares, international shares, property, fixed-interest securities and cash.

Supply and demand

Before you invest in a company, it is essential to understand what they produce, how strong the demand for their goods and services is, and what the competition is doing. Understanding the relationship between supply and demand for the products made by a company you're interested in can be a useful guide to what their future prospects are.

For example, if a situation arises where a leading oil company makes an announcement about a massive new oil discovery, this will generally push the demand for that company's share price up, as the market believes that this should have a positive impact on future earnings. However, the following day a vehicle manufacturer announces the design of a new engine that runs on water, and will be cheaper, more efficient and less polluting than its petrol-guzzling counterpart. The net effect of this announcement is the demand for oil products will fall, the oil company will be left sitting on a large supply of oil that is no longer as valuable, and the share price will generally also fall, as the market re-evaluates the company's long-term future earnings. Now running cars on water is pretty extreme, but I'm sure you get my point!

Management

Now I can prattle on about logical reasons why shares may rise and fall, but, in the final analysis, if idiots or crooks are running the company you invest in, regardless of the fundamentals, you'll end up losing money. So check out the directors and senior management with care.

Government policy

Government policy can also play a significant role in changing the playing field within a particular sector and therefore the companies within it. The most obvious examples that spring to mind are the banking and telecommunications sectors that experienced deregulation in the 1980s and 1990s. An individual decision by a government (such as deregulation, the introduction of a new tariff regime, or the removal of trade protection) can also have a huge impact on a sector and the companies operating within it.

WHAT SHARES?

When it comes to choosing shares that will perform in this century, the starting point is to think about how we will be living. Businesses can't just grind out any old product and make loads of money. I'm sure prior to electricity, kero lamps were huge sellers, and the introduction of electric lights was seen as just a novelty. But a business that refused to adapt to a new era soon went broke, taking its shareholders' money with it. The changes we are experiencing in our economy today are just as dramatic as the shift in the late 1700s from a rural to an industrial society. Some 200 years later we are making the move from the Industrial to the Information Age.

In the early 1700s, to find wealth you needed to look at the owners of rural land, but in the early 1900s you turned to the industrialists, such as Henry Ford who had adapted to new industries and new consumer demands. Today you need to look at those involved in information and communication technology. In 1999, I spent a day with Jerry Yang, one of the co-founders of Yahoo. Five years ago his net wealth was $50. At one stage this had grown to $4 billion. Due to the April 2000 tech crash, his personal wealth is significantly less, but this is still a good example of wealth creation.

Information Age

Without doubt the most exciting stocks in this century will be those linked to the Information Age. People will continue to evolve. We'll be big users of all forms of technology. We will end up using a much simpler version of the Internet to buy day-to-day goods, talk to friends, buy a car and book a holiday. For those of you who doubt this, I ask you to reconsider. There is a bit of the luddite's refusal to accept change in all of us, but let me leave you to reflect on this point by reminding you that one of the first comments made about the telephone was 'it will never catch on'.

We'll also live in a world of two-income families with smaller numbers of children. We'll live longer, work hard, but use our relatively higher incomes to try to balance work and lifestyle. We'll be concerned about job security and accept that in order to eventually live comfortably away from work, we'll need to build up our investments. We'll also be big users of rapidly advancing medical technology.

WHAT SECTORS TO INVEST IN

This broad picture then takes us to a few specific sectors of the share market. (A sector is simply a group of similar companies. For example, the tourism and leisure sector is made up of companies involved in things like casinos, cinemas, holiday destinations and resorts.) Exactly how many sectors of the stock market there are depend upon how you want to categorise shares. For example, you could lump all mining companies in the mining sector, or you could put gold miners in the gold sector. (Equally, you could go completely overboard and set up a 'gold miners who have never found gold' sector!)

Some argue there are around 50 sectors, but to keep my life reasonably simple I've lumped these into somewhat larger groups giving me 24 sectors, namely:

* energy
* diversified industrials
* engineering
* infrastructure and utilities
* building materials
* tourism and leisure
* gold
* other metals
* retail
* health care and biotech
* diversified resources
* chemicals
* developers and contractors
* food and household goods
* miscellaneous industrials
* insurance
* property trusts
* investment and financial services
* paper and packaging

- transport
- banks
- telecommunications
- alcohol and tobacco
- media.

As a small aside, it is really interesting (well, to me anyway) to look at the share market in any year (I've chosen 1998) and see what happened. In 1998, the All Ordinaries Index rose a comfortable 11.6%, but just take a look on the next page at how the 24 sectors performed.

Here you can see the risk of selecting one sector. The energy sector fell nearly 40%, while telecommunications rose over 60%. A good argument for diversification indeed.

Money Tip

A diversified portfolio of shares will make you money over the long term.
But don't just punt on one company.

This certainly highlights the perils of going for a small number of sectors, and while I am happy to nominate three sectors that I reckon are looking very exciting, please do note that I certainly will not have 100% of my share portfolio in these three sectors, nor would I advise you to. While it makes sense to have a good exposure to the most likely growth sectors, punting your wealth on a small part of the market is a fool's game.

That said, let's turn now to my favoured sectors. These are listed in no particular order.

Banking and finance

We are becoming more and more concerned about our money. We use mortgages, credit cards and negative gearing

Sector Performance 1998

Sector performance	Yearly (%)
Energy	-36.33
Diversified industrials	-7.82
Engineering	-18.54
Infrastructure and utilities	16.43
Building materials	-27.13
Tourism and leisure	1.83
Gold	9.05
Other metals	-8.74
Retail	14.82
Health care and biotech	4.13
Diversified resources	-11.40
Chemicals	-18.23
Developers and contractors	36.96
Food and household goods	-17.60
Miscellaneous industrials	6.01
Insurance	0.70
Property trusts	10.16
Investment and financial services	-8.17
Paper and packaging	-10.15
Transport	22.92
Banks	17.02
Telecommunications	61.32
Alcohol and tobacco	45.17
Media	19.81

more than ever. At the same time we're trying to manage our cash flow better, building up our super and saving for the future.

This basic consumer trend, linked to exciting developments in technology, means that our banks are in a very powerful position. Let's hope banks become smarter about minimising the bank fees we pay, but the banks that adapt to the new era will do very well.

Telecommunications and information technology

I don't think I need to say too much here. Just look around you at mobile phones, e-mail, video conferencing and the Internet. Even more scary is the fact that this is only the start. Compared to what telecommunications will look like in a decade, today it is like a steam-driven motor car.

The advances in consumer-friendly telecommunications systems will astound you – and will make those companies which move with the times a fortune.

Health and biotechnology

As I was writing this I was reflecting on how just the other day I had inhaled the new reduce-the-effects-of-the-flu drug, Relenza. It's only available on a prescription basis from a doctor and costs a pretty serious amount ($65), but if this means I can still put a TV show together for next week, it's a cheap investment. According to the chemist, I wasn't the only person thinking this. The fact is that young and old Australians will be very demanding users of new drugs, genetic medicine and technology to keep us healthier. Expect this sector to generate significant amounts of revenue in the near-future.

So these are the three sectors that I reckon have terrific prospects for our century. But the question is of course, which shares do you buy? Well, this question cannot be answered in a book, I'll keep you up to date on my TV show and in *Money Magazine*, but any broker can give you their recommendations on shares in these sectors in a flash.

SELECTING WHAT SHARES TO BUY AND SELL

Obviously seeking the advice of a broker or financial adviser could prove to be the best way of selecting shares that best suit your financial needs. However, it's also helpful if you have some idea of what to look for. I'd generally recommend either mature or growth companies.

Mature companies

A mature company is generally an established brand name like Coles Myer, Woolworths or Coca Cola. Mature companies usually depend on strong management, whose chief business goal is to protect the company's existing share of its market.

Growth companies

As well as selecting a number of mature companies to invest in, I also recommend that you look at investing in growth companies. These are generally companies who look for new opportunities like mergers, takeovers or new technologies to grow the size of their existing business. Such companies include Telstra, News Limited, Commonwealth Bank and some of the other big banks. As I said earlier, the growth companies tend to be those competing in the telecommunication, information and technology, banking, and biotechnology sectors. These sectors should continue to grow over the next ten years at least.

One way of differentiating a mature company from a growth company is by looking at the size of its pay-out ratio. To calculate the pay out, you can divide the dividend paid per share by the profits per share. The significance of this calculation is that it shows you the percentage of profits being paid to shareholders as well as the per cent reinvested into the business. Generally, a mature company will pay

80% of profits back to shareholders. On the other hand, a growth company is more likely to reinvest around 70% back into the business, leaving 30% for shareholders.

An easy way to invest in emerging and smaller growth companies is in a smaller companies managed share fund.

Different types of shares

But there's more to understanding shares. While we have looked at what a share is, it is worth noting that there are different types of shares that companies issue to investors that are traded on the Australian Stock Exchange (ASX). It's worth understanding the basics of the different types of shares because they do involve different risks and return characteristics.

Ordinary shares

This is the most basic and common form of share. An ordinary share entitles an investor to a share of the company's profits through dividends, a share of the proceeds from the sale of the company's assets should it be liquidated or bankrupted, and a say in the company's direction through their voting rights at the annual general meeting. A share is usually called an 'ordinary share' if it is fully paid. This means that the investor owns the share outright, and there are no deferred or outstanding payments to be made at a later date, as is the case with other types of shares.

Preference shares

Preference shares differ from ordinary shares in that they normally pay a fixed rate of return (still called a 'dividend'). This fixed dividend rate is expressed as a percentage of the issue price.

The benefits of holding preference shares include receiving dividend payments before ordinary shareholders; and if the company folds, any capital left over, is paid to preference shareholders before ordinary shareholders.

Though a preference share might in theory sound more attractive than the ordinary share, this isn't always the case. They can be restrictive. Take the situation where the company is performing very well, having a fixed dividend can be very restrictive given the dividends paid to ordinary shareholders can be much higher than those for preference shares. However, if the company experiences a difficult period, the preference shareholder will generally receive a dividend that outstrips the dividend received by the ordinary shareholder.

Contributing shares

Unlike ordinary shares, contributing shares are not fully paid. This means that the company issuing the shares will make demands, or calls for further payments at a later date. The benefit of investing in contributing shares is that you get the share for a lesser amount than would otherwise be the case. Like other shares, contributing shares are traded on the ASX where you can sell them for a profit.

RESEARCH

For many of us, working out whether a company will perform and what its prospects are is just as important as working out whether or not we should invest in it. The following resources may be useful in assisting you to choose the right shares.

A *prospectus* should explain how much money a company is seeking to raise, how it plans to use those funds, what its assets are, what its actual business is, who its directors and other office holders are, and what they think the future direction and performance of the company will be. Of course, the directors will tend to put a positive slant on this material, but the prospectus is still a very important source of information.

The *balance sheet* reflects the company's financial health, showing its assets (what it owns), liabilities (what it owes), and cash flow (how much money is flowing into the coffers). Balance sheets can be found in either a prospectus for a new company or an annual report for an existing company.

An *annual report* includes the company's balance sheet and profit and loss (P&L) statement. The P&L statement indicates what the company has earned during the previous year and how those earnings have been distributed.

Other company reports include the final statements, six-month interim reports on the company's performance, and company announcements to the ASX about any new ventures that they might be participating in, such as a merger or takeover. These reports are available from the ASX.

Financial and investment journals and magazines provide extensive information and helpful articles each month.

Stockbrokers' newsletters are provided by many stockbroking firms to give clients advice on market trends, industry sectors and individual companies.

Books and other specialised publications on finance, investment, economics and company management can be obtained through the ASX and bookshops.

Understanding the daily share tables

Since 1837, when the *Sydney Morning Herald* first published its share market information, newspapers across Australia have provided daily information on share prices, as well as news reports on specific industries and companies that may have an impact on share prices. Typically the information is presented in what are called 'share-trading tables' and you will find this information in the business section of most Australian metropolitan newspapers. These published share-trading tables contain a wealth of information, most of which is relevant to your share portfolio. But how do you interpret it all?

Let's look at some of the more important information you can find in the share-market trading tables as they appear in the *Australian Financial Review*.

52-week high and low lists the highest and lowest price the share has traded on the ASX in the year to date. Some investors look at the current share price and compare it to the 52-week high and low as a guide to whether to buy or sell a share. If the share price is trading well below the high, they might consider buying the share and if it's moving in the opposite direction, sell the share. I would not recommend using this method on its own, rather use it in conjunction with other research to make an investment decision.

Day's high and low gives the range of prices the share traded between on the latest ASX business (trading) day. This is a good indicator of volatility (the ups and downs) of the share price. It is more useful for professional traders than long-term investors.

Company name is, obviously, the name of the company that has issued the shares.

Last sale is the price at which the company's shares traded on the last sale of the previous business day. This is the most accurate figure used for measuring the value of your share holding.

+ or − is the difference in cents between the price of the share at the close of business the previous trading day, and the price of the share at the close of business the trading day before that. For example, XYZ closed at $1.50 on Monday, 27 March, having closed at $1.42 on Friday, 24 March. This would be shown as '+8' in the newspapers on Tuesday, 28 March.

Vol 100's gives the total volume of shares (in hundreds)

traded in the company on the previous trading day. This indicates the level of market interest in a particular stock. But be warned, if the volume of a stock is up, this is not always a good sign. The volume could be up because investors have been trying to sell the shares. Selling generally leads to a fall in the share price. On the other hand, it might also mean that buyer demand for the stock is high and that shareholders are being offered prices that they can't refuse.

Quote (Buy) is the highest price at which a buyer is prepared to buy a share in a listed company. It is also known as the 'bid' or 'buying price'. Shares may not always be traded at this price if a seller is not prepared to sell at that price.

Quote (Sell) is the lowest price at which a seller is prepared to sell shares. It is also known as the 'offer price' or the 'selling price'. Shares may not always be traded at this price if buyers feel that this isn't a reasonable price to pay for the share.

Dividend c per share represents the size of the latest annual dividend distributed by the company per share (in cents and fractions of a cent). The 'f' that follows some entries indicates that the dividend was franked.

Earn share c stands for the 'earnings per share' (EPS). It shows the amount of profit earned for every ordinary share issued. It is calculated in the following way:

$$\frac{\text{Earnings available for ordinary shareholders}}{\text{Number of ordinary shares}}$$

P/E ratio or Price/Earnings ratio is probably the most often used indicator of future earnings. The P/E is generally a very good guide to how much the market is prepared to pay for a share. This ratio provides a means of measuring investors' expectations of the company's performance. A low P/E normally indicates a bargain. A relatively high P/E on the other hand, indicates that the stock is overpriced.

$$\frac{\text{Current selling price for an ordinary share}}{\text{EPS}}$$

There are other ratios and price information and a brief explanation of these can generally be found above the tables in the newspapers.

Analysing share ratios

As investors, it can be dangerous to use these ratios in isolation as a guide to future earnings. What you need to do, is combine an analysis of these indices along with a basic understanding of what the company is involved in. Let's consider the example (adapted from one presented by Arun Abey in *Fortune Strategy*) of two fictitious mobile phone companies – CityPhones and TeleLink – to illustrate this point.

Let's assume that both companies are trading at around the same price, $1.30. However, CityPhones has recently paid a dividend per share of 13 cents, compared to only 6 cents for TeleLink. Let's also assume that, CityPhones has an EPS of 16 cents (and P/E of 9) compared to 9 cents for TeleLink (P/E of 16). On the basis of these share ratios alone, investors would appear to be crazy paying this price for TeleLink. CityPhones pays a higher dividend, and with a lower P/E would appear to be better value than TeleLink.

CityPhones Versus TeleLink

	Dividend per share	Net asset backing	EPS	P/E ratio
CityPhones	13	$1.30	16c	9
TeleLink	6	$1.90	9c	16

Source: Adapted from *Fortune Strategy*

However, we need to look at the broader picture and ask why the shares are trading at the same price. With a bit more research, the canny investor would have discovered that the net asset backing for TeleLink is almost twice as high as CityPhones (i.e. $1.30:$1.90). The reason for this is that TeleLink is developing a revolutionary new mobile phone and has decided to reinvest more of the profits back into the business rather than paying it to shareholders. The share market is aware of this and is anticipating that the new mobile phone will be a winner. And investors will continue to pay the asking price for TeleLink despite the higher P/E ratio because they are sure they will do well over the long term.

Money Tip

Don't invest in anything that you don't understand.
Do your research first.

Understanding share-market indices

How often do we sit down in front of the TV after a long day, and switch on the news for the regular nightly line up of politicians, car accidents, wars, robberies, animals, sportspeople, isobars and the All Ords? Every night the newsreader refers to share market indices like the All Ords, the Nikkei, the Dow Jones, or the FTSE, but for many of us, they remain a bit of a mystery. So, for those of you who would like to know more, let me try and explain.

Stock exchanges worldwide have developed indices as a quick way of keeping an eye on what's happening in a particular market. Put simply, an index reflects the change in value of a sample selection of shares in a share market, over a period of time. There are two types of indices.

- A *price index* measures changes in the market's value based on movements in share prices on a daily basis.
- An *accumulation index* also takes into account the value of dividends or interest payments, thus giving a more complete picture of market return.

When an index is created, the first day is given a base value of say 1,000. Changes in market direction from then on, are measured in relation to that value on a daily basis. Consider the following example, where activity on a fictitious share market was strong over a period, say a month, and the index rose to 1,034. This would mean that the value of the market (or more accurately, the value of the sampled shares in this market) had risen by 3.4%. The following is a sample of some of the indices most often quoted on the news:

- The All Ordinaries Index is based on a sample of around 500 actively traded companies listed on the ASX. The key criteria for companies chosen includes their market value, between them they represent approximately 90% of the ASX's total share turnover. The base value of the All Ords was set at 500 on 31 December 1979. It only measures changes in the market's price and does not include dividends or interest payments.
- New York's Dow Jones Industrial Average indicates the average share price of a group of 30 major companies actively traded on the New York Stock Exchange. These companies include Exxon, IBM, Ford and General Motors. There used to be a saying that 'if the Dow Jones sneezes, the rest of the market catches a cold'. For Australian investors, movements in the Dow Jones can be a very good indicator of what to expect on the Australian market.
- London's FTSE 100 is the UK equivalent of our All Ordinaries or New York's Dow Jones. It's commonly called the 'footsie' and the letters stand for Financial Times

Stock Exchange (Index). The index is based on the average share price of 100 leading UK-listed companies.

- The Nikkei is the market index for the Tokyo Stock Exchange. Once called the 'Nikkei-Dow Jones', this index reflects the value of 300 of Japan's leading listed companies.

There are countless other indices in existence and more are being developed all the time. For example, at last count there were 52 different indices offered by the ASX for investors to look at on their web site: www.asx.com.au. So long as you know what they are measuring, they can be very useful in showing what direction a market or market sector is travelling, and how it has performed over a certain period. When you come across an index that you're not familiar with, ring your stockbroker, your fund manager, or the ASX, and they should be able to tell you how the index is constructed, what it measures and what it can mean to you.

SO HOW DO YOU INVEST?

Well, if you know what you want to buy, the cheapest way to go is to use a discount broker or an Internet broker. If you think you need a bit of help, use a full-service broker. You'll pay more, but good advice is usually worth every cent. If you don't know a full-service broker, give the stock exchange in your capital city a ring and they'll give you a list of suitable brokers.

An excellent way to find out about a suitable managed share fund is to talk to a professional financial planner.
The Financial Planning Association can send you a list of qualified planners, if you call them on 1800 626 393.

Another really good way of buying shares is through a managed share fund. The expert fund managers like AMP, Macquarie and Rothschild all have managed share funds that will give you access to these sectors and other important sectors, generally for around a minimum of $1,000.

BUYING AND SELLING SHARES

Buying and selling shares has never been easier. At the click of a computer key or a telephone call, you may buy or sell any shares trading on the ASX. There are two types of brokers who can help you buy and sell shares:

- The full-service (traditional) broker, at the barest minimum, offers you advice on whether to buy, sell or hold a particular stock. This advice is usually based on your overall investment needs. Full-service brokers will also buy and sell shares on your behalf, and all you need to do is contact them by telephone, fax or email to give them the authority to do this.

- The do-it-yourself (DIY) broker offers online services only, meaning they allow investors to buy or sell shares themselves via the Internet or telephone. Generally, investors who use DIY brokers have planned their own investment strategy and the shares that will help them meet their financial needs. DIY brokers also offer research, which can be accessed via their web sites. Investors can choose to use this information or ignore it at their own discretion.

Investing online

Ten years ago the share-broking industry was transformed, following demands from some investors to unbundle the traditional research and advisory functions from buying and selling shares. For example, an investor who did their own research would pay the same brokerage fee as another investor who received lots of advice and research, generally over the telephone from the broker, before making their investment decision.

Not surprisingly, DIY investors believed that they shouldn't have to pay brokers for a service they didn't require. They demanded cheaper brokerage fees, and, in response, a number of execution-only broking firms sprang up. This meant that an investor could phone or fax a stockbroker who would buy or sell shares on their behalf, at a discounted rate to what a traditional (full-service) broker would charge.

However, about four years ago some smart marketing gurus realised that the Internet offered a new way of providing all investors with research, advice, and a quick and inexpensive way of buying and selling shares. In fact, many investors, who had used either execution-only or full-service brokers, realised that the Internet could fill both roles. For example, the DIY investor can now use the Internet to place an electronic order to buy and sell shares, monitor changes in the markets, and access company information – all from a computer screen. For investors who had traditionally required investment advice, these services mirrored very closely what they received from the full-service brokers, so online trading became a very attractive option for them too. Added to this is the relatively low cost of online brokerage, hence its popularity. If you are considering buying and selling shares on the Internet, or thinking about opening up an Internet account, you might like to consider the following information.

> **Internet broking is here!**
> One in five trades are now conducted online.

Understand what happens to your online orders. Most online broking services require an employee of the broker to enter your online orders into the ASX's trading system (SEATS). In this case, sending the order via the Internet is in some ways similar to making an order by telephone or by facsimile – you do not have immediate access to the market. Alternatively, some brokers like Etrade can offer 'straight through processing' which is direct access to SEATS without the need for human intervention. If you are using the services of a 'direct access' broker, it is very important to make sure that the order details you type in are totally correct.

Alternatively, if you use a 'traditional' or a 'non-direct online' broker, you won't have to worry about doing this, as it's the broker's responsibility to do it for you. If you provide the broker with the right instructions by either telephone or email and a mistake is made, the broker wears the cost.

Understand the process before you use an online broker. Before you start trading online or even through a full-service broker, make sure that you understand the use of market and limit orders.

- A market order is an order to buy or sell shares at the existing market price. When you place a market order, you can't control the price at which the order will be filled. You could end up paying more for a purchase and receiving less for a sale than you wanted.
- A limit order operates only within a specified upper or lower price limit. For example, you can request a limit order to buy shares in Bonzer Ltd at a price below $1.20 only. If the market price quickly goes to $1.30, your order might not be filled. However, you won't be paying more for shares in Bonzer Ltd than you wanted to pay, or could afford.

Understand online confirmation procedures. You should

also be familiar with your online broker's order confirmation procedures. Monitor the progress of your online orders. Make sure you get timely confirmation from the broker that your electronic order has been received, has been placed on the market, and has been executed. You can only change or cancel an order up until the time it is executed.

Using a full-service broker

It's important to remember that full-service brokers offer very similar services to one another. For example, they generally have extensive research departments that provide information and advice on specific companies and industries. The range of services that the full-service broker may provide include:

- advice on traditional investments, such as shares, debentures, government bonds and listed trusts
- advice on a wide range of non-listed investments, including cash management, property and equity trusts
- tailored investment plans, including portfolio planning, structuring and monitoring, and retirement planning
- research on national and international investment trends and developments.

Selecting a broker

Selecting a sharebroker is generally easier if you have some idea about the services that you require. To select a suitable broker, I recommend you consider the following steps:

- Contact the ASX who will provide you with a list of sharebroking firms. All share brokers operating in Australia must be licensed by the Australian Securities and Investment Commission (ASIC).
- Once you have a list from the ASX, telephone a few firms and ask them to send you a copy of their *Advisory Services Guide (ASG)*. If you want a broker to provide investment

advice, then as a private investor you are entitled to protection under the law. This protection will be outlined in the *ASG* which your adviser is obliged by law to provide, and will confirm that the broker is licensed, how they deal with customer complaints, and what complaint-resolution procedures are available should something go wrong.

- Select three broking firms and call and speak to a broker at each firm, giving them a general outline of your financial position and investment goals.
- Analyse the responses from each and decide which one you feel most comfortable with, make an appointment to meet the adviser you have selected to find out more about them, like how long they have been providing advice, what their qualifications are, what type of clients they specialise in, what type of ongoing service they provide, and how they are paid for their services. (I have spoken in more detail about how to choose a financial adviser in Chapter 5, 'Financial Planning'.)

> I strongly recommend you do an introductory share course run by the Australian Stock Exchange.
> For information, ring 1300 300 279.

FEES AND COMMISSIONS

Full-service brokers charge brokerage rates on buy and sell orders, but also offer investor's advice, research, portfolio management and other services. The brokerage rates usually comprise a minimum charge or a percentage rate on the value of the order, or whichever is the greater. The brokerage fee charged on the transaction varies with the size of the order.

For a smaller order of up to about $5,000, they charge around 2.5%, but this drops down to a negotiable 0.5% to 0.75% for orders greater than $100,000 (which is normally the domain of institutional investors such as banks and super-annuation companies).

The online brokers, on the other hand, charge lower brokerage costs on share transactions. And much to the pleasure of online investors, the costs seem to be falling practically on a daily basis.

SHARE FLOATS

Recently big share floats such as Telstra 1, the Commonwealth Bank and TAB have proved a very successful way for investors to get into the share market. A share float generally occurs when the owners of a company (this can be the government) decide they want to make some significant changes to the way the company does business, but can't afford to pay for the changes out of existing capital. The owners of the company will then generally offer part of the business for sale to the public via a share float in order to raise the additional capital.

Companies have various reasons for floating. They might need to free up some of the capital tied up in the business to enter new markets, undertake factory updates or purchase new equipment. Before floating, companies must provide investors with a prospectus. This document outlines the detail of the float offer, and should explain how the funds raised will be used.

One reason that recent floats like Telstra 1 and the Commonwealth Bank have done so well is that the companies involved have been well-established businesses in viable industries, with good cash flows, and good scope to do better.

They have not been start-up operations relying, for instance, on the successful development of new products, new markets, and new technologies.

But it would be very costly to assume all floats are winners. Take a look at the following table of companies that floated in January 2000, and you will see that not all share floats are guaranteed winners.

Some Share Floats, January 2000

Share	Issue price	Last sale (31/12/00)	Change
Aboriginal Australia	$1.00	$0.29	-71%
ESec Ltd	$0.40	$0.33	-18%
Max Multimedia	$0.30	$0.05	-82%
Milnes Mines	$1.00	$1.05	5%
P.O.S. Media Online Ltd	$.025	$0.07	-74%
Pilbara Mines Ltd	$0.20	$0.27	35%
PocketMail	$0.40	$0.07	-84%
Seafood Online.com.Ltd	$0.20	$0.105	-48%

Source: ASSIRT

So how do you avoid the bad floats? You need to do some research before you invest in a float. If you don't feel that you are experienced enough or have the time, then you should consider seeking the advice of an independent financial adviser or stockbroker.

How to apply for shares in a float

Applying for shares in a float has always been a fairly competitive process, with many of us missing out on an allocation more times than we succeed. It's worth reviewing the share-float allocation process at this point.

Applications for shares can be made on a form attached

to the prospectus. Amongst other information, the prospectus will tell us how much we will be able to buy the shares for. In most prospectuses we are referred to as 'retail investors', and at times we can purchase shares at a discount to what the big institutional customers like the banks and superannuation companies pay for the shares. If you've wondered about this, it's called politics. Shares of the major government institutions that have been floated have been bought by millions of investors, who are generally voters!

Role of the underwriter

One of the best ways to get an allocation of shares as an investor is through the underwriter of the share float. An underwriter is usually a sharebroker who undertakes to sell a certain number of shares on behalf of a company to retail investors like us. In return, the company issuing the shares pays the underwriter a commission that can range from between 10% and 20% of the money raised in the float. The size of the fee generally depends on how difficult it is to sell the shares.

Do it yourself

You can still pick up shares through a share float, even if you choose not to go through a broker. Many companies allocate a proportion of their shares to the general public, but it's worth understanding some of the factors that guide the allocation of these shares.

Picking up shares in a public share float can be a case of 'first come, first served'. In the event that more people apply for shares than there are shares to allocate, the earlier you return your application, the more likely you'll receive preferential treatment. Another issue you should be aware of when applying for shares is the geographic location of the company. For example, when the Bank of Western Australia was floated, those applicants with a Western Australian address received preferential treatment. With AMP and NRMA which belonged to members, only the members (people who had bought a product and held onto it) got free shares. The general public could buy only after they listed on the stock exchange.

In some of the larger floats like Telstra, TAB and the other government privatisations, all applicants generally receive some shares. But to accommodate demand for these floats, a company might stipulate a maximum allocation. This is the highest number of shares that each investor will receive, to ensure that every applicant receives an allocation. If the demand is stronger than initially expected, the maximum subscription may be reduced. For example, the demand for TAB shares was so strong, that the final maximum allocation for retail investors was 243 shares, when many investors were expecting closer to 1,000.

INTERNATIONAL SHARES

So far we've concentrated solely on Australian shares and the Australian share market, but there's a world of shares out there trading on share markets from New York to London to Tokyo. In fact, the share investment opportunities are staggering when you start thinking globally. Australia is only 1.3% of the world's total share markets, as the chart on the next page shows.

In the fifteen years to 31 December 2000, Australian shares returned an average of 12.5% per annum based on the All Ordinaries Accumulation Index. Over the same period, international shares, as measured by the MSCI World Accumulation Index, returned an average of 14.36% per annum. This means that an investment of $10,000 made in Australian shares on 1 January 1986, would have grown by

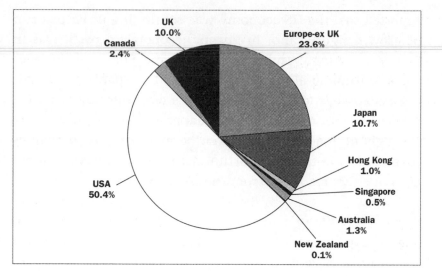

Source: MSCI as at 31/12/2000, compiled by ASSIRT

31 December 2000 to around $60,000, whereas the same investment in international shares would have returned more than $74,000, according to ipac's research.

Some benefits of investing in international shares

International shares offer a number of benefits to the Australian investor. You might be looking for a wider choice of companies and industries in which to invest. For example, while there seemed to be a technology company floating on the Australian market every second week, an investor could have an even greater choice of investing in this sector by investing in the American share market.

Diversification

Given that the world's economies don't all perform in the same way at the same time, international share investment presents a very good way of diversifying your portfolio – which is a foundation stone of effective personal investment. For example, at the beginning of 2000 economic analysts reported that the US economy was continuing its record run of growth figures and, in Europe, economic growth was in fact accelerating. While both the US and Europe economies were continuing along the growth route, Japan was recording negative-growth figures. But it's worth noting that despite this, foreign investment in Japan continued to increase throughout 1999 and into 2000, because foreign companies identified investment opportunities as the Japanese economy continued its recovery from the 'Asian Crisis'.

Emerging markets

Many people I speak to suggest that investing in shares overseas is a riskier venture than investing in the Australian share market. But this is not the case. The risk involved in investing in international shares may depend on which share markets you decide to invest in. Some are more risky (more volatile and more variable) than ours, others aren't.

In general, the share markets of the developing world, the so-called 'emerging markets', are the most risky. They have the potential for the wildest swings, which means they may be more prone to plunging – as those who invested in the region when the economic crisis hit in 1998, will testify. But according to research from ASSIRT, in the decade preceding this crisis, the Asian markets returned almost 11%, while the world share market returned 11.7% during the same period.

Western Europe and North America

The mainstream markets of Western Europe and North America tend to have lower rates of growth, but also don't experience the dramatic downturns that the emerging markets can. And, importantly, investing in these markets is no riskier than investing in the Australian market. If you look at the table on page 133, 'Returns for Australian and International Shares, 1986–2000', you will note how the incidence of negative returns is less frequent for international shares than for Australian shares.

Over this period, the returns from the international share markets measured by the MSCI were less volatile and therefore less risky than the returns from the Australian share market – while at the same time producing a higher average annual return. This goes against the normally accepted principle that the higher the return, the higher the risk. The relationship that existed between risk and return for local and international shares between December 1993 and December 2000 is plotted in the following graph.

Risk Versus Return for Major Asset Classes (December 1993–December 2000)

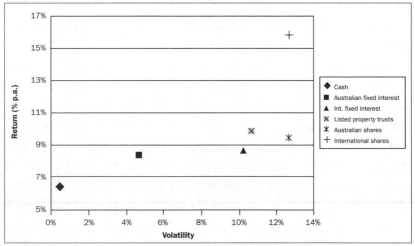

Source: ASSIRT

Again, note how the risk level of investing in all Australian shares (as determined by the annualised standard deviation percentage of returns) was just over 12.61%, with an average annual return of around 9.6%. At the other end of the graph, the risk level of investing in all international shares was about the same at 12.71%, while the return from international shares was 15.8%.

Don't lose sight of the fact that we have been looking here at historical figures over a single (sixteen-year) period. However, ipac research has shown that in most ten-year periods, international shares do slightly outperform Australian shares with a slightly lower level of risk. So, assuming that this pattern is repeated (and there is no reason to think otherwise) diversification into certain international markets makes a lot of sense.

WHICH OVERSEAS MARKETS?

'Which overseas markets should I invest in?', 'How much money should I invest?', and 'How do I do it?' are questions that I am regularly asked.

The first consideration is their risk-and-return characteristics. For convenience, we have classified the world's share markets into 'mainstream' (or 'established') markets and 'emerging' markets. Typically, emerging markets are more volatile than mainstream markets. The ratio of how much money you hold in emerging markets depends on how much risk you are prepared to wear. Personally, for long-term-growth investors, as a rule of thumb, I recommend a ratio of 20% to 30% emerging markets with 80% to 70% in mainstream markets. This is a sensible mix that should generate good growth, with an acceptable level of risk. But naturally this is a very personal issue and needs to be looked at carefully.

Let me stress again how important it is to treat international shares as a long-term proposition. By this I mean, hold on to them for at least five years, preferably ten. All share markets have good and bad years, so if you are investing for only one, two or three years, you may get lucky and get all good years. Or you could just as easily catch one or two bad ones!

HOW MANY INTERNATIONAL SHARES?

To answer the question 'What proportion of my share port-folio do I allocate to international shares?', I generally recommend a minimum of around 30% international with the balance in the Australian markets. In fact, I would like to see investors put 40% of their money into overseas investments. But, given that the international shares appear to be such strong performers, why not invest more? There are at least five good reasons worth mentioning:

1 By investing in the Australian share market you can invest solely in companies that pay fully franked dividends. This benefit does not apply to international shares.
2 When you invest in shares listed on the ASX you are investing to a significant extent in Australia. Companies that operate here (even foreign-owned) provide employment, reinvest in Australia, pay local taxes, and generate wealth that benefits all of us. There's also a bit of room for nationalism here, even if, strictly speaking, it's not normally a yardstick for investment advice.
3 It is relatively harder to keep track of international shares than Australian ones. Indeed, knowing what overseas companies to invest in and keeping tabs on them can be a difficult task for the average investor.
4 Many Aussie companies own off-shore businesses, giving you international exposure from a local company.
5 Finally, you should keep a reasonable percentage of your assets in the community you live in – unless it's a complete basket case, which I am very pleased to say, Australia is not.

HOW TO INVEST OVERSEAS

For many people, direct investment in overseas share markets fits into the too-hard basket. However, the Information Age has made it easier to buy and sell international shares directly. The World Wide Web and email are helping investors access the international market. You can now research markets and sectors, have research sent to you from around the world, and access the charts of thousands of companies from around the world from your home computer. But a word of caution, you may need to appoint an overseas sharebroker, who is not registered with the Australian Securities and Investment Commission (ASIC) and is therefore not answerable to Australian law should you find something goes wrong.

Investing in international share funds

Therefore, the simplest way to go about investing overseas is through an international managed fund. A number of companies offer these to Australian investors: Bankers Trust; Rothschild; AMP; MLC; Invesco; Dresdner; HSBC, among others. Any financial adviser can give you full information about these as well as other managed international share-fund products, or you can contact the managers directly.

The details of managed funds are discussed in Chapter 10, but briefly, managed international share funds can give you access to a large range of investment options. Some funds concentrate on Asian markets, others on the US market, some on a mix of mainstream international markets, and others solely on emerging markets. The choice is very wide.

SHARES AND TAX
Dividend imputation

Although international shares provide us with a great way of diversifying our portfolio and creating wealth, one of the major advantages of investing in local shares is dividend imputation. Dividend imputation refers to the system that allows an Australian company to pass on franked dividends to shareholders. When dividends are franked, it means that they have been paid to the shareholder from company profits after the company has already paid tax on those profits at the company tax rate of 30%. Unlike Australian shares, an investment in international shares doesn't afford investors this benefit.

Franking

Companies can pay dividends that are fully franked, partly franked or unfranked:

- A fully franked dividend indicates that the dividend has been paid from company profits, fully taxed at the company tax rate.
- A partly franked dividend indicates that the dividend is paid from profits not fully taxed at the corporate tax rate.
- An unfranked dividend is paid before a company pays any tax on it.

A company will generally advise shareholders of the status of the dividend at the time of the payment. If you are chasing franked dividends, any basic piece of company research will tell you how much of a company's dividends will be franked over the next couple of years.

Prior to the introduction in July 1987 of the current franking system, a company paid tax on its profits and declared a dividend from the profit. A dividend was then paid to the shareholder. The dividend was treated as income in the same way that interest on a savings account is, and taxed at the shareholder's marginal rate – which may have been as high as 48.5% (including the Medicare levy). So dividend imputation was introduced.

Now when a shareholder receives a fully franked dividend from a company, it means that it has been distributed from the company profits that have been taxed at the full company rate. This means an investor on the top marginal tax rate may only have to pay the difference between the company tax rate – if the shares are fully franked – and their top tax rate of 48.5% on their dividend.

> *To illustrate the benefits of imputation, let's say Bonzer Ltd pays you an annual dividend of $6,000. Bonzer Ltd advises you that these dividends are fully franked with an imputation tax credit of $3,091 in tax paid on them on your behalf. The total of your taxable dividend income is $9,091 which is the sum of the money you have actually received ($6,000) and the imputation tax credit ($3,091).*
>
> *Let's say that you also earn $15,000 from other sources. Adding the taxable dividend income of $9,091 to the $15,000, gives you a taxable income of $24,091. Now, the tax liability on $24,091 is $3,607, but Bonzer Ltd has already paid $3,091 in tax on the dividend, which remember is tax that is effectively paid in your name. So, the amount of tax now outstanding on the $24,091 is reduced to $516 ($3,607 – $3,091). Many other types of investment income (such as interest earnings) are taxed at the full marginal rate, so you can begin to see the real value of dividend imputation.*

For more information and personal advice on the tax implications of share-market investment, and the benefits of dividend imputation and franked dividends, you should contact your accountant or the Australian Tax Office.

Capital gains tax (CGT)

I might have given the impression that share dividends were the only things taxable in share investment. Not so. Similar to other assets – most notably property – when you sell your shares you are required to pay capital gains tax on any after-inflation capital gain they have made. CGT is a tax on the profit you make from the sale of your shares. A capital gain occurs when you sell your shares for more money than you paid for them. If you sell the shares for less than you paid for them, a capital loss is realised.

As part of the Federal Government's 1999 tax reforms, CGT has changed. The treatment of capital gains now depends on the date you bought your shares, and the period of time you held the shares for. The Australian Tax Office (ATO) has established the following categories:

- shares sold prior to 21 September 1999
- shares purchased and sold after 21 September 1999
- shares purchased before, but sold after, 21 September 1999.

For more information on CGT see pages 384–386 in Chapter 12, 'Tax'. For other CGT inquiries, I suggest you talk to your stockbroker, financial planner or contact the ATO on 13 28 61.

RIGHTS ISSUES AND BONUS ISSUES

One of the best things about paying capital gains tax (if there is anything good about a tax), is that it means you have made a profit on your share investments. We have spoken about capital gain through increases in the share price, another way that capital growth can occur is through something called 'rights issues'.

Rights issue

A rights issue is a capital-raising strategy where companies invite existing shareholders to buy new shares at a discount to the current market price. A discount is offered to investors as an inducement to participate in the rights issue. The amount of new shares the shareholder is invited to buy is proportional to the number of shares he or she already owns.

According to stockbroking firm, JB Were, in early 2001, Australian communications company, Powertel offered shareholders one new share for every four shares held, at a price of $0.54 per share. The trading price was $0.75, so the rights issue represented a discount of almost 39%.

There are two types of rights issues offered by companies to shareholders. The first, a renounceable rights issue, means that the shareholder's right to the issue can be sold on the share market. If you, as a shareholder, choose not to take up the renounceable rights issue it can be sold by the company on the share market to another investor. On the other hand, a non-renounceable rights issue, can't be sold by either the shareholder or the company and will lapse if not taken up by the shareholder.

Bonus issue

Similar to a rights issue, a bonus issue is also an allocation of new shares in a company to the existing shareholders. But it's important to realise that a bonus issue does not represent an immediate capital gain for the investor.

Let's consider the example of Australian company Millers Retail Limited that is traded on the ASX. In September last year Millers announced a five-for-one bonus issue. This meant that if a shareholder held 100 Millers shares, they now held 120 shares.

Companies tend to do this, in my experience, mainly for marketing reasons. Sadly, it is true that investors don't like buying 'expensive' stocks. Personally, I reckon this is a waste of shareholders' money.

OTHER TRADABLE INVESTMENTS

Although we have looked at what a share is, it is important to note that there are different types of securities that companies issue to investors that are traded on the ASX. It's worth understanding the basics of the different types of securities because they do involve different risks and return characteristics.

Options

Investing in shares is generally viewed as a high-risk investment choice. Since 1976 when the Australian Options Market opened for business, some people have attempted to manage their share risk by investing in equity options. On the other hand, some investors have used options successfully for purely speculative trading purposes.

What is an option contract? An option contract (which represents 100 ordinary shares) is a bit like an insurance policy that an investor can take out to protect his or her investment against share price changes that may go against them. There are two types of options, the put option and the call option.

If you are interested in trading options, I recommend that you speak to a stockbroker first or call the ASX in your capital city and ask for a copy of the *Options Explanatory Booklet*.

Warrants

Warrants are a way of owning a share without paying the full price for it up-front, while still receiving all the dividends and franking credits that are paid on the ordinary share. Typically, warrants belong in the high-risk, high-return category meaning that they aren't necessarily for those looking to get rich slow. Warrants require a good deal of research and a strong view of the growth potential of the ordinary share upon which the warrant is based. Ideally, they need to be constantly reviewed and re-evaluated.

There are generally three ways that a warrant can be obtained. These include buying the warrant directly from a warrant issuer, such as a bank or financial institution. You can also purchase warrants through the ASX. Alternatively, you can obtain warrants by swapping ordinary shares you own for them. In each instance, you gain or retain an ownership interest in the ordinary share for a part payment that could be anything from 20% to 50% of the existing share price.

Once an investor purchases a warrant, there are a number of choices to be made. Firstly, the investor can sell the warrants via the ASX to realise a capital gain. Or they can make another payment on the warrants and convert them to ordinary shares. Investors can also rollover the existing warrant into a new warrant contract. This allows the investor to defer payment again for a further twelve to eighteen months.

For more information on warrants, you can contact the ASX in your capital city and ask for a copy of the *Warrants Explanatory Booklet*.

CONCLUSION

Look, I can make shares as complicated as you like, but let's get back to basics. Shares are a part of a business. The world population is growing. Demand for goods and services will increase, hence businesses will grow in size and value. Some will do better than average, some will fail, so you should hold many shares to minimise your risk. Over several centuries, after stripping out inflation, shares have returned 6% to 8% per annum.

Buy shares when you can, sell them when you must, wait a couple of decades and you will have built genuine wealth. It's not too hard, is it?

chapter 8

INTEREST-BEARING INVESTMENTS

Talk to anyone with a mortgage, a personal loan or a credit card and they will be able to tell you about the pitfalls of debt. Nobody gets a kick out of paying interest to somebody else. But imagine an investment where you could be the lender? Do you like the sound of this? Well, that's what interest-bearing investments are.

Whether you put your money in a bank term deposit, invest in government bonds, or buy finance company debentures, you're basically lending your own money to somebody else (such as a big company, the Federal or State Government) on the understanding that they will pay interest to you for the privilege of using your money. And, as with any loan, at the end of its term, you get your original amount (or principal) back.

Traditionally, interest-bearing investments have provided investors with a safer, more secure form of investment with regular cash flow, than other asset classes such as shares and property that are considered more volatile and a higher risk. Interest-bearing investments can be broken down into two camps or 'asset classes': fixed interest (such as bonds) and cash.

FIXED-INTEREST INVESTMENTS

A fixed-interest security is an investment where you effectively lend a company, a semi-government authority, or the Federal or State Government money for a fixed term at a fixed interest rate. The interest due on it is paid to you in fixed amounts on a regular basis. This could be every month, or every three, six or twelve months. As a rule, the more frequently payments are made to the investor, the lower the effective interest rate you receive. This is because of the higher costs involved in distributing the income more frequently and the fact that you get your interest sooner. The original amount is repaid to you in one lump sum at the end of the term (at 'maturity').

BONDS

In Australia the word 'bond' is generally taken to mean a fixed interest-bearing security issued by the Commonwealth or State Governments, but semi-government authorities also issue them. This government backing makes them generally pretty safe investments.

Bonds pay interest, called a 'coupon'. The use of the word 'coupon' apparently dates back to the nineteenth century when bond traders tore off coupons attached to the bond certificate to present to the issuer of the bond in order for them to receive their interest payments.

A bond is basically a debt, with the amount of the loan called the 'principal'. Although interest rates of bonds are higher by comparison to those of bank accounts or term deposits, over time they earn less than shares. Nevertheless, bonds still improve portfolios for a number of reasons such as:

- The economic forces that lower share prices tend to boost bond prices.
- Bonds provide a predictable stream of high income.

Bonds can favourably complement your investment portfolio since they help reduce risk. In general, the conditions that make share prices drop tend to raise the value of bonds as investors move their money away from shares and into the relative safety of bonds. Therefore, losses in shares will often be offset by gains in bonds.

The value of the bonds you hold generally moves in the opposite direction to interest rates. If interest rates go up, new bonds will offer higher yields while your bond still pays at the original lower rate, thus decreasing its value. Conversely, when interest rates go down and new bonds offer lower yields, your old bond still earns interest at the previous high rate, thus increasing its value.

Money in History

1st–5th centuries A.D.

The earliest recorded use of bonds was by the government of Rome in the 1st century A.D. At the time, Rome controlled an empire of nearly 70 million people. The Government of Rome faced similar problems to those of modern governments, such as finding money to build roads, feed armies and find jobs for the unemployed. To help raise money, the emperors decided that government bonds were a good option. For the investor, the bonds were a relatively safe investment, because they were guaranteed by allocations of public lands or lucrative government business contracts (such as tax collecting, border duties or the sale of supplies to the military).

TERM DEPOSITS

If you can afford to have your money tied up for from three months to five years, then you might like to consider a term deposit with a bank, building society or credit union. With these securities, you deposit a lump sum with the institution on the understanding you don't have access to the money until the end of the agreed term. At that time you get your money back plus interest which is paid to you at set intervals. To compensate you for tying up your money in this way, term deposits pay a higher rate of interest than normal bank accounts.

The good thing about term deposits is that your money isn't locked away totally. You can get your hands on the money quickly if you need it, even before the investment expires. However, there is a catch – you may have to pay a penalty fee for taking your money out early and your interest will be recalculated at a lower rate that's more in line with that of a regular savings account.

DEBENTURES, UNSECURED NOTES AND CONVERTIBLE NOTES

As we have discussed earlier, with a bond you are lending to a government (Federal or State). However, you can also lend your money to a company by buying debentures, unsecured notes and convertible notes. In general, these investments pay a higher rate of return, but, since you are dealing with a company and not a government, they also involve a higher risk.

- *Debentures* are similar to bonds, the only difference being that they are loans to companies, typically industrial and finance companies, rather than loans to government or semi-government bodies. Debentures don't come with government guarantees, so they are riskier than bonds and consequently normally pay a higher rate of interest. I would recommend that you consider buying debentures in blue chip companies only to manage this risk.

- *Unsecured notes* are similar to debentures in that they are for a fixed-term, fixed-rate loan to a company. However, these loans are not secured against the company's assets. This puts them higher up the risk curve than debentures but, in compensation, they tend to pay higher returns.

- *Convertible notes* are fixed-term, fixed-interest loans to companies, not unlike debentures. The major difference is that they have a set date and a set price when the note can be converted into shares in the issuing company, if the note holder so wishes. Up until the time the note is converted into shares, the holder receives regular, fixed-interest payments from the issuer. If the holder of the note chooses not to convert the note to shares, the issuing company repays the principal value of the note to the investor on the note's maturity.

Money in History

1660

Because goldsmiths' promissory notes are accepted as a medium of exchange, they are a convenient alternative to handling coins or bullion. The realisation by goldsmiths that borrowers would find them just as convenient as depositors, marks the start of the use of banknotes in England.

CASH

A cash investment can range from depositing your money in a bank account to investing in a cash management trust – which is a managed fund investing in a diversified range of short-term interest-bearing securities. 'Cash' also covers investments in the short-term money market or in bank bills with terms of usually no more than 180 days.

The reason that many private investors may invest in cash is because they are reluctant to lock away money in longer-term fixed-interest securities such as ten-year bonds. They are fearful that a rise in interest rates may bring better rates on long-term products and leave them with an uncompetitive rate of return. Instead, many have chosen to spread their fixed-interest funds across short-term, highly liquid offerings, such as cash management trusts, the short-term money market, and bank bills.

This strategy reflects the general rule that if interest rates are going up, fixed-interest investors should keep their money in shorter-term or highly liquid fixed-interest securities. On the other hand, if you thought interest rates were going to fall, you would need to have some longer-term investments (such as shares and property).

PERFORMANCE

Research from ipac shows that over the long term, traditional after-inflation annual returns for cash and fixed-interest investments have been:

Australian cash	0% to 1%
Australian fixed interest	0% to 3%
International fixed interest	1% to 2%

In certain periods, as you can see from the following table, after-inflation returns have been far better than these.

Date	Australian fixed interest (%)	International fixed interest (%)	Cash (%)	Inflation (%)
1986	18.92	25.13	18.12	9.77
1987	18.60	13.78	15.33	7.14
1988	9.36	13.34	13.28	7.60
1989	14.40	18.83	18.37	7.83
1990	19.10	13.51	16.24	6.85
1991	24.75	18.14	11.20	1.51
1992	10.41	9.62	6.92	0.28
1993	16.32	14.31	5.39	1.95
1994	-4.69	-3.02	5.34	2.55
1995	18.64	19.89	8.06	5.05
1996	11.90	10.67	7.57	1.52
1997	12.23	10.65	5.63	-0.25
1998	9.54	10.80	5.14	1.58
1999	-1.22	0.30	5.01	1.80
2000	12.08	10.36	6.27	5.80

Source: ipac securities

LIQUIDITY

Without doubt cash is the most liquid of the asset classes. You can get access to your cash investments immediately in the case of a bank deposit, or within 24 hours in the case of a cash management trust. This is one of the best things about cash – it's there when you need it.

While not quite as liquid as cash, fixed-interest securities are also very liquid. This is because you can trade them either via the stock exchange, through a professional money-market trader working for a bank, or, in some cases, by selling them back to the issuer (either a government or company), depending on the investment.

Under normal circumstances there should be a buyer for any fixed-interest security you wish to sell. The exception to this would be in the case of a company that was struggling financially – finding a buyer to purchase the security might prove difficult.

You also need to be aware that if you decide to sell fixed-interest securities before they mature, the price that you get will depend on the interest rates at the time, which means you could actually end up getting less than you paid for them.

RISK

Cash is an extremely safe investment. When you deposit your money in a bank, or invest in bank bills and treasury notes via a cash management trust, the risk of losing your money is minimal. Risks include a bank closure (which in this age of big bank profits is highly unlikely) or the collapse of an entire financial system (which could be a possibility in one of the weaker economies in Latin America, for instance, but is unlikely in Australia).

As discussed in Chapter 6, 'Savings and Investment', since cash is the safest of the major asset groups this factor makes its returns amongst the lowest. Of course, cash doesn't always do badly. Take 1994 as an example. Cash proved to be the best performing of the major asset classes. But this is a rare occurrence.

Fixed-interest investments, on the other hand, generally are a riskier investment than cash and therefore you can expect higher returns under normal market conditions. However there are exceptions to this rule. You could argue that there is nothing safer than a Commonwealth Government bond and, in most cases you'd be right given the gilt-edged government guarantee. However, this only applies if you hold the bond until maturity. If you sell it early, you can lose money, as we'll see next.

FIXED-INTEREST SECURITIES AND VARIABLE MARKET VALUE

This will probably surprise you, but the daily bond market turnover is typically many times greater than the turnover of the Australian share market. But how does it all work?

When you invest in fixed-interest securities, such as bonds and debentures, you will know exactly how much you receive in interest payments during the life of the security. You also know that you will get your original investment back when the security matures. In addition, with many fixed-interest securities, you are free to trade them on the open market before they mature at what is called their 'market price' or 'capital value'. The market price generally reflects the future direction that bankers and economists think interest rates are headed. The capital value can only be realised if you intend trading the fixed-interest security before its maturity date.

Typically, it's only flustered money-market traders who get involved in trading fixed-interest securities. They are looking for short-term capital gains by trading enormous dollar values. Most investors tend to stick to the tried and true strategy of holding onto these securities rather than trading them, because of the regular and dependable income and security that they offer.

While trading fixed-interest securities may not be part of your investment strategy, it's still a useful exercise to understand how these securities work.

> *Let's say an investor buys a $1,000 three-year bond that pays 6% ($60 p.a.). Two years pass and the investor decides to sell the bond. However, during the two-year period, interest rates have risen and new three-year bonds are now yielding 8%.*
>
> *Obviously, a prospective investor would be pretty silly*

to pay $1,000 for a bond paying 6% ($60 p.a.) when they could buy a $1,000 bond paying 8% ($80 p.a.). But if the seller were to offer a cheaper price than $1,000 for the bond then the buyer who pays the lower amount for the bond could earn an effective yield of 8%. Look, I won't get into the mathematics of this, but I'd suggest that you let a broker do it for you.

Alternatively, if interest rates head south, the seller can ask more than $1,000 because if interest rates have fallen to 4% a bond paying 6% is obviously a pretty attractive proposition, so its price goes up.

There is another factor that we need to consider here. The longer the security has to go to reach maturity, the more pronounced the changes in its market value are in response to interest-rate speculation. For example, if economists and fund managers started predicting interest-rate rises, the value of ten-year bonds would fall further than a bond with three years to maturity.

We can sum all this up by saying that if interest rates are expected to rise, the capital value of a fixed-interest security will fall and if interest rates are expected to fall, the value of fixed-interest securities will rise. The longer the term to maturity, the greater the rise (or fall) in the value of the security as expected interest rates fall (or rise).

> Fixed-interest securities with longer terms to maturity are riskier than those with shorter terms to maturity.

Trading fixed-interest securities

Fixed-interest securities can be traded in a number of ways. You can pick them up:

- as part of a new issue (similar to a share float)
- via the stock exchange
- via banks and other financial institutions 'over the counter'.

New issues A market for interest-rate securities is created when a company initially offers them for sale to the public. Just as Telstra, TAB and Optus sent out a prospectus to members of the public offering the opportunity to buy shares in the company as part of its public share float, companies seeking to raise funds by issuing bonds outline an offer in writing for investors.

Exchange-traded markets The ASX has introduced an Interest Rate Market that enables investors to buy and sell bonds in much the same way as they trade shares. Prior to the introduction of this market, investors found it difficult to trade bonds issued by companies, and to calculate their value and the return that they should be receiving. In most cases, investors could only buy the bonds directly from the companies issuing them.

> For more information on exchange traded securities, go to the ASX's web site at www.asx.com.au.

Over-the-counter markets In Australia, fixed-interest securities have traditionally been traded in an over-the-counter market. 'Over the counter' essentially means 'not centralised'. Unlike the equity market, which has a recognisable physical location to trade shares, the bond market has no central focus, no one meeting place and transactions occur verbally or electronically between market participants such as the Reserve Bank, investment banks, fund managers, and individual investors.

TAX IMPLICATIONS

Logically, as the name implies, interest-bearing investments such as bonds, debentures and term deposits earn interest during the course of their product lifetime. In Australia, the government taxes interest earned on these investments as income.

The tax treatment of fixed-interest securities is therefore pretty straightforward and particularly unattractive for higher income earners. The amount of tax paid is calculated in accordance with your marginal rate of tax. Therefore, if you are earning more than $60,000, you can expect to pay 47%, plus the Medicare levy on any interest you earn from these investments. This means that you lose almost half of the interest you earn on a fixed-interest investment to the ATO.

The tax factor and the benefits of dividend imputation (discussed in Chapter 7) account, in large part, for the popularity of shares among high-income earners. However, there are still good reasons why you should consider fixed-interest investments as part of your overall portfolio. So why should you consider this sort of investment?

SHARES VERSUS BONDS

Had an ancestor invested $1 in the stock market way back in 1882, it would have been worth about $500,000 by 1997. On the other hand, the same dollar invested in bonds would have returned only $250! The reason for this startling difference in performance is that shares yielded an annual return of more than 12%, whereas bonds returned only 5% during this period.

Now don't go and cross bonds off the shopping list immediately – they can be a useful investment tool! Bonds issued by the Commonwealth or State Governments, which guarantee returns, can peak at around 3% after tax and inflation. So, for example, if you are a retiree, who is interested in maintaining a steady income flow to live on in retirement, bonds offer peace of mind by ensuring this.

However, if you are a bit younger and prepared to invest over the longer term, then shares, with their higher returns (and higher risk) may provide a better way of growing your money.

> Which investment best serves you? Shares or bonds? – it's largely a matter of your age and the risks you can bear.

Finally, many personal financial advisers recommend interest-bearing securities because typically they have a predictable stream of payments and repayment of principal. Many people invest in them to preserve and to increase their capital, or to receive dependable interest income. Whatever the purpose (saving for your children's university education or a new home, increasing retirement income, or any of a number of other worthy financial goals), investing in fixed-interest securities can help achieve your objectives.

chapter 9

PROPERTY

Property is very close to the heart of all Australians and this reflects in our extremely high home-ownership rate. Some argue that our attachment to property stems back to our colonial days when many came to Australia in the hope of obtaining a plot of land, but, when you think about it, it goes back to our earliest origins. Property has always been a symbol of wealth and power and I wonder how many fights broke out over access to a dry and draft-free cave!

Unsurprisingly, property has generally been a sound investment in Australia. Only two centuries ago our land had little value to the first European settlers, but since then our population has grown steadily, creating a demand for property. And that demand, in our large but arid continent, is naturally focussed where we tend to cluster – near the ocean, especially on the eastern coastline.

Originally rural land was more valuable than land in our emerging cities. A close friend of mine still wonders about his great-great-grandfather who swapped what he considered was a useless stony piece of ground (now a fabulously expensive chunk of harbourside real estate in Sydney's eastern suburbs) for a far more fertile parcel of land on the New South Wales western plains. At the time he was probably correct in his judgement, but you see how land values change!

The Industrial Revolution had a major impact on property values. In less than a century, we went from having 90% of our jobs on the land to less than 10%. People moved to the cities and most new arrivals landed in a major Australian city and stayed there.

Property values are driven by supply and demand and ever-rising city values have made home owners better off, and property investors and developers very wealthy, while rural land has generally provided lower returns due to the shift in our population to the cities. Of course, rural land on the outskirts of development which is absorbed into an expanding city commands a high price.

PROPERTY OWNERSHIP IN CHANGING TIMES

For the first time in Australian history, many have started to question if the dream of property ownership is still relevant. They are asking: How will property respond to the Information Age and will it become obsolete as a primary source of wealth for most Australians? This is a challenging question and one that is vital to home owners and in particular to property investors. It is quite possible to construct an argument that with increasing job mobility, small families, millions of young retirees and people working from home the very nature of the property market will change. We may well be better off to rent all our lives and invest in super and shares instead.

As history shows, shares have consistently been a better investment over the longer term than property. I demonstrated this in the first 'Money' show for 1998 when I ran a comparison of my first home against shares.

Back in 1983, my wife and I bought a small semi-detached home in the Sydney suburb of Artarmon. Sure, for the $90,000 we paid, we could have bought a bigger home further out, but Artarmon was a bit over ten minutes by train to the city, had excellent restaurants and was near most facilities and services such as universities, hospitals and sporting grounds. Some years later we sold the semi to buy a freestanding home in Artarmon, but early in 1998 our original home came on the market again, and sold for $385,000. Now $90,000 to $385,000 in fifteen years is pretty good – in fact, an average return of 10.17%.

But it was an interesting exercise to compare $90,000 invested in the Australian stock market over the same period. Quite frankly, I was extremely surprised to find out that even after allowing for the fact that I would need to rent a property, the share portfolio in early 1998 would have been valued at $984,144. As you can see some so-called 'new' ideas worked just as well in the past.

So what is the outlook for property?

Seven out of every ten of Australia's 7 million households were living in homes they either owned outright or were paying off in 1997–98.

Sydney had the highest housing costs with households who had a mortgage paying an average of $269 per week, while renters were paying an average of $210 per week.

Hobart had the lowest housing costs ($142 for purchasers and $129 for private renters).

Source: Howard Brenchley, *Property Trusts – The Next 10 Years*, ASX Perspective, 1st Quarter 1999, pp. 64–67

POSITION, POSITION, POSITION

Position, position, position has been the real-estate agents' catchcry, and is still a very valid concept. While position is still crucial, first of all you've got to ensure you've picked the right area to buy in, and then worry about the position. The best-positioned property in an area where the population is shrinking will still lose you money. The dominant driver of property values is demand and while none of us are sure about the impact of technology on how and where we work, we can still draw some firm conclusions:

- Our population is growing. Today there are nearly 19 million Australians. According to the Bureau of Statistics this is likely to grow to between 25 and 28 million by 2051.
- We are getting older. Today we have just under 2 million Australians aged 65 plus. In 30 years time we will have over 5 million Australians aged 65 plus.
- We are forming permanent relationships later in life and most couples plan on having small families (or no children at all).
- Most also believe that apart from short 'times out' from work, that both partners will be at work.
- We are retiring earlier. The average age at retirement in 1998 was estimated to be 58.
- We are living longer.
- While we are working harder, we want more emphasis on lifestyle.

My conclusion from these points is that, given the growth in population, property in the right area will do well, but you can expect to see younger and childless two-income couples and the millions of young, active retirees placing a significant emphasis on owning or renting property in a convenient location. By 'convenient' I mean near public transport, close to work, restaurants (these groups won't cook too often), entertainment, culture and education facilities (both the young and the new retirees want to keep on learning).

Affordability of Houses Worldwide

Agents in various major cities were asked to provide examples of the best homes (biggest home for the money) available for $US250,000 ($AUD430,000). Other criteria included commuting distance, desirability of the area and proximity to schools, parks and transport. On this basis, Sydney looks pretty cheap!

Starting with the most affordable, here's the list:

1 Mexico City
2 Muntinlupa (Philippines), Jakarta
3 Antwerp
4 Escazu County (Costa Rica)
5 Sydney, Montreal and Shanghai
6 Atlanta
7 Auckland and Miami
8 Beijing
9 Vancouver
10 Waterloo (Belgium)
11 Caracas
12 Los Angeles
13 Toronto and Chicago
14 Singapore
15 Honolulu and New York
16 Barcelona and Madrid
17 Taipei
18 Seoul
19 Boston
20 London
21 Tokyo
22 Paris and Hong Kong.

A family of four moving from a home in Castle Hill, Sydney, to a home in Mexico City would find themselves with three times the living space for the same investment. You could buy a 10,333 square-foot palatial luxury in the prestigious Club de Golf Hacienda neighbourhood. The home would include three bedrooms, four bathrooms, a family room, dining room, recreation room, playroom and a three-car garage.

Castle Hill, Sydney, ranks fifth. $AUD430,000 would secure you a 3000 sq/ft residence consisting of four bedrooms, separate ensuite, formal lounge, formal dining, combined family kitchen overlooking a glass atrium, in-ground pool, double lock-up garage and spacious landscaped gardens.

By contrast, in Hong Kong and Paris – tied at the bottom of the rankings – US$250,000 will buy little more than the proverbial oversized broom closet. In Paris, the family could get a 753 sq/ft two-bedroom apartment in the Fifteenth Arrondissement, near City Hall. There's a living room, but a garage would cost extra. In Hong Kong, an option would be a 753 sq/ft apartment in Tseung Kwan O. It would have three bedrooms, but no garage.

Source: Century 21, May 2000.

Bigger homes, smaller back yards

While we won't want to live in smaller homes, we will certainly trade off big backyards for closeness and convenience. This will, in my opinion, continue the trend for properties in the better locations near our city centres to grow in value faster than those in the middle and outer suburbs. But regardless of our lifestyle dreams, properties that will do well will be in areas that are experiencing job growth.

Impact of jobs on property

The days of starting work for a major company at 16 and retiring from the company at 65 are just about gone. Executives have been highly mobile for work purposes for two decades and this trend is spreading rapidly. Young Australians have no hesitation about moving for advancement, better money and a more exciting lifestyle, and this has been a bonanza for property owners in areas with significant job growth.

But not only is it jobs, it's the right jobs – in finance, technology and communications. Here Sydney and Melbourne have done very well, not only attracting people, but highly skilled, highly paid people who then rent or buy property. This is why Sydney and Melbourne property values in the 'right' locations have exploded. The large Sydney suburb of Mosman had an average sale price in 1999 of just under $1 million, with two of its harbourside areas of Clifton Gardens and Balmoral both averaging over $1.5 million.

Compare this to the flat values in the very attractive cities of Hobart and Adelaide. In many ways both offer a far more pleasant and relaxed lifestyle, and much cheaper housing. But property values have been flat because the quantity and quality of jobs have not been created. Both have suffered a 'brain drain' of bright young people and closures of head offices. This has resulted in a lower rate of population growth (0.08% in Tasmania in 1995/96 and 0.37% in South Australia against a national average of 1.33%). Moreover, the 1996 census tells us that both had a higher than average age for their population and higher than average proportion of people over 65 years old compared to the rest of Australia.

So Australia has not one property market, but many markets and sub-markets inside each location. (There will be more on this later in the chapter.) While no one can predict with any certainty the movement of property or share markets in the short to medium term, the basic facts about our population speak for themselves. A growing population and a growing economy will continue to see demand for property both to live in and to rent.

WHY BUY YOUR OWN HOME?

While I accept the 'rent is better' argument as being technically correct, I'm still going to encourage you to own a home for a few pretty simple reasons:

- Borrowing money to buy a home forces you to pay the loan off. This forces you to save and, even if your property performs poorly as an investment, at the end of the day you'll own it.
- I fear that, unless you are very disciplined, you won't rent and buy shares. You'll rent and blow your surplus money on lifestyle. This leaves you at retirement with no house and no shares.
- You won't have a landlord who can kick you out at his or her whim. Moving house is a major pain!
- With your own house you can knock down walls, dig holes and paint it pink and purple if you wish. This is highly therapeutic, if not terribly economically logical – but the lifestyle benefits of home ownership are high.

> If you want to own a property as a home or investment and make money, I strongly recommend phoning the Australian Bureau of Statistics to get their excellent information on population trends. I certainly know where I'd buy property and it's going to be in an area with job growth, convenience, modern facilities and access to those crucial lifestyle facilities, such as the beach and parks that both young and old Australians dream about.

HOW TO BECOME A PROPERTY TYCOON

Do you have to be Kerry Packer or own a string of successful hair boutiques to get started as a property tycoon? Apparently not. Let's look at the case of Patricia Monaghan, aged 29, who works as a manager in Sydney and has a property portfolio worth $2,000,000.

As 'Money' show reporter Kim Watkins found out, Patricia isn't your typical property tycoon. To start with, she's young, she doesn't earn millions and she still works at McDonald's — the same company she began with as a teenager.

When Kim introduced Patricia to the show in 1999, her story grabbed the attention of many viewers. After all, here was an ordinary young person who just happened to buy twelve units valued at more than $1.5 million.

'People are amazed by this,' Patricia says. 'But it really comes down to not being afraid of debt.' And right she is, because on the other side of her balance sheet was a debt of $730,000.

'Debt doesn't worry me,' Patricia says. This probably explains why she continues to add to her portfolio, even today. 'The rents go in every week and then there's capital gains and negative-gearing benefits, too.' Like most shrewd property investors, Patricia lets the rent do the work for her. By paying the minimum amount off her mortgages, she not only maximises her tax benefit, but she's able to save up for her next deposit as well. 'That's how I started,' Patricia says. 'A little bit can go a long way.'

But like all investments, there are risks. Put everything into one basket and you could find yourself out in the cold. Interest rates can rise, tenants can move and jobs can be lost. Fortunately, Patricia has spread her risk by negatively gearing around $300,000 into the share market.

It's hard to believe Patricia started off with next to nothing. She had saved for her first deposit by age 19 and since then hasn't looked back. 'I'm an ordinary person,' Patricia insists. 'Anybody can do it. Even if you buy one

*property, it's a great start. All you need to do is get out
there and build up some confidence.'*

OUR MOST POPULAR INVESTMENT

When Australians think of investment, many think of property, particularly residential property. Indeed, around 20% of Australian dwellings are rented to private-sector tenants, which is a massive show of support for residential property as an investment. Similar to buying a home to live in, buying a property to rent out and, hopefully, sell at a profit one day is an easy concept to grasp. Property is a more tangible investment than shares or bonds, and I am sure this goes a long way towards explaining its great popularity.

It may look easy, but it would be wrong of me to leave you with the impression that investing in property is a cinch. Getting it right is not as simple as it looks. You could probably argue that Blind Freddy could have gone out and invested in the Sydney market (which according to the *Property Market Review* of Macquarie Bank Limited posted a 50% increase in property prices between May 1997 and May 2000) or the Melbourne market (70% increase in property prices across the board) and won.

But the reality is that if you don't do your homework and choose carefully, you may find that your returns (income and capital growth) are low or even negative. It's fair to say that direct investment in property (residential or commercial) normally requires greater care, is more complex, and has more pitfalls than any other investment. I should also point out that the information in this chapter is intentionally skewed towards providing you with information about property as an investment rather than as an asset to live in. Obviously there are plenty of similarities between buying a home and investing in property, but if you want to know more about buying a home, I'd suggest taking a look at Chapter 6, 'Owning a home', in my other book, *Making Money* (2000 edition and forthcoming in 2001 edition).

RETURNS

Like all investments, returns from residential property depend on which period you look at, because all investments have their good and bad years. To get a more accurate picture of how well an investment has performed, you need to look at returns calculated over the longer term. Research from ipac indicates that over this century, residential property increased in value at an average rate of 1% to 3% above the rate of inflation. This is not to say that the residential property market always beats inflation, because there are times when in fact the property market has performed poorly.

> The Real Estate Institute of Australia reports that during the March 1987 quarter the median price of a two-bedroom apartment or unit in Sydney was $76,000. By June 1989, it had risen to a then peak of around $149,000. However, by the December quarter 1990, the median price had fallen to a bit over $128,000. It only returned to its June 1989 levels by the September quarter 1993.

I reckon one reason that property always looks good in most of our major cities over the years is that we ignore transaction costs and renovation costs.

Earlier I mentioned my experience with my first home, a semi in Artarmon. Now let's look at my next home, a bigger three-bedroom property. I bought it, again in Artarmon in Sydney, in mid 1988 for $385,000 and sold it for

$425,000 in mid-1993. Sounds good, as on paper I 'made' $40,000. But did I?

Well, I paid a bit over $13,000 in stamp duty, $1,200 in solicitor's fees, $21,000 for a major kitchen renovation, $3,500 on carpets, $3,000 on painting and over the five years $3,000 on rates. When we sold, the agent's commission was $10,000 and selling costs, including the solicitor and advertising came to $4,000: a total of $58,700.

Yes, I saved by paying no rent, which would have come to nearly $100,000, but I paid $145,000 in interest and had some of my own money tied up in the house which I could have invested and earned around $40,000 in interest. So let's see how my 'profit' looks in reality.

Profits

On sale	$40,000
Rent saving	$100,000
Total	**$140,000**

Costs

On purchase	$14,200
Renovations	$21,000
Maintenance	$6,500
Council rates	$3,000
Selling costs	$14,000
Interest	$145,000
Loss of interest	$40,000
Total	**$243,700**

So when we take a realistic look, my so-called profit, was in actual fact a loss of $103,700 – after allowing for rent on an equivalent property!

Anyway, I do accept that this was a poor period for property, so let's look at some longer-term returns.

When talking about how well you've done out of property, you need to look at the full picture. How well have you done after *all* of your costs are taken out? It makes quite a difference!

A Comparison of Housing with Other Asset Classes (January 1980–December 1998)

Asset sector	Average growth p.a.	Standard deviation
All industrials	12.72%	9.95%
House total returns (HTR)	11.59%	3.41%
Unit total returns (UTR)	9.29%	3.78%
Property trusts	8.89%	6.69%
All ordinaries	8.39%	10.45%
Bonds	7.63%	4.63%
Treasury notes	5.14%	0.78%
All resources	1.23%	12.96%

Source: Residex Pty Ltd

As you can see from this table calculated by property analysts Residex and extracted from one of their many readily available investment reports on the housing market, the gross real returns from residential property investments have been excellent, being surpassed only by the all industrials share market index, but do note my previous point on the costs of owning and selling property. However, the returns from an investment are only part of the story. When one makes an investment, you need to consider the risk of the investment. This is discussed in Chapter 6, but I will recap some key points.

'Risk' is the term we use to describe the chance that an investment might make or lose money for us. One of the methods property analysts such as Residex use to calculate risk is something called 'standard deviation'. The standard deviation measures how much the short-term return from an investment might deviate from the long-term average. The smaller the standard deviation, the greater the chance an investor has of achieving the average return from their investment and, consequently, the smaller the risk. If an investment has a larger standard deviation, then you can expect it to be riskier.

To put this into plain English, look at the table opposite. The all resources index (shares) is the most risky with a standard deviation of 12.96%. Treasury notes (guaranteed by the Government) are the least risky at a standard deviation of 0.78%. Property at 3.41% for houses and 3.78% for units is a medium-risk investment.

MARKETS AND POPULATION MOVEMENTS

According to a KPMG study, Sydney remains the place many Australians and immigrants flock to in record levels. Sydney added almost 60,000 people to its population (1.5% growth) in the twelve months to June 1999 and benefited from a number of factors like the Olympics, the development of the information economy, and a new transportation infrastructure – all of which are drivers of city growth.

Move West

During this period, almost 13,000 people moved to Sydney's West, including a record 3,500 who decided to make Baulkham Hills their home. In Melbourne, there was a similar migration west of the CBD, where the population increased by 12,600, especially to Hume in the north-west, which is up a record 3,400.

The reason for the shift westward in both cities is thought to be a response to the development of new transportation

Sydney Median House Prices, 1930 to 1999

Year	Growth per decade (%)	Reasons for returns
1930–1939	1.7	Great Depression
1940–1949	0.3	World War II
1950–1959	12.6	Golden era – baby boom, government incentives to encourage home ownership, increased immigration
1960–1969	7.7	Credit squeeze (early 1960s)
1970–1979	12.2	First home ownership scheme, high inflation
1980–1989	12.3	Massive influx of immigrants, removal of negative gearing forced investors out of the property market in 1985. Negative gearing reintroduced in 1987 led to investors returning en masse to the property market. The crash of 1987 saw investors move money from shares into property. 1980s was the high point of property purchase for baby boomers.
1990–1999	5.4	Recession, high interest rates and high unemployment in the early 1990s. Low inflation and with it low capital growth caused investors to look at alternatives to property, such as shares in mid to late 1990s. Share floats made buying shares more popular. Also baby boom and migrant demand for property had been satisfied in the 1980s. Government cut immigration.

Source: Real Estate Institute of New South Wales

infrastructure such as the M2 in Sydney, and the Western Ring Road in Melbourne, both completed in 1997. 'The West' in both cities has been revived as a consequence.

Inner city

The move to the west was offset to a certain extent by the record almost 16,000 Australians who shifted into the inner suburbs of all capital cities over the year to June 1999, up from 14,000 in the previous year.

Almost 7,000 new residents moved into Sydney suburbs within five kilometres of the GPO, followed by Melbourne with more than 5,200 added to its inner city. CBD living is also increasing with almost 1,900 new residents moving into an apartment within the CBD of a capital city in the twelve months to June 1999.

The Bush loses

What won't surprise you is that less and less of us are moving to the bush. Some 120 local areas in rural Australia lost more than one per cent of their population in the twelve months to June 1999, compared with three such areas in metropolitan Australia. The KPMG study sees no let up in this trend away from the Bush.

The beach

During the 1990s a new demographic trend emerged. Traditionally, Australians have made a choice between the city or the bush, but now there's a third option: the beach. The City of the Gold Coast heads the nation for the most people added to a single municipality in one year: 12,797 (3.4%) in the year to June 1999. This signals the first upturn in the Gold Coast's rate of growth since 1993. Similar increases were recorded in other beach destinations like Queensland's Sunshine Coast and New South Wales's Central Coast.

MARKETS AND TRENDS

Baby boomers

Over the next decade and half, the housing decisions of the 50- to 65-year-olds – the ageing baby boomers – will have a huge influence on the residential property market. The first of the baby boomers are now in their mid 50s and by 2010, nearly all boomers will be within the 50 to 65 age group. This age group is forecast to grow at a massive rate of between two and three times the average population growth during the first decade of this century.

Where will boomers live?

To take advantage of this growth, investors need to work out what sort of housing the boomers will choose. I am confident that, in general, boomers will not conform to their parents' retirement. (The baby-boom generation has a real aversion to the idea of ageing – so forget nursing homes or retirement villages.) As Macquarie Bank points out in its *Property Market Review* of May 2000, where previous generations tended to stay in the family home until forced out by sickness, old age, or worse, it is expected that boomers will sell up earlier. They will move into low-maintenance

Importance of demographics

In my line of work, people are always seeking tips on the individual property investments likely to produce the best returns both in terms of capital (price) and income (rental) growth. Well, we've seen above how hard it is to answer this question just by looking at the short-term property results for specific areas. Typically, the media tends to focus on the short-term when reporting on property prices. My view is that we need to look not only at changing lifestyles, but also at emerging demographic trends – and particularly the impact of the baby-boom generation.

(little or no gardens), high-density housing (like apartments or town houses) that provides good security and a more convenient lifestyle (close to shops and transport). It is also expected that these dwellings will include a guest room for visiting children and grandchildren and a large lock-up garage for hobbies and recreation.

Boomers' impact on the property market

As Macquarie Bank points out this is not the first time that the baby boomers have had a major impact on the residential property market. They are becoming old hands at driving the property market in a direction that suits them and their lifestyle. No doubt this is due to their sheer weight of numbers – 5 million boomers today in Australia. Where the boomers went, the market was always sure to follow. The most obvious example of this phenomena was the property boom of the late 1970s and early 1980s. During this period, the earning power of the baby boomers was at its greatest and didn't they let everybody know about it, driving the property market to new heights.

At present, the only housing that is providing the features we talked about earlier, are the new upper-priced developments of high-density apartments in inner-city fringe areas. Here the problem is pricing. These apartments will fill the gap for a minority of wealthy boomers, but for the majority the overall solution will require cheaper-than-average pricing for established detached dwellings in suitable suburbs.

If you want to buy an investment residential property, I recommend you buy something that fits these parameters. The type of housing that will appeal to many of the ageing boomers will remain in greater demand than the type of housing that will appeal to less populous demographic groups – and hence show greater growth. It should also mean that the general localities best suited to baby boomers' needs should show relatively stronger price and rental growth than other localities.

GENERATION X

Generation X refers to the generation born between 1965 and 1976. It's expected that the so-called 'Gen X' will also have an impact on property investment. Generation X and the gay male community are driving the market for lifestyle housing in select inner-city fringe suburbs. Generation X café society and, in particular, the gay male demographic are typically characterised by high disposable incomes and the desire to make fashion or status statements.

According to Macquarie Bank research, gay men are recognised as not only earning more ($49,981 p.a.) income than the average for the total male population ($40,800 p.a.), but they also have a strong interest in design and fashion issues and more importantly are prepared to pay large amounts of money to be close to cafés, cinemas, nightlife and their place of work. They are also extremely selective about the choice of location and style of housing. The gay community has already had a major impact on micro markets such as Darlinghurst and Paddington in Sydney, as well as St Kilda and Prahran which are only about three kilometres from the centre of Melbourne, and this trend will no doubt continue across other inner-city locations.

There are a number of reasons why the gay community should not be overlooked when selecting investment locations:

* Gay men have the capacity to spend a higher proportion of their income (compared to the total population) on mortgage and rental payments.

- Research shows that gay men are almost three times more likely to own an investment property.
- Anecdotal evidence suggests the gay community has a higher propensity to buy and sell property more often – adding to demand and market liquidity.

Whilst the gay community is only a small segment of the total Australian population, the available evidence suggests that they can have a very strong influence on select micro markets. As an investor it's worth knowing about their influence in these select markets and the type of residential properties that they buy or rent.

MICRO MARKETS

Before you start trying to work out which direction the property market is headed, you should be aware that there are markets within markets. These are called 'micro markets'. A micro market could be a particular suburb within a city or a local government area and may or may not produce higher or lower returns than its neighbouring suburbs. To further confuse you, you can't take it for granted that the prices of home units and houses within the same suburb, let alone the suburb next door, will always go in the same direction either.

For example, according to the Real Estate Institute of New South Wales, for the year to 31 December 1999, the average price for a three-bedroom home in Manly increased by 12.7% to $625,000, while during the same period, the average price of home units in Manly fell by over 10% to $327,000.

Houses, in terms of capital growth, have historically done better than home units because of the land component. However, this trend may change if more and more of us decide that surplus land is time consuming and a hassle and therefore less appealing to the property investors of the future. To illustrate these anomalies further, the average price of a three-bedroom home in Ashfield rose by 21% to $427,000, while in neighbouring Strathfield, the average price for a similar home fell by 6% to $450,000.

According to the Real Estate Institute of Victoria, in 1999 the average price of a two-bedroom unit in Balwyn North fell by 9% to $287,000, whereas the average price for a similar property jumped by 24% to $227,500 in neighbouring Balwyn. Local real-estate agents suggested that one major reason for this discrepancy might lie in the increased demand from the retiree market for new units. Cashed-up retirees aren't interested in moving into older units that may require more maintenance and are therefore happy to pay a bit more for peace of mind. Balwyn has a bigger supply of newer units than does Balwyn North and therefore has outperformed it in more recent times.

For those of you not familiar with Melbourne, Balwyn and Balwyn North lie about twelve kilometres east of the CBD (not far from Camberwell, the Melbourne suburb that played home to Australia's favourite 1970s TV series 'The Sullivans'). Both are good middle-class suburbs, with the major attraction for property buyers being their close proximity to Melbourne's private schools.

FUTURE RESIDENTIAL PROPERTY PROBLEMS

So far I have given you some tips on the up side, but there are other issues of which you should be aware. Again the biggest is linked to demographics.

Slow population growth

Many investment experts have expressed their concerns about the slowing rate of natural population growth. In 1950 at the high point of the post-war baby boom and with the influx of migrants from overseas, Australia's population was growing at 3.3% per year, but by 1999 the ABS reported that this growth had slowed to 1.2%. The relevance of this to residential property is that population growth is the key driver of real (after-inflation) property growth. So, all being equal, if there is a decline in population growth – due to either natural causes or reduced immigration – there should also be a corresponding relative decline in property returns.

Lack of control

It's important to understand that residential property is different to owning a business. Other than renovating the dwelling and upgrading the grounds, or getting the land rezoned, you don't have a lot of influence over its financial performance. To what extent it appreciates is largely beyond your control. You're in the hands of the market – and where population growth is slow, market growth is also likely to decelerate. Now, I don't believe that our population growth will ever be allowed to get so low that it leads to a sustained decline in property values. However, I'd be very surprised if residential property could sustain the same level of returns that we have seen in the past. The combination of low population growth and demographic changes are partly to blame for this.

Let me explain. As I said earlier, baby boomers are currently the fastest growing segment of the working population. This segment will continue to grow until about the year 2020, when the other age segments will be in decline. Significantly, over this period the 25- to 45-year age group will fall sharply as a proportion of the total working population. The reason that this is important is because many people in this age segment start a family and buy a home. Having fewer people in this age segment could result in the relative demand for housing falling. However, the impact of this probably won't be felt for another decade or so.

PRICING

Why is it that some properties listed for sale take months to sell whereas others are snapped up in a few days or weeks? Plenty of real-estate agents will tell you that if a house or unit doesn't sell within 90 days it is probably overpriced. However, overpricing isn't the only reason why a property doesn't sell. There are many factors that can help you get the best price for your property. These include the strength of the local economy, the number of homes for sale, demand from buyers, the condition (external and internal) of your home, and how it stacks up against similar properties on the market. Property investors and home buyers are also willing to pay more for near-perfect homes in 'move in' condition.

But what types of homes are for sale? In an older area, heritage-type homes tend to attract top dollar, but a run-down 1960s red brick with aluminium windows will tend to take longer to move. I could go on, but I'm sure you get the

A splash of paint can add value

So before you put your home on the market, take a walk around each room and the exterior of your property and jot down the best and worst aspects. Treat this exercise as if you were a home buyer looking at your place for the first time. Honestly consider how well the paint is holding up both inside and on the exterior of the property. New paint is generally a cheap but profitable way of freshening up your property. How clean and orderly is your home and garden, and what needs fixing? Throw out any clutter that you don't need. The goal should be to get your home into model-home conditions, if you want to get the best price. (A hot tip is to bake some bread or cake just before open inspections to give your house that homey feeling. Just be sure you leave yourself time to clean up – and don't let the baking burn!)

idea why some homes don't sell as quickly and as profitably as others. The onus is on the vendors to present the property at its best. Avoid attracting negative comment from potential home buyers. So, if a house needs some work, do it before putting it on the market. A house needing $30,000 of work is generally in pretty bad shape. There are very few home buyers who have enough money to purchase a home that also requires major repair work. Sure, there are plenty of home renovators around, but they will usually only buy at discounted prices. Typically, these prices are well below the house's market value were it in better condition.

SHOULD YOU USE AN AGENT?

Many people choose to use a real-estate agent when buying or selling a property, but some do it themselves. If you have the experience to price the property correctly yourself, are prepared to advertise it adequately, and have the time to show people through it during the week, then there's no reason why you shouldn't try and sell it yourself. This strategy could save you a lot of money in agent's fees.

The reality is that most property owners don't have the experience or the skill to price and then market their properties properly. The result is that either it takes a long time to sell the property, or it doesn't sell at all. An even more distressing scenario is that you might have undervalued the property and sold it too cheaply. Employing the services of a real-estate agent can be the right move in most cases, making sure, of course, that you negotiate a fair selling fee first.

I also must say that selling your own house is not easy as you are emotionally attached to it. If you do your own selling, keep your emotions well in check.

Choosing a real-estate agent

> 'You can get rid of the estate agent, but you cannot get rid
> of the estate agent's work' is an old caution for those who
> intend to sell their homes privately.
> *– Anon*

Choosing a real-estate agent is an important decision. Whether you are buying, selling, or looking for a property manager, you obviously want to find a professional with the right blend of skills and experience. Unfortunately, real estate is one of those industries with more than its fair share of dubious practices and the very last thing you need is a dud agent.

The Real Estate Institute of Australia (REIA) recognised this issue way back in the 1960s when it introduced an Accreditation Program to help property consumers identify good professionals. The best thing about the REIA accreditation process is that it recognises and identifies real-estate agents and property managers who are specialists in their field of practice. To achieve and maintain accreditation, a real-estate professional must have the skills and experience required and commit to continuing education. Accreditation is only available to REIA members who abide by a strict Code of Ethics.

Before deciding on an agent, ask them whether they have REIA accreditation. Some agents are accredited in different specialities. There is accreditation for residential sales, strata management, property management, auction, business agency, valuation and commercial/industrial. The real-estate agent may also display an accreditation logo in the office window.

Once your home is in the best condition possible, you

should interview at least three real-estate agents about listing it for sale. *Do this even if you plan on selling your home by yourself.* They should be local agents and they should be successful. Each agent should give you a Comparative Market Analysis (CMA) that will show recent sales prices of nearby comparable homes, asking prices for homes in the area, and the agent's opinion of your home's fair market value.

Average out the suggested values from each real-estate agent to give yourself a ball-park guide as to what your property is worth. Don't let deliberately inflated appraisals win your business – this is a fairly common and particularly irritating practice that usually leads to disappointment for the seller. You don't need to be Albert Einstein to work out that many vendors sign up the agent promising the best price, even if it is unrealistic. Go and look at comparable local houses or units being offered for sale and, most importantly, those that have sold recently in order to establish what is a reasonable price.

Commission tip

You'll get agents arguing against this, but I reckon you should negotiate a way of paying your agent in a way that motivates them. This is unlikely to work if you live in a street where every house or unit is pretty much the same, but if your property is in a high-demand area, or has unique features, then I think the old 2% to 3% commission is not best for you.

You want the agent busting to get you that extra $5,000, $10,000, or even $50,000. Consider this. If your property has a fair value of $400,000, put the agent on, say, 1% to 1.5% commission if this result is achieved. But you could offer 5% on every dollar achieved above a sale price of $400,000 and even 7.5% for anything above $450,000.

This has two advantages:

1 It really gets the agent fired up to achieve the best price.
2 The agent will be less likely to quote you more than the property is worth when trying to get your business, if he or she thinks you will only pay 1% to 1.5% for an average result.

Now, you've got to know what your property is worth to be able to negotiate a deal like this, but it really can work. Poor sale price equals poor agent fee. Average sale price equals average agent fee. Excellent sales price equals excellent agent's fee – sounds fair to me!

HOW TO BUY AND SELL PROPERTY
Selling by auction

After you've chosen an agent, the next question is: should you sell your property by auction or by private treaty? Most city agents associated with the large franchise real-estate groups will push the auction barrow pretty vigorously – generally more so than independent agents. One reason for this is that the franchise networks have well-established auction procedures and regular auction dates in place, and a culture that is described as 'auction oriented'.

The advantages

There is little doubt that your property will gain maximum exposure in the marketplace through auction promotional activities. The auction marketing campaign, which normally includes site signs, media advertising and 'open for inspection' signs builds awareness of the property. This has the effect of creating a sense of urgency and attracts bidders to the auction day, which may be held on site or in the real-estate agent's auction room.

With all this pre-auction publicity, prospective bidders

know they have to complete all their pre-purchase checks so that they are ready to bid for the property at auction. Some properties can sell before the auction day because an interested party makes a top-dollar offer. If the property makes it to auction, the reserve price can be exceeded as bidders compete for the property and if the property does not sell at auction, negotiations can begin with the highest bidder.

The best thing about the auction process is that everyone concerned knows that a decision to buy has to be made on a set day. A sale on auction day is a sale with an immediate exchange of contracts. This ensures genuine bids for the property.

As a vendor you will be asked to approve a promotional budget which will be managed by the estate agent. This is an important factor in the success of the auction and an important commitment by the owners of the property.

The disadvantages

Whether you're buying or selling, auctions can be a traumatic experience. Auctions aren't always successful. In fact only 55% to 60% of properties sell at auction. Here are some of the main disadvantages to consider:

- Under longstanding tradition, where properties are being sold by private treaty (simply being offered for sale), real-estate agencies generally pay for the advertising. Consequently, though the ads are normally fairly modest, they still do the job effectively. However, when it comes to advertising an auction, it's the vendor who pays the bill. The reason for this has never been convincingly explained to me. The ad campaign for an auction can be quite expensive (thousands of dollars) depending on the property, location and the persuasiveness of the real-estate agent. It's become a bit of a standing joke that auction advertisements in local newspapers are more a promotional piece for the real-estate agent than for the property. The joke falls a bit flat when you realise that it's all paid for by the vendor not the agent. Some agents are also known to quote you full advertising rates, and then get a rebate from the newspaper for the volume of ads. A nice little earner indeed!

One amazing story I heard recently was the response of a real-estate agent based on the upper North Shore of Sydney to an offer made by a couple on a property that they were renting. Incredibly, the agent told them that he couldn't respond to their offer until he had spoken to the vendor and worked out what the marketing costs would be. What marketing costs? The agent already had a potential sale!

- The intensive advertising/marketing period under auction is relatively short: an average of three to four weeks of inspections prior to the auction day. This may be too short a time to find a buyer who will be prepared to pay top dollar for it.
- Under normal market conditions, only about 50% of properties are sold at auction. When times are a bit harder, such as during a property market slump or a recession, clearance rates can be even lower. The failure to get a sale on auction day can be demoralising and can also lead to pressure from an agent to drop your asking price. The result of this is that you end up receiving less for the property than it is worth.
- You need to be aware that some agencies levy non-refundable marketing charges of up to $1000 whether you sell on auction day or afterwards. This money goes towards costs like hiring an auction room, the auctioneer's fees, signboard and pamphlets. I should point out that an auction involves more than just trying to sell a property under the hammer. It can be sold before, during or after

the auction, but trying to sell the property on the day is still the primary focus. This is because it's believed that the auction is where the highest price is obtained. Despite arguments to the contrary, if I had a property with the potential to attract many buyers, I'd go to auction, if not, I'd use private treaty. Read on.

Private treaty

A private treaty sale – where a property is simply offered 'for sale' – can take longer than sale by auction, but it's not such a pressurised, time-specific approach. It is often a slower method which can provide the seller with more time to find that buyer who will pay top dollar. In most cases selling by private treaty can be less stressful than by auction. There's also minimal or no advertising charges levied on the seller, so it can also be cheaper than auction.

One major criticism of this method of sale is that the buyer isn't penalised if they pull out of the sale. By reneging on a private treaty sale, the buyer only loses the deposit, which generally is around 0.25% of the sale price of the property. In many States, the buyer has a five-day cooling-off period in which they can pull out of the sale. With auctions, however, the buyer can lose up to 10% if the sale doesn't proceed.

Whatever you do when selling by private treaty, don't give your property to a number of agents to sell. This is called an 'open sale' and almost guarantees that your property will sell slowly or not at all. The reason is pretty simple, Agent A will be loathe to spend too much time marketing the property if there is a chance that Agent B ends up making the sale.

I recommend that you go for an 'exclusive listing' – where there's only one agent authorised to sell your property, normally for a specified period of a month or two. This gives the agent the incentive to have a real go at selling your property and if they do a poor job, they lose the listing at the end of the exclusive period. Remember if you go for an exclusive listing, this not only excludes other agents from selling your property, it also excludes you. So if you find a buyer, you must pay the full commission to the agent.

Buying on the web

One of the biggest burdens involved in buying property (whether it's a home or an investment) is finding the time to do it – unless you're a professional property speculator with the time to pore over the real-estate pages of the newspapers, spend endless hours on the phone to agents, and then visit properties that are just so wrong you wonder why you bothered.

Consequently, more and more people are turning to the Internet to help them find the right property. One of the biggest pluses of the Net is that it allows you to easily narrow the contenders down by matching you with people either wanting to buy or to sell property. Web sites such as www.realestate.com.au, www.domain.com and www.property.com.au allow you to type in the parameters of the type of house you are seeking. You will be asked how much you want to spend, where you would like to live, what type of home (house, unit, town house) you are looking for and when you want to move in. There also are pictures on the web site to give you some idea of what the property looks like, as well as information on properties sold in that suburb during the past year. Once you have entered the details about your ideal investment, the property web sites keep this information on file and send out regular emails to let you know about market movements in your special segment.

You can choose how often these emails are sent to you and for how long you want to receive them. Another great feature is that the information can be downloaded as a brochure and emailed to friends and family, so you can gauge their thoughts on the property you are considering.

Some of these sites also offer investors the opportunity to take a virtual tour of some of the properties that are listed – but only a very small proportion thus far. This service is dependent on things like modem speed – the faster the better and whether the real-estate agent offering the property for sale is prepared to invest time in the technology to offer the virtual tour. The tours replicate visiting the property yourself: you can view rooms, yards, walls and ceilings at the touch of your mouse. You can zoom in on features that capture your interest or take a broader view of the home. And best of all you can ask others who have access to the Internet to go to the web site and get their first-hand view of the property. Of course, it's not the same as visiting the property in person, but especially if you're an interstate investor, it can save you heaps of time and money.

Anecdotal evidence suggests that investors are ten times more likely to take the jump into residential property investment if they use the web. Typically, these investors like to do a lot of research (which the web is great for) and know what they are looking for and are less likely to allow real-estate agents to waste their time showing them the wrong properties.

Buying costs

Do remember that apart from the price of property you must take into account many additional costs. If you borrow money, you will have to pay interest on the loan. You may also have to pay an application fee, valuation fees, settlement fees, registration fees on the mortgage itself, solicitor's fees, stamp duty, and – depending on the size of the loan in proportion to the total cost of the property – mortgage insurance.

Property price: $200,000
Location: Summer Hill, Sydney
Mortgage: $160,000

Stamp duty on property	$5,800	(2.9% of $200,000)
Stamp duty on mortgage	$580	(0.29% of $200,000)
Buyer's legal fees	$1,500	
Bank loan application fee	$600	
Total	**$8,480**	

In this example, buying costs represent 4.24% of the $200,000 purchase price.

Above is the approximate breakdown of what buying a home unit for $200,000 (with a mortgage of $160,000) can cost. I must stress that all these costs, apart from stamp duties, are open to market forces and negotiation and there may be no need to pay for pest and/or building reports when you are buying a home unit.

Selling costs

When you sell your property you will be up for some or all of the following costs: agent's fees; advertising; solicitor's fees (to prepare the mortgage and exchange documents); early mortgage pay-out fee; building and pest reports (for homes); surveys and possibly cosmetic renovations.

Agent's fees vary from State to State and, in some instances, are simply arrived at through negotiation between the vendor and the agent. As a guide, work on the agent's selling fee being 2% to 2.5% of the value of the property.

Here is what it would cost to sell the same property for $200,000 in Summer Hill. (Bear in mind that lenders might not charge an early repayment fee or may charge more than is quoted here. Also, some vendors make no financial contribution towards a property's advertising campaign, while others contribute significantly more than quoted here.)

Solicitor's fee (includes contract preparation)	$1,800
Early mortgage pay-out bank fee	$500
Agent's fees (2.5%) negotiable	$5,000
Advertising	$500
Total	**$7,800**

In this example, selling costs are 3.9% of the $200,000 selling price.

BORROWING TO INVEST

It's only when the tide goes out that you learn who's been
swimming naked.
– *Warren Buffett*

Using other people's money to buy property investments has
a long tradition and lots of people have tried it. Some have
succeeded, others have achieved moderate results, while
others have failed dramatically. The late 1980s was littered
with the corpses of failed entrepreneurs who borrowed too
much at the wrong time.

But investors who understand the risks and do their
research can make borrowing work for them. Now, borrowing is a perfectly good way to fund an investment in
property – but you need to be aware that you are investing
money that is not yours. If the investment goes badly, you
still owe the lender their money and you have to pay it back.
The obvious attraction is that gearing amplifies the gains and
any losses along the way are tax deductible. But to work, of
course, prices must rise and hopefully interest rates won't
blow out like they did at the end of the 1980s. Gearing up
simply for the tax losses is a big mistake.

If you are keen on this subject, take a look at Chapter 11,
'Borrowing to Invest'.

Selecting a lender

Basically, the banks have recognised there is less chance of wearing a loss if they lend against property than if they lend against shares – a far more risky venture. As a consequence the leveraging that banks will allow against a property is much higher. In fact, some lenders will allow up to 100% on residential property. This means that investors can improve their returns or own more (in dollar terms) than you could if you were investing in stocks and shares. With this in mind, plus the fact that there is also a relatively lower level of risk, and our feeling that we understand property better than shares accounts for property's popularity.

Clearly there is no point in borrowing if the interest rate on the debt is higher than the total net returns being generated from the investment. This can happen, so be careful. There are a very large number of lending products in the market and it is now very difficult to determine which is the best.

LOANS

Variable loans are probably the most common mortgage, however, there are other options that you can choose including fixed-interest loans, split loans, capped-interest loans, honeymoon loans and interest-only loans.

Variable loans

The most common mortgage is the variable loan. The interest rates on these loans are described as variable because the lenders can change them at any time. Typically they change when the official Reserve Bank of Australia (RBA) rates move. When the RBA amends its rates, the lenders normally follow. Many cynics claim that the banks seem quick to move when the rates go up, but are much slower to pass on the benefits to their customers when the Reserve Bank reduces official rates.

Standard variable loans can offer a number of features of which redraw and mortgage offset are the most common:

- *Redraw facility* offers you a way of paying extra money into your mortgage. You can then withdraw it when you need it. You should be aware that, if you withdraw money, there are fees and charges and minimum withdrawal amounts. You should find out what these are before you opt for this feature. You can ask your lender for more information about the redraw option.

- A *mortgage-offset account* allows a normal bank account to be linked to your home loan. The benefit of this is that the interest in your savings accounts can be used against the interest on your mortgage to help reduce it. This can help you pay off the loan faster and save you money at the same time. Your lender will have more information about mortgage-offset options.

Fixed-interest loans

A fixed-interest loan allows you to fix the interest rate on your loan over a set period of time. Most lenders offer fixed loans from one to five years. By choosing a fixed loan, you are limited in how many repayments you can make (i.e. CBA allows borrowers to pay back only an extra $10,000 a year in repayments). However, what you lose in flexibility, you can make up for with peace of mind – you know what your regular repayments will be. Another argument for fixed loans is that they can be a buffer against rising interest rates. But, as a friend of mine found out, locking in a fixed rate can also prove costly if interest rates fall. My friend locked in a fixed loan in 1990 at 15%, but was left scratching his head as the rates on variable loans headed south for the next couple of years to the extent that by September 1993 they were at 8.75%.

Split loans

Split loans are a bit like an each-way bet on interest rates. These loans offer you the option of a part fixed and part variable loan, and in any ratio that suits you. With split loans, it doesn't really matter what way rates go, you win some and you'll lose some either way. The real benefit of these loans is that you can make extra repayments even though part of the loan is fixed. You should also remember to make sure that you don't pay monthly fees on both (variable and fixed) parts of the loan.

Capped-interest loans

These are similar to fixed-interest loans and are generally part of an introductory offer lasting for the first six to twelve months when they revert to a standard variable rate. They work like this: the interest rate is variable below the capped rate and can't go above the capped rate. When the loan reaches the capped rate you effectively have a fixed-rate loan.

Honeymoon loans

Honeymoon or teaser-rate loans offer rates that generally look pretty attractive, but be warned they can have hidden traps for the unsuspecting. Often the rates offered after the honeymoon period expires will be higher than a standard variable-rate loan and there can be penalties if you decide to terminate the loan early.

Interest-only loans

Interest-only loans differ from most types of loans (which stipulate that you repay both the principal and the interest). With an interest-only loan your repayments are comprised of interest charges only. You don't repay any of the principal (capital) at all. Interest-only loans were designed primarily with the property investor in mind. They enable you to hang onto a property, which during the term of the loan will generate some rental income and possibly some capital gain. Interest-only loans often involve selling the property to repay the principal.

PROPERTY MANAGEMENT

Obviously finding the right property and then obtaining a loan that suits your needs is only the start of the property investment process. As a property investor, you now have to contend with a range of issues that you should know a little about before you invest. There are the ongoing costs of owning a property and tax issues. Let's look at some general property management issues.

To maximise your returns, it's imperative that you manage your property effectively by maintaining its value and minimising the cost to you. From choosing tenants and appointing a managing agent, to routine maintenance and emergency repairs, your property will require a sound management strategy if it is to provide the sort of returns you envisage.

Property costs

Property costs include:
- council and water rates
- insurance
- body-corporate fees
- property-management fees to real-estate agents
- maintenance
- bookkeeping fees
- accountancy fees
- legal fees (for drawing up leases)
- advertising costs to find tenants

- bank charges
- petrol, phone, postage and stationery.

While ongoing costs vary from property to property, a reasonable rule of thumb is that residential outgoings average 20% of gross rentals. (This is the percentage used by the REIA, based on three-bedroom houses. Net rent is, therefore, around 80% of gross rent.)

Some property costs are unavoidable, such as insurance and rates, but it may be possible to save some money by managing your own property, doing your own mainten-ance or finding your own tenants. These chores might give you a headache, but they will help you to achieve a better than average net return (yield) from your investment property.

Choosing tenants

Obviously there are two ways for you to make money from your investment property. The first is by selling it for a profit, but the second, and often the most predictable way, is to collect rent from tenants. Maximising your rental income is more easily achieved by maintaining consistent, reliable tenants than by undertaking expensive renovations or by pricing the rent at the very top of the market.

Long-term tenants are a guaranteed source of income. So if your residential property investment is part of a long-term investment strategy, it is best to keep the same tenants for as long as possible, providing that your tenants:

- are responsible
- don't damage the property
- pay the rent on time.

The reason it is best to keep the same tenants for as long as possible is simple: the longer they stay, the more you'll be able to maximise rental income and minimise any outgo-ings and expenditure. This is because whenever you have to find new tenants you incur new costs such as:

- advertising
- agent's fees
- zero rental income while the property is vacant.

DIY property management versus real-estate agent

Investors can either choose to manage the property themselves – which can be a bit of drag on time, especially when in most instances they really don't have the experience to do the job efficiently – or they can choose an agent. The agent will find tenants for you and ensure that the property is maintained properly. However, this will be done at a cost.

There's more to selecting an agent than just feeling comfortable with them. Most importantly, consider finding an agent who is well known and successful in the local area. Passing traffic is important and the estate agent's window is often the first place prospective tenants look. Other factors to consider include the level of commission they are asking and their length of experience.

Interviewing and finding the right tenant can be a trying experience for the inexperienced. There are plenty of horror stories about tenants who seemed great at the interview, but, when it came to paying the rent regularly and caring for the property, they fell way short of expectation. Of course it's not all doom and gloom. But if you're going to manage your own property, there are a few things you can do to ensure you rent your property to the best possible tenant.

It will pay for you to take the management of your investment property seriously. It's critical that all prospective tenants have references – and not just work references. Work references only indicate whether or not they can afford your property, not how well they will care for your property. I can't stress enough how important references from previous real-estate agents are. Obviously first-time renters won't have references from other agents and therefore you'll have to rely on character references and other relevant information. So if any potential tenants have poor references or can't provide references, keep well clear. I would also suggest at the final stage of the selection process you phone the referees to double-check the references.

Some questions to put to prospective tenants at the interview:

- What was the longest period of time they rented a residential property for?
- What was the shortest time they have rented for?
- Why did they leave the last rental property?

What you should also keep in mind is that you want a tenant who:

- has clean habits
- will look after your property like it's their own
- will pay the rent on time
- will contact you or your agent if there are any problems.

You and your tenant

Good people skills play an important part in sound property management. If you treat your tenants fairly, they should treat you well in return. So it's important to build a good relationship with your tenant. Be friendly, but always remember that the relationship is a business one, not personal. When you feel you have found the right tenant for your property, it's best to make sure you get everything clear from the start. This includes:

- conditions of the lease
- when the rent is due
- how often it is to be paid
- to whom and where it should be paid
- the details of the bond.

How much rent should you charge?

Before you begin to think about searching for the right tenant, you should work out how much rent you should charge. The best place to find this out is in the 'To Let' section of your local and metropolitan newspapers' classified sections. Why not even visit a few of these properties to get a better idea. Another option is to look in the windows of local real-estate agents to check out how much rent is being charged for similar properties in the local area. You can also contact an office of the Real Estate Institute in your State. You can find their contact details by visiting the Real Estate Institute of Australia's web site at www.reia.asn.au and following the links to your State's site.

Even if you want to manage the property yourself, it won't hurt to ask an agent to give you some feedback on how much rent you can ask a tenant to pay. Ask an agent:

- how much rent you are likely to get
- what work needs to be done and will that work increase the rent you can charge
- what type of tenants are likely to be interested in the property.

Following are some indicative rental return figures for Australia's capital cities which you can use as a very broad benchmark to begin your research. Obviously rental returns will vary widely from suburb to suburb.

Median Rents for Three-bedroom Homes ($ Per Week)

Year	Sydney	Melbourne	Brisbane	Adelaide	Perth	Canberra	Hobart	Darwin
1995	260	155	170	140	125	170	150	240
2000	235	195	175	160	154	210	155	220

Source: Real Estate Institute of Australia

Median Rents for Two-bedroom Flats/Units ($ Per Week)

Year	Sydney	Melbourne	Brisbane	Adelaide	Perth	Canberra	Hobart	Darwin
1995	190	130	155	110	100	150	120	180
2000	260	180	100	125	138	190	125	180

Source: Real Estate Institute of Australia

TAXATION

Tax is an important issue you need to consider before you invest in property. The major taxes on property include stamp duty, land tax, capital gains tax (CGT) and Pay as You Go tax (PAYG). Tax on property is a major issue for the Federal and State governments due to the huge amounts of revenue derived from it. According to the REIA, in 1995–96, for instance, the State and Territory governments collected more than $5,600 million in stamp duties and land taxes. In the same year, local governments raised over $5,000 million through rate payments on property. The combined total of nearly $11,000 million, represents over $1,500 for every household in Australia.

Property taxes account for about one-quarter of all State government tax revenue, and more than 95% of all taxes collected at the local government level. Though we know that taxation makes a major impact on investments, it is impossible to determine the precise benefit/cost this has on individual investors since it depends on an individual's marginal tax rate.

Generally, the following should be noted with respect to taxation:

- Higher-income earners will reap more valuable tax benefits from investing in property.

- Housing has more tax benefits than any other investment due to things like building-allowance deductions and depreciation benefits.
- Lenders will generally lend you more for property. This, in turn, has a positive taxation benefit because you can offset any income (rent) against interest costs on the loan. We call this 'negative gearing'.
- Property attracts the benefits of capital gains tax. I'll explain this in more detail later in the chapter.
- It's sensible to gear your investment, provided the net returns are not less than the cost of financing your mortgage. This will enable you to hang on to a property even in the bad years or if you lose a tenant.

Land tax

Land tax is an annual tax generally imposed by each State government (including the ACT, but excluding the Northern Territory) on land of higher value. The rates at which land tax applies vary widely across the States – the Victorian Government hits property investors hardest with a maximum rate of 5%, while the ACT has the lowest rate at 1.5%.

In all States, except Victoria and New South Wales, taxpayer's homes are exempt from land tax, although very expensive properties whether they are homes or not are subject to land tax. It is usually calculated on the unimproved value of the land as determined by local council land rate notices. This means that any structures or buildings on the land aren't subject to land tax. Sure, it cuts in at over $1 million, which can get pretty nasty in New South Wales if you are lucky enough to own a harbourside property.

Stamp duty

Stamp duty is a tax on many types of transaction such as property, shares, insurance policies and powers of attorney. Stamp duty on property accounts for between 40% and 50% of all stamp duty revenue. Stamp duty is paid on the purchase price of the property. You will also pay stamp duty on any loans that you take out to help you acquire a property. All States have stamp duty concessions for first home buyers, and some extend concessions to your principal place of residence.

The various State governments, rather than the Federal Government, administer stamp duty. The net effect of this is that stamp duty taxes are calculated differently in each State.

The State departments below can tell you how much stamp duty you will pay on a property purchase:

Australian Capital Territory
ACT Office of Financial Management
Phone: (02) 6207 0028
Web site: www.act.gov.au

New South Wales
Office of State Revenue
Phone: (02) 9685 2122
Web site: www.osr.nsw.gov.au

Northern Territory
Stamp Duties Office
Phone: (08) 8999 7949
Web site: www.nt.gov.au/ntt/revenue

Queensland
Office of State Revenue
Phone: (07) 3227 8733
Web site: www.osr.qld.gov.au

| **Victoria** |
| State Revenue Office of Victoria |
| Phone: (03) 9628 6777 |
| Web site: www.sro.vic.gov.au |
| **Tasmania** |
| Department of Treasury and Finance |
| Phone: (03) 6233 3068 |
| Web site: www.tres.tas.gov.au |

Source: Real Estate Institute of Australia

Capital gains

The impact of capital gains (CGT) on your overall property investment returns can be significant, so it's important that you understand its impact before you invest. CGT is complicated and we look at it in more detail in Chapter 12, 'Tax'.

Briefly if you hold an asset for more than twelve months, and you bought it after 19 September 1985, you will be liable to pay CGT if you have made a profit on it when you sell. The Tax Office regards a capital gain as the difference between the cost of an asset and the amount you receive when you sell it. The cost of the asset, as discussed above, can include acquisition fees like stamp duty and conveyancing costs.

Since September 1999, the ATO has used two methods of calculating capital gains. For all property investments bought and sold before 21 September 1999, the ATO used a system of indexation to revalue the purchase price of the property. Indexation increased the value of the purchase price of the property by the rate of inflation. You then pay CGT (at your highest marginal rate of tax) on the difference between your new purchase price and the sale price.

If you purchased your investment property after 21 September 1999 and then sold it twelve months later, the capital gain is taxed at half of your highest marginal rate of tax.

Under the new system, there is no indexation of the purchase price. If you didn't hold onto your property for twelve months, then there are no concessions under either system, and you will be liable to pay the full value of the capital gain. And finally, if the investment property was purchased prior to 21 September 1999 but sold after this date, you can choose either the discount or indexation method. Certainly the significant drop in CGT will have a positive effect for property investors.

GST

GST has had a great impact on property. For example, you pay GST on new homes where all or most of the building work was completed after 1 July 2000. In fact, you incur GST on any work done to your home from 1 July 2000.

Building depreciation allowances

You can deduct certain kinds of construction expenditure for tax purposes. In the case of investment properties, the deductions can be spread over a period of 25 or 40 years (depending on their date of construction) and are called 'special building write-off deductions'. The deduction is limited to 100% of the construction expenditure.

Deductions based on construction apply to: a new building or an extension, such as a new room or garage; alterations, such as the removal of an internal wall; or an improvement, such as the building of a patio or pergola. Deductions are only allowable for the period that the property is rented.

You need to be aware of a number of rules in relation to the special building write-off:

- If you purchased the property before 18 July 1985, you can not claim a special building write-off.
- If you purchased a property constructed between 18 July 1985 and 15 September 1987, the annual special building

write-off allowable is 4% of the construction expenditure. This can be claimed over 25 years.

- If you purchased a property constructed after 15 September 1987, the annual special building write-off is 2.5% of the construction value and this can be claimed over 40 years.

Building depreciation allowances provide strong incentives for investing in newer rather than older properties, and can make the difference between a good and a poor return on your investment property.

Depreciation of furniture and fittings

If you are the landlord of furnished premises that contain large household items which have a limited life, you can depreciate these and claim them as a deduction against the property's taxable income.

You can claim things like above-ground swimming pools, air-conditioning units, carpets, curtains, furniture and fittings, radios and refrigerators, and much more. You should talk to your accountant about what you can and can't claim. For example, you can't claim clothes hoists, electrical wiring, wash basins and toilet bowls, driveways and paths and other items that have a long life span. As with building depreciation, depreciation on furniture and fittings also has rules you need to be aware of that can have an impact on your claims and, ultimately, your investment returns.

There are two methods of working out depreciation deductions. You can choose the prime-cost method or the diminishing-value method.

The prime-cost method uses the cost of the item, for example, a blind, as the basis for calculating depreciation. If you purchased blinds for $2,000, with a prime-cost rate of 13%, you can claim the same amount of deductions (13% of $2,000 for the next 20 years). Each item is given its own effective life span by the ATO. For a stove it's 20 years, for a television it's 10 years, while for a washing machine, its life span is 7 years. You can find more information on effective life spans in the ATO's *Guide to Depreciation* which can be downloaded at www.ato.gov.au or by ringing 13 28 61 for help.

The rate used in the diminishing-cost method, on the other hand, is generally about one and a half times the equivalent prime-cost rate. So for the blinds, the prime cost rate is 20%. The depreciation allowed under this method is worked out each year on the undeducted cost of the item. So in Year One you can claim a $400 (20% of $2,000) deduction. In Year Two it's a $320 (20% of $1,600) deduction, and so on.

To confuse us further, the ATO also applies different prime-cost and diminishing-cost rates depending on when the item was purchased. For example, if you decided to use the prime-cost method for calculating your deductions on the blinds, the rate prior to 27 February 1992 is 6%, while the post 27 February 1992 rate is 13%. If you decide to use the diminishing-cost rate, pre 27 February 1992 you can claim a 9% annual deduction on the purchase price of the blinds, but if you bought the blinds after this date, the deduction is 20%. So again, you can see there are strong incentives to invest in newer fittings in your investment property.

If you're confused about all this, I suggest you talk to your accountant about depreciation.

Rental expenses

As most of you are aware, buying an investment property and then maintaining it is not exactly a cheap proposition. We've already looked at the costs of buying and selling property – the transaction costs.

Though you can't claim buying and selling costs such as conveyancing and advertising (although if you purchased the property after 19 September 1985, these costs can be included as part of the cost base of the property for capital gains purposes), there are plenty of other expenses that you can claim during the period that your property is available for use by tenants.

Some of the expenses that you might be able to claim include:

- advertising for tenants
- bank charges
- body-corporate fees
- cleaning
- council rates
- electricity and gas
- gardening
- insurance
- land tax
- legal and accountancy fees
- lease costs
- pest control
- property agent's fees
- quantity surveyor's fees
- repairs and maintenance
- travel and car expenses
- telephone, and more.

You can't claim stamp duty, nor expenses incurred by the tenants (such as water or electricity).

Pay As You Go (PAYG)

If you make a profit from renting out your property, you will need to be aware of PAYG. PAYG requires you to pay instalments either quarterly or annually during each income year. You will need to pay PAYG if you earn more than $999 from rental income. We have discussed PAYG in more detail in Chapter 12, 'Tax'.

A quick summary

Tax is an important issue to consider before you invest in property. The major taxes on property include stamp duty, land tax, capital gains tax (CGT) and Pay As You Go tax (PAYG).

But remember you can reduce the size of your tax bill on your property investments by understanding what you can and can't claim as depreciation allowances.

What enhances and diminishes returns

The following should be avoided as they will reduce your property investment returns:

- buying a property in a poor location
- buying property in an area showing below-average growth
- buying property in poor condition with high maintenance costs
- buying property that lacks aesthetic appeal and has no potential to improve
- buying when the market is expensive
- paying too much
- selling when the market is weak
- investing too much money (overcapitalising) in the property
- poor maintenance
- difficult tenants
- long vacancies
- being a bad landlord
- inadequate planning for capital gains, PAYG and land taxes
- relative high land value to property value, which generates relatively higher land tax
- rising interest rates
- economic downturn or recession causing low rates of growth
- inadequate insurance to cover damage caused by tenants or neighbours

- inadequate insurance to cover damage to tenants, like an injury caused by an electric shock from old wiring
- ineligibility for depreciation allowance
- poor record keeping and poor control of costs.

These factors, on the other hand, will increase your returns:
- buying a property in a good position in a strongly performing area
- buying an aesthetically pleasing property, or one with potential for improvement
- buying property that appeals to ageing baby boomers and other key investor groups
- buying a property with a unique and positive feature
- buying a property that is in good order
- buying when the market is cheap
- paying a fair price
- selling at the top of the market
- a property rezoning in your favour (i.e. company title flats converted to strata title)
- low maintenance and other costs
- relatively low land value compared to property value, resulting in relatively lower land tax
- good tenants on a long-term lease
- short vacancies
- being a good landlord
- an appropriate degree of renovation that enhances the property
- a healthy economy
- low interest rates
- adequate insurance cover
- sufficient tax planning
- eligibility for depreciation allowances
- good records, good bookkeeping, good accountancy and good overall control of costs.

COMMERCIAL PROPERTY

We should also look at investing in commercial property as it is a major investment sector and has been a source of extraordinary wealth for some people. Traditionally, small investors have stayed away from investing directly in commercial property. That's not because it's a second-rate investment – returns for commercial property are generally higher than residential – it's just that most investors steer away from commercial property because they think it's very specialised, too expensive, and just too difficult.

There are also investors who nevertheless reckon that because they own a house, they are property market experts. I wish I could agree, but as you can see from the information in this chapter, there is a whole lot you need to know.

What experience do you need?

While I'm not trying to discourage you from investing in commercial property, you need to be aware that there are quite a number of factors to consider. Property experts suggest that the key factors include:

- location – for which more or less the same rules apply as for residential properties
- the level of supply and demand for the property you are investing in
- what future tenants might be looking for
- what sort of floor space they might need
- the type of business that will be attracted to your property
- what services they might expect (such as air-conditioning, toilet facilities and lifts)
- how you might develop your property to meet future tenant demand
- what the local council's zoning laws are for commercial property.

Generally, these are areas we don't need to venture into when buying a residential property and, even if we did, it's doubtful whether we would have the necessary experience to deal with them. In most instances when we buy residential property, we buy in areas that we know something about. In effect, we draw upon our own in-built research database. We know what is good and bad about the area, what sort of facilities the area has, and what the property prices are like. While this is very useful when you are buying residential property, it's not really enough when you begin to look at commercial property. Sure there are research houses to help you, but this just underlines the major differences between investing in residential versus commercial properties.

Leases and tenants

Commercial property investors are interested first and foremost in finding good tenants who will pay good rental income. This is not dissimilar to landlords of residential units hoping that the tenant will stay for a reasonable amount of time. The advantage of investing in a shop, for example, over a residential investment is that as the landlord you are protected by the *Retail Tenancies Act*. The Act stipulates that leases should be signed for a minimum of five years. Usually, a commercial tenant worth his or her salt will plan to be around for longer than the average six months that tenants stay in residential properties.

Tenants who cannot afford to pay the rent are the biggest problem that retail investors face. As a landlord, you rely heavily on the business acumen of your tenant. Sometimes tenants can be very good, but when they are bad, it can cost you lots of money. So it's important that you choose tenants wisely:

* know who they are and what they do
* find out what sort of space they want

- work with them to develop the property to meet their needs.

Yields

The yield (rental return) from commercial property is generally higher than for a residential investment. In Sydney, for example, shops have returned between 7% and 10% per annum in recent years compared with 4% to 5% for residential returns. This reflects the higher risk associated with retail property, where success is crucially dependent on choosing both the right location and securing a suitable tenant.

Yields depend very much on the forces of supply and demand as well as general economic conditions, but not always in the way you would expect. If, for example, interest rates were low, you would expect this to be good for commercial property. However, this is not always the case. For example, if there is an oversupply of property, it doesn't matter how strong the demand is, rents will fall. Now, if there is an undersupply, it won't matter if interest rates are going up, demand will still be strong. According to CB Richard Ellis, in August 2000 in Sydney's CBD there was about one year's supply of commercial property against four years' worth of demand. So, even if interest rates go up, rents are predicted to rise during this period by up to 50%.

COMMERCIAL PROPERTY OPTIONS

I would recommend that anyone contemplating a direct property investment start with residential first. If this works for you – and there is no reason why it shouldn't, if you do it properly – after a few years think about a small commercial property investment, such as a shop. By this stage you will have developed a feel for property. You'll understand the value of good tenants, you'll understand leases, the role of property management, and just how much time and money is involved in investing in property. In other words, you will no longer be a complete novice, which is something you can't afford to be when investing in commercial property. There are plenty of things that can go wrong that are outside your control, so it's good if you have some experience to deal with problems should they occur.

Shops

'Over the years, owning a small shop in an inner-city suburb has delivered excellent returns,' wrote my colleague Pam Walkley in the May 2000 edition of *Money Magazine*. And, according to the results of a study by KPMG, this is set to continue. The report indicates that almost two-thirds of shoppers prefer to shop in suburban strips rather than big malls. Combine this with continued high levels of consumer spending and it's not hard to see that small shops will continue to be a very attractive investment option.

It's also worth noting, as BIS Shrapnel pointed out, that while retail construction boomed in recent years – peaking at over $2 billion in the 2000 financial year – most of the development has been in medium to major shopping centres and very little in strip shops. This means that there is a very real shortage of street (strip) shopping properties.

Over recent years, there have been a number of 'strip' stars across Australia. According to Burgess Rawson Property Consultants, in Melbourne, Burke Road in Camberwell, Lygon Street in Carlton, Brunswick Street in Fitzroy and Church Street in Brighton have been the pick. In Sydney, it has been Oxford Street, Paddington; King Street, Newtown; Darling Street, Balmain; and Victoria Avenue, Chatswood. Strips have improved significantly over the past four years, according to research by CB Richard Ellis. Yields levelled at around 6% to 7% – after peaking at around 9% to 10% in 1991. On the flip side, capital values have increased as demand from investors grew.

Specialty shops in malls

If you are considering specialty shops in a prime CBD mall, Melbourne would appear to be a good investment with shops in Bourke Street Mall recording a 2% rental growth during 1999 to $2,750 a square metre, according to Knight Frank. In the other major malls – Pitt Street in Sydney, Queen Street in Brisbane, Rundle Mall in Adelaide and Hay Street in Perth – rentals did not move much in 1999.

In other capital cities, CB Richard Ellis research found lower rentals and higher yields. Brisbane rentals ranged from $500 to $600 gross and yields averaged 8.5%; Perth strips recorded rentals of $350 to $400 with yields ranging between 7% and 8.5%. Finally, shopping strips in Adelaide returned $400 to $500 in rents, a yield of 8.5% to 9.5%.

Rental income

Rental income is of greatest interest to retail investors. Like an investor in residential property, the retail investor hopes to find tenants who will stay for a reasonable amount of time. As we discussed earlier, the *Retail Tenancies Act* is a big help: stipulating retail leases should be for a minimum of five years – a big difference from residential leases of generally six months.

As I said earlier, the yield from shops is generally higher than for residential property (as much as twice as high), reflecting that commercial property is a riskier investment than residential property. Factors such as choosing the right

location and suitable tenants are even more important in relation to shops. The success of your investment can also be
hampered by such external factors as the performance of
neighbouring shops.

Do's and don'ts of strips

So when you are considering buying a strip shop, there are
a number of factors that you need to consider. What businesses will do well along shopping strips? In recent years,
butcher shops and fruit shops haven't fared well along strips,
having lost out to supermarkets which are open for longer
hours and offer one-stop shopping. To take their place along
the strips have come real-estate agencies, restaurants and
boutique clothes shops.

The viability of the shopping area is crucial to the investor's success. Unlike residential property, the physical qual-
ities of a retail investment are not nearly as important as the
location and the traffic flow. Many shops depend on impulse
buyers – and you have a far better chance of finding them
with 5,000 people passing rather than 1,000. It's also important to pick the right side of the street. Post offices, Medicare
offices or banks tend to attract plenty of passing traffic.
However, with many of these facilities closing or relocating,
it's important that investors find out about any planned
changes. If you are considering a destination shop like a
video shop or a liquor store, passing trade is not so critical,
and these are often best located on the edge of a centre where
customers can park outside.

Strata units

The small investor does not need to be confined to shops
only. There is a vast array of choice of strata units (including
car spaces, office suites and industrial units). In a strata
scheme, each unit owner owns some of the property – such

as an office block, car park or industrial unit – individually (this is called a strata lot). There are strata units available in a wide price range. At the lowest end you can get a car-space in Melbourne for around $35,000, although these are scarce. As with all property investments, you need to keep the fundamentals in mind. There's no point buying a real-estate asset if there is limited demand for it, regardless of how cheap it is, or attractive it might be.

Let's look at some strata-unit possibilities.

Car spaces

Car spaces are probably the least glamorous of strata options, but if you bought one in Sydney a few years back you would have done very well indeed. That is because demand for the product outweighed the supply. This in turn pushed up rental income and prices.

According to a report from Stanton Hillier Parker, investors in car spaces have done well over the past couple of decades. For example, between 1982 and 2000 prices for car spaces in a Clarence Street car park rose from $30,000 to $60,000. When you consider that a Porsche Boxster S Convertible and the like retail for more than $130,000, paying $60,000 for a parking spot doesn't appear to be quite so excessive.

Research from CB Richard Ellis showed a wide variation in yields for car spaces across Australia. In Sydney yields range from 6% to 7% for a space, while in Melbourne yields range from 8% to 10%. Typically location and the condition of any management agreement create the huge variations in car-space investments. Clearly, the option of having the space managed by a recognised operator will push yields down as buyers will pay more for a quality manager.

Industrial units

Industrial units are essentially four concrete walls to which the property mantra 'location, location, location' does not really apply since views aren't a high priority. (I can't think of too many panel beaters who have panoramic views of Sydney Harbour!) What the industrial sector does need is access to transport hubs for distribution and access to population centres for a skilled work force. But typically, industrial units accommodate small manufacturers, warehouses, and auto electricians and are more or less just enclosed space with access.

In Sydney one of the key industrial areas is the southern region around Botany and Alexandria. This is close to both the main airport and dock facilities. This area will benefit from a shortage of land, close proximity to the airport, and the new rail and motorway links. According to Sydney-based Bennett Real Estate, industrial sites don't offer particularly great capital growth, but what they do offer is extremely healthy rental returns (9.5% or better). Remember that residential property returns between 4% and 5%.

Industrial sites have also proven to be an investment favourite of retirees because they require minimum ongoing maintenance and provide a good income stream which, as we know, is a more important financial goal than capital growth for many retirees.

Other factors that attract retirees to strata industrial sites is that the tenants are generally easier to work with. They sign up for a reasonable period of time – three years with either a two- or three-year option to extend – they pay all outgoings like rates, electricity and so on. When a tenant moves on, you don't have to repaint rooms or replace carpets. All you need is a high-powered hose, a couple of minutes and the job is done. That's all it takes to clean four concrete walls.

Don't get me wrong, there is a dodge that even the experts can't explain. For some reason, no matter where your strata industrial unit is located, you can almost always expect a three- to six-month lag between the outgoing tenant leaving and the new tenant setting up shop.

Strata office suites

These make up another subset of the commercial property family that has captured the interest of smaller investors. From a location perspective, office suites have to be in areas where people want to set up business, chiefly central business districts, although business parks can also be an alternative.

Not surprisingly, Sydney and Melbourne represent the biggest slice of the strata title office market, with Brisbane the next largest, according to information provided by CPM Research. Average Sydney strata prices in 2000 were approximately $4,300 per square metre, with yields of 7.5%. In Melbourne a square metre of office space was valued at $1,850, with a yield of 9.5%. Brisbane recorded a yield of 9%, at $2,700 per square metre.

The strength of demand for office suites in Sydney's CBD is responsible for pushing prices up. Of the 750 buildings in Sydney's CBD, 75 are strata titled, of which 80% are owner-occupied. Of the remaining 20%, there is only the equivalent of three buildings up for grabs. According to CB Richard Ellis, strata office suites in Sydney's CBD start at $75,000, with the majority of suites sitting between $200,000 and $600,000, averaging around $350,000.

More affordable strata-title office units are found in secondary CBD markets, rather than in the big-end-of-town, flash, new office towers. According to Westpac research, rentals for secondary office space in Sydney are expected to increase by a total of 17% until 2003. In Melbourne, secondary rentals are predicted to grow by 24% over the same period. However, Melbourne rentals are coming off a much lower base, as rentals there fell for a number of years due to an oversupply of space.

SYNDICATION

Investment in property generally offers investors the benefit of capital growth, but not everybody has enough money to invest directly in it. Property syndicates offer smaller investors with as little as $10,000 a chance to invest in larger, quality properties that they would not normally be able to afford. Property syndicates invest in shopping centres, hotels, office towers and industrial sites.

According to research from Stanton Research Hillier Parker, property syndicates have proved popular with many investors over recent years for a number of reasons: the favourable differential between low-interest rates and higher property yields; and the fact that many baby boomers are currently in their peak saving period and are looking for suitable investments. They are also a good way for inexperienced investors to get a feel for the commercial property market. Landmark Property Syndicates reports that there is about $3 billion currently invested in property syndicates throughout Australia.

Lawyers, accountants and other professionals with a client base of investors and access to suitable properties have traditionally 'arranged' many property syndicates that have proven to be a successful sideline to their main line of business. In a syndicate, the manager is known as the 'arranger'. More recently a number of property specialists who exclusively manage property syndicates have emerged, including MCS Asset Management, York Capital and Landmark Property Syndicates.

Now for those of you wondering, syndicates are legal and

well regulated. They are policed by the Australian and Securities Commission (ASIC) under the terms of the Corporations Law. ASIC ensures that all arrangers are licensed, have appropriate tertiary and graduate qualifications, plus industry experience. Arrangers must also have a property qualification or real-estate licence.

Once a property has been purchased and placed in a syndicate, offers to investors must be made through a prospectus that is registered with ASIC. This prospectus requirement can be circumvented for professional investors (those investing $500,000 or more). While these regulations are designed to protect investors against fraud and incompetence, protection against ineptitude is harder to guarantee. Therefore, many investors have tended to trust their money with arrangers who have a solid track record, such as lawyers and accountants.

But I should caution that there are limitations to property syndicates:

- You need to be aware that the individual investor has little input into the investment process. Decision making begins and ends with the arranger, and there have been cases where some investors have disagreed with an investment strategy but have been thwarted because they weren't in the majority.
- There is also the problem of liquidity. For example, if an investor dies, the estate has no choice but to hang onto the investment or find somebody else to replace them in the syndicate.

All investors should read the prospectus that includes the trust deed setting out your rights as a unit holder in the syndicate. As with all forms of investment, there is no substitute for reading all the relevant documents before you decide to invest.

But beware: there are lots of syndicates springing up, so

you can be pretty certain that some will turn out to be dogs! We don't need to ignore this type of property, but as with all property investments, you need to exercise caution.

PROPERTY TRUSTS

Property trusts are managed funds that invest in apartment blocks, large shopping centres or city offices which are generally out of the financial scope of most smaller investors. Property trusts have grown in popularity in recent years because they make investing in commercial property easier. In fact, many fund managers, reports Stanton Hillier Parker, recommend that the appropriate level of property in an asset allocation strategy is 10%. However, currently, this is down to as low as 5.5%. More investors are starting to fill this void through investing in property trusts.

The relative advantages of property trusts over direct property are that they are much more liquid and can be bought and sold more swiftly on the market. As I discussed earlier, selling a property can be a long drawn-out process requiring a marketing period, exchange of documents and settlement.

A minimum investment in a property trust is usually $1,000. It's a lot less money and a lot less risky than a direct investment in commercial property which, as we know, can run into hundreds, even millions of dollars.

For more information on property trusts, contact a fund manager or talk to your financial planner.

CONCLUSION

To some extent you could argue that 'Blind Freddy' could have invested in some of Australia's major property markets over recent years and won. And in plenty of cases you might be right. But it would be wrong of me if I left you with the impression that investing in property is a licence to print money. So as Julius Sumner Miller used to say – why is this so?

Some of the more common mistakes property investors have made include overcapitalising, not doing their research properly and paying too much or buying into a suburb that traditionally has a history of low growth. Now to get around these problems, I recommend that you do your homework and don't buy the first property you see, as well as learn what a fair price is in the locality you're looking in. Do all these things right, then over time, an investment in property can become one of your most important assets.

Commercial property investment tips

- Research the property thoroughly. Attend seminars, read books, subscribe to magazines on the topic; watch out for property prices in the area where you intend to buy for several months before you take the plunge; keep your eyes on fluctuations in interest rates.
- Know exactly what you can afford to buy, and what you can afford to repay. Prepare your monthly budgets in advance, and stick to them.
- Keep on top of the unforeseen: consciously and carefully manage the risks (location, interest rates, damage to property, loss of rent, etc.)
- Deal only with people you trust. This applies to real-estate agents, managing agents, solicitors, accountants, as well as builders, repairers, etc.
- Don't buy property when everyone is buying, as you may be paying too much. Wait until prices go down.
- Don't fail to do your own research on the properties offered. Although you should try to deal only with agents you trust, even

so, it's best to satisfy yourself that everything is as you believe it to be.

- Don't hold out for a lease that's more than tenants are willing to pay. Any lengthy vacancies will finish up costing more than the difference between what you want to get and what you can get.
- Don't put up with a poor managing agent. Look around until you find a good one, one whom you can trust.
- Don't neglect to protect your investment from such unforeseen events as the loss of your regular income.

chapter 10

MANAGED FUNDS

Now that you have read through the previous chapters on shares, interest-bearing investments, and property, you'll know that they satisfy certain investment objectives and that your short-, medium- and long-term needs and goals ought to determine what proportion of each you hold in your investment portfolio.

If your goal is long-term growth, you will tilt your portfolio towards shares and property. If you need regular income and security, you should have more cash and fixed interest in your portfolio. If you want both growth and income, then you should have a spread of investments across all of these assets.

OK, but what is the best way to achieve all of this? How do you know how much of each asset class you should hold and what investments to select within each class? Will you have time to monitor the progress of your investments? Though the Internet is great for accessing up-to-date information, the problem remains: what to do with all this information?

This is where professionally managed investment funds come in very handy.

Decades ago (in fact, in 1924), investment experts realised that investing in the many asset classes was difficult for the average investor, so the idea of managed funds emerged. The idea was very simple. You let investment professionals do some or all of the work for you. They charge a fee for this service, but in return they save you time and effort in stock selection and monitoring. In theory, they should also be able to produce better returns than you should, because it's what they do full time. Obviously the theory doesn't always stand up in practice and some managed funds have been bad news for investors. But in my opinion, managed funds are an excellent way for most people to build and manage wealth.

Whether managed investments suit you depends on:

- to what extent you want to control the investment selection process yourself
- how much you want to be involved in your portfolio's ongoing management.

As I said earlier, if you are confident of doing this yourself and have some experience, go for it. But for others with limited investment experience, limited confidence in their ability to pick the right stocks, limited time and, perhaps, minimal interest, a managed fund is a perfectly sensible and simple alternative. Many must agree with these sentiments since there are more than three million Australians now investing in managed funds.

WHAT ARE MANAGED FUNDS?

'Managed (investment) fund' is a generic term that covers a range of related investment products, including:

- balanced funds

- property trusts
- equity or share funds
- superannuation trusts
- insurance bonds.

Although they are structured differently and may have varying taxation implications, there are some basic similarities.

Sometimes managed funds are called 'managed trusts', 'pooled funds', 'investment trusts' or 'unit trusts'. Americans call them 'mutual funds'.

The table below examines the basic types of managed funds and helps you understand which may be appropriate for you.

Types of Managed Funds

Type of managed fund	Volatility (risk)	Returns	Minimum time frame (years)	Possible tax benefits	Income/ Growth
Shares/Equity	High	High	5+	Yes	Both
International shares	High	High	5+	Yes	Both
Property	Medium–High	Medium–High	5+	Yes	Both
Balanced	Medium	Medium	3–5+	Yes	Both
Fixed interest	Medium	Medium	1+	No	Income
Mortgage	Low–Medium	Low–Medium	1+	No	Income
Cash	Low	Low	24 hours on call	No	Income

Source: IFSA

So a managed fund is a vehicle in which the investments of a large number of smaller investors are pooled together and managed as one large investment portfolio by a professional manager.

The manager can invest in shares, property, fixed interest

or cash, or all of them. The investments can be direct or indirect through other managed funds.

Managed funds can specialise in Australian, international, European, American or Asian assets. They can also invest in fish farms, pine plantations and movies. In fact, the mix and type of assets and ventures you can invest in through a managed fund is only limited by the imagination of those offering them.

Investors in a managed fund are effectively part-owners of the assets held by the fund. Earnings generated from the fund's assets can be distributed as income to investors on a monthly, six-monthly or yearly basis, or, alternatively, its earnings can help increase the capital value of the investors' units. The capital growth of the units is only realised when the units are sold.

Most funds have a minimum initial investment level, which is usually between $500 and $5,000.

FUND MANAGERS

The investment manager of a fund is usually an experienced and reputable investment organisation, such as AMP, ANZ, MLC, Colonial, Perpetual, BT or Rothschild. Working within the defined investment parameters of the fund, the fund manager's job is to invest the pooled money in a range of assets. The manager is responsible for shifting the fund's money in and out of assets when they see fit and generally in response to changing market conditions. The manager's objective is to achieve the best return possible within certain risk limits, which should be set out in the prospectus.

When selecting a fund manager you can appreciate that it is extremely important to get it right. In fact, recently it became even more important to choose the right manager, because the manager now has even greater responsibility for your money than in the past.

Prior to 1998, the law required a two-tier system that included the fund manager who invested and managed your money, and a trustee who oversaw the investment decisions of the manager and generally represented the rights of the investors. The trustee was also responsible for ensuring that the terms of the Trust Deed were met. The Trust Deed sets out how the fund's income is to be distributed and in general, where the fund's monies are invested. The key details of the Trust Deed are included in any managed fund's prospectus.

The problem with this system was that both the fund manager and the trustee charged investors in the fund a fee for their services. But with the introduction of the *Managed Investments Act (MIA)* in 1998, the law no longer requires this two-tiered system and the role of a trustee has generally been assumed by the manager.

External complaints resolution scheme

It is the job of the Australian Securities Investment Commission (ASIC) to ensure that any fund manager offering funds to the public is registered under the auspices of the *Corporations Law*. Not only do the fund managers need to be registered, but also they need to obtain a licence from ASIC. One of the conditions they need to satisfy in order to get a licence is that they are members of the 'external complaints resolution scheme'. The scheme was set up to protect the rights of investors.

UNITS

Managed funds are divided into units of equal value. Like an ordinary share, they give you part ownership of an asset – in this case the investments in the managed fund. Although shares and units are technically quite different, the concept is the same. Some units, such as listed property trusts, are actually traded on the Australian Stock Exchange.

The number of units issued for sale in some funds is fixed (this is generally the case with listed trusts). In other funds, new units are always available to anyone who wants to buy them (generally these are available in unlisted trusts).

Unlisted trusts can be either open or closed. An 'open' unlisted unit trust means that it is open to the public and will continue to issue units, and it does this by updating its prospectus every six months. Managed funds (such as superannuation, insurance or friendly society bonds) are nearly always open – you can increase your stake in them by as much as you like at any time.

Valuing units

Except for listed trust units, managed funds value their units daily or at least weekly. There are actually two prices, a price for buying and another for selling. Confused? The reason is pretty simple, the cost of buying and selling the units can differ.

The buying price of a unit is calculated by taking the current valuation of the fund's total assets, adding a loading to cover purchase costs, such as stamp duties and brokerage, and then dividing this amount by the number of issued units. The selling price is determined by taking the current valuation of the fund's total assets, adding a loading to cover the selling costs, and then dividing this amount by the number of units on issue. The difference between the two prices can be as high as 6%, which reflects these costs, as well as commissions payable to a licensed adviser.

> *Let's look at a very simple example of how changes in a unit's value affect you. Robert invests $5,000 in an unlisted managed trust with units selling for $1; this buys him 5,000 units.*
>
> *Remember the value of units fluctuates in line with the value of the fund's underlying assets. If Robert wished to redeem 2,000 of these units and the unit price had risen to $1.10 (because the value of the fund's assets had risen), he'd get back $2,200, representing a profit of 10%.*
>
> *If, however, Robert had paid an entry fee of 6%, his $1 unit would have a resale value on the same day of 94 cents. His investment would need to rise by nearly 7% to get him back to his original dollar.*

This is the reason why it is very important to minimise entry fees by negotiating with your adviser or using a discount broker. Paying an entry fee must be looked at very seriously as it reduces your investment capital, and unlike ongoing fees it is a capital cost and not tax deductible.

LIQUIDITY

Some managed funds are liquid, others aren't. Some cash management funds offer same-day redemptions (withdrawals). However, converting your units in an insurance bond into cash can take a couple of days, while it could take up to two weeks to get your money back from a share fund – which is about the maximum length of time it should take to cash-in any type of unit.

Having said this, real problems with liquidity have occurred with property trusts in the past. These have been

due to the relative lack of liquidity of the property investments in tough market times. The collapse of unlisted property trust values in 1990 meant that redemptions were
frozen, since the property assets could not be sold to pay
back investors who wanted to get their money back.

There are chiefly two ways of buying units and two ways
of redeeming them. When a managed fund is listed, its units
can be bought and sold through a stockbroker at a price set
by the market, just like shares. How quickly a buyer or seller
is found for units depends on the mood of the market, but
generally a transaction should take place almost immediately.

On the other hand, if the managed fund is unlisted, then
you can normally only buy and redeem units directly from
the fund manager. There is no other simple way of buying
or redeeming units in an unlisted fund. This is why it's
important that you invest only with reputable and competent fund managers, who are likely to stay in business.

You can also trade units directly between individuals,
bypassing stockbrokers and fund managers, though this
type of trading is rare.

SAFETY

Competent investment professionals who take their jobs
seriously and act in good faith manage the vast majority of
our mainstream managed funds. Fund managers are a fairly
conservative bunch by nature and training and are aware of
their enormous responsibilities and manage accordingly.

Well-documented disasters, such as the collapse of the
Estate Mortgage unlisted mortgage trust in 1990, are a rarity.
Collapses of this kind can happen, but they should remain
uncommon events. However, remember, if all the marketing
and publicity about a particular fund sounds too good to be
true, then it usually is.

There are thousands of managed funds in which Australians can invest. If you need any reassurance, think about this. There is a greater proportion of companies listed on the ASX that have failed taking shareholders' money with them than managed funds which have experienced losses. And the number of those who have lost money in managed funds would certainly be nowhere near as great as the number of direct property investors who have lost out by buying on a market downturn or by losing control of costs, purchasing poor rentals, getting bad tenants, or experiencing long delays with the approval of development plans, and so on.

Money Tip

Spread your risk.
These days with as little as $100 a month you can invest in a managed share fund.

Having said this, different funds have different risk profiles. The ones with the lowest risk of management failure are those mainstream funds managed by banks, major insurance companies and reputable financial houses that invest in the major asset classes, such as shares, bonds, property and cash.

At the other end of the spectrum come the more speculative managed investments, specialising in areas such as feature films, horticulture and even exotic animals. Usually these schemes rely on money from investors to get them off the ground. Be warned that the failure rate of these non-mainstream managed investments is pretty high and I would generally recommend that you invest your money elsewhere. They are risky because:

• All new ventures are riskier than established ones.
• The fund manager is generally the person who operates

the business and therefore may not have a huge amount of managerial or operational experience.

- Even the best fund management team in the world would have difficulty making profits in the investments that many of these speculative funds promote.

HOW MANAGED FUNDS WORK

Let's recap. With most managed funds, you are allocated a number of units based on the amount you invest and the current unit price. The units are the building blocks of the fund.

In simple terms, if the fund was worth $100,000 and was divided into 100,000 units, each unit would be worth $1. If you invested $2,000, you would receive 2,000 units. These are unlikely to be worth $1 each if you sell on the same day, due to entry and/or exit fees. Let's look on the next page at a few examples of buy and sell prices.

The unit price reflects the value of the fund's investments. If the value of the investments rise, the unit price will also rise. If the value of the investments fall, the unit price falls too.

The return on the fund's investment is paid out in proportion to the number of units you own. So investors who invest a few hundred dollars get the same investment return per dollar as those who invest hundreds of thousands of dollars.

To determine the current value of your investment, you need to multiply the current unit price by the number of units you hold.

In many funds, the unit price can go up or down each day depending on what is happening to the value of the fund's investments. Most fund managers can tell you the current unit price of your investment over the phone and via the Internet, and the prices are also listed in the newspapers each week.

Sample of Buy/Sell Prices for a Selection of Managed Funds as at 31 December 2000

Fund name	Size ($M)	Entry price	Exit price	Buy/Sell spread
Perpetual Industrial Share	$1,975	$1.49	$1.48	0.87%
Commonwealth Balanced Fund	$944	$1.56	$1.54	0.99%
MLC Platinum Global Fund	$1,148	$1.88	$1.78	5.00%
Merrill Lynch Imputation Fund	$889	$2.85	$2.71	4.80%
BT International Fund	$2,129	$3.59	$3.48	3.07%
Colonial First State Imputation	$3,362	$3.84	$3.82	0.70%

Source: ASSIRT

INVESTMENT PHILOSOPHY

An important question to ask any fund manager is their investment philosophy or investment style. It isn't too hard to work out that a share fund is different to a property fund, but you really need to know exactly how the manager will invest your money.

In a mortgage trust, for instance, you need to ask: Are the loans secured by relatively conservative completed residential property investment or highly risky commercial development sites? Does your share trust manager focus on large companies or more risky small companies? Are they a value manager who looks for shares that are good value today (that is, the manager thinks they are inexpensive), or a growth manager who will happily pay for an 'expensive' stock today, providing it has good growth prospects?

It really is important to know what your manager intends to do with your money! I have provided an overview of the investment philosophy of some of Australia's leading fund managers at the end of this chapter.

Know your manager's investment style.

MANAGED FUNDS – THE GOOD STUFF

Instead of purchasing individual stocks and bonds, many investors choose managed funds as their main investment. What makes these investments so appealing? For many individuals, managed funds provide an easy way to enter the market without a great deal of additional work on their part, but there are other benefits as well:

- *Diversification* A managed fund invests in dozens to hundreds of securities. It would be very difficult for the average investor to buy such a wide variety of investments individually, because the cost would be prohibitive for most small investors. As I've discussed elsewhere, owning many different securities (including bonds, shares, cash and property) lowers the overall risk of losing money on your investments. Diversification can reduce the risk of any one security causing the fund's value to decline.
- *Pooled money* By pooling money from a number of people, a managed fund can provide greater buying power for each investor. And, because the fund buys and sells many securities at a time, its brokerage costs are often lower than you would pay as an individual investor.
- *Affordability* You can usually invest in a managed fund for a low minimum initial investment from as little as $1,000 – which you can then top up with regular

investments. The fund managers generally refer to these as 'savings plans'.

- *Dollar-cost averaging*   Saving plans help you benefit from dollar-cost averaging. Dollar-cost averaging is pretty simple: instead of trying to time the highs and lows of the market, you invest the same amount of money regardless of the unit price. In this way you reduce the chances of mis-timing the market.

  And by investing the same amount each month, you automatically buy more units when prices are low, and fewer units when prices are high, and over time you reduce the average cost of the units you hold. (It's also a great way of forcing you to save on a regular basis.)

- *Regular source of income*   Certain managed funds provide a monthly, quarterly or half-yearly income distribution to unit holders that reflects the level of income earned by the fund's investments. Unit holders can take the regular distributions in cash or have them reinvested as additional units in the fund.

- *Access to expert investment professionals*   When you buy shares in a managed fund, you also effectively buy the advice of full-time investment professionals. The fund's manager analyses hundreds of securities and makes decisions on what to buy, when to buy, and when to sell. With professional management, once you've chosen a fund that's right for you, there's no need to constantly monitor the stock market or economic conditions in order to make changes – the fund manager does it all for you.

Money Tip

Compound interest is your best friend.
Invest $10,000 and leave it for 20 years at 8% and you'll have almost $47,000. Over 40 years it becomes over $217,000.

MANAGED FUNDS – THE BAD STUFF

- *Fees* But, of course, you don't get this expert support for free. Normally, there are entry, exit and ongoing management fees. Some funds may not charge an entry fee, but they may charge a higher-than-average exit fee, or vice versa. Some funds have no entry or exit fees, as long as you maintain your investment for a minimum number of years. This is set out in the fund's offer document. Fees vary enormously and are a source of real competition across the industry.

  Generally speaking, entry fees range from 0% to 5% of the value of your initial investment. Ongoing annual fees that primarily go to the fund manager (often referred to as the 'Management Expense Ratio' or MER) range from 0.5% to 3% of the value of your investment, and exit fees usually range from 0% to 2% of the value of your withdrawal.

- *Loss of control* Managed funds reduce the degree of control you have over your asset selection. When you invest with a managed fund, your money is invested in shares in companies that the fund manager selects, not companies that you select. Unlike listed companies on the stock market which hold annual general meetings for shareholders, fund managers don't offer unit holders this opportunity to vent their spleen publicly if they aren't performing.

- *Price fluctuations* Like all investments, managed funds may go up, but they also may go down in price. You need to be aware that unit prices can be worth less upon redemption than when they were bought.

  Should the fund experience a major devaluation of its underlying assets, or the manager is thought to be doing a poor job, a run may be made on it. A 'run' is the label given to the situation where a group of investors attempt simultaneously to pull their money out of the fund.

TYPES OF MANAGED FUNDS
Share or equity funds

As we discussed earlier, an investment in shares makes you a part-owner of a company. You can buy shares through the share market or through a share fund. The advantage of a share fund is that you can benefit from the knowledge and expertise of the fund manager. A fund manager can give you the best chance of superior returns because:

- they follow economic trends and choose shares in companies that are most likely to benefit from these trends
- they analyse companies and identify those that are well managed and likely to perform well
- they have a depth of research and resources that no individual investor could hope to match.

You can also select from a range of share funds. Some, for instance, invest solely in Australian shares or international shares. Others invest in the shares of companies involved in emerging or developing markets, while others are linked to shares in the gold, mining or energy sectors.

While the capital returns from share funds can be volatile, these funds can generate strong capital growth and good income over the long term. Most 'growth' and even 'balanced' funds invest in shares. More on this later.

By investing in an Australian share fund, you can also take advantage of the tax benefits associated with dividend imputation. Many of the companies that a share fund invests in pay franked dividends, which, depending on your highest marginal tax rate, can reduce the amount of tax you pay. A franked dividend is a dividend that has already had tax paid on it at the full company rate of 30% (the company tax rate changed to 30% from 34% on 1 July 2001). If your highest marginal tax rate is less than 30%, then you will receive a tax credit. A more complete explanation of the benefits of franked dividends is given in Chapter 7.

International funds

The Australian share market represents about 1.5% of the world's total share markets. This means that if you only invest in the Australian market, then you are missing out on investing in companies in many of the world's most profitable economies.

The best way I know of investing in these companies is through an international share fund. So, instead of limiting your investments to Australia, you can diversify across the world.

Some fund managers also offer international fixed-interest funds for even greater diversification.

Property trusts

For many Australians, property has always been a popular investment, but it does have some limitations. For instance, an investment in property generally:

- requires a large amount of money
- your money is tied up in one investment
- it takes time to buy and sell
- it's difficult to calculate your actual return because of the ongoing expenses, maintenance, improvements, and the buying and selling costs.

Fortunately, property trusts provide us with a very good alternative to investing directly in property. Property trusts invest your money across a range of property investments (such as entire apartment blocks, shopping centres or city offices) that are generally well out of the reach of smaller investors.

Many property trusts are listed (so-called 'listed property trusts') on the ASX. This allows you to sell your units in the trust at any time, which is a lot easier than selling a property investment. The other major benefit of a property trust is that you don't have to worry about rents, insurance, repairs, vacancies, refurbishment, or buying and selling, the fund manager does it all for you.

Fixed interest or bond funds

Governments, banks and other companies normally raise money using fixed-interest investments (commonly referred to as 'bonds'). The attraction of bonds is that they can be less volatile than shares or property, but can pay higher returns than cash.

The problem with bonds is that they are expensive to buy and out of the financial reach of most investors. This is where a bond fund can help. Bond funds allow you to invest in a range of bonds and benefit from the higher interest rates that are usually the domain of large institutional investors, such as banks.

Bond funds can generate good income and capital growth, but generally the growth is not as good as share funds.

In Australia the word 'bond' is generally taken to mean a security with a fixed interest rate. However, the value of bonds within a bond fund can change depending on trading activities and the value of the bonds in the market in which the fund invests.

Sure, if you buy a $100,000 government bond paying 7% for ten years, you'll get your 7% each year for ten years, and then get your money back. But if interest rates increase to 10% per annum and your manager owns a bond paying 7% and wants to sell the bond before the ten years are up, they are not going to get $100,000.

Why would anyone pay $100,000 for a 7% bond when they could buy one that pays 10%? So the bond is only saleable at a discount. But if the manager gets it right and buys ten-year bonds at 10% and then rates fall to 7%, your bond will increase in value.

Cash management trusts

Cash management trusts (or cash management funds) invest in securities (such as bank bills, treasury notes and overnight deposits) that can easily be converted to cash. Typically, they are very safe and liquid, meaning you can get your money almost as soon as you need it.

Many managed investment companies – such as banks and fund managers – offer Cash Management Trusts (CMTs). A CMT can be used in the same way you use a bank account: for parking money for short periods of time while you work out the best way to invest it. They offer similar features to bank accounts, such as chequebook facilities and periodic payments, but, unlike bank accounts, they pay higher interest rates. You are also required to keep a minimum balance in the account at all times to keep the account open.

I strongly recommend one of these for any money you have sitting around for the short term.

Multi-sector or diversified funds

As an alternative to choosing a managed fund that invests primarily in one asset class (such as shares or property), you can choose funds which invest in a selection of asset classes. These funds are known as diversified funds or multi-sector funds.

Multi-sector funds are a great way to diversify your investments across all asset classes and reduce the risk of volatile returns. While individual markets move up and down, your overall return is likely to be reasonably steady. There are three types of multi-sector funds:
• capital stable funds
• balanced funds
• growth funds.

To give you a better idea of how capital stable, balanced and growth funds can be structured, the three charts following show the actual asset allocation (the proportion of the whole fund that each asset class comprises) of ipac's strategic investment services diversified funds in December 2000.

The asset allocation in each of these funds is designed to produce the best long-term risk and return outcomes considered appropriate by ipac. These asset allocations can be adjusted at any time as varying market conditions dictate.

Capital stable funds

These funds invest primarily in a range of cash and fixed-interest securities, with a small percentage of share and property assets usually thrown in too. They're designed for investors looking for a regular and reasonably secure source of income over a relatively short term, say one to three years minimum. They are particularly good for retirees.

These funds are characterised by:

- low risk
- low capital growth
- strong income

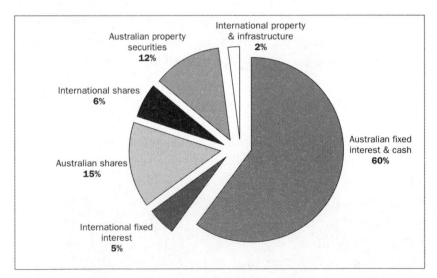

Source: ipac securities

- short-term horizon
- few, if any, tax breaks.

Balanced funds

These are for investors looking for medium- to longer-term capital growth, accompanied by some regular income during the term of the investment. An appropriate investment in a balanced fund would be three to five years minimum. These funds should have a ratio in the vicinity of 75% growth assets (shares and property) to 25% income assets (cash and fixed interest). These are good for people who are closer to the end than the start of their working career.

Balanced funds are characterised by:

- low to moderate risk
- moderate to good capital growth
- low income
- medium-term horizon
- reasonable tax breaks (due to share dividend imputation and property allowances or depreciation).

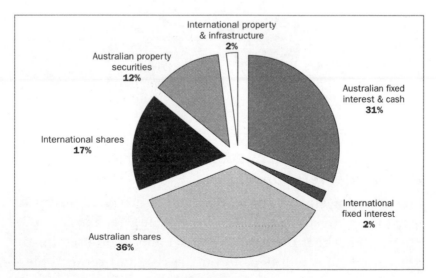

Source: ipac securities

Growth funds

These funds have a higher proportion of growth assets and a lower proportion of income assets than do balanced funds. If you still have a long way to go to retirement and are gathering together the funds for a nest egg, then you should consider growth funds.

They are characterised by:

- moderate to higher risk
- strong capital growth
- low income
- long-term horizon (five years minimum)
- better tax breaks than balanced funds.

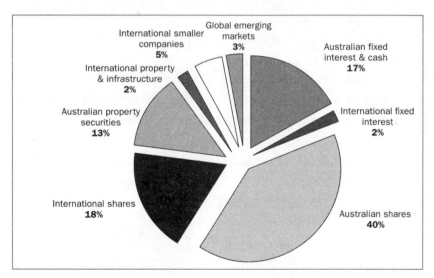

Source: ipac securities

Risk–return relationship

The following table shows the risk and return relationship for ipac's three diversified funds with similar asset allocations.

Remember that the particular asset allocation used in any diversified fund will depend on the risk and return objectives of the manager. For example, the objective of ipac's

Risk–Return Relationship, ipac securities
Multi-Sector Funds

	Capital stable	Balanced	Growth
Minimum recommended term	2–4 years	3–5 years	5 years plus
Income/Growth assets	65%/35%	30%/70%	15%/85%
Range of expected annual returns over:			
1 year	-0.6% to 15%	-5.7% to 24.3%	-12% to 38.4%
3 years	2.5% to 11.5%	0% to 17.3%	-1.6% to 21%
5 years	3.5% to 10.5%	1.8% to 15.2%	0.7% to 18.2%
Likelihood of a negative return	1 year in 12	1 year in 8	1 year in 6

Source: ipac securities

capital stable fund is to provide returns of 1% to 3% per annum in excess of the current rate of inflation.

The objectives other managers have for the capital stable funds (or any other funds for that matter) may be quite different to ipac's, and this will be reflected in them having different asset allocations. Just make sure that you find out what their objectives are before you invest with them, and that these objectives match yours.

Mortgage funds

Mortgage funds invest in residential, industrial and commercial property mortgages. They pool together the money you invest with them with other investors' money and then lend it to companies or individuals looking to buy mortgages secured by real estate. These funds aim to maintain a stable unit price. They generate income rather than capital growth. They offer investors the security of putting their money into mortgages backed by real estate.

It's worth noting that investors should take care with mortgage funds offering unusually high returns, which invariably means that the quality of the mortgages is not crash hot. As I've said several times, thousands of Australian investors lost some or all of their money with the collapse of Estate Mortgage in 1990 – a trust offering high returns on, as it was later revealed, high-risk mortgages, often secured over partially completed developments. Equally, be just as careful with investing in solicitor-arranged mortgages. In the final analysis, your security is only as good as the property underpinning the mortgage and the quality of the borrower. No matter what you are told, no quality borrower ever pays a rate of interest much above the going bank rate.

> A quality borrower will never pay you a rate of interest much higher than bank lending rates.

Insurance bonds

Insurance bonds are managed investment products offered by life insurance companies and are nothing like the fixed-interest securities offered by governments and semi-government authorities. In fact, calling these investments 'bonds' is really a misnomer.

While technically insurance bonds are life insurance policies (and this does cause some confusion), managed insurance bonds are more appropriately regarded as managed investments that possess the flexibility of other managed investment vehicles.

Insurance bonds are effectively managed funds that may be balanced, may invest primarily in growth assets, or may invest primarily in industrial shares and fixed-interest securities. The choice of the underlying asset is broad and, as with all managed funds, the higher the potential for growth, the greater the potential returns – but also the higher the risk of potential losses.

Like unit trusts, a bondholder gains entitlement to units in the fund in proportion to his or her contribution, with the bond price reflecting the performance of the fund's under-lying investment. Insurance bonds are structured to provide capital growth rather than income. The only way to get your hands on this return is to redeem (the hopefully much more valuable) units when the bond matures.

You need to be aware that insurance bonds are taxed dif-ferently to other managed funds due to their insurance status.

Redemptions from insurance bonds are not subject to tax and, therefore, no imputation credits are passed on to inves-tors at redemption. Tax is paid on the investor's behalf. This means that all returns are 'tax paid' (tax free) in investors' hands.

Should you wish to close the investment and get your hands on the cash within the ten-year period, you can. However, your investment earnings will be taxed at your highest marginal rate, though you are entitled to a 34% rebate against these (taxed) earnings. This will change to 30% from the 2002–2003 tax year.

This applies at any time during the ten years, but this doesn't mean that a short-term investment in these funds is the best way to go. It means that if your marginal rate of tax is less than 34%, you'll get a rebate that actually generates a tax credit that can be used to offset some of the tax that you are obliged to pay on your other assessable income.

Friendly society bonds

These are basically the same as insurance company bonds in that they are managed funds designed to be held for ten years, at which point they mature tax-free and are yours to cash in. They simply happen to be managed by friendly societies rather than insurance companies.

Like insurance bonds, cashing in a friendly society bond early will ensure that any earnings are taxed at your highest marginal rate. However, like insurance bonds, you also get paid a tax rebate which could mean that eventually you get all your tax back. You may even end up with a tax credit to be offset against other assessable income.

The size of this tax rebate is effectively equivalent to the rate of tax that has already been paid on your investment by the friendly society. During much of the 1980s this rate was 20%. It has changed a number of times since then and now sits at 33%. This is set to change in 2002–2003 to 30%.

Ethical managed funds

So far we have discussed the characteristics of a good managed fund: good returns, the risk and capital growth levels that you are comfortable with, and competitive management fees. But in recent years a new factor has become important for fund investors – ethics. Like other managed funds, ethical funds generally invest in conventional assets like cash, shares, property and bonds. However, they also select assets for their positive impact on the environment, community and their ability to earn a good return on your money.

 Money in History

1960s
Ethical funds sprang up as a response to the Vietnam War. Many people were keen to invest their money but not in companies that were supporting the war effort.

The emergence of ethical funds has been somewhat slower in Australia than the rest of the developed world. This trend is changing and some of the larger institutional investors, such as Westpac and BT, have begun to incorporate ethical parameters into some of their fund products.

Overseas ethical funds have become major players in the overall managed fund landscape. In the USA, $3.5 trillion are invested in ethically managed funds or about $1 in every $8. In the UK, ethically managed funds have grown from $500 million in 1989, to more than $6.3 billion in 1999.

Most ethical funds will operate a process known as a 'negative screen'. This device screens out whole areas that are widely held to be unethical. These include sectors such as gambling, tobacco, alcohol, armaments and, more recently, genetically modified organisms. Companies dealing in those areas are excluded from the fund.

Alternatively, some funds will employ a 'positive screen'. This is the process of actively seeking out sectors and companies which are considered to be making a positive contribution to social wellbeing or sustainability. Popular among those chosen in Australia are environmentally friendly technologies, such as waste reduction or emission-reducing products. Others include certain biotechnologies, solar energy, natural gas, healthcare and pollution reduction.

> For more information on ethical investments call the Ethical Investments Association on 02 9214 8411.

There's not a huge choice of fund manager, but their returns have been pretty good. Ethical share funds have generally performed as well as traditional funds over the past few years, recording returns between 5% and 8% a year after tax, inflation and fees.

So, if you want to feel assured your investments are doing good out in the world and are not involved in any business that offends your values, yet get a good return at the same time, ethical funds could be just the tonic to get your money working for you.

Indexed funds

Everyone wants to beat the market. Unfortunately, it's more difficult to do than you might think – especially over the long term. This is because:

- It is almost impossible to pick only winning investments. Unless you own a crystal ball, it's inevitable that you will choose some losers.
- If managed funds had no costs, then in theory it would be pretty easy to match the market's returns. But because of costs (fees, taxes and brokerage charges), few investors don't do as well as an index, because the index doesn't take into account fees and charges.

One way that you can at least try and match the market is via an index fund. An index fund (also known as a 'passively managed fund') seeks to match the investment performance of a specific market index, such as the All Ords. Instead of trying to beat the market by actively trading shares, an index fund manager will simply hold all (or a representative sample) of the shares in the index. In contrast, an active fund manager buys and sells securities regularly in an attempt to maximise gains.

An index fund has several advantages:

- *Lower costs* Traditional managed funds are actively managed by professionals, who charge annual management fees of between 0.5% and 3%. Because managed funds trade the securities in their portfolios frequently, they have a greater capital gains tax liability. On the flip side, since index funds don't trade as often, theoretically they should pay less tax.

- *Reduced risk* When there is a market correction or crash, there is usually no place to hide. However, an index fund can help you avoid having too much money in the wrong sector at the wrong time. At the same time, indexing can also help you to have some of your money in the hottest sector when the market takes off. With index funds, you don't have to worry about poor market timing.

- *Returns that mirror the market* Because they are designed to provide returns that closely track returns on market indices, index funds carry all of the risks typically associated with the underlying assets held in the fund. So, when a share market correction occurs, you can expect the unit prices of an index fund to reflect this by falling too. Likewise, the unit price of a bond index fund will (like the price of bonds) fall when interest rates rise. In short, an index fund does not lessen market risk, it merely ensures that your returns will not stray far from the returns on the index that the index fund mirrors.

PERFORMANCE OF MANAGED FUNDS

As we have discussed, managed funds can be comprised of one asset class, such as all shares, all property or all bonds, and perform similarly to the main market indices for those asset classes. Real, after-inflation, long-term average performance figures for the main asset classes are examined in Chapter 6, 'Savings and Investment', but to recap, they have traditionally been as follows on the next page.

Hopefully, the fund that you've invested in will do better than the average market returns for that asset class, though there is no guarantee of this. Indeed, it is of great and understandable concern to investors when their managed fund underperforms the market.

Returns for the Major Asset Classes

Major asset classes	Projected real annual long-term returns
Cash in the bank	0% to 1%
Term deposits (1 to 3 years)	0% to 2%
Long-term fixed interest and bonds (3 to 10 years)	0% to 3%
Residential property	1% to 3%
Commercial property	3% to 5%
Australian shares	5% to 8%
International shares	6% to 9%
Emerging markets (e.g. South-East Asia, Latin America)	10% to 25%

Source: ipac securities

WHY PAY A FUND MANAGER?

In fact, this raises the vexed question as to why you'd bother paying a fund manager to do worse than the index. Managed funds are no different from any other investments. Before you invest you need to do your research. You should know what your investment goals and objectives are, then match these to the goals of the fund manager. Before you invest, it's also important that you look into the performance and reputation of the fund and its manager. So, before you choose a fund:

- establish your own financial goals
- decide how much risk you can afford to take
- consider the cost, services and track record of the particular managed fund.

Prospectus

It is important to obtain and read the fund's prospectus. A prospectus is a document or brochure given to potential investors interested in a particular managed fund. It outlines all the relevant information about the fund manager, such as its history, operations, financial conditions, management structure and key personnel. Most also include a description of the general nature of the fund and a description of the fund's assets. Managed funds are required by law to provide prospectuses.

The prospectus also contains the investment objectives of the fund. The success of the fund is measured by how well the fund achieves these objectives. Some of the most common objectives are 'conservation of capital', 'growth' or 'steady income'. Your decision to purchase units in a managed fund should begin with a careful examination of its investment objectives. Every fund's prospectus must also disclose all fees, and provide information on performance, including one-, three- and five-year averages of annual total return.

The fees and charges argument

We have already talked at some length about fees and charges, but I know many people who tell me that they refuse to use managed funds because of all the fees and charges, preferring to buy investments directly. The fact is that managed funds have generally delivered strong returns, after fees and taxes have been taken into consideration. Comparing fees between different investments is like comparing apples and oranges. It's more useful to decide whether the fees are reasonable in light of the return and service you receive.

I think this issue requires more attention. When you compare managed funds to direct investments (such as shares and property), don't forget to compare all of the costs, such as the transaction fees you pay on your bank account, the brokerage charged by a stockbroker or the real-estate agent's commission. I want you to do your best to minimise your fees, but at times paying a fee to get good value makes sense. Don't forget that if you buy and sell an investment property, including all government, solicitor, bank and real-estate agent charges, it's not hard to spend 10% of the value of your asset!

At the end of the day, you are paying fees for professional advice. We will talk more about the managed fund versus the do-it-yourself option later in the chapter.

BUYING INTO RETAIL AND WHOLESALE FUNDS

There are two kinds of managed funds you can invest in:
- retail funds – those that you can buy into directly 'off the shelf', or through the stockmarket in the case of a listed trust
- wholesale funds – those you can only invest in indirectly through another managed fund.

Retail funds

Retail funds are those that you see advertised regularly in the media. You can buy into them for as little as $500, by either approaching the fund manager directly, or by going through a financial adviser or stockbroker.

If you buy listed units through the ASX, you will pay brokerage on top of the unit's trading price, as you would for shares. With unlisted products you will pay anywhere between 0% and 5%, regardless of whether you buy them directly or from a financial adviser. Although, as we discussed in Chapter 5, 'Financial Planning', if you buy these products through a fee-for-service financial adviser, he or she can rebate all or part of the entry fee – so ask!

Discount brokers such as E*Trade, TD Waterhouse and Commonwealth Bank Securities advertise regularly in the 'Business Section' of the major newspapers, and are an inexpensive way of buying into managed funds if you know what you want. But if you don't, I would recommend that you seek the assistance of a financial adviser. I also recommend you shop around for a financial adviser who rebates managed fund entry commission fees.

Wholesale funds

Wholesale managed funds have lower fees, but the average independent investor can not invest in them. The main reason for this is the prohibitive price involved in purchasing minimum parcels that can start at $50,000.

You can access wholesale funds indirectly by investing in a retail managed fund which in turn invests in them (many managed funds invest very heavily in other managed funds), or through mastertrusts. Many of the big banks and stockbrokers offer mastertrust options. Let's have a look at what mastertrusts are.

MASTERTRUSTS

A mastertrust (also known as a 'masterfund') is a managed fund that invests not only in other funds, but also in assets such as shares, cash and bonds. When you invest through a mastertrust your money goes into a selection of its own funds, which in turn invest primarily in other managed funds – many of which are wholesale funds beyond the financial reach of most independent investors.

So, given that the cost of investing in a mastertrust is similar to investing directly in a fund, the real benefit lies in the fact that your investment dollar is exposed to an even wider range of assets than in a single retail fund.

Mastertrusts also claim to offer investors a high level of customer support that includes regular meetings with an adviser to monitor investment results, and to adjust if necessary the strategy (most mastertrusts allow you to switch between their funds at no charge). This extra service generally includes reports detailing where your money has been invested, performance data, tax obligations, as well as a tax statement to help you at tax time.

It's not really as confusing as it sounds. For more information on mastertrusts and how to invest in one, talk to a financial planner.

Let's look at the two types of mastertrusts: fund-of-funds and discretionary. The major difference between the two is the amount of choice you have as to which assets the mastertrust invests in.

Fund-of-funds mastertrust

With a fund-of-funds mastertrust you, together with an adviser, select the appropriate broad asset area or areas that you want to invest in (in terms of risk versus return and growth versus income). You might, for example, decide to invest in the mastertrust's Australian bond fund (for income) and the international share option (for capital growth). These two funds will, in turn, invest in a wide range of assets appropriate to their investment parameters.

Or, you may prefer the strategy we use at ipac in which clients target a return above inflation that relates to their personal goals and objectives, and then invest in a balance of assets designed to give a return that beats inflation.

While you have been free to select the mastertrust's funds that invest in certain broad asset classes, as is the case with other managed funds you can't select the individual assets in which they invest. This is the fund manager's job.

Discretionary mastertrust

On the other hand, a discretionary mastertrust is structured to enable investors who prefer to have a greater control over their own asset selection. The fund manager will give you a recommended list from which to choose.

MANAGED VERSUS DO-IT-YOURSELF (DIY) FUNDS

So how on earth do you make the decision to use a managed fund or invest directly? Well, managed funds are a very popular way for many Australians to achieve their investment goals. For my part, I do own some direct property and direct shares, but I use managed funds for the majority of my Australian investments and all of my international investments.

There are many reasons why you would choose to invest in managed funds. For me, it's a pretty simple choice. I am busy and I know that my investment returns will come from the asset mix I select. In other words, it's more important to me whether I have 30% to 50% of my investment portfolio in shares, rather than whether or not I buy Telstra or Cable and Wireless Optus.

My advice is that you choose which option best suits you. Some people who create wealth will buy direct. Others will use managed funds. The thing they have in common is that they actually do something. Either of these options work, *just do something*!

SNAPSHOT OF SOME FUND MANAGERS

I thought it would be remiss of me not to provide you with a snapshot of how some of the major fund managers have performed over the past seven or so years.

With the help of research house ASSIRT, I have chosen the four major banks (Commonwealth, ANZ, National Australia and Westpac), AMP, BT, Colonial, MLC, Perpetual and Rothschild and have provided information on philosophy, investment objectives, volatility and returns across a range of their funds. This information should be used as a reference for your own research rather than as a list of my favourite funds.

AMP

Owned by	AMP Limited
Philosophy	AMP is a multi-style investment house. This means that across the various asset classes AMP uses both active and passive strategies and within some asset classes both investment approaches are offered. AMP also offers growth, value and style-neutral approaches across the various asset classes. A style-neutral approach means that the fund manager has neither a growth nor value bias. The AMP Equity Trust, for example, is managed using a style-neutral approach.
Contact details	AMP Building, 33 Alfred Street Sydney Cove NSW 2000 GPO Box 4134, Sydney NSW 2001 Phone: 13 32 67 Email: trustinfo@amp.com.au Internet: www.amp.com.au
Key services	$1,000 minimum initial investment. No exit fees. Entry fees range from 0%–4%. MERs range from 0.55%–2%.

List of products and returns

AMP Equity Trust – Diversified Shares

3 yr rtn %	5 yr rtn %	7 yr rtn %	Volatility	Size at 31/12/00 (millions)	Yearly returns %				
					2000	1999	1998	1997	1996
17.3	16.7	13.4	82	305.9	7.4	30.9	14.8	13.2	18.3

Investment objective

To provide capital growth and tax-effective income over the medium to long term. Invests in shares which appear to be under-valued or have the potential to generate higher returns in the longer term.

AMP Multi-Manager Global Share – International Shares

3 yr rtn %	5 yr rtn %	7 yr rtn %	Volatility	Size at 31/12/00 (millions)	Yearly returns %				
					2000	1999	1998	1997	1996
13.7	15.9	12.6	82	144.4	3.7	13.4	25.1	33.7	6.2

Investment objective

Invests in a diversified portfolio of international shares, using a multi-manager approach. Aims to provide growth and some income.

AMP Property Securities – Australian Property

3 yr rtn %	5 yr rtn %	7 yr rtn %	Volatility	Size at 31/12/00 (millions)	Yearly returns %				
					2000	1999	1998	1997	1996
9.2	11.4	9.6	39	211.0	14.4	-1.0	15.0	17.5	11.9

Investment objective

To provide tax-effective income and capital growth over the long term. Invests in a range of commercial, retail and industrial properties.

AMP Cash Management – Cash

3 yr rtn %	5 yr rtn %	7 yr rtn %	Volatility	Size at 31/12/00 (millions)	Yearly returns %				
					2000	1999	1998	1997	1996
4.2				126.6	4.9	3.8	4.0	4.6	

Investment objective

To provide security, ease of access and competitive returns by investing in bonds and bank bills.

AMP Australian Bond – Fixed Interest

3 yr rtn %	5 yr rtn %	7 yr rtn %	Volatility	Size at 31/12/00 (millions)	Yearly returns %				
					2000	1999	1998	1997	1996
4.8	6.8		I	206.2	9.7	-2.5	7.8	10.3	9.4

Investment objective

To provide income with moderate capital stability over the medium term. Invests in government bonds, bank bills, debentures, etc.

AMP Conservative – Capital Stable

3 yr rtn %	5 yr rtn %	7 yr rtn %	Volatility	Size at 31/12/00 (millions)	Yearly returns %				
					2000	1999	1998	1997	1996
7.2	8.0	7.0	I	138.3	7.3	5.7	8.6	9.7	8.6

Investment objective

To provide mostly income with some growth over the medium term. Invests in fixed-interest securities and cash, with some investments in property and shares.

AMP Balanced Growth – Growth

3 yr rtn %	5 yr rtn %	7 yr rtn %	Volatility	Size at 31/12/00 (millions)	Yearly returns %				
					2000	1999	1998	1997	1996
10.4	11.5	9.5	39	352.0	7.1	10.9	13.2	14.8	11.5

Investment objective

To provide a balance of income and capital growth over the medium to long term. Invests in cash, fixed-interest securities, property and shares. The fund may hold up to 80% of its investments in growth assets.

Source: ASSIRT (www.assirt.com.au)

ANZ ASSET MANAGEMENT

Owned by   ANZ Limited

Philosophy   ANZ Asset Management aims to deliver strong investment returns, consistently. They do this through an investment process based on detailed research, a focus on quality assets and disciplined risk management. As an active fund manager, they are selective about the securities purchased and held in portfolios. They do not aim to replicate or invest passively in financial markets. They attempt to outperform each financial market by identifying and selecting only those investment opportunities that will provide a return above the market over the long term.

Contact details   16th Floor, 68 Pitt Street
Sydney NSW 2000
GPO Box 4028, Sydney NSW 2001
Phone: 1800 022 893
Internet: www.anz.com

Key services $5,000 minimum initial investment. No exit fees. All funds offer both entry-fee and nil-entry-fee options. If you select the entry-fee option, expect to be charged 5%. But here's the dodge. Some of the nil-entry-fee options require a 0.05% entry fee. You'd also expect that the MER fees would reflect which entry-fee choice. If you chose a nil-fees option then you'd normally expect to pay a higher MER than for the entry-fee option. But that's not always the case. With the ANZ

International Markets Fund, for example, the MER for the entry-fee option is 1.88%. Whilst on the nil-fee option, the MER is 1.84%. MERs range from 1.59%–1.9%.

List of products and returns

ANZ Australian Share Market Trust – Diversified Shares

3 yr rtn %	5 yr rtn %	7 yr rtn %	Volatility	Size at 31/12/00 (millions)	Yearly returns %				
					2000	1999	1998	1997	1996
16.8	15.2		82	22.9	9.9	21.4	19.3	11.2	12.3

Investment objective
To provide capital growth and tax-effective income over the long term. Primarily invests in shares selected from the top 50 companies listed on the ASX which are likely to pay franked dividends.

ANZ International Markets – International Shares

3 yr rtn %	5 yr rtn %	7 yr rtn %	Volatility	Size at 31/12/00 (millions)	Yearly returns %				
					2000	1999	1998	1997	1996
14.5	15.4		82	46.2	1.5	15.6	28.4	30.7	0.2

Investment objective
To provide capital growth with a low level of income over the long term. Primarily invests in the major world markets seeking quality shares that are expected to outperform the various markets. May also invest in smaller and emerging markets.

ANZ Property Securities – Property Securities

3 yr rtn %	5 yr rtn %	7 yr rtn %	Volatility	Size at 31/12/00 (millions)	Yearly returns %				
					2000	1999	1998	1997	1996
7.7	10.6	8.7	69	73.0	17.3	-7.2	14.8	17.8	12.7

Investment objective

To provide regular income with some capital growth over the long term. Primarily invests in a range of property trusts and companies listed on the ASX to obtain exposure to the retail, commercial and industrial property sectors.

ANZ Australian Bond Trust – Fixed Interest

3 yr rtn %	5 yr rtn %	7 yr rtn %	Volatility	Size at 31/12/00 (millions)	Yearly returns %				
					2000	1999	1998	1997	1996
5.6	7.1		1	10.0	11.3	-2.0	8.2	11.7	8.6

Investment objective

To provide regular income and potential for moderate levels of capital growth in the medium to long term. Primarily invests in Australian fixed-interest securities and liquid investments seeking attractive income yields.

ANZ Monthly Income – Capital Stable

3 yr rtn %	5 yr rtn %	7 yr rtn %	Volatility	Size at 31/12/00 (millions)	Yearly returns %				
					2000	1999	1998	1997	1996
6.2	7.0	6.4	1	86.5	6.9	2.9	7.9	8.8	7.4

Investment objective

To provide regular income and a low level of capital growth over the medium to long term. Primarily invests in fixed interest and money market securities, with some exposure to Australian and international equities to enhance growth potential.

ANZ Quarterly Income Trust – Balanced

3 yr rtn %	5 yr rtn %	7 yr rtn %	Volatility	Size at 31/12/00 (millions)	Yearly returns %				
					2000	1999	1998	1997	1996
7.9	8.6	7.3	39	170.8	8.6	4.5	10.7	11.1	8.4

Investment objective

To provide regular income and some capital growth over the medium to long term. Primarily invests in fixed interest and money market securities, with some exposure to Australian and international equities to enhance growth potential. Invests in listed property trusts.

ANZ Balanced Trust – Growth

3 yr rtn %	5 yr rtn %	7 yr rtn %	Volatility	Size at 31/12/00 (millions)	Yearly returns %				
					2000	1999	1998	1997	1996
11.3	11.2	8.3	39	120.4	8.3	10.7	15.2	13.2	8.9

Investment objective

To provide capital growth with a moderate level of income over the long term. Primarily invests in Australian and international equities and fixed-interest securities, with some exposure to Australian property and listed property trusts.

Source: ASSIRT (www.assirt.com.au)

BT FUNDS MANAGEMENT

Owned by Principal Financial Group

Philosophy BT is a manager with a very active investment style. The investment team is prepared to take very significant positions that differ markedly with the competition and the market index if a strong view is held. BT believes strongly in their ability to make decisions that will add value over the returns provided by the market benchmarks. BT's philosophy on active management is consistently applied to the management of all asset classes.

Contact details The Chifley Tower
2 Chifley Square, Sydney NSW 2000
GPO Box 2675, Sydney NSW 1117
Phone: 13 21 35
Internet: www.btonline.com.au

Key services $5,000 minimum initial investment. Entry fees range from 0%–4% and MERs range from 1.61%–2.09%. Entry fees may apply for nil-entry-fee options.

List of products and returns

BT Equity Imputation Fund – Diversified Shares

3 yr rtn %	5 yr rtn %	7 yr rtn %	Volatility	Size at 31/12/00 (millions)	Yearly returns %				
					2000	1999	1998	1997	1996
8.5	12.3	9.7	69	1,605.4	-6.3	19.3	14.2	14.4	22.3

Investment objective

To provide capital growth and some tax-effective income over the long term by primarily investing in Australian shares whose market prices do not reflect the long-term value, and are expected to appreciate over time.

BT International Fund – International Shares

3 yr rtn %	5 yr rtn %	7 yr rtn %	Volatility	Size at 31/12/00 (millions)	Yearly returns %				
					2000	1999	1998	1997	1996
16.2	18.6	15.0	82	2,129.0	-1.6	34.1	18.7	34.1	11.5

Investment objective

To provide capital growth over the long term by investing in a variety of international companies whose market prices do not reflect the long-term value, and are expected to appreciate over time. No investment in the Australian share market.

BT Property Securities Fund – Property Securities

3 yr rtn %	5 yr rtn %	7 yr rtn %	Volatility	Size at 31/12/00 (millions)	Yearly returns %				
					2000	1999	1998	1997	1996
4.0	6.5		69	59.1	15.4	-5.0	2.5	3.3	18.2

Investment objective

To provide capital growth and some income over the long term. Primarily invests in a range of property trusts and property-related companies in the commercial, retail, industrial, residential, tourism and rural property sectors in Australia and New Zealand.

BT Cash Management Trust – Cash

3 yr rtn %	5 yr rtn %	7 yr rtn %	Volatility	Size at 31/12/00 (millions)	Yearly returns %				
					2000	1999	1998	1997	1996
4.3	4.8	5.0	1	490.3	5.1	3.9	4.0	4.8	6.0

Investment objective

To provide capital security and income over the short term. Primarily invests in short-term securities backed by governments or banks. This Fund is AAA rated by Standard and Poor's.

BT Australian Bond Fund – Fixed Interest

3 yr rtn %	5 yr rtn %	7 yr rtn %	Volatility	Size at 31/12/00 (millions)	Yearly returns %				
					2000	1999	1998	1997	1996
5.2	7.0		39	37.0	9.9	-1.8	7.7	9.4	10.0

Investment objective

To provide income over the medium term. Primarily invests in a portfolio of Australian and New Zealand fixed-interest securities. The Fund uses the Warburg Dillon Read Composite Bond All Maturities Index as its performance benchmark.

BT Split Income Fund – Capital Stable

3 yr rtn %	5 yr rtn %	7 yr rtn %	Volatility	Size at 31/12/00 (millions)	Yearly returns %				
					2000	1999	1998	1997	1996
5.4	7.7	6.5	1	297.0	4.8	4.5	6.9	9.0	13.6

Investment objective

To provide mostly income, but with some capital growth over the medium term. Invests primarily in a portfolio of fixed interest and cash investments, but will have some exposure to shares and property.

BT Income Plus Fund – Balanced

3 yr rtn %	5 yr rtn %	7 yr rtn %	Volatility	Size at 31/12/00 (millions)	Yearly returns %				
					2000	1999	1998	1997	1996
6.2	8.4	7.4	39	352.1	3.1	6.6	8.9	9.9	13.8

Investment objective

To provide tax-effective income and some capital growth over the medium to long term. Invests across a full spectrum of asset classes. Investment in shares is not anticipated to exceed 45% of the value of the fund.

BT Balanced Returns Fund – Growth

3 yr rtn %	5 yr rtn %	7 yr rtn %	Volatility	Size at 31/12/00 (millions)	Yearly returns %				
					2000	1999	1998	1997	1996
8.1	11.1	9.6	39	1,076.4	1.8	13.3	9.5	17.1	14.6

Investment objective

To provide capital growth and income over the long term. Invests across a range of asset classes, including property and fixed-interest securities. Investment in shares is not anticipated to exceed 60% of the value of the fund.

BT Split Growth Fund – Growth

3 yr rtn %	5 yr rtn %	7 yr rtn %	Volatility	Size at 31/12/00 (millions)	Yearly returns %				
					2000	1999	1998	1997	1996
13.6	18.2	15.0	82	1,899.2	-3.1	28.9	17.5	34.1	17.1

Investment objective

To provide capital growth over the long term. Predominantly invests in a carefully selected portfolio of international shares with some exposure to Australian shares.

Source: ASSIRT (www.assirt.com.au)

COLONIAL FIRST STATE (CFS)

Owned by   Commonwealth Bank of Australia

Philosophy   CFS is an active manager that seeks to add value through stock selection. They apply fundamental (bottom-up) analysis to each security – portfolios are not constructed with close reference to market indices such as the All Ords. For example, the Australian and Global share funds seek to identify stocks with earnings growth ahead of GDP (economic growth). The benefit of this approach is that, during a market correction that might impact negatively on an index, active stock selection can help you to avoid having your money in the wrong stocks at the wrong time.

Contact details   Level 17, 52 Martin Place
Sydney NSW 2000
GPO Box 27, Sydney NSW 1007
Phone: 13 13 36
Internet: www.colonialfirststate.com.au

Key services $1,000 minimum initial investment, no exit fees, most funds require entry fees ranging from 2.5%–4% and MERs range from 0.97%–2.25%.

List of products and returns

CFS Australian Share Fund – Diversified Shares

3 yr rtn %	5 yr rtn %	7 yr rtn %	Volatility	Size at 31/12/00 (millions)	Yearly returns %				
					2000	1999	1998	1997	1996
15.7	15.9	14.1	82	224.7	2.9	20.3	25.3	7.7	26.1

Investment objective

To provide capital growth and income over the long term. Invests in a diversified portfolio of listed Australian shares. It has no particular bias towards any shares and will invest in small, medium or large companies, industrial or resource companies or high-dividend payers.

CFS Global Share – International Shares

3 yr rtn %	5 yr rtn %	7 yr rtn %	Volatility	Size at 31/12/00 (millions)	Yearly returns %				
					2000	1999	1998	1997	1996
17.2				184.9	6.4	18.3	28.0		

Investment objective

To provide capital growth over the long term, by investing in a diversified portfolio of international shares.

CFS Property Sector – Property Securities

3 yr rtn %	5 yr rtn %	7 yr rtn %	Volatility	Size at 31/12/00 (millions)	Yearly returns %				
					2000	1999	1998	1997	1996
9.8	12.3	8.9	69	153.4	19.4	-5.6	17.5	19.1	13.3

Investment objective

To provide capital growth over the medium to long term. Primarily invests in property securities listed on the ASX, with exposure to commercial, retail, industrial, hotels, leisure and some infrastructure projects.

CFS Cash Management Trust (CMT) – Cash

3 yr rtn %	5 yr rtn %	7 yr rtn %	Volatility	Size at 31/12/00 (millions)	Yearly returns %				
					2000	1999	1998	1997	1996
4.2	4.7	4.9	I	219.2	5.0	3.7	3.9	4.5	6.3

Investment objective

To provide income over the short term with a strong capacity to repay your investment in full at call. Invests in government and semi-government securities, bills of exchange, negotiable certificates of deposits and promissory notes.

CFS Conservative – Capital Stable

3 yr rtn %	5 yr rtn %	7 yr rtn %	Volatility	Size at 31/12/00 (millions)	Yearly returns %				
					2000	1999	1998	1997	1996
8.2	8.9	8.3	I	91.5	8.3	7.5	8.7	9.9	10.3

Investment objective

To provide a capital stable investment with a regular tax-effective income stream over the medium to long term. Primarily invests in money market and fixed-interest securities, with some exposure to leading Australian shares to provide growth and income.

CFS Balanced Fund – Balanced

3 yr rtn %	5 yr rtn %	7 yr rtn %	Volatility	Size at 31/12/00 (millions)	Yearly returns %				
					2000	1999	1998	1997	1996
10.8	12.7		39	201.7	10.0	9.9	12.6	13.8	17.5

Investment objective

To provide both capital growth and tax-effective income over the medium term. Invests in Australian money market and fixed-interest securities and Australian shares.

CFS Diversified Fund – Growth

3 yr rtn %	5 yr rtn %	7 yr rtn %	Volatility	Size at 31/12/00 (millions)	Yearly returns %				
					2000	1999	1998	1997	1996
12.1	13.5	11.0	39	765.2	8.5	10.6	17.3	17.3	14.2

Investment objective

To provide consistent returns with low volatility over the long term. Invests in a broad range of asset classes, including Australian and international shares, fixed-interest securities, listed property trusts and cash.

Source: ASSIRT (www.assirt.com.au)

COMMONWEALTH FINANCIAL SERVICES

Owned by	Commonwealth Bank of Australia
Philosophy	Commonwealth Investment Management offers either indexed or active investment management, or a combination of both. It applies highly disciplined investment methodologies and processes that focus on achieving clients' return objectives. Risk control is a priority at each step in the investment management process.
Contact details	Level 6, 48 Martin Place
	Sydney NSW 1155
	Reply Paid 3306, Sydney NSW 2001
	Phone: 13 20 15
	Email: service@cba.com.au
	Internet: www.commbank.com.au
Key services	Minimum initial investments start at $2,500, no exit fees, some funds require entry fees of 3% and MERs range from 0.96%–1.66%.

List of products and returns

Commonwealth Imputation Share Fund – Diversified Shares

3 yr rtn %	5 yr rtn %	7 yr rtn %	Volatility	Size at 31/12/00 (millions)	Yearly returns %				
					2000	1999	1998	1997	1996
8.7	10.5		69	72.6	5.8	16.4	4.4	15.2	11.1

Investment objective

To provide regular tax-effective income and capital growth in the medium to long term by investing predominantly in high yielding Australian company shares expected to pay franked dividends.

Commonwealth International Share Fund – International Shares

3 yr rtn %	5 yr rtn %	7 yr rtn %	Volatility	Size at 31/12/00 (millions)	Yearly returns %				
					2000	1999	1998	1997	1996
15.2	16.2		82	138.7	0.0	14.3	33.8	29.5	6.7

Investment objective

To provide capital growth over the long term by investing in major international share markets with no restrictions on the amount which may be invested in any one market or sector.

Commonwealth Property Securities – Property Securities

3 yr rtn %	5 yr rtn %	7 yr rtn %	Volatility	Size at 31/12/00 (millions)	Yearly returns %				
					2000	1999	1998	1997	1996
9.1				74.9	19.7	-6.1	15.4	16.8	

Investment objective

To provide income and capital growth over the medium to long term by investing in property securities listed on the ASX. The fund may invest in shares of property development companies and international property investments.

Commonwealth Cash Management Trust – Cash

3 yr rtn %	5 yr rtn %	7 yr rtn %	Volatility	Size at 31/12/00 (millions)	Yearly returns %				
					2000	1999	1998	1997	1996
4.6	4.9	5.1	1	4,706.6	5.4	4.2	4.2	4.6	6.3

Investment objective

To provide regular income, stability of capital and ready access to funds over the short term by investing in short-term assets, such as bank bills, overnight deposits, promissory notes and floating rate securities.

Commonwealth Australian Bond – Fixed Interest

3 yr rtn %	5 yr rtn %	7 yr rtn %	Volatility	Size at 31/12/00 (millions)	Yearly returns %				
					2000	1999	1998	1997	1996
5.0	6.5	6.2	1	157.1	7.9	1.6	5.8	8.6	9.1

Investment objective

To provide an income stream and potential for some capital growth over the medium term by investing in a variety of Australian government, semi-government and corporate bonds with a high credit rating.

Commonwealth Income Fund – Capital Stable

3 yr rtn %	5 yr rtn %	7 yr rtn %	Volatility	Size at 31/12/00 (millions)	Yearly returns %				
					2000	1999	1998	1997	1996
5.3	6.0		1	659.8	6.6	4.4	5.0	6.6	7.6

Investment objective

To provide income and the potential for some capital growth over the medium term by investing in cash and domestic bonds and a small exposure to domestic shares.

Commonwealth Balanced Fund – Growth

3 yr rtn %	5 yr rtn %	7 yr rtn %	Volatility	Size at 31/12/00 (millions)	Yearly returns %				
					2000	1999	1998	1997	1996
8.9	9.9	8.2	39	944.1	4.6	9.8	12.5	14.8	7.9

Investment objective

To provide a balance of capital growth and income over the medium to long term by investing in a diversified selection of assets, such as shares, bonds, cash and fixed interest.

Source: ASSIRT (www.assirt.com.au)

NATIONAL AUSTRALIA FINANCIAL MANAGEMENT (NAFM)

Owned by   National Australia Bank

Philosophy   NAFM applies an active, value-based style, which it describes as 'value active'. This means that it looks to buy into markets or securities that are cheap relative to their sector. For example, in Australian equities, NAFM would look to buy companies that are out of favour with the market (and therefore cheap), but that have the potential to improve within a reasonable time frame. NAFM would expect that such improvement would be reflected by a rise in the share price, thereby adding value to its portfolio.

Contact details   342 Flinders Street
Melbourne, Vic 3000
GPO Box 4373, Melbourne VIC 3000
Phone: 13 22 95
Internet: www.national.com.au/nfm

Key services   Minimum initial investments range from $2,000 to $5,000. Some funds offer nil-entry-fee options, while for those that charge entry fees, expect to pay anywhere between 1.6%–4.0%. In some cases where there is no entry fee you might pay an exit fee. MERs range from 1.6%–2.5%.

List of products and returns

NAFM Investment Trust Dividend Imputation – Diversified Shares

3 yr rtn %	5 yr rtn %	7 yr rtn %	Volatility	Size at 31/12/00 (millions)	Yearly returns %				
					2000	1999	1998	1997	1996
11.5	11.5	9.2	69	42.8	5.1	20.2	9.9	8.6	14.7

Investment objective

To provide income and capital growth over the long term by investing in a range of equities and property trusts listed on the ASX and short-term securities.

NAFM Investment Trust Global – International Shares

3 yr rtn %	5 yr rtn %	7 yr rtn %	Volatility	Size at 31/12/00 (millions)	Yearly returns %				
					2000	1999	1998	1997	1996
13.2	15.0	11.6	69	81.9	1.7	12.8	26.6	29.5	6.9

Investment objective

To provide capital growth over the long term by investing in individual equity investments from a range of international stock markets.

NAFM Investment Trust Property – Diversified Property

3 yr rtn %	5 yr rtn %	7 yr rtn %	Volatility	Size at 31/12/00 (millions)	Yearly returns %				
					2000	1999	1998	1997	1996
8.9	7.8	6.8	39	192.9	14.5	1.5	11.1	9.1	3.3

Investment objective

To provide income and capital growth over the medium to long term by investing in a balanced portfolio of commercial, retail and industrial property.

NAFM Investment Trust Conservative Income Fund – Capital Stable

3 yr rtn %	5 yr rtn %	7 yr rtn %	Volatility	Size at 31/12/00 (millions)	Yearly returns %				
					2000	1999	1998	1997	1996
4.3				12.8	4.3	3.2	5.4		

Investment objective

To provide regular income over the medium term with low capital growth by investing in a range of government, semi-government, corporate and mortgage-backed securities of varying maturities. ('Maturities' is a term used to describe the period for which you invest your money.)

NAFM Investment Trust Balanced Fund – Growth

3 yr rtn %	5 yr rtn %	7 yr rtn %	Volatility	Size at 31/12/00 (millions)	Yearly returns %				
					2000	1999	1998	1997	1996
9.4	10.1	8.1	39	541.5	5.5	9.4	13.6	11.6	10.4

Investment objective

To provide income and capital growth over the medium to long term through investing in a diversified portfolio of Australian and international equities, fixed interest and short-term money market securities and Australian property trust securities.

Source: ASSIRT (www.assirt.com.au)

MLC INVESTMENT LIMITED

Owned by	National Australia Bank Limited
Philosophy	MLC uses a multi-manager investment process. This process is based on the philosophy that different investment managers have different investment styles and specialise in different asset classes, geographic regions and industry sectors. Some fund managers are aggressive, some are conservative and by combining their styles, MLC aims to diversify investment risk and produce less volatile returns.
Contact details	Level 10, MLC Building 105–153 Miller Street, North Sydney, NSW 2060 PO Box 1042, North Sydney NSW 2059 Phone: 13 18 31 Email: mlcinvestor@mlc.com.au Internet: www.mlc.com.au
Key services	Minimum initial investments range from $2,000 to $5,000. MLC does not charge exit fees, but entry fees range from 3%–5%. MLC charges no entry fee on its Cash Management Trust. MERs range from 1.38%–2.22%.

List of products and returns

MLC MasterKey Unit Trust Australian Shares – Diversified Shares

3 yr rtn %	5 yr rtn %	7 yr rtn %	Volatility	Size at 31/12/00 (millions)	Yearly returns %				
					2000	1999	1998	1997	1996
9.1	10.2	8.8	69	284.4	5.2	16.8	5.7	9.0	14.9

Investment objective
To provide capital growth and some tax-effective income over the long term through a diversified portfolio of shares listed on the ASX.

MLC Platinum Global Fund – International Shares

3 yr rtn %	5 yr rtn %	7 yr rtn %	Volatility	Size at 31/12/00 (millions)	Yearly returns %				
					2000	1999	1998	1997	1996
13.6	16.1	12.7	82	282.5	1.3	26.9	14.1	29.6	10.8

Investment objective
To provide capital growth over the long term. Primarily invests in securities listed on international share markets that appear to be undervalued by the market.

MLC MasterKey Unit Trust Property Securities – Property Securities

3 yr rtn %	5 yr rtn %	7 yr rtn %	Volatility	Size at 31/12/00 (millions)	Yearly returns %				
					2000	1999	1998	1997	1996
8.5	11.6	8.8	69	493.7	17.0	-5.0	14.9	18.7	14.1

Investment objective
To provide income and capital growth over the long term. Invests in a diversified portfolio of listed property securities, including prime retail, commercial and other types of properties over broad geographic regions.

MLC MasterKey CMT – Cash

3 yr rtn %	5 yr rtn %	7 yr rtn %	Volatility	Size at 31/12/00 (millions)	Yearly returns %				
					2000	1999	1998	1997	1996
4.1	4.5	4.7	1	1,098.5	4.2	4.1	4.1	4.1	6.0

Investment objective

To provides investors with a convenient alternative to a traditional bank account. Investors are able to earn a competitive market interest rate with an AAA rating while maintaining ready access to funds.

MLC MasterKey Unit Trust Australian Bonds – Fixed Interest

3 yr rtn %	5 yr rtn %	7 yr rtn %	Volatility	Size at 31/12/00 (millions)	Yearly returns %				
					2000	1999	1998	1997	1996
5.1	7.3	6.3	39	95.7	10.0	-1.7	7.3	10.2	11.4

Investment objective

To provide income over the medium to long term. Primarily invests in a diversified portfolio of Australian interest-bearing securities, including government-backed securities, local and semi-government backed securities, corporate and cash securities.

MLC MasterKey Unit Trust Income Fund – Capital Stable

3 yr rtn %	5 yr rtn %	7 yr rtn %	Volatility	Size at 31/12/00 (millions)	Yearly returns %				
					2000	1999	1998	1997	1996
6.9	8.3	6.9	39	78.4	9.3	1.9	9.7	10.8	10.1

Investment objective

To provide regular income with some tax advantages and also some capital growth over the medium to long term. Invests in cash, interest-bearing securities, property securities, Australian and international shares.

MLC MasterKey Unit Trust Balanced Fund – Balanced

3 yr rtn %	5 yr rtn %	7 yr rtn %	Volatility	Size at 31/12/00 (millions)	Yearly returns %				
					2000	1999	1998	1997	1996
9.3	10.6	8.7	39	1,001.2	6.0	11.6	10.6	13.6	11.6

Investment objective

To provide a balance of income and capital growth over the long term. Invests in a balanced mix of cash, interest-bearing securities, property securities and Australian and international shares.

MLC MasterKey Unit Trust Growth Fund – Growth

3 yr rtn %	5 yr rtn %	7 yr rtn %	Volatility	Size at 31/12/00 (millions)	Yearly returns %				
					2000	1999	1998	1997	1996
10.2	11.4	9.4	69	125.2	5.9	14.1	10.9	15.1	11.5

Investment objective

To provide capital growth over the long term through a diversified portfolio that focuses on assets with strong growth potential. Invests in cash, interest-bearing securities, property securities and Australian and international shares.

Source: ASSIRT (www.assirt.com.au)

PERPETUAL INVESTMENT MANAGEMENT LIMITED

Owned by	Perpetual Group
Philosophy	Perpetual Investment's overall philosophy and style is based on identifying value. Perpetual's analysis and research is focused on the company and what it does. This follows its belief that company characteristics and qualities are the most important determinants of share prices over time. Perpetual seeks to buy shares at levels where it believes the fundamental value of the company is greater than the current market price. Perpetual has appointed Fidelity International Ltd to manage its international equity funds.
Contact details	1 Castlereagh Street Sydney NSW 2000 GPO Box 4171, Sydney NSW 2000 Phone: 1800 022 033 Internet: www.perpetual.com.au
Key services	Perpetual offers a standard minimum initial investment of $2,000 on all its products. It also offers both nil-entry-fee and entry-fee options on some of its products. On all other products, entry fees are generally 4%. MERs range from 0.95%–2.69%. Perpetual doesn't generally charge exit fees, but there are exceptions. For example, if you choose the nil-entry-fee option for the international share fund, you still pay an exit fee of 0.2%.

List of products and returns

Perpetual Investor Choice Australian Shares – Diversified Shares

3 yr rtn %	5 yr rtn %	7 yr rtn %	Volatility	Size at 31/12/00 (millions)	Yearly returns %				
					2000	1999	1998	1997	1996
12.6	16.2		69	38.1	11.2	16.1	10.7	10.9	33.5

Investment objective
To provide capital growth and tax-effective income over the long term. Primarily invests in quality Australian industrial and resource shares and other securities.

Fidelity Perpetual International Fund – International Shares

3 yr rtn %	5 yr rtn %	7 yr rtn %	Volatility	Size at 31/12/00 (millions)	Yearly returns %				
					2000	1999	1998	1997	1996
16.4	18.2	13.9	82	521.0	1.7	19.7	29.4	40.0	4.6

Investment objective
To provide capital growth over the long term by investing, through Fidelity's four regional share funds, in a diversified portfolio of international investments.

Perpetual Investor Choice Property Securities – Property Securities

3 yr rtn %	5 yr rtn %	7 yr rtn %	Volatility	Size at 31/12/00 (millions)	Yearly returns %				
					2000	1999	1998	1997	1996
7.9	10.2		69	6.2	16.9	-5.8	14.3	15.7	11.7

Investment objective
To provide capital growth and income over the long term. Invests in Australian listed property securities and listed property-related companies.

Perpetual Cash Management Trust – Cash

3 yr rtn %	5 yr rtn %	7 yr rtn %	Volatility	Size at 31/12/00 (millions)	Yearly returns %				
					2000	1999	1998	1997	1996
4.4	4.8	5.0	1	673.9	5.1	4.0	4.0	4.6	6.4

Investment objective

To provide income and security of capital by investing in short-term government, corporate and bank-backed securities and bank deposits. The Fund has a AAA credit rating from Standard and Poor's Australia Limited.

Perpetual Investor Choice Conservative – Capital Stable

3 yr rtn %	5 yr rtn %	7 yr rtn %	Volatility	Size at 31/12/00 (millions)	Yearly returns %				
					2000	1999	1998	1997	1996
6.5	7.4		1	11.3	8.0	4.6	7.0	8.4	8.9

Investment objective

To provide moderate growth and income over the medium to long term. Invests in a diversified portfolio, with an emphasis on cash and fixed-interest securities.

Perpetual Investor Choice Balanced Growth – Growth

3 yr rtn %	5 yr rtn %	7 yr rtn %	Volatility	Size at 31/12/00 (millions)	Yearly returns %				
					2000	1999	1998	1997	1996
10.7	11.2		39	93.0	8.4	11.7	11.9	11.7	12.4

Investment objective

To provide capital growth and income over the longer term. Invests in a diversified portfolio with an emphasis on Australian and international shares.

Fidelity Perpetual Split Growth – Growth

3 yr rtn %	5 yr rtn %	7 yr rtn %	Volatility	Size at 31/12/00 (millions)	Yearly returns %				
					2000	1999	1998	1997	1996
				57.9	5.2	15.7			

Investment objective

To provide capital growth over the long term by investing, through other Perpetual managed funds, in a diversified portfolio of quality international and Australian shares.

Source: ASSIRT (www.assirt.com.au)

ROTHSCHILD AUSTRALIA ASSET MANAGEMENT LIMITED

Owned by	Rothschild Group
Philosophy	Rothschild is a multi-style investment house. Across all asset sectors Rothschild is an active manager, however active positions are generally bound by the use of quality filters (such as credit ratings or debt limits) and risk-management constraints (such as benchmarking a fund closely against movements in its market index).
Contact details	Level 12, 1 O'Connell Street Sydney NSW 2000 GPO Box 7081, Sydney NSW 1008 Phone: 1800 227 100 Email: client.comms@rothschild Internet: www.rothschild.com.au
Key services	Minimum initial investments range from $5,000 to $100,000. Entry fees range from 0%–4%. There are no exit fees and MERs range from 0.696%–3.07%.

List of products and returns

Rothschild Five Arrows Australian Share – Diversified Shares

3 yr rtn %	5 yr rtn %	7 yr rtn %	Volatility	Size at 31/12/00 (millions)	Yearly returns %				
					2000	1999	1998	1997	1996
9.8	9.6	8.6	69	296.8	5.7	20.5	4.0	6.8	11.9

Investment objective

To provide capital growth and tax-effective income over the long term by investing in Australian industrial and resource companies which appear to represent good value.

Rothschild Five Arrows International Share Fund – International Shares

3 yr rtn %	5 yr rtn %	7 yr rtn %	Volatility	Size at 31/12/00 (millions)	Yearly returns %				
					2000	1999	1998	1997	1996
				19.4					

Investment objective
To provide capital growth over the long term by investing in a diversified portfolio of international shares. The fund will usually be fully invested in shares with less than 10% held in cash. The fund uses the Morgan Stanley Composite International World Index as a benchmark.

Rothschild Five Arrows Cash Management – Cash

3 yr rtn %	5 yr rtn %	7 yr rtn %	Volatility	Size at 31/12/00 (millions)	Yearly returns %				
					2000	1999	1998	1997	1996
4.2	4.7	4.9	1	32.7	4.9	3.8	3.9	4.2	6.6

Investment objective
To provide income and security of capital by investing in bank-accepted bills, promissory notes from large corporations and bank-issued certificates of deposits. The trust may also invest in short-dated fixed-interest securities issued by the Commonwealth Government.

Rothschild Five Arrows Property Invest – Unlisted Property

3 yr rtn %	5 yr rtn %	7 yr rtn %	Volatility	Size at 31/12/00 (millions)	Yearly returns %				
					2000	1999	1998	1997	1996
9.7				5.9	19.5	-1.9	12.5		

Investment objective

To provide capital growth and income over the long term by investing in a portfolio of Australian property trusts. The Fund also has the ability to invest in infrastructure investments. The Fund uses the S&P ASX 300 Property Accumulation Index as a benchmark.

Rothschild Five Arrows Balanced Fund – Balanced

3 yr rtn %	5 yr rtn %	7 yr rtn %	Volatility	Size at 31/12/00 (millions)	Yearly returns %				
					2000	1999	1998	1997	1996
8.3	9.9	8.1	39	314.5	6.4	8.7	9.9	15.9	9.0

Investment objective

To provide a balance of capital growth and income over the long term by investing in a balanced portfolio of Australian and international shares, listed property trusts, Australian and international fixed-interest securities and cash.

Rothschild Five Arrows Growth Fund – Growth

3 yr rtn %	5 yr rtn %	7 yr rtn %	Volatility	Size at 31/12/00 (millions)	Yearly returns %				
					2000	1999	1998	1997	1996
10.0	11.2	8.9	69	49.5	3.4	15.9	11.0	16.2	10.2

Investment objective

To provide capital growth over the long term by investing in Australian and international shares, including smaller companies, listed property trusts and cash.

Source: ASSIRT (www.assirt.com.au)

WESTPAC INVESTMENT MANAGEMENT (WIM)

Owned by Westpac Group

Philosophy WIM is an active, value-based fund manager whose philosophy is fixed firmly on the belief that all asset classes and securities are either overvalued or undervalued at various times during the market cycle. WIM aims to protect customers' money by identifying the best combination of asset classes and securities when this occurs.

Contact details Level 4, 130 Pitt Street
Sydney, NSW, 2000
GPO Box 5354, Sydney NSW 2000
Phone: 13 18 17
Internet: www.westpac.com.au

Key services Initial investments are generally $5,000. Most funds have an entry fee of 3%, except the Conservative Growth Fund (1.75%) and Enhanced Cash (nil). There are no exit fees and MERs range from 1.1%–2.11%.

List of products and returns

**Westpac Investor Choice Australian Tax-Effective Shares –
Diversified Shares**

3 yr rtn %	5 yr rtn %	7 yr rtn %	Volatility	Size at 31/12/00 (millions)	Yearly returns %				
					2000	1999	1998	1997	1996
10.7	11.8	9.3	82	119.9	9.8	17.7	4.9	14.8	12.3

Investment objective

To provide tax-effective income and capital growth over the long term and achieve returns comparable to the Australian share market by investing in a diversified portfolio of Australian shares, most of which are expected to pay imputation credits.

**Westpac Investor Choice International Share Fund –
International Shares**

3 yr rtn %	5 yr rtn %	7 yr rtn %	Volatility	Size at 31/12/00 (millions)	Yearly returns %				
					2000	1999	1998	1997	1996
14.1	14.3	10.7	82	143.6	1.3	15.1	27.6	28.4	2.4

Investment objective

To provide capital growth and some income over the long term and achieve total returns in Australian dollars comparable to those of overseas share markets by investing in companies listed on all the world's major share markets.

**Westpac Investor Choice Australian Property Securities Fund –
Property Securities**

3 yr rtn %	5 yr rtn %	7 yr rtn %	Volatility	Size at 31/12/00 (millions)	Yearly returns %				
					2000	1999	1998	1997	1996
9.4	11.7	9.1	69	133.9	19.0	-4.7	15.3	17.3	13.5

Investment objective

To provide tax-effective income and capital growth over the long term, as well as to achieve returns comparable to those of listed property trusts on the Australian share market. This is achieved by investing mostly in listed property trusts.

Westpac Investor Choice Money Market Fund – Cash

3 yr rtn %	5 yr rtn %	7 yr rtn %	Volatility	Size at 31/12/00 (millions)	Yearly returns %				
					2000	1999	1998	1997	1996
4.4	4.8	5.1	1	751.8	5.3	4.0	4.0	4.5	6.4

Investment objective

To provide a high level of capital security and to maximise interest earnings over the short term by investing in money-market securities, such as bank bills.

Westpac Investor Choice Australian Bond Fund – Fixed Interest

3 yr rtn %	5 yr rtn %	7 yr rtn %	Volatility	Size at 31/12/00 (millions)	Yearly returns %				
					2000	1999	1998	1997	1996
5.4	7.4	7.0	1	92.2	11.0	-2.0	7.6	11.1	10.0

Investment objective

To provide quarterly income with the potential for capital growth over the long term and achieve total returns comparable to those of the Australian bond market by investing in short-term interest-bearing securities, mortgages, and mortgage-backed securities.

Westpac Investor Choice Conservative Growth Fund – Capital Stable

3 yr rtn %	5 yr rtn %	7 yr rtn %	Volatility	Size at 31/12/00 (millions)	Yearly returns %				
					2000	1999	1998	1997	1996
5.6	6.8		1	166.0	7.7	2.8	6.3	7.3	10.0

Investment objective

To provide a conservative level of capital growth over the medium term and a relatively high level of interest earnings by investing so that the majority of the underlying assets are income providing, such as bank-backed bills and cash on deposit.

Westpac Investor Choice Moderate Growth Fund – Balanced

3 yr rtn %	5 yr rtn %	7 yr rtn %	Volatility	Size at 31/12/00 (millions)	Yearly returns %				
					2000	1999	1998	1997	1996
6.8	8.2	7.0	39	885.4	8.6	3.3	8.5	10.7	10.3

Investment objective

To provide a moderate level of capital growth and income over the medium term by investing in a diversified portfolio with the majority of the underlying investments being income assets, such as, bank bills, cash and bonds. There is also some share exposure in the fund.

Westpac Investor Choice Balanced Growth Fund – Growth

3 yr rtn %	5 yr rtn %	7 yr rtn %	Volatility	Size at 31/12/00 (millions)	Yearly returns %				
					2000	1999	1998	1997	1996
9.1	10.1	8.3	39	803.3	8.5	7.5	11.5	14.4	8.7

Investment objective

To provide investors with a high level of capital growth over the long term by investing in a balanced portfolio of assets with a larger proportion in high-growth investments, such as Australian and international shares and property.

Source: ASSIRT (www.assirt.com.au)

chapter 11

BORROWING TO INVEST

NEGATIVE GEARING

Let me start by saying that I think the benefit to our community of individuals being able to negatively gear our favourite investment asset (residential property) is extremely marginal. But more on this later. Certainly one of the most common questions I get asked is in regard to negative gearing. This is not too surprising as it has historically been an excellent wealth-creation strategy.

The questions asked have been focussed around the following issues:

- Is negative gearing still a good strategy?
- How does it work?
- Will I make money?

I am always amused by the last question, it certainly gets to the crux of the issue! But first things first. Most Australians are now familiar with how negative gearing works, but to summarise, if you borrow money to buy an income-producing investment (such as shares or property) that you believe will be profitable over the long term (if you buy aiming to make a permanent loss, the tax office could disallow your tax deductions), then the interest costs on the money you borrow, plus costs associated with running and maintaining the property, less any rent you receive, will be able to be claimed by you as a tax deduction.

Let's look at a simple example, a $120,000 property is purchased as an investment with a $100,000 mortgage at 8% interest. It rents for $120 a week. Yearly rates and water are $800, insurance is $220, agent's fees for rent collection are $450, maintenance is $500 and body corporate fees are $600.

Money Tip

Negative gearing, where you borrow money to buy an investment is a perfectly valid strategy, providing the investment increases in value.

So before you get excited about tax deductions, choose a solid investment.

It works out like this:

	Costs	Income
Rent		$6,240
Interest	$8,000	
Rates	$800	
Insurance	$220	
Agent's fees	$450	
Maintenance	$500	
Body corporate fees	$600	
Total	**$10,570**	**$6,240**

Your loss (costs less income) is $4,330 which is tax deductible in most circumstances. Assuming your tax rate was around 42%, plus 1.5% Medicare levy (meaning you earn over $50,000), then your tax refund would put around $1,880 in your pocket, meaning the property actually costs you about $2,450 to run over a year.

Simple logic would say that if the property grew in value by $2,450 in the year, you would break even, but don't forget the purchase and sale costs which are very significant.

So that's how it works, but is it a good strategy and will you make money?

The simple answer is 'yes' to both of these questions if the property rises in value in excess of all of your costs. But I think that in many parts of Australia this is a dangerous bet. Unless you purchase your residential property in an area with population growth, sustainable job growth, access to leisure and entertainment, health services, schools and public transport, your negative gearing may simply become a brilliant way to multiply your losses, rather than multiply your profits.

My previous example assumes a deposit of $20,000. If the property falls in value by around 16.5%, you've lost the value of your deposit (i.e. $120,000 × -16.5% = $19,800). Let me repeat that point. Before we even consider any costs of buying and selling, that 16.5% fall in value triggers a 100% loss of your invested capital if you sell.

A rise in value of the property of just over 16.5% would see your property now worth $139,800, or a $19,800 profit (again before costs), giving you close to a 100% return on your $20,000 deposit – again ignoring buying and selling costs.

Paul's key rules for negative gearing

- Don't overcommit yourself. Plan for emergencies such as a significant rise in interest rates or the loss of a tenant.
- Only purchase a property in an area with population and sustainable job growth. Consider the impact of the ageing population on your strategy.
- Don't invest for a tax deduction. Make the right investment decision first and then consider tax.
- Remember that negative gearing can multiply your profits, but can also multiply your losses.

- Only use negative gearing if you are in a high tax bracket.
- Take out income protection insurance in case you have an accident or get ill, and have a serious think about your job security.

And finally, why do I think negative gearing residential property has only marginal benefits to our community? Well, when you think about it, we should never live in a home that we own. We're technically better off renting and owning property as a negatively-geared investment.

Negative gearing does nothing to help home owners, but really only helps high income earners to own two, three or, in the case of one of my clients, in excess of 60 properties. In the final analysis, we'd be better off helping all Australians to own a home to live in, and not just a minority who have the income and the knowledge to take advantage of a peculiar piece of tax legislation.

THE OVERSEAS EXPERIENCE

Most other major economies have tax breaks that help their citizens to buy one home and live in it. We, on the other hand, have decided to make it really difficult for Australians to own their own home, but very simple for a minority to own dozens of investment properties, paid for with someone else's money and all funded by the taxpayer – who happens mainly to be the hard-working salaried employee, struggling to pay off their own home.

Frankly, it's a complete joke, but I suspect it's funnier if you're playing by these silly rules, rather than battling along from day to day. The sad thing is that large numbers of people who want to get ahead just can't get into the game.

However, after this minor dummy spit, let me give you another example of how you can use negative gearing to your advantage.

The most obvious is the person who has his or her mortgage under control and can buy an investment property. Let's assume they earn $45,000, making their top rate of tax 31.5% (including the Medicare levy), and that they borrow $200,000 to buy a property valued at $200,000, using the new property and their home as security.

To keep it simple, let's say that the net rent after all costs of running the property, is $200 a week and let's use a lower rate of interest than in the previous example (i.e. 6.5% on their loan). The numbers look like this:

Interest on $200,000	$13,000
Rent	$10,400
Loss	$2,600
Tax refund at 31.5%	$819
Total cost of property p.a.	**$1,781**

In other words, it costs around $34 a week to own this property, and it would have to grow in value by under 1% per annum for its increase in value to exceed the annual costs of $1,781, which in a decent location isn't a bad bet.

Please remember though that I've left out all the nasty bits such as unexpected repairs, tenants trashing the place, costs to buy the property and so on, but no doubt you get the idea.

Negative gearing is a fantastic way to get into a home, for young people living at home and paying little or no rent, and also for people renting a home who want to buy now and move in at a later date.

But to again point to the absurdity of our laws, remember in this country you should never live in the house you own – and if you know someone buying a house at a similar value and location to you, you could always consider buying their house, renting it to them and negatively gearing it, and they do the same for you. Sure, this sounds illogical and really quite silly, but a quick look at the mathematics will soon show you that you will both be much better off.

Okay, so you can make money by negatively gearing the right property in the right locations, but what about shares?

BORROWING TO BUY SHARES

'SeaChange' was a popular ABC television program about lifestyle choice. And I'm not surprised at its popularity, as many people I know are contemplating how to get out of the rat race. But at the same time another huge seachange is taking place: our changing attitude to investment.

It really is quite incredible. Twenty years ago 'investment' meant a bank savings account or an investment property. Less than 4% of adults owned shares. Ten years ago negative gearing became the rage, and dinner party conversation revolved around when and where to buy investment property using borrowed money. But today with property performing badly in many parts of Australia, one of the most commonly asked questions is 'Should I borrow money to buy shares?'.

I guess I shouldn't be so surprised, given that over 50% of adult Australians now own shares, not to mention the fact that we are in the ninth year of a bull market.

If you had invested $100,000 in a broad group of shares in January 1991, your money would have grown to nearly $300,000 by 2000.

Despite very minor losses in 1992 and 1994, tripling your money over nine years is not a bad result – and I don't know of too many properties that have tripled in value since January 1991!

If, however, you had borrowed $100,000 to invest, you would be so far in front it's scary. Allow me a little poetic licence here and forget about the benefits of franked dividends (the fact that tax has already been paid on these only makes the story look better), this is how it would have gone for someone who borrowed $100,000 on 1 January 1991.

Please note that the annual returns have been separated into capital growth and dividends (income), with these assumed to be 3% per annum.

I've also assumed the investor is earning over $50,000, but under $60,000, and therefore is paying 42% tax plus 1.5% Medicare levy on this part of their income. Again the results would look better for an investor earning over $60,000, because their tax would be 47% plus Medicare levy, or a total of 48.5%. I've also rounded out all the numbers to make it easier to follow. Sorry about all these figures, but hang in there, you'll soon get the point.

Example of Negative Gearing

Year	Income (divi-dends)	Interest cost	Loss	Tax refund at 43.5%	Loss after tax refund	Capital value of a $100,000 initial investment	All Ords Accumulation Index annual return
1991	3,000	8,000	5,000	2,200	2,800	126,200	29.04%
1992	3,900	8,000	4,100	1,800	2,300	118,800	-6.15%
1993	3,600	8,000	4,400	1,900	2,500	167,300	40.24%
1994	5,100	8,000	2,900	1,300	1,600	147,900	-12.00%
1995	4,500	8,000	3,500	1,500	2,000	170,100	15.18%
1996	5,200	8,000	2,800	1,200	1,600	187,900	10.06%
1997	5,700	8,000	2,300	1,000	1,300	203,100	7.91%
1998	6,100	8,000	1,900	800	1,100	218,700	7.53%
1999	6,600	8,000	1,400	600	800	245,500	12.05%
2000	7,400	8,000	600	300	300	250,100	1.66%
Totals	51,100	80,000	28,900	12,600	16,300		

Source: ipac securities

By the end of 2000, our investor has seen the $100,000 grow to $250,100. They've paid $80,000 in interest, but earnt $51,100 in dividends, leading to a loss (negative gearing) of

$28,900 and at their tax rate of 43.5%, a total tax deduction after the eight years of some $12,600. After the tax refund, the actual cost of holding the investment over the years has been $16,300.

Assuming they don't sell the investment, at the end of 2000 they are $133,800 in front, which is worked out like this:

Investment value	$250,100	
Plus tax refunds	$ 12,600	
Plus franked dividends	$ 51,100	$313,800
Less loan owing	$100,000	
Less cost of interest	$ 80,000	$180,000
		$133,800

Now this is a handsome return and one that every share salesperson seems to have tucked away in their back pocket. But while the facts for this particular period of history are true, I fear that the selective return of the years chosen to do the numbers are highly deceptive.

Borrowing against your home to buy shares

A whole industry has sprung up around getting people to borrow against their home to buy shares. The sales pitch is generally based around the types of returns we have seen during the 1990s, which as I said before, has been an extended boom period. A number of sales groups have quickly realised that if the commission to get into a share fund is in the region of 3% to 5%, then someone willing to borrow $100,000 is worth $3,000 to $5,000 in commission, plus additional commission on the loan if they organise it.

You can pick the representatives of these groups. The sales pitch is exclusively positive, computer print-outs show vast profits, and the chance to pay out your mortgage early, or just make money. I am strongly against borrowing money against your home to buy shares on this basis. Risk is simply not explained in any detail – and there is plenty of risk.

Imagine that instead of borrowing $100,000 in January 1991, you did so in October 1987. Four years later your capital would have been worth $61,300, not to mention the interest payments. Here I have deliberately chosen the worst four-year period in the last two decades, which is as silly as choosing the best ten years in the last couple of decades (1991 to 2000), but I hope it makes my point clear.

When it comes to considering borrowing against your house to buy shares, I am not against the idea, *providing* you take note of these key points:

- Shares are a risky investment in the short to medium term.
- You should take a long-term (ten years or more) view.
- Assume the market falls 50% just after you invest. If you think you would panic and sell, don't borrow against your home to buy shares in the first place.
- In any projections given to you by a salesperson, get them rerun with dividends at 3% and capital growth at 5%. This is historically more realistic.
- Also run the numbers with interest rates increasing by 3% to around 10%. How does this look now?
- Don't borrow against your house if you are not confident about your job security. You still have to make the interest repayments.
- Have disability insurance so you can make the repayment if you get ill or have an accident away from the workplace.

Above all, make sure the investment passes the can-I-sleep-at-night test. If you are worried about losing money and losing sleep, you just shouldn't do it. But providing you follow these rules, history shows borrowing to buy shares has been a profitable investment – but it is not something you should do without considering all the facts. And let's not beat around the bush. If you borrow a large amount against your home to buy shares, and the market falls severely causing you to panic and sell, the end result could be that you lose your home. I appreciate that this is not likely, but as always when high returns are projected, let's not pretend there is no risk.

Margin lending

Now let's take a look at a different strategy to borrow money to buy shares. We'll leave the poor old house alone and borrow money directly against the shares we buy. The bad news is that this generally means we'll need to put in some money of our own, unlike our house where it becomes the security.

The broad name for this way to borrow money to buy shares is 'margin lending'. Typically the margin you put in is around 30%, and the 'margin lender' lends you 70% against the securities you buy. These can be direct shares or managed share funds.

One of the major margin lenders is BT Margin Lending. It commenced margin lending in 1979 and was the first to do so, but today you have plenty of choices with some eighteen institutions with a margin lending product. BT has a pretty simple 'basic' facility. You choose from 500 Australian shares or managed funds and they will lend you 70 cents for every 30 cents you put in, with a minimum loan of $40,000.

JB Were are another big player in this field, but they rate products individually. This means that you would only need to put in 10% to buy National Income Securities, but 60% to buy Novus Petroleum. They will lend to 70% on most managed funds, with more volatile funds such as a Resources Trust rated at 50%.

The benefits or risks involved in a margin loan are pretty simple to see, and the JB Were example below illustrates this point very effectively.

Example of a Margin Loan

Investor	Geared	Ungeared
Investor's own equity	$30,000	$30,000
Loan obtained	$70,000	$0
Initial market value of portfolio	$100,000	$30,000
10% rise in market value of portfolio		
resulting market value of portfolio	$110,000	$33,000
Loan outstanding	$70,000	$0
Resulting value of investor's equity	$40,000	$33,000
% gain in investor's equity	33%	10%
10% fall in market value of portfolio		
resulting market value of portfolio	$90,000	$27,000
Loan outstanding	$70,000	$0
Resulting value of investor's equity	$20,000	$27,000
% loss in investor's equity	(33%)	(10%)

Source: JB Were

A 10% rise in the market, sees someone with a 70% loan on paper at least, up by 33%. But where there are swings there are roundabouts, and a 10% drop in the market sees paper losses of 33%.

Of course there are a couple of other negatives investors should consider. The major one of these is the dreaded margin call. Margin calls don't happen when you borrow against your house because the lender is protected by the value of your home, but your margin lender starts to get very nervous when markets start falling, and for a very good reason. If you put in 30% and the markets fall 30%, your securities only just cover your loan. If the market falls by 40%, you've lost all of your 30% margin and 10% of the lender's money. This makes lenders very jumpy and so, to protect themselves, they will issue you with a margin call, meaning simply that you need to put in more money to make sure the lender is protected.

This can have some severe repercussions if you are not prepared or able to meet a margin call. In this situation your lender would sell some or all of your securities, depending on the severity of the fall and their own particular rules for margin lending. This would magnify your loss. If markets then rebounded (as in September 1998), you would be left licking your wounds.

In other words, it is essential to understand exactly how your lender's margin calls work, and to have a plan in place to meet the inevitable market downturns. This plan could, depending upon your situation, see you borrow a smaller percentage, have a buffer put aside somewhere else, or possibly a mortgage facility in case of emergencies.

Other strategies to reduce the likelihood of a margin call include diversifying your investments, keeping up with the interest payments on the loan, reinvesting dividends to reduce your loan as a proportion of your total portfolio and finally by keeping a close watch on the performance of your portfolio.

I am certainly not against using a margin loan. The benefits can be very attractive. Deutsche Bank Equity lending pointed out on the Australian Shareholders Association web site (www.asa.asn.au) that $30,000 invested in Lend Lease ten years ago would today be worth $130,000 and $170,000 in National Australia Bank. But if you borrowed another $70,000 and invested $100,000 also ten years ago, today your Lend Lease shares would be worth $434,000 and $573,000 in National Australia Bank.

This is good stuff and music to investors' ears, but they don't point out that $100,000 invested in Christopher Skase's Quintex ten years ago, would today leave you with nothing except a $70,000 debt to your margin lender.

Fees

Another point not often highlighted is the cost of getting a margin loan set up. To their credit, JB Were do highlight the costs in some detail in nice large print, and they are as follows:

- Company or Trust Registration fee = $250.
- Margin buffer of 7.5% of market value of portfolio.
- Variable rate interest payable monthly in arrears.
- Fixed-rate components must be $50,000 or greater.
- Minimum loan balance of $20,000 for first six months. No penalty for lower loan balance.
- Government stamp duty is payable on total loan (@ 0.4%).

Protected loans

Most margin lenders also offer a 'protected' option. Now this gets quite interesting. BT, for example, offers a 100% protected loan with a minimum loan size of $50,000.

By taking a '100% protected' loan, you don't get margin calls and you don't need to invest equity of your own. If the value of your shares rise, the profits are yours if you sell. If they fall, BT will take back your shares as full repayment at the end of the agreed term.

You can also take a 90% or 80% gearing option, but you'll find that you pay for this protection via a higher interest rate on your loan.

Late in 2000 this type of product was reviewed by the Australian Tax Office (ATO) and it announced it will disallow a proportion of tax deductions, for interest on protected margin loans. An example may help here. Let's say that a typical normal rate for a margin loan is 7.5%. If you were paying 10% per annum for a 'protected loan', the ATO would move to disallow your claims for the entire 10% interest, only allowing you to claim the 7.5%.

The ATO's view is that because a portion of the 'interest' charged on these products is for a capital protection fee, that portion can't be deducted under the general deduction provision. Generally deductions can only be claimed for fees that are incurred to service or maintain borrowed funds. The capital protection fee however doesn't do this. It protects the taxpayer against a share-price fall.

Frankly, this is really a bit of a red herring. It doesn't strike me as terribly unreasonable that the ATO only wants interest to be tax deductible. But what is really important with margin lending is that you understand exactly how your loan works, the costs involved, the risks you are taking, what your strategy is for, and the inevitable reality of a falling market.

Providing you can hang on in the tough times, history shows that a well-managed share portfolio, or a quality managed share fund, will produce very solid returns over the long term. Gearing can help to enhance these returns, but let's not pretend that this is without additional risk.

Remember, at its most basic, gearing multiplies your profits as the market goes up, and it also multiplies your losses as the market goes down.

The only way to avoid this is to take out a protected loan. I worry that the higher costs of these loans and the now non-tax-deductible nature of the 'capital protection' part makes the loan too expensive. If investors earn long-term average return on shares, these factors make the exercise hardly worthwhile.

CONCLUSION

Let me be blunt. If I hadn't borrowed money to buy my first house or to start my business, I have little doubt that my personal wealth today would be considerably less. So I accept that the use of leverage, at any time in history, has been one path to wealth.

But let's also face facts. Many people have gone broke over borrowing to invest. Often it's through no fault of their own. It could be a recession, rising interest rates, an illness, an unexpected job loss, or even a divorce.

Negative gearing works, but you have to accept the risks involved. Above all, you must not be conned into buying an overpriced asset, as was the case with Queensland property sold via marketing seminars to interstate buyers. You must also have the health and financial resources to ride out any personal or economic dramas that come along.

But if my aim were to create additional wealth over the next decade or two, I'd use negative gearing and use it to buy quality assets.

chapter 12

A quick look at history reveals that the paying of taxes has been a constant thorn in the side of communities worldwide. Here in Australia, tax lies at the heart of the famous mutiny at Ballarat's Eureka Stockade during the gold rush in the 1850s when the miners got very angry about paying a miner's licence (or tax) on their prospecting.

Inevitable and irritating as taxes are, we shouldn't lose sight of the fact that if we all pay our fair share of tax, our governments will have sufficient funds to provide the services we all take for granted.

I am always fascinated when people come up to me and complain about the small fortune they pay in tax. In most cases I can't see a problem. If they are paying so much tax, then they are obviously making a bucketload of money — which, to my mind, is not the world's biggest problem.

That's not to say that you should pay more tax than you are obliged to by law. There are a number of sound and legal ways of reducing your tax bill which you should take advantage of if you can. What this means is that you should attempt to minimise your tax, as opposed to evading tax.

You should also keep in mind that it can be counterproductive if you participate in an investment strategy just to reduce your tax. You should only invest to increase your wealth and you should treat the tax reductions that the investment produces as a bonus. I've been in this game for almost twenty years now and as far as I know, nobody has ever got rich by taking a loss of $1 that reduces their tax bill by around 50 cents!

Money in History

1642–1651 A.D.
The English Civil War is fought because Parliament disputes the King's right to levy taxes without its consent.

STEPS TO MINIMISE TAX

Regardless of any tax benefits that may flow onto you from participating in certain investments or by the way you receive your income, there are a few simple tax-reducing steps you need to follow.

Step 1: Check permissible tax deductions

The most fundamental step is to be aware of what tax deductions relate to your job. The latest statistics from the ATO say that about 6 million taxpayers claimed over $6.5 billion worth of work-related expenses. Considering that there are about 9 million taxpayers, this means that on average two out of every three taxpayers are claiming work-related deductions.

Work-related deductions

Whilst it would be impossible to list all the deductions available to every occupation and the reasons why you can claim them, it's fair to say that employees in some occupations can probably claim deductions where others can't. For example, the ATO has deemed that a funeral director can claim the cost of a black suit because it relates directly to the service that he provides. However, if an office worker shows up to work in the same garb, he can't claim this as a deduction. Rightly or wrongly, the ATO does not deem the suit, in this instance, to be essential to the office worker's business. Other curious deductions include the costs of rehydrating moisturisers for flight attendants, gowns and wigs for lawyers, repairs to a fob watch for nurses, and maintaining and training police dogs for police officers.

Other general work-related deductions include car and travel expenses. The expense must be work-related and not be a private cost. For example, the normal cost of travel to and from work, no matter how many times you might do it in a day, isn't a business expense and can't be claimed as a tax deduction. Remember, you can't claim an expense for which your employer has or will reimburse you. You can, however, also claim the cost of buying, renting, repairing and cleaning certain work uniforms.

Generally a work-related expense is incurred after you have spent the money or paid for it by cheque or credit card.

You need to be aware of some basic rules about what you can and can't deduct. Information on these deductions can be found by contacting the ATO. You can also ask your accountant what work-related expenses you can and can't claim.

Self-education expenses

Self-education expenses can also be tax deductible if they are directly related to your work. For example, a writer could claim the cost of a creative writing course, but could not claim the cost of a wine appreciation course (unless they were a wine author!). If your self-education was to help you get a new job, then you can't claim these expenses. You could claim deductions for other self-education expenses such as textbooks, stationery, student union fees, course fees and even the depreciation of your computer.

Step 2: Keep good records

Making sure you record all your expenses might seem a bit of a drag at times, but it's essential to good tax management. In the likelihood of undergoing a tax audit, make sure that you can verify whatever work-related expenses you have claimed as deductions. If your records are incomplete and you can't prove your claims, you may have to pay additional tax and a fine. In the worst-case scenario, you could also end up facing tax fraud charges.

The ATO also requires us to provide evidence of all of our deductions if the total is more than $300, so make sure you keep good records. Just to be on the safe side, you probably should keep records of those deductions under $300 because the ATO may require an explanation of how you came up with this figure, if and when you are audited. More on this later.

Remember that the ATO requires us to keep all our tax records for a minimum of five years. If you have lost your records or they have been destroyed, call the ATO's general inquiries line on 13 28 61.

Step 3: Strategies and investments

There are a number of worthwhile tax-minimisation strategies and preferentially taxed investments available to everybody, no matter what your occupation is. These include:
* income splitting
* income timing
* negative gearing

- franked dividends
- superannuation and managed investments in retirement
- interest-offset accounts
- end-of-year tax schemes
- rebates.

Income splitting

Income splitting is a highly effective way in which couples can minimise the total amount of tax they pay. The principle is very simple: income is held in the name of the partner on the lower marginal tax rate so that the actual amount of tax paid is minimised. (Your marginal rate is the highest level of income tax that you pay.)

> *Let's say we have a couple, Pat and Clare. Pat earns $60,000 per annum and Clare, who does some part-time work as a physiotherapist when she's not looking after her young baby, earns $4,000. Clare's income is well below the tax-free threshold of $6,000, so she pays no tax. Pat has $16,480 deducted from his annual pay. This includes the 1.5% Medicare levy.*
>
> *Now, let's assume that the couple has $25,000 in cash that they have saved and wish to put into a one-year term deposit paying interest at 6% p.a. ($1,500). If the term deposit is put in Pat's name, his annual income will rise to $61,500 ($60,000 plus $1,500). At this income level his marginal tax rate will be 47%. Therefore he will pay $705 in tax retaining only $795 ($1,500 × 47% = $705).*
>
> *It would make much more sense from a tax point of view if the term deposit were invested in Clare's name. The $1,500 income flowing from it would raise her overall income to $5,500, which is still below the tax-free threshold of $6,000. Therefore Clare – and of course Pat – will pay no tax on the $1,500 income.*

Income timing – Year-end moves

Income is generally taxable to individual taxpayers in the year in which it is received. In general, a taxpayer may defer payment of tax by deferring receipt of the income.

A good strategy for people in stable tax brackets is to postpone payment of taxes by deferring income and accelerating deductions. For example, delaying a financial year-end bonus until July 2002 means the taxes are not due until October 2003. So if you did some extra paid work towards the end of the financial year knowing that you were going to do less paid work the following year, it would be a good idea to defer payment until July. This payment would be counted as income for the new financial year where your lower overall level of income could attract a lower marginal tax rate.

You might also be able to control the timing of income by controlling events that create income. For example, a self-employed person could delay June billings until July; your employer may be willing to delay your bonus until July; and a retiree could save themselves thousands of dollars in tax liabilities by retiring in July rather than in June.

We will talk more about capital gains later in this chapter, but it's worth noting here that the situation described above is reversed. If you exchange contracts on an investment property on 1 June 2001, but don't settle until 31 July 2001, any capital gain will be included in the 2000/2001 not the 2001/2002 return.

Negative gearing

(See also Chapter 11.)

Negative gearing has become a popular tax-saving device in recent years. Negative gearing involves borrowing money to buy an income-producing asset (such as a rental property or shares).

An investment is said to be negatively geared when the

costs of holding it, including the interest on the borrowed money, exceeds the income it produces. In other words, the investment is negatively geared if it produces a running loss when all income and costs are taken into account.

The significance of running this loss is that it can be used as a tax deduction against other assessable income, such as salary or wages. This has the effect of reducing the real size of the loss, especially if you are in a higher marginal tax bracket.

> *Let's say, for example, you borrowed money to buy an investment property that after twelve months generated a loss of $2,000, including interest payments on the loan. The $2,000 would be tax deductible against other sources of income, such as wages or commissions.*
>
> *If your marginal tax rate is 47%, this tax deduction would reduce the real cost of holding the property to $1,060 (47% of $2,000 equals $940). If your marginal tax rate is 17%, this would reduce the real cost to $1,660 (17% of $2,000 equals $340).*

Negative gearing, as this example shows, is a perfectly legitimate way of creating wealth (particularly for those of us who are paying a higher rate of tax), but be very aware that when you borrow to invest, you are using money you don't own. If the investment fails, you still owe this money – and that won't make you all that happy.

You should never participate in an investment simply because it promises good tax deductions. You should only invest in an asset if it stands a reasonable chance of returning good profits. Treat any tax deductions that come your way as a bonus, not as a reason for investing.

Dividend imputation

Dividend imputation refers to the system that allows an Australian company to pass on franked dividends to shareholders.

To say that dividends are 'franked' means that they have been paid to the shareholder from company profits after the company has already paid tax on those profits.

Companies can pay fully franked, partly franked or unfranked dividends. A fully franked dividend indicates that the dividend has been paid from company profits fully taxed at the company tax rate of 30% (the company tax rate changed from 34% on 1 July 2001). A partly franked dividend indicates that the dividend is paid from profits not fully taxed at the company tax rate, whilst an unfranked dividend is paid before a company pays any tax on it. A company will generally advise shareholders of the status of the dividend at the time of the payment.

But what does all this mean come tax time? If you receive fully franked dividends (pre-taxed at 30%) and your tax rate is 30%, you will pay no further tax on this dividend. If your tax rate is, say, 42%, then you will owe the ATO some tax on these dividends, being the difference between the fully franked rate of 30% and your rate of 42%.

On the other hand, if you sit in the 17% tax bracket, you will receive a tax credit equivalent to the difference between the fully franked rate of 30% and your rate of 17%. You can use this credit against other income sources such as salary, interest or other dividends to reduce your overall tax liability.

Again, don't buy shares for their dividend benefits only. You need to look at a whole range of issues, such as whether the share will provide you with decent and steady growth over time. (See Chapter 7 for more information on dividend imputation.)

Superannuation and managed investments

Superannuation is a way of saving for retirement. Eventually your superannuation contributions build into a larger and larger sum that earns investment income and continues to grow for your retirement. When you retire, this money is paid to you either as a lump sum or a superannuation pension.

Over time, superannuation can give a high return on savings invested for you by your employer – you can also top it up yourself   and the Government taxes superannuation favourably at 15% for the complying superannuation funds. For most Australians this is why superannuation is one good way you can save for retirement. Because superannuation usually can't be paid out until you retire, it's an excellent long-term way of ensuring greater financial security in your retirement.

Once you have retired, your superannuation pay-out can be put towards a range of other preferentially taxed managed investments, including annuities, rollovers and allocated pensions. The tax provisions applying to these investments are considerable and can be complicated, particularly in the case of exiting super early. These are detailed in Chapter 13.

Again, I wouldn't recommend investing in superannuation simply to receive good tax treatment. Super generates respectable returns that make it worthy of an investor's attention. At ipac securities our research shows that you can expect real long-term returns after tax and inflation from balanced super funds in the vicinity of 3% to 5%. The story is even better for growth super funds that have recorded between 5% and 8% returns.

Money Tip

Minimise tax by keeping good records and using simple strategies such as income splitting and making salary sacrifice payments into your super fund.

Interest-offset accounts

If you have a savings account earning interest, you'll pay tax on it. But instead of having the interest added to your savings account, you can offset this interest against a loan account, such as your mortgage, where it will reduce the size of the debt – and attract no tax. Interest earned on one account and offset against debt in another account is tax-free, because you haven't earned any income. The other advantage of this strategy is that you can also put a real hole in your long-term interest repayments.

According to the Commonwealth Bank which offers an offset facility called the MISA Offset Account, an additional $25 per month (in this case, offset interest) coming off a 25-year $100,000 variable mortgage at an average interest rate of 7.8% would reduce the interest costs by around $13,640 over the term of the loan and cut more than two years off it. One of the best things about this sort of debt reduction is that you are effectively saving an extra $13,640 on your investment which is not subject to tax.

End-of-year tax schemes

End-of-year tax schemes sit at the end of the tax minimisation spectrum – the bad end. I have lost count of the number of stories I've heard about unsuspecting investors who have wasted their money by investing in schemes that promise them that they will no longer have to pay tax.

It is important that people realise that tax is a fact of life and that, if we earn an income, most of us are going to have to pay tax. While there are a number of legitimate ways of reducing the amount of tax you pay, you should be especially cautious about schemes that seem too good to be true, because often they are!

It is clear that there are a number of schemes on the market using tax minimisation as the main incentive for consumers. While many may be legitimate, my general advice is to forget them as they offer little more than a way for shonks to get their greedy mitts on your money.

In one particular scheme that caught the attention of the ATO, the promoters claimed that for an investment of between $6,000 and $9,000 they could ensure that investors 'would never be bothered by the tax office again'. The promoters claimed that the Australian Constitution was extinguished when Australia joined the League of Nations (the precursor to the United Nations) at the end of World War I and therefore the tax system didn't apply. Sounds more like a crazy April Fools' prank and the ATO agreed, describing this particular scheme as 'wacky' and warning investors that any attempts to contest the validity of the Constitution would be thrown out of court. Incredibly, despite the warnings, some people invested money in the scheme. Not paying your tax has serious implications, including heavy fines and potentially a stint behind bars.

There is normally nothing intrinsically wrong with the products at the heart of the schemes. They may be farmed prawns, pine plantations, vineyards or feature films which, with good management and given the right conditions, can generate returns. But like the example above, there are many that are put together by con artists whose main interest is in hijacking your money.

Investors claiming deductions for schemes should be aware that, if necessary, the ATO can amend tax returns several years after they are submitted. Potential investors should check for a 'product ruling' on a scheme on the ATO web site at www.ato.gov.au. A product ruling gives an investor certainty that a scheme has tax benefits allowable under the law – provided the arrangement is implemented in the way described in the product ruling. But investors should note that it does not give any assurance of a scheme's commercial viability.

Rebates

Rebates can reduce your tax bill, so it pays to know which ones are available to you. The most recent statistics from the ATO state that more than 6.7 million people claimed rebates totalling more than \$8 billion. The rebates you can claim depend on the nature and level of your income and your family circumstances, such as whether you're married or not.

For example, if you have a spouse (married or de facto) whose income is below \$5,641 (\$6,089 if you have dependent children), you could get up to \$1,452 off your tax bill by claiming the spouse rebate. If you're a sole parent, you could get a rebate of up to \$1,258, as long as none of your children earn more than \$1,785. Remember the rates on the rebates can change fairly regularly.

There are other rebates too. For an older person on a low income, or for those with medical expenses (over \$1,250) or for those looking after an invalid relative, these rebates can mean money off your tax bill. If you make contributions to a complying super fund or retirement savings account, and your assessable income is less than \$31,000, or if you make contributions on behalf of your spouse, you can also claim a rebate.

And don't forget, if you have private health insurance cover there is a 30% government rebate, no matter what you earn. This was introduced for the first time in 1999. It means you can get back 30% of your insurance premium – through your tax return, or from Medicare through reduced payments to your health fund.

For more information contact the ATO or your tax accountant.

As was reported in the July 1999 issue of Money Magazine, *Belinda Abel, a part-time TAFE worker and single
mum with two children, is one of many people who see
great value in going to a tax accountant rather than doing
their own tax claim.*

*A couple of years ago Belinda was receiving an $800
tax rebate. However, after seeking professional advice and
becoming more organised with her receipts and records, she
now gets back around $3,000.*

*Before the advice, Belinda was unaware of how much
she could claim on items such as professional development
courses and associated books, and work-related travel
expenses (mileage and cost of petrol), nor was she taking
full advantage of Social Security rebates. Because of her
part-time work, her sole-parent pension fluctuates and can
range from nothing to $350 a fortnight.*

*She also bought an investment property in Sydney
because she couldn't afford her own home at that stage,
and while she was negatively gearing the interest on that
loan, she hadn't been aware of the other deductions available. However, the amount that Belinda now gets back
accounts for around half of her refund.*

*The interest on her investment loan totalled $12,196 a
year. Her rent was $12,750 a year. Once the extra expenses
of her investment property were added in, Belinda received
a rebate of $1,756.80. The extra expenses included agent's
fees, bank charges, cleaning costs, council rates, repairs
and maintenance, body corporate fees, water rates and
depreciation.*

SHOULD YOU DO YOUR OWN TAX?

One of those vexed questions that many of us face at tax time
is whether or not we should do our own tax return. If we

take care and have the support of the various computer products on the market, there is a definite opportunity for some of us to save money by preparing our own tax return. In fact, about 2.7 million or 30% of all Australian taxpayers prepare their own forms.

But when you take into consideration your preparation experience in doing one tax return per year compared to that of a professional accountant who does hundreds of returns every year, then you really need to question whether the do-it-yourself approach is the best way to go.

By using an accountant, you get support that a computer program just can't provide: the accountant's professional counsel, expertise, plus their ability to deal with the ATO and all of its regulations on your behalf. This is likely to be worth much more than the fee you pay to have your tax return professionally prepared. By engaging a professional, you are guaranteed that in most cases, this will not only save you time and stress, but also money.

If you are a salaried employee with simple work deductions and no involvement in say, a family trust or company, you probably don't really need to consult an accountant. But remember, you can seriously short-change yourself if you don't know what work-related deductions you can claim, or if you don't keep adequate records. Any accountant worth their salt will make sure that this won't happen – though not even a tax accountant can claim for items for which you have no receipts or records. That remains firmly your responsibility.

My advice is that if your financial affairs are a bit more complex and you do things like refinance your home mortgage, or buy and sell other investments (such as a rental property, shares, bonds, or managed funds), then you'd be wise to use professional assistance when preparing your return.

Remember that the correct approach to tax planning is to

start on July 1 this year, not on June 1 next year. Making tax decisions in consultation with a tax accountant and making sensible investment decisions throughout the year will see you much richer in the long term, and much less stressed in the lead-up to the end of the tax year on 30 June.

e-tax 2000

Since July 2000, the ATO has offered those who prefer to do their own tax the opportunity to do it over the Internet. e-tax is an 'intelligent' *TaxPack* which asks the relevant questions, does calculations and gives you immediate access to helpful tax information.

One benefit of doing your tax return electronically is you'll get your refund sooner (within 14 days) and, even if you have a tax bill, the earliest you will have to pay is 1 December. To help you do your own tax, e-tax checks for oversights (picking up typing errors and pointing out any questions that you have missed). It also gives you simple tips, such as to keep records of all deductions worth more than $300.

e-tax is free of charge (excepting normal Internet connection charges) and is available to all Australians. You can log onto e-tax via the ATO web site at www.ato.gov.au or Channel 9's 'Money' web site at www.ninemsn.com.au/money.

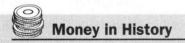 **Money in History**

1162 A.D.
Henry II levies the first of a series of taxes to finance the Crusades.

NEW TAX SYSTEM

Unless you've been lost in the Simpson Desert for the past three years, you are probably well aware that the Australian

Government launched the 'New Tax System' on 1 July 2000. If you somehow missed all the hype at the time, the new reforms were introduced because the old system had reached its use-by date and was affecting Australia's business and investment opportunities leading into the new millennium.

As expected, there have been some serious teething problems that are still being overcome and we have all struggled to become more comfortable with the changes. So, for those of you who have been living in a cave or under a rock, here is a quick update on the major changes to the tax system.

Probably the most talked about reform prior to 1 July 2000 was the introduction of a consumption tax on goods and services. It's not well known, but the introduction of a Good and Services Tax (GST) had been a hot topic of debate for 25 years before the Howard Government introduced it. In fact, Australia's obsession with the GST began way back in 1975 when the Asprey Taxation Review Committee, with little fanfare, handed down a report recommending that a broad-based consumption tax replace the outdated wholesale sales tax regime. Not surprisingly, the recommendations were soon forgotten given the political eruptions that occurred at the time due to Gough Whitlam's dismissal. Not much was heard of a consumption tax until the bureaucrats at the Treasury proposed one in 1985 at the infamous Tax Summit. It was rejected out of hand at the Summit and again eight years later when, during the 1993 Federal Election campaign, John Hewson failed to convince voters of the need for a consumption tax.

Many thought the issue was then dead and buried, but it resurfaced again prior to the 1998 Federal Election when the Coalition Government decided to make tax reform and the GST, a central issue of the campaign. The Coalition won the election and declared that the electorate had given them the green light to revamp the tax system. After much haggling with the minor parties in the Senate over the finer details of the GST, the New Tax System kicked off on 1 July 2000 – more than a generation after the idea was first floated in 1975.

Given this long gestation period, it's still too early to judge the impact of the New Tax System and the GST. The GST is a consumption tax on the supply of most goods and services and anything else consumed in Australia. As we are all well aware, there is no GST on basic food, health, education, childcare services, hospitals, nursing homes, bank fees and charges, or local government rates. The GST has been locked in at ten per cent and replaced dinosaurs like wholesale sales tax and financial institutions duty.

But the GST wasn't the only new reform. Just as important are the changes to income tax, the introduction of the Pay As You Go (PAYG) tax, and the alteration to the way Capital Gains Tax (CGT) is calculated.

PERSONAL INCOME TAX

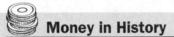 **Money in History**

1799–1816
The first modern income tax was levied in Britain to fund the Napoleonic Wars, but it did not become permanent until 1874.

Your income is composed of more than your salary or wages. It includes other financial returns, such as interest earned from term deposits, dividends from shares, and rents from property. This investment income, over and above the income you generate from your paid employment, is fully taxable at your highest rate of tax (known as your marginal rate) as per the current personal income tax rates.

The income tax rates are subject to change at any time, but in 2000-2001 were as follows:

Income Tax Rates, 2000 to 2001

Taxable income	Marginal tax rate	Tax payable
$0–$6,000	0%	Nil
$6,001–$20,000	17%	Nil + 17% of excess over $6000
$20,001–$50,000	30%	$2,380 + 30% of excess over $20,000
$50,001–$60,000	42%	$11,380 + 42% of excess over $50,000
$60,001+	47%	$15,580 + 47% of excess over $60,000

Source: ATO

As you can see from the above information, you do not pay tax on all your income. The amount of income you can earn before you start paying tax is called the tax-free threshold. The basic tax-free threshold is currently $6,000.

In addition to income tax you need to add the Medicare levy. The normal levy is 1.5% of your taxable income, however this may vary according to your circumstances. If you earn $13,550 or less, you won't pay the levy. Those earning between $13,550 and $14,649 pay a reduced levy. This is calculated at twenty cents for every dollar above $13,550 but below $14,649. There are also other exemptions which you can check out by calling the ATO.

From 1 July 1997, the Federal Government also introduced a Medicare levy surcharge. The Medicare levy surcharge is a fee on all individuals who earn more than $50,000 (or couples who earn more than $100,000) and who do not have private patient hospital cover. The surcharge is 1% of taxable income and is in addition to the normal 1.5% Medicare levy.

To put all this information into perspective, let's take the example of Tran who earns an annual income of $55,000. Based on the scale above, he pays $11,380 on the first $50,000 he earns. The $5,000 between $50,000 and $55,000 is taxed at 42% or $2,100 (his marginal or highest tax rate).

Tran's total tax will therefore be $13,480, which represents an average tax rate (see below) on his salary of 25%. To this $13,480, Tran must add the Medicare levy of $825 ($55,000 × 1.5% = $825) making the total tax payable $14,305.

But there's more. Tran decided that he didn't need private medical cover, so he is liable to pay the Medicare levy surcharge of $550 (1% of taxable income) which he must add to his tax bill. His total tax liability is now $14,855.

If on top of his salary, he had earned up to $990 in dividends and interest income, the $990 would be added to Tran's salary and taxed at his highest marginal rate, that is 42%. (Note that the Medicare levy and the Medicare levy surcharge would be calculated on $55,990.)

Average tax rate

It's not uncommon for people to misunderstand the way the ATO works out their taxes. That's why it's worth explaining what average tax rate is all about.

Let's consider the case of Helga who earns $60,001. This doesn't mean she pays 47% in tax on all her earnings, only that income above $60,000. Rather than paying $28,200 (47% of 60,001), Helga in fact pays only $15,580 (which is 26% of $60,001).

Here's how the ATO works this out. None of us, not me, Kerry Packer or Helga pay any tax at all on the first $6,000 that we earn. The ATO calls this the tax-free threshold. Once Helga earns a dollar more than $6,000 she enters the second threshold at $6,001 where she pays 17% on any income earnings up to $20,000. Remember she pays 17% only on the income between $6,001 and $20,000 and not on the first $6,000.

The third income threshold starts at $20,001 where Helga will pay 30% on all income up to $50,000. Earn another dollar and she enters the next threshold at $50,001 where the ATO slugs her 42% on all earnings from this point up to and including $60,000. The final threshold is reached at $60,001 and she pays 47% on all income earned above this rate.

So to work out how much tax Helga would pay with earnings of $60,001, she needs to work out how much tax she pays in each threshold and then add them together.

To work out her total average tax rate, divide her tax payable by her gross income ($15,580.47 ÷ $60,001 × 100 = 26%).

Calculating Average Tax Rates

Taxable income	Marginal tax rate	Total tax payable#	Average tax rate per threshold*
$6,000	0%	$0	N/A
$20,000	17%	$2,380	12%
$50,000	30%	$11,380	23%
$60,000	42%	$15,580	26%
$70,000	47%	$20,280	29%

\# Tax payable on taxable income excludes Medicare levy
* Average tax rate equals tax payable on taxable income ÷ taxable income
Source: ATO

Pay As You Go (PAYG)

If you earn more than $1,000 from interest earned in a deposit or cash management account or from dividends paid out on shares and other stocks, then you have a PAYG liability. If your only income is from a wage or a salary, PAYG doesn't affect you, but it's still worth knowing about because plenty of us earn more than $1,000 from interest or dividends. Take our example of Tran and his $990 worth of dividends and interest income. If he had earned $10 more of such income, he would have been liable for PAYG.

PAYG is a way of reporting and paying tax on business and investment income. It can be paid in either quarterly or annual instalments after the income has been earned.

Prior to PAYG, business owners and investors were asked to forecast how much income they would earn over the next twelve months and then pay what was known as provisional tax on this prediction.

Forecasting earnings on investments was not an exact science. As we learned in Chapter 7, shares are a good long-term (five to seven years) investment. But within this time-frame, the performance of some companies within your share portfolio can fluctuate significantly. Some years you earn more in dividend income, in other years not so much. Predicting this was pretty tough, with many investors paying more provisional tax than required. Sure this was adjusted at tax time, but it meant that investors were out of pocket for some months before the adjustment.

Now under PAYG, paying tax on your investment income is a bit more sensible. You pay your tax after you have earned it, so that if you earn less, you pay less and if you earn more, you pay more tax.

For individuals, especially those with fluctuating incomes, paying PAYG in instalments provides more flexibility in meeting tax commitments. Your payments can be closely matched to your income.

Alternatively, if you aren't comfortable with this approach, you can choose to have the ATO calculate your PAYG liability based on your previous tax returns. I recommend that you speak to your accountant about what is the best method of calculating PAYG for you.

PAYG is normally paid quarterly, although some taxpayers can make annual payments. The ATO will let you know if its records indicate that you may be eligible to make an annual payment. If you wish to pay on this basis, you will have to complete and lodge an activity statement by 21 October. If you don't lodge the form by this date you will have to pay your instalments quarterly. If you are paying quarterly, instalments will be due 21 days after the end of each quarter. So if your income year starts on 1 July, your instalments will be due on 21 October, 21 January, 21 April and 21 July.

Unless you're in business, it's unlikely that you'll need an Australian Business Number (ABN). You can continue to use your Tax File Number (TFN) in your dealings with the ATO.

If you have lost or can't remember your TFN, call the ATO's tax file numbers inquiry line on 13 28 63.

Finally, just a quick reminder on how to report your PAYG liability. All PAYG obligations and entitlements should be reported on a form called an Instalment Activity Statement (businesses that are registered for GST will use a similar form called a Business Activity Statement). The ATO will send an Instalment Activity Statement to you before you have to pay PAYG tax.

If the ATO's records indicate that you have to pay PAYG, a set of instructions will be sent to you to help you complete your Instalment Activity Statement. It can either be sent to you or your accountant. You can also get this information by calling the ATO on 13 61 40.

Capital gains tax (CGT)

We talked earlier about the benefits of engaging an account- ant to help us at tax time, especially if we have more com- plicated tax returns. Capital gains tax (CGT) is one of the more complex parts of my tax return that convinced me to seek the advice of an accountant. Even if you do decide to seek the help of an accountant, it's worth understanding the principles behind CGT.

CGT is a tax on any increase in the capital value of what the tax office calls a capital gain asset, the most recognisable being shares, property or bonds. Other capital gain assets include options, foreign currency, jewellery, paintings, pre- cious coins, rare books and stamps. And there are many more!

When you sell such assets, any profit you make must be added to your taxable income for the current tax year. A capital gain occurs when you sell your asset for more money than you paid for it. If you sell the asset for less than what you paid, the ATO calls this a capital loss.

There are a number of items that escape the CGT tax web. For example, your home is exempt if it's your principal place of residence, but is taxed if it is an income-producing prop- erty. The family car is also exempt, as are most superannuation funds, compensation claims, betting or gambling winnings. However, you should be aware that if you won a house in a competition and then sold it, you would be liable for CGT.

As part of the Government's tax reforms, CGT changed in 1999. The treatment of capital gains now depends on when you bought your asset, and how long you have held it. The ATO has three categories to deal with capital gains declarations:

- assets sold prior to 21 September 1999

- assets purchased and sold after 21 September 1999
- assets purchased before, but sold after 21 September 1999.

Assets sold prior to 21 September 1999
Indexation rules apply

If you purchased and sold your assets prior to 21 September 1999, the old CGT system will apply to you. Under the old CGT system, your tax is calculated on the capital gain and is included in your taxable income and is taxed at your marginal tax rate.

The ATO used a system of indexation to revalue the purchase price of the assets. Indexation increased the value of the purchase price of the shares by the rate of inflation. To be entitled to indexation, an investor needed to hold assets for longer than twelve months prior to the sale.

Assets purchased and sold after 21 September 1999
Discount rules apply

If your assets were purchased after 21 September 1999, the new CGT system applies to you. If the assets were sold twelve months or more after the date of acquisition, then the realised gain from the disposal of these assets will be included in your tax return as income, but taxed at 50% of your highest marginal rate of tax.

If the holding period was less than twelve months, no concession under the new system will apply to you and the full value of the capital gain will be included in your return as income and taxed at your highest marginal rate of tax. Under the new system, there is no indexation of the purchase price.

On 27 September 1999, Caroline bought 1,000 XYZ ordinary shares at $2.50 each. She subsequently decided to sell all of her XYZ shares on 28 October 2000 at $3.00 each.

As she bought these shares after 21 September 1999, any capital gains she made will be taxed under the new system. As she held these shares for more than one year, she will qualify for the 50% reduction. If she was a high-income earner earning more than $60,000, any capital gain on investments held for more than twelve months after 21 September 1999 are taxed at 24.25% (that is, half of her highest marginal tax rate of 47%, plus Medicare levy of 1.5%). This means she will pay approximately $121.00 in CGT.

Assets purchased before, but sold after 21 September 1999

If the assets were purchased prior to 21 September 1999, but sold after this date, you have a choice as to how to calculate the taxable capital gain and can apply either the discount option or indexation. This choice only has relevance if the assets are held for more than twelve months. Neither the indexation nor discount options are available for assets held for less than twelve months.

On 15 November 1997, Roy bought 1,000 First Instalment Receipts of Telstra at $1.95. A year later, Roy paid an additional $1.35 for each of the Instalment Receipts to complete his acquisition of 1,000 Telstra shares. He then sold all of his Telstra shares on 20 December 1999 at $8.00. Roy acquired his Telstra shares prior to 21 September 1999, sold them after that date, and held them for longer than one year. In this situation, there are two options available to Roy: he can apply the indexation option or the discount option.

TAX OFFICE SCRUTINY

With all these changes in mind, I repeat my earlier recommendation and suggest you leave dealing with the ATO over things like CGT to an accountant – it's all just too specialised and time consuming. But if you still feel confident that you want to have a go yourself, then it's worthwhile knowing a bit about what the ATO expects from you at tax time.

Self-assessment, which was introduced in 1986, means that the ATO uses the information you provide in your tax return to work out your refund or tax bill. You are required by law to make sure you have shown all your assessable income and claimed only the deductions and rebates to which you are entitled. Even if someone else, including an accountant, helps you to prepare your tax return, you are still the person legally responsible for the accuracy of the information.

Australian taxation is based on self-assessment: the ATO trusts you to work out your own tax liability with or without the help of an accountant. Paying the correct amount of tax is your responsibility. You are obliged to be truthful and reveal what you owe in taxes or what the ATO owes you, keep good records, take reasonable care in preparing and lodging your tax return, and finally pay your taxes in full by the due date.

However, the ATO performs both random and targeted checks (known as audits) just to keep us on our toes. And if a tax officer finds a mistake in your return (your mistake, not theirs), you may be fined and forced to repay the out-standing amount. Remember, it's not a case of if you will be audited or when, every taxpayer needs to be as accurate as possible with returns and keep good records which must be retained for five years. Short of running off to become a Buddhist monk and adopting a vow of poverty, what can you do? My advice is to be prepared.

There are three different ways you can be audited:

1 In the case of the simple mail check, you receive a letter from the ATO seeking a clarification and/or documentary proof of one or more deductions that you have claimed.

2 In the case of the income-matching check, the ATO asks your bank to provide it with financial details on matters such as the amount of interest you have earned.

3 Then there's the full audit – the big daddy of the family. Contrary to popular belief, tax officials don't suddenly leap through your window in the middle of the night or break down the door demanding you show them your receipts. It's a much more civilised process than that, but nonetheless unsettling.

Some of our phobias about tax audits come from US media reports of overzealous tax officials, who created so much anxiety amongst American taxpayers that Congress passed the *Taxpayers' Bill of Rights* in 1988, followed by the *Taxpayers' Browsing Protection Act* in 1997, to protect taxpayers from snoopy tax officials.

Fortunately, our tax office doesn't treat all taxpayers like crooks and bandits, preferring instead to take a more conciliatory approach to those who make mistakes. It looks at each case on its merits and works with the taxpayer to make sure that the problem is rectified.

With a full audit you will receive either a letter or a phone call requesting a meeting. At this and any subsequent meetings you can expect a pretty thorough examination of your books, records, receipts and deductions. The audit can go back five years, so you must keep all your documentation for at least that long.

If you have an accountant who has been doing your tax returns, you should contact him or her immediately after you're contacted by the ATO and discuss the situation. If the ATO is conducting a full audit, it would be a very good idea to have your accountant with you at all meetings. If you don't have one, this might be a good time to find one to help you out.

Find all your receipts and documents needed for the audit,

put them in order for the appointment. One word of warning – don't turn up for a meeting with a bag of receipts and dump them on the auditor's desk, the auditor will probably make you take them home and sort them out, which is waste of your and the auditor's time.

What are the odds of being audited? Pretty high. In recent years, around 350,000 taxpayers have been audited annually out of a total population of 9 million-plus Australian taxpayers.

What interests the ATO?

Few things are more unnerving than having your tax return selected for an ATO audit. But it doesn't have to be this way if you have some idea of what is likely to interest a tax official.

Work-related expenses

Of the 9 million taxpayers in Australia, about 5 million claim work-related expenses. Recently the ATO introduced (yet another) new form or schedule: the Work-Related Expense (WRE). The WRE is sent to a sample of taxpayers (not necessarily people that the ATO has their eyes on) who claimed work-related expenses during the previous tax year. This schedule asks them for greater detail when making their work-related claims for the tax year just finished. In June 2000 for example, 162,000 (3.2% out of the 5 million) were contacted to fill out the WRE for the 1999–2000 tax year.

Rental expenses

If you claimed rental expenses on your tax return during the previous year, you might receive a Rental Income and Deductions schedule from the ATO. This is currently sent to about 25,000 of the 1.2 million taxpayers who claim rental expenses on the tax return.

According to the ATO, these schedules are an aid rather than a reprimand – helping taxpayers to get their returns right, which in turn helps them to steer clear of any potential troubles come tax time. The ATO claims that the result of the introduction of these schedules has reduced deductions by about 15%. I would urge you to seek the advice of an accountant if you receive one of these schedules, as the ATO will be taking particular interest in the information you provide in your tax return.

Income matching

Another area of interest to the ATO is the declaration of other income such as interest, dividends and capital gains. The ATO's greater concern with capital gains and dividend declarations has been driven by the boom in share ownership and the proliferation of new investors who may not be as well-versed as more experienced traders in their tax obligations in relation to share transactions.

With the sophisticated electronic income-matching systems and procedures now available to the ATO, it's much easier for them to contact financial institutions to ensure that your declarations are correct. There are about 5 million taxpayers who declare other income and the ATO audits about 180,000 or 3.6% of them each year. Unlike the schedules mentioned above, income matching is conducted after you lodge your return and the ATO tends to choose to audit those with higher 'other income' declarations.

You should also be aware that at the time of the introduction of the GST, the ATO acknowledged the huge workload that accountants and other tax agents had, so they backed off on auditing the tax returns they lodged on behalf of their clients. However, if you think that this trend is going to continue, think again, because now the tax reform dust has settled, tax agents are back in the ATO's firing line.

Look, nobody enjoys being audited, and it can be the cause of much anxiety. However, if you keep all your receipts, maintain good records, and don't fudge on your tax returns, you won't have a thing to worry about.

chapter 13

SUPERANNUATION

The Australian superannuation system is a product of fear and hope: fear that the pension will not support the growing ranks of greying Australians; and hope that Australians can be encouraged, through super, to save for their retirement.

For those of you who have read my book *Making Money*, have watched 'Money' on Channel 9, or have seen my musings on superannuation in *Money Magazine* or newspaper articles, you'll know that I think superannuation is a brilliant idea, but that it's heavily flawed by constant rule changes – around 2,000 between 1988 and 1998 alone. I am the first to admit that super can be very complicated, nonetheless it's worth knowing about. And if you plan ahead, superannuation should play a very important part in ensuring that you have enough money to live on when you retire.

How very important it is can easily be seen when you consider that one industry survey found that many people estimate they will need around 60% of their annual pre-retirement earnings to maintain a comfortable lifestyle. In many cases this represents a far larger sum than is provided by the age pension – which is slightly less than $200 a week, or 25% of average total male earnings, only just scraping in above what Australian economic and social researchers regard as the poverty line.

For the average baby boomer to retire on a government-funded age pension is almost out of the question, as they are likely to demand a far higher standard of living than this provides. Lifting the age pension to 30% isn't really an option because it would increase Government spending on the age pension by a staggering $12 billion above today's level by the year 2050.

There is no publicly set yardstick or target determined as the optimum level of income in retirement. But to achieve a 60% of earnings target, an individual would have to save 15% of their wages for 40 years. Compulsory contributions, which are scheduled to rise to only 9%, would provide about half this target savings (28%) after 30 years of contributing and 43% after 40 years.

For example, someone earning around average weekly earnings ($730 per week) before retirement and contributing 9% of wages for 30 years would end up with a total retirement income of 40% of average weekly earnings. A third of this would be a part-age pension.

WHAT IS SUPERANNUATION?

Superannuation is a way of saving for retirement. All superannuation contributions, or premiums, are paid into superannuation funds. More on superannuation funds later.

For most of us, superannuation is the best way to accumulate the significant amounts of money we'll need to set us up for life after work. In fact, for many Australians super will grow to be their largest asset – worth even more than the family home.

This alone makes super an important investment. But

that's the good news. The bad news is that it's confusing, your money is locked away for a very long time and the Federal Government keeps moving the goal posts.

But there is another reason why super is so important: the fact that Australia has an ageing population. If you are in your 40s or early 50s, you are part of the largest group in Australia's population – the baby boomers. Over the next five years, the first baby boomers will start to retire. This will have a dramatic effect on the structure of our population.

Today there are five working people for every one retired person. Those five working people are paying taxes that go partly towards supporting one retired person on the age pension. (Currently most people in retirement receive either a full or part age pension.)

Is the pension enough?

In 2020, there will be only three working people paying taxes for every one retired person. Under these circumstances it may become more difficult for the Government to continue to provide the same level of support to retired Australians.

The age pension will probably always be there in some form, but unfortunately in future it may be increasingly difficult to qualify for pension benefits. If you are retiring in 20 years or more, the chances are you may have to provide for your own retirement – and this could mean selling your home!

I need to reiterate that whilst you may own your own home, you don't want to be forced into selling it to fund your retirement. Spreading your money across a number of investments – such as superannuation, managed funds, shares, and property – over the course of your working life is the best way to fund a comfortable retirement. And the success of how you invest depends on your ability to save.

If you don't save, you don't invest. If you don't invest, you'll have nothing apart from your home to retire on.

The problem is we aren't good savers. In fact, we are amongst the worst savers in the world. A recent survey conducted by the International Monetary Fund (IMF) ranked Australia equal last out of 21 OECD countries in terms of household savings. The study found that Australia's household saving ratio stood at 4.3% in the early 1990s and that this was down from 11.1% in the late 1970s. Now, if you're a Kiwi and think you've finally found something to give us Aussies a hard time about, sorry. New Zealand joined Australia on the lowest rung of the savings ladder according to the same report.

This more than anything else is the reason why the Federal Government has forced us to save and the way they have chosen to do this is through compulsory superannuation. The key word is 'compulsory'. If there was only voluntary superannuation, there's little chance we'd contribute enough to provide for a comfortable retirement. And the statistics back me up on this. According to a report by the Association of Superannuation Funds of Australia (ASFA), nearly 28% of Australians do not save beyond compulsory superannuation and the proportion of non-savers is growing (from 17% in 1995).

Who is covered by superannuation?

Superannuation coverage for Australian employees has more than doubled since 1984, rising to around 98% for permanent full-time workers and to 59% for part-time and casual employees.

Coverage outside the compulsory regime is lower. For example, only 39% of the self-employed have superannuation, despite the tax breaks available for contributions.

Source: ASFA

WHAT IS A SUPER FUND?

A super fund is an investment fund for superannuation money that is given favourable taxation benefits by the Government. More on tax and superannuation later in this chapter. There are two basic forms of superannuation fund.

Defined benefit fund

A defined benefit or 'benefit promise' fund is a super-annuation fund where the employer promises to pay a set amount to the employee on their retirement. This payment is usually worked out by factoring in how long the employee has worked for the employer and how much money the employee is earning when they retire. For example, you may get four times your salary if you retire at 55 years, five times at 60 and so on. You know in advance what you'll get.

These schemes have tended to be very generous: the employee receiving both a large lump-sum payment and favourable taxation advantages. Politicians, judges, public servants and senior managers have been the major benefi-ciaries of these funds in the past.

The advantages of these schemes are that you know how much you'll receive when you leave or retire. The down side is that if you leave or retire early, you don't receive the same benefits. This can be a lose/lose situation for both the employer and the employee. The employee may hang around long after they have lost interest in the job because they can't afford to leave and miss out on the payout. Their morale and subsequently their productivity is compromised as they bide their time until retirement.

With a defined benefit fund, the performance of the invest-ments in the fund is of no consequence to the employee. Your final payment is guaranteed (unless the company goes belly up and can't pay you). Investment performance is more important to your employer because the better the fund does, the less they have to put in.

There are plenty of arguments about who has the rights to any surplus money in a defined benefit fund should it perform well. In those cases where there is more money in the fund than is required to pay members' entitlements, I believe that this surplus belongs to the employer. I base this premise on the fact that the employer guarantees that the member will receive a set benefit when they retire and dips into the company coffers if the money isn't there. So, given the fact that the employer must meet any short-fall, they should therefore be entitled to any surplus monies.

Accumulation fund

Most of the new superannuation funds tend to be 'accumulation' or 'defined contribution' funds. An accumulation fund is a superannuation fund where the benefit received by the investor is determined by the contributions that have been invested, plus the investment earnings, less any fees and taxes.

Since compulsory superannuation (also known as the 'Superannuation Guarantee Charge') was introduced in 1992, the employer alone, or the employer along with voluntary contributions made by the employee, pays contributions weekly into an accumulation fund. This money is invested in the fund, and on retirement the employee receives a payment for the amount that has accumulated in the fund. The performance of the investments in the fund is critical to how much money you get when you retire. With an accumulation fund, the final payout is not known in advance.

COMPULSORY CONTRIBUTIONS

The following are the basic requirements that will make it easier for you when you consider your superannuation investments. Government legislation ensures that minimum levels of contributions are made to superannuation on behalf of all employees. The required rates are:

Superannuation Guarantee Contributions

Financial year	Superannuation guarantee contributions
1999/2000	7%
2000/2001	8%
2001/2002	8%
2002/2003 (and subsequent years)	9%

Source: ATO

If you recall, the Coalition Government scrapped the proposed compulsory employee contributions that were set to start in 1997. A combination of 9% employer contributions plus 6% Government and employee contributions would have ensured a minimum compulsory super contribution of 15% by July 2002. This would have been great, because for many younger people entering the work force, this would almost surely have taken care of their retirement. So the logic of the Government's decision has been lost on me.

A figure of 15% is not without precedent if you look at other developed countries across the globe. Take our near neighbour, Singapore. The combined contributions of employee and employer in Singapore are 40%. In Spain, the story is similar with combined contributions ensuring 45.8% is invested in workers' retirement savings. Whilst Spain and Singapore stand at one end of the spectrum, there are plenty of other countries whose contributions to retirement saving hover between 15% and 20%. According to figures presented by the Senate Select Committee into Superannuation in 1992, Australia's 9% ambition by 2002/2003 falls well short when compared to the rest of the world.

> **Money Tip**
>
> Salary sacrifice, where you take less money home so as to add to your superannuation, is a sure-fire way to build up your wealth.

VOLUNTARY SUPERANNUATION

But will the employer contributions alone give you the lifestyle you want when you stop working? To make sure that we will have enough, most of us will need to top up our super.

If you are an employee, your employer is already investing a portion of your pay into super through the compulsory 'Superannuation Guarantee' or SG. As we discussed earlier the SG is set to rise to 9% by 1 July 2002.

Many people think this will be enough to provide for a good quality of life when they stop working. However, as I said earlier, you will need to put in much more than 9% of your pay. I would suggest that a figure of 15% of your salary over your working life would be closer to the mark.

This may sound like a lot, and may be more than you can afford to commit to super at the moment, but even a few extra dollars invested now can make a big difference to the amount that you will accumulate during your working lifetime. You may find that as the years go by you can gradually increase the amounts you are investing into super. The important thing is to start now.

Making extra contributions is also known as 'salary sacrifice' and some superannuation funds require that you do this, while your employer may offer incentives to make further contributions by offering to put in extra money if you do.

Added to these incentives are the tax breaks on monies invested in supcrannuation. Like your employer's contributions that are taxed at 15%, if you add your own money, this contribution is also taxed at 15%. For this reason, you can often earn more by investing in your own superannuation than you could by investing in other assets, like shares and property. However, once you earn more than $81,493 the 'high income superannuation surcharge' kicks in. (More on the superannuation surcharge later in the chapter.)

SOME BASIC SUPERANNUATION ISSUES

There are three simple things that you can do right now that will help maximise the amount of your super. These are:
- consolidate your super
- consider investing your super for growth, and
- add to your super.

Consolidate your super

On average, Australians change jobs every six or so years. This means that you could have as many as six or more different superannuation accounts by the time you retire. In fact according to a recent NRMA report, there is currently about $3.5 billion sitting in lost members' accounts and an average 2.7 lost accounts for every Australian. You can call the ATO on 13 10 20 and ask them about lost accounts. And you might be surprised (pleasantly in many cases) when you add up all the super funds that you knew about and others you'd lost track of – it could be a significant amount of money.

Into which fund should you consolidate?

Now here's the tricky part. If you have an employer whose super fund is flexible and offers full investment choice, then you should consider consolidating your super into this fund. But if you find that your employer's fund is less flexible, then consolidate it into a personal fund (which you use to consolidate your other accounts). Then, whenever you leave an employer in future, you can continue to rollover that super into your personal fund.

If you are currently self-employed, it's easy to consolidate your entire super into your personal fund. Most personal funds are quite flexible. Look for one that offers full investment choice and good customer service (such as information and transaction services via the phone and Internet) – and low fees.

Once you have worked out where all your super money is, the best advice I can offer you is to consolidate it into one fund. Consolidation will reduce your paperwork and your fees! If you have more than one super fund, each fund will send you statements and other information on a regular basis and this means plenty of paperwork. In most cases, you'll also pay multiple sets of fees. By consolidating your super, you will be charged only one set of fees.

With your super money spread over different funds, your investment strategy may not be as effective. Without a clear investment strategy you may not be getting the earnings you need to accelerate your super. Consolidating your super allows you to have a more focussed investment strategy that can lead to a better return.

Consider investing your super in growth assets

As super is invested for the long term, it is important to consider putting an amount in investments that have the potential to increase in value over time, like shares and property (known as 'growth assets'). However, most Australians invest their super very conservatively. According to BT Australia, Australians currently have more than $10 billion of their hard-earned super lying idle in cash and fixed interest investments where there is little potential for their money to grow. For super, as with any long-term investment, there is one golden rule: consider investing a proportion of your money in growth assets.

Once you have consolidated your super, why not accelerate its growth? Most super funds offer a choice of investment strategies. This allows you to choose whether your money is invested conservatively such as in a capital stable fund (usually around 70% fixed interest and 30% shares), rather more aggressively in a balanced fund (a mix of shares, property and fixed interest), or even more aggressively in shares only. Exercising investment choice is one of the best ways to take control of your super. Not taking advantage of this opportunity could mean missing out on hundreds of thousands of dollars over your working life! (If you don't already have investment choice, ask your employer.)

A young employee of, say, 25, earning the average wage, would be some $500,000 worse off over 40 years by investing in a capital stable fund rather than a growth fund. Investing your super conservatively may be the easiest and safest option in the short term, but it could be the worst option in the long term. Many people are afraid to invest their super in shares because they think they will lose their money. In the long term, however, shares have been proven to provide far greater investment returns than cash.

Add to your super

Once you have consolidated your super and started investing for growth, you are well on the way to achieving control.

But will you have enough super to give you the lifestyle you want when you stop working? To make sure we will have enough, most of us will need to top up our super.

RESTRICTIONS ON ACCESS TO SUPERANNUATION

Superannuation is a long-term investment and the Federal Government has placed restrictions on when you can access your benefits. In general, you can't get access to your super until you reach the age of 65, or you have reached the preservation age of 55 and have retired. Your preservation age can be worked out using the following table.

Preservation Age for Superannuation

Date of birth	Preservation age
Before 1/7/1960	55
From 1/7/1960 to 30/6/1961	56
From 1/7/1961 to 30/6/1962	57
From 1/7/1962 to 30/6/1963	58
From 1/7/1963 to 30/6/1964	59
On or after 1/7/1964	60

Source: Assetlink

Early release of preserved superannuation benefits is permitted only in certain restricted circumstances. Let's look at some of these circumstances.

Financial hardship

Superannuation fund trustees administer the early release of super benefits on the grounds of severe financial hardship according to a simple objective test, as well as a subjective test.

To be granted early release of benefits you must:

- have received a Government support payment for the previous 26 weeks; and
- satisfy the trustee that you are struggling to pay for your family's day-to-day living expenses.

Support payments include things like social security or service pensions, certain social security benefits, income support supplements, and drought relief payments.

If you satisfy both of the above criteria, the trustee may, in any twelve-month period, release to you one lump sum payment. The lump sum payment is to be no more than a gross amount of $10,000 and no less than $1,000 (or the balance of your benefit if it is less than $1,000).

If you are aged 55 years and 39 weeks or more, there's an alternative, optional test. That is, you must:

- have received a Commonwealth income support payment for a cumulative period of 39 weeks after turning 55; and
- not be gainfully employed on a full-time or part-time basis on the date of your application to the trustee.

If you satisfy this test, the trustee provider may release your entire benefit. In all cases, applicants will need to provide a letter from Centrelink, the Department of Veterans' Affairs or a CDEP grantee organisation before the trustee will release any benefits.

Grounds for release

If you cannot gain early access to your superannuation benefits on severe financial hardship grounds, you may consider seeking approval from the Australian Prudential Regulation Authority (APRA) to release some or all of your benefits on specified grounds. Some of these include:

- medical treatment for a life-threatening illness or injury, or to alleviate acute or chronic pain or acute or chronic mental disturbance, and where treatment for such conditions is not available through the public health system;

- modifications to the family home and/or vehicle to meet the special needs of a disabled member or his/her disabled dependant; or
- palliative care or death, funeral, or burial expenses for a member or their dependant.

It is also possible for a member to have some of their funds released to prevent the foreclosure of a mortgage. It is APRA's role to rule on whether your financial position is such that you require early release of some of your superannuation. For more information call APRA on 13 10 60.

Permanent departure from Australia

Up until three years ago, people who decided to move overseas permanently could take their superannuation with them. All you needed to do was write a letter to the super fund manager and provide them with evidence of your permanent move. This could be a copy of a one-way plane ticket or paperwork that showed that you had sold your property.

While providing this evidence was a relatively easy assignment, the problem was that many permanent emigrants tended to change their minds and wanted to come back after only a couple of years. In fact, it appears some people had never intended leaving Australia permanently in the first place!

Therefore, from 1 July 1998, Treasury tightened up the laws relating to permanent departure to the extent that now emigrants can't take their super with them and can only get their hands on it when they satisfy the conditions of release, such as reaching the retirement age of 55. As you can imagine, not everybody was pleased with the change in the law. So now Treasury is looking into establishing agreements with other countries so that people leaving Australia permanently can roll their money over into a fund of their choice in their new country.

DIY SUPERANNUATION

If you're like most people, the thought of managing your own superannuation can be a daunting one. But as my colleague Anthony O'Brien wrote in the February 2001 edition of *Money Magazine*, for a growing number of Australians, DIY super funds have become a flexible and economical way of saving for their retirement. In fact, their popularity has grown to such an extent, that by 30 June 2000 there were over 210,000 DIY funds, representing 14% ($68 billion) of total super-annuation assets. This was up from 174,937 or 12% ($43.8 billion) of the total superannuation industry in 1988.

Industry experts suggest that if your existing super-annuation assets are between $100,000 and $200,000, you should seriously consider a DIY fund as the most cost-effective super option. However, as the Australian average for total savings per capita in super sits at around $50,000, this would seem to indicate that for many of us, DIY super is out of reach and is the domain of high net-worth individuals (such as, small business owners, professionals, executives or contractors). But according to research figures this isn't necessarily the case. More investors are attracted to DIY super because they are beginning to understand that super-annuation is not as complicated as they had previously been led to believe. The school of thought that super is a complex process that only banks and superannuation companies can control is gradually being overturned. As a result, more people are travelling down the DIY path. Not only has DIY super given them more control, it has also saved them money in establishment and management fees.

According to Robert Hodge of the Association of Super-annuation Funds of Australia, there are three variants of the DIY fund:

- the self-managed super funds (SMSF)
- the small APRA funds (SAF), regulated by Australian Prudential Regulation Authority (APRA)
- superannuation mastertrusts

All three have a role to play and provide investors with different levels of control over their super. Let's look at the SMSFs first.

Self-managed super funds (SMSF)

Technically a SMSF is a fund with less than five members where all members of the fund are trustees and are fully involved in the decision-making process of the fund. The major advantage of a SMSF is complete control. That is, you choose how your assets are invested, you monitor how those investments perform and you make investment decisions based on that knowledge.

This is in sharp contrast to a retail super fund, where you are unable to influence investment decisions, and often aren't aware of how well your investments are performing until you receive a statement from the manager.

The reality is that trustees are relatively free to chart their own investment course. Indeed, they can invest in literally anything (even ostrich farms!) provided it fits the fund's overall investment strategy, and is within the legal guide-lines.

One of the major concerns for many contemplating a SMSF: the fear of penalties from the ATO if a trustee fails to follow the rules. Relatively speaking, the regulations for SMSF are not as complex as those for managed super funds because the SMSF members and the trustees are one and the same. Therefore, the trustee is unlikely to knowingly make mistakes or do anything illegal that may have a negative impact on the performance of their super fund. On the other hand, the rules for the trustees of the managed super funds are more complex, since they are responsible for the retirement savings of a much larger pool of members and may not necessarily be members themselves.

As such, the ATO has tended to take a more conciliatory approach in their dealings with trustees of SMSF. When trustees make small mistakes like failing to keep paper work up to date for tax purposes or don't pay dividend income into the correct account, the ATO tends to work with them to fix the problem rather than taking legal action and imposing stiff penalties. However, if you do something illegal, you can be sure that the ATO will eventually catch up with you.

Even with the conciliatory stance of the ATO, some trustees have taken the step to outsource compliance issues to third parties such as solicitors, accountants and DIY specialists like Super Concepts. Whilst this may add to the ongoing cost of managing the SMSF, it can free the trustees up to do what they do best, which is to manage their superannuation without the worry of compliance.

Small APRA funds (SAF)

The small APRA funds (SAF) on the other hand are regulated by APRA. Unlike the SMSF, the investors aren't the trustees of the fund. But unlike the managed super funds, the SAF members can provide the trustee with an investment strategy and the trustee then has the responsibility to carry it out on their behalf, including compliance issues. The trustee assumes all the accounting and reporting obligations for the member.

Approved trustees are professional trustee companies that are required to meet stringent financial and regulatory criteria set down by APRA. You can find a list of approved trustees at APRA's web site (www.apra.gov.au) and follow the links to the superannuation page.

Superannuation mastertrusts

The final instalment of the DIY trilogy is the superannuation mastertrust offered by the likes of BT Funds Management and AMP. With a mastertrust, the fund manager is the trustee and members are offered a broad range of investments into which they can deposit their super. However, while the choice is wide, it's not as wide as that of a SMSF. For instance, mastertrusts don't invest in direct property nor do they invest in exotic ventures such as ostrich farms! BT, for instance, offers members a choice of investments from the Top 100 shares traded on the ASX, in addition to 80 managed funds. Whilst mastertrusts don't offer the same level of control as a SMSF, or even a SAF, it's still a higher level than you get with the retail or public super funds.

Similar to the other DIY funds, the mastertrusts offer you choice, while removing the worry associated with compliance issues and other paperwork. Though the costs aren't as competitive as that for the SMSF, BT Funds Management's Mastertrust charges 2.5% on a $200,000 investment – which covers all compliance work and the trustee's fee.

Giving up some control for greater peace of mind in uncertain times is another major attraction of superannuation mastertrusts. Letting the professionals call the shots makes very good sense for many investors with neither the time nor the qualifications to monitor the impact that factors like a slowing economy, interest-rate changes and currency fluctuations have on their superannuation savings.

Currently, most superannuation mastertrusts are only available through financial planners like Count Financial and Lonsdale, as the trustees don't offer them directly to the public.

No matter which type of DIY super fund they choose, more individuals and families want to take at least some control of their superannuation. DIY super funds provide the opportunity to do this, whilst offering a tax-effective investment environment like all super funds. They also offer cost savings, flexibility in relation to managing compliance issues, and a greater range of investments for your superannuation savings.

SUPERANNUATION AND TAX
High-income superannuation surcharge

The Superannuation Contributions Surcharge is a tax on 'surchargeable' superannuation contributions. It was introduced in August 1996 and only applies to higher-income earners – those who have an adjusted taxable income that is above the superannuation surcharge's lower threshold amount. The adjusted taxable income is usually calculated by adding the member's taxable income to their superannuation contributions.

The adjusted taxable income lower surcharge threshold was set at $70,000 from 20 August 1996. The lower threshold amount is indexed to general salary increases and is currently $81,493 for 2000–2001. For every $1,000 you earn over $81,493, the surcharge adds an extra 1% to your super contributions tax until you reach $98,955. At this point you'll pay 15% – meaning that someone on this salary or above will pay 30% on their super contributions. If your adjusted taxable income is below the lower surcharge threshold there is no surcharge payable.

The thresholds are indexed annually as set out in the following table.

Superannuation Contributions Surcharge Thresholds, 1996–2001

Financial year	Surcharge minimum threshold	Surcharge maximum threshold
1996/97	$70,000	$85,000
1997/98	$73,220	$88,910
1998/99	$75,856	$92,111
1999/2000	$78,208	$94,966
2000/2001	$81,493	$98,955

Source: ATO

There has been a lot of debate about whether higher-income earners should be burdened with this surcharge. My position has always been that they are already slugged with high-income tax. If this surcharge applies to you, you're probably not comfortable paying this tax, but think of it this way: paying 47% in income tax, plus the Medicare levy if you take the money home is much worse than paying the surcharge which can be a maximum of 30%.

From a tax planning point of view, how you manage your income levels will be very important to minimising the impact of the surcharge. I would contact a financial planner or an accountant and talk to them about the best way to minimise the impact of the tax.

SPOUSE SUPER

You should try and take advantage of the rules relating to spouse super. Taxpayers can claim an 18% tax rebate on superannuation contributions of up to $3,000 made on behalf of their low-income or non-working spouse. The maximum rebate allowed is $540.

To be eligible to claim the full rebate your spouse must

411

be receiving $10,800 or less in assessable income a year, although a reduced rebate is payable for spouses earning up to $13,800 assessable income per annum.

A 'spouse' includes another person who, although not legally married to you, lives with you on a bona fide domestic basis as your husband or wife, but does not include a person who lives separately and apart from you on a permanent basis.

So, if you can cut your tax bill by up to $540 and make an investment for your spouse, it's certainly worth considering.

SUPER AND DIVORCE

The proposed introduction of the Federal Government's Family Law Amendment (Superannuation) Bill potentially opens the door to superannuation tax breaks. However, as my colleague Anthony O'Brien wrote in the January 2001 edition of *Money Magazine*, it does seem a real pity that you have to visit the divorce court in order to take full advantage of the thousands of dollars due to be freed up by the new legislation.

The aim of this new Superannuation Bill is to provide separating or divorcing couples with the capacity to split their superannuation entitlements. In its current form, the focus is solely on couples facing this unpleasant predicament, and so it seems that the Government may be missing a great opportunity to simplify and broaden the attraction of superannuation for all couples, not just those facing divorce.

The law, as it stands, doesn't allow a couple (married or separated) to split superannuation entitlements between them. This seems rather unusual given that couples generally share ownership of most things like the family home, bank accounts and other investments. The problem with this situation is that in many cases women are far more likely to take time out of the work force, or work part-time to look after children or other family members. Such a broken employment pattern reduces the period in which super benefits can be accumulated and, therefore, the size of the end benefit. In other words, men tend to accrue more super than women do.

But this is only part of the issue. By not splitting these entitlements, couples going through a divorce end up paying far more in lump sum tax than they should have to pay. Currently, if you wait until you're 55 to retire, you can take your superannuation entitlement as a lump sum. The benefit of taking a lump sum is that you now have full control of your money and you are free to invest it as you wish. If you decide on taking a lump sum, the first $100,696 is tax-free. The amount above this tax-free threshold and up to $506,092 is taxed at 15% (plus the Medicare levy).

Now, if a couple could split their superannuation money, they could both take advantage of the $100,696 tax-free threshold and pay only 15% on any superannuation up to $506,092. They would also maintain control of their money rather than having it tied up in allocated pensions. You don't have to be a genius to work out that this could save you some serious money (perhaps tens of thousands of dollars).

Due to the restrictions in the way that the law is currently written, these options are not available as yet. But under the Government's proposed Superannuation Bill, couples deciding to divorce or separate will be able to split their money and take advantage of all the great tax breaks and benefits mentioned above.

SHOULD I TAKE A LUMP SUM OR A PENSION?

One of the biggest choices you need to make prior to retirement is whether you take your superannuation in one single

413

cheque, known as a 'lump-sum payment' or as a 'pension' paid for by your employer.

The first step in making this decision is to analyse your employer's pension scheme. Take a close look at it and see whether it is indexed to inflation. This is important because if the cost of living rises (as it will) your pension needs to rise accordingly. Also be sure that you understand what happens to it if you die. Is it 'reversionary', meaning it will then be paid to your spouse for the rest of their life? You also need to find out if your money is paid to your estate in the event of both you and your spouse dying at the same time.

By taking a pension you know how much you'll get every payment (usually monthly). Those paid to public servants are also government guaranteed. That's the good stuff. However, choosing a pension means that:

- you lose control of your money
- your monthly income can be less than if you had invested the money yourself
- in many cases, you won't ever have the chance to take a lump sum again or leave it to your heirs (if that's important to you)
- you're hampered by the set annuity payout schedule that prevents you from taking out larger sums for an emergency.

By choosing a lump sum, on the other hand, you don't have these issues to deal with and you get everything you're entitled to from your company's pension plan, even if you die early in your retirement.

The catch is that by taking a lump sum payment you don't have the same level of security that is offered by a pension. You must be prepared to provide for your own monthly income – for the rest of your life. The prospect of losing this money can be too much for many people, so they choose the pension option.

Most private enterprise schemes only offer a lump sum at retirement, but, believe me, if offered, I'd be very tempted by a guaranteed monthly payment, linked to inflation and reversionary to my spouse. This provides certainty, no hassles and a regular income. And remember a good each-way bet may be to take part pension and part lump sum.

At this point, you might consider rolling some or all of your superannuation into a managed superannuation fund, a 'Do it Yourself' (DIY) super, or a lifetime pension or annuity.

CONTRIBUTIONS

Superannuation funds can accept both Eligible Termination Payments (ETPs) and contributions. ETPs are a payment from a superannuation fund, approved deposit fund or employer to a person upon resignation, retrenchment, disablement, death or retirement. Sometimes such payments can be taken in cash, at other times they must be rolled over. We will discuss this in more detail in the following section.

Contributions refer to the regular payments of money made by you, the employee, into a super fund during your working life. This is a similar process to making regular investments in managed funds. In the superannuation context, this is called 'salary sacrificing'.

As discussed earlier, salary sacrifice is an amount of pre-tax salary that an employee decides to contribute to super or allocate to a fringe benefit, such as a car, instead of taking as cash salary. As we've seen, salary sacrificing is one of the most tax-effective ways to add to your super. You need to ask your employer if they will allow you to invest your before-tax dollars into super through salary sacrifice. Remember that salary that is sacrificed can't be withdrawn from the super fund until retirement.

ROLLING OVER YOUR BENEFITS

As I have said many times, I have plenty of sympathy for those people who tell me that super is too hard to understand, that the system changes too much, and that they want their money out of it. However, there are definite benefits of rolling over your Eligible Termination Payment (ETP) and staying in the super system. These include:

- The lump sum tax isn't paid, therefore, you have more money working for you.
- You continue to pay a maximum tax rate of 15% on investment earnings in lump sum rollovers to, for example, approved deposit funds or deferred annuities, and zero tax if you rollover into an annuity or pension.
- If you continue to rollover until you turn 55, your lump sum tax on taking the money drops quite significantly.

But what are your rollover options? You can rollover into:

- another superannuation fund
- an approved deposit fund (ADF)
- a deferred annuity (DA)
- an allocated pension or annuity
- a lifetime pension or annuity
- a term-certain annuity.

Following is a brief description of some of these options.

- *An approved deposit fund (ADF) and deferred annuity (DA)* are concessionally taxed investment funds for superannuation monies. They are similar to a superannuation fund, however an ADF can only accept ETPs and rollovers and doesn't allow contributions. For this reason superannuation funds have become more popular. There's not a huge difference between approved deposit funds and deferred annuities. It really depends who is offering them. Many banks, fund managers and credit unions offer ADFs, whereas life insurance companies and friendly societies offer DAs. You can invest in an ADF or DA until you're 65.

- *An allocated pension or annuity* is a retirement income investment. An individual invests their super money and receives an income periodically. The value of the account depends on the investment earnings and the amount of income taken. The capital is accessible and the income is flexible. There is no guarantee that the income will be paid for life.
- *A lifetime pension or annuity* (also known as 'immediate annuities') are retirement income investments. An individual invests their superannuation or other money and receives an income periodically. The capital is not accessible, and there is little income flexibility. The payments are guaranteed to be made for the person's lifetime and the amount of income you get depends on your age, sex and the interest rate at the time you bought the policy. You can go for a lifetime annuity but I'd suggest you'd want to be in good health when you buy it. With traditional lifetime annuities, if you buy it one day and die the next all your money is lost.
- *A term-certain annuity* is similar to a lifetime annuity. The major difference is that payment is guaranteed for a fixed period. If you bought a ten-year annuity one day and died the next, your estate would receive the annuity payment for the next ten years. This is a much better result for your beneficiaries.

For more information on which is the best rollover option for you, I suggest you talk to a financial planner.

CONCLUSION

Despite all the complexity and constant changes, superannuation still stacks up as an effective way of saving for our retirement because it ensures that we set aside a percentage of our earnings. It is also tax effective and most decent super funds generally invest in quality, long-term asset classes, such as shares and property. And finally, probably the best thing about super is that you can't touch it until you retire.

There are two battles still to be fought with those who control our super. One is to simplify it, the second is to win the right for all of us in super to have genuine choice about how our money is invested. I'll keep you in touch with developments in these areas on my 'Money' program and in *Money Magazine*.

chapter 14

PENSIONS

Australia was one of the first countries in the world to introduce a government-provided age pension. Tens of thousands of single men from around the world had flocked to Australia during the gold rushes of the 1850s and 1860s. Few struck it lucky, and most ended up doing labouring work, and as they aged, they found they had no savings or families to support them. By the 1890s the proportion of aged people began to increase dramatically. Convict transportation had ended 30 years before and other immigration had stalled. The depression and strikes of the 1890s left many unemployed and homeless – and a vast number of these people were too old to work. Remember in those days, the average life expectancy was around 50 years, compared with today's 80 years. Jails were packed with the elderly and destitute as the private charities could not handle the numbers.

Due to this social crisis, the community appealed to the colonial governments (remember, this was before Federation) for support and aid. Consequently, the New South Wales Colonial Government introduced a government-funded social security scheme in 1900 and Victoria and Queensland followed suit during the next decade. The New South Wales scheme was based on the first-ever model of a government-funded pension introduced in the 1880s by Germany's famous 'Iron Chancellor', Otto von Bismarck, who is better known for subduing the French than for his concern for social policy.

For most of the twentieth century, Australians didn't view retirement as something that they needed to plan or save for. There was always the expectation that once you finished working, the Federal Government would step in and pay you the age pension. For many, it was the final reward for paying taxes all their working days. As is the case today, life on the pension had to be frugal, but people's lifestyle expectations in retirement were remarkably low for most of the 1900s. But how things have changed!

According to the ABS, in 1997 some 74% of people 65 years and over were dependent on government pensions and allowances for their principal source of income. The problem is that today we are retiring earlier, living longer and expecting a much higher material standard of living than a century or even half a century ago, so we are looking at a time bomb of significant proportions.

But, please don't feel depressed if you are already retired or are close to retirement and have saved very little. After all, Australians have never been great savers and the current generation of retirees were never asked to save. It's only in the last few years that we have started to understand the importance of saving. What this chapter intends to do is to look at the best way of making your pension income work for you.

WHO CAN GET THE AGE PENSION?

To get the age pension, you must be an Australian resident and in Australia on the day you lodge your claim with Centrelink. Moreover, to qualify for residency status, you must have been an Australian resident for a total of at least ten years and have had at least one stay of five years. For instance if you came to Australia in 1980 and lived overseas every second year from that time onwards, then you wouldn't be eligible to get the age pension. If you are a man, you must be aged 65 and over. If you are a woman, your age will depend on when you were born. (The age pension qualifying age for women has been progressively increased from 1 July 1995. From 1 July 1997 the qualifying age for women was extended to 61 and will increase by an additional six months every two years until it reaches 65 in July 2013.)

Entitlement to the Age Pension for Women Aged 61.5 or Over

Women born between	Eligible for age pension at age
1 July 1935 and 31 December 1936	60.5
1 January 1937 and 30 June 1938	61
1 July 1938 and 31 December 1939	61.5
1 January 1940 and 30 June 1941	62
1 July 1941 and 31 December 1942	62.5
1 January 1943 and 30 June 1944	63
1 July 1944 and 31 December 1945	63.5
1 January 1946 and 30 June 1947	64
1 July 1947 and 31 December 1948	64.5
1 January 1949 and later	65

Source: Centrelink

There are a few exemptions to this situation. Australia has reciprocal agreements with some countries (such as Austria, Canada, Cyprus, Ireland, Italy, Malta, Netherlands, Portugal and Spain) that may count towards Australian residence. You should contact Centrelink on 13 16 73 if you require information about this.

You may also qualify for an exemption if you arrived as a refugee or via a special humanitarian program or you were widowed in Australia when both you and your late husband were Australian residents and you have 104 weeks' residence immediately prior to making a claim. You are also exempt if you were receiving the widow pension, widow allowance, mature-age allowance, or partner allowance immediately before qualifying for the age pension.

BASIC RATES OF PAYMENT

Pension Rates, July 2000

Status	Pension rate (per fortnight)
Single	$394.10
Couple	$382.90 each

Source: Centrelink

Be advised that payment rates change on a regular basis and, therefore, to ascertain the latest rates and eligibility criteria you should telephone Centrelink on 13 23 00 or visit a Centrelink office. You could also visit its web site at www.centrelink.gov.au.

AGE-PENSION BENEFITS

All age pensioners and those on the mature-age allowance can get a Pensioner Concession Card to access Commonwealth, State and local government, and some private organisation concessions. Benefits of the card include:
- discount fares on Great Southern Rail services
- free mail redirection from Australia Post if you change address

- free eyesight tests from optometrists that bulk-bill Medicare
- free hearing aids
- discounts on chemist bills.

One valuable benefit is the Health Care Card which entitles the holder to prescription medicines generally at $3.30 a script (the normal cost is around $16) offered by the Pharmaceutical Benefits Scheme (PBS) if your taxable income is less than $40,000, or under $67,000 for a couple. Both figures are indexed to inflation. After spending $171.60 in a calendar year, the card holder and dependents are entitled to free PBS medicines for the rest of that calendar year (purchases must be recorded on a Prescription Record form).

There is also a Telephone Allowance which is paid every three months with your pension or benefit if you have a home phone in your (or your partner's) name. Also, the State/ Territory and local governments chip in to provide additional concessions such as reduced property and water rates if you are a householder; possible reductions on your energy bills (gas or electricity); reductions on public transport fares; and reductions on motor vehicle registration charges.

You may be able to get other concessions so it is certainly worth asking your local council about pensioner's and senior's benefits.

RENT ASSISTANCE

Rent assistance is another Federal Government funded scheme that is available to most people receiving social security payments. Rent assistance isn't generally used to pay the whole rent, but is used to make up the difference between what you can afford and what the landlord is asking you to pay. It's not paid to those who are in government housing, but can be used to assist in paying for the rent on a house, unit or townhouse, site fees for a caravan, tent or mobile home; retirement village (if you aren't considered an owner) or nursing home fees.

Rent Assistance

Family situation	Maximum payment per fortnight	No payment if fortnightly rent is less than	Maximum payment if fortnightly rent is more than
Single, no dependent children	$85.00	$73.80	$187.13
Single, sharer, no dependent children	$56.70	$73.80	$149.40
Couple, no dependent children	$79.80	$120.20	$226.60
One of a couple who are separated due to illness, no dependent children	$85.00	$73.80	$187.13
One of a couple who are temporarily separated, no dependent children	$79.80	$73.80	$180.20
Single, 1 or 2 children	$99.20	$97.00	$229.27
Single, 3 or more children	$112.20	$97.00	$246.60
Couple, 1 or 2 children	$99.20	$143.60	$275.87
Couple, 3 or more children	$112.20	$143.60	$293.20

Source: Centrelink

MEANS TESTING

Right up until the early 1980s there was no means test on income or assets. Every male over 65 and female over 60 received a pension. But the ageing population proved too great a drain on government money, so initially an income test was introduced. Very sensibly, retirees switched to growth assets to avoid this test (there was also no capital gains tax at this time). Soon afterwards the government introduced an assets test, and very cleverly said that you would be judged under both tests and the lowest payment would be made to you.

So, any entitlement to the age pension is subject to means testing, and this is done by a separate valuation of any income you might earn and any assets you might own. Assets include shares, bonds, investment property, managed funds, the present value of any life insurance policy, cars, furniture, and so on.

To be eligible for a full pension, you have to earn less than $106 a fortnight for a single and $188 a fortnight for a couple. If you earn more than this, you can still earn a part pension, with the level of pension decreasing as your earnings increase. To get a part pension you have to earn less than $1,105.75 per fortnight if you are single and $1,847 if you are married. You also have to qualify by owning less than a certain amount of assets (such as money in the bank, a car, furniture, shares, and suchlike).

The limit on assets for a single person who owns their own home and is on a full pension is $133,250, for a couple it is $189,500. To be eligible for the part pension, a single person owning their home must have less than $266,750 whilst a couple must have less than $411,000 in other assets. Note that under the assets test, the home you live in and own is excluded from the calculations until you sell it.

Thresholds are set higher for non-homeowners and range from less than $228,750 of assets for a single person on a full pension to less than $285,000 for a couple; and for those on a part pension the limits are less than $362,250 of assets for a single person to less than $506,500 for a married couple.

One of the most common questions I am asked is: How do I value my household contents? Well, don't forget it's not the insured value. It's the price you'd get if you flogged your clothes and furniture to a second-hand goods company, or in a garage sale. In other words, not much!

The assets test
Assets Test for Homeowners

Family situation	For full pension/Allowance	For part pension
Single	up to $133,250	less than $266,750
Partnered (combined)	up to $189,500	less than $411,000

Source: Centrelink

Assets Test for Non-Homeowners

Family situation	For full pension/Allowance	For part pension
Single	up to $228,750	less than $362,250
Partnered (combined)	up to $285,000	less than $506,500

Source: Centrelink

Assets over these amounts reduce the pension by $3 per fortnight for every $1,000 above the limit (single and couple combined).

The income test

From July 2000 you were permitted to earn the amounts listed in the following table, per fortnight, in order to qualify for the age pension under the income test.

Income over these amounts reduces the rate of pension payable by 40 cents in the dollar (single), 20 cents in the dollar each (couple). So if you are a couple and earn up to $48,022, you are eligible for a part pension, while a single person can earn up to $28,749.75 and still earn a small pension.

Earnings Permitted to Qualify for Age Pension

Family situation	For full pension (per fortnight)	For part pension (per fortnight)
Single	up to $106	less than $1,105.75
Single + 1 child	up to $130.60	less than $1,130.35
Couple (combined)	up to $188	less than $1,847.00
Additional children	add $24.60 per child	

Source: Centrelink

Deeming

Under the income test, 'income' includes normal things such as salaries and wages, rent, interest and dividends. But I'm afraid to say that there's more. There's also income that's 'deemed' to have been earned from a wide range of financial assets such as bank, building society and credit union accounts; term deposits; managed funds; shares; loans and debentures; gold and superannuation investments. Deeming was introduced in 1991 to discourage retirees from putting all their money into low or zero-interest savings accounts. They were doing this to keep their earnings low to make sure that they qualified for the pension. To discourage this the Government decreed that these low-return investments were 'earning' more interest than they actually were, based on a prescribed interest rate known as 'the deeming rate'. The key point being that the theoretical income earned from these investments was included under the terms of the income test for the age pension.

The current deeming rules commenced in July 1996. Before July 1996, there were numerous income test rules for different types of financial investments and it was all very confusing. At the time, an independent review of the income test reported that pensioners and pensioner organisations had major concerns about the complexity of these rules,

427

particularly the 'rate of return' rules used to assess income from shares and managed investments. There was also concern about the frequent changes the rules caused to pension payments. The report of the review recommended that a broad deeming approach be adopted.

As the Commonwealth Department of Family and Community Services made clear in July 2000, deemed income is worked out by adding together the values of a person's 'financial assets'. The first $31,600 of the total value ($52,600 for pensioner couples and $26,300 where one of the couple is eligible for the pension and the other isn't) is deemed to earn 3.5% as income, while any amount over $31,600 ($52,600 for pensioner couples) is deemed to earn 5.5%. The actual income earned from financial assets is not counted.

To illustrate this, a single pensioner with $100,000 worth of managed funds is deemed to be generating $4868 annual income for the purposes of the income test, calculated thus:

$31,600 × 3.5%   = $1,106
$68,400 × 5.5%   = $3,762
Total deemed income = $4,868 ($187.23 per fortnight)

Once the deeming income has been worked out it is added to any other income sources (such as wages, rents or interest payments). The total income is then used to determine the amount that can be paid under the income test.

The Minister for Family and Community Services sets the deeming rates and they are monitored regularly, taking into account factors such as market returns on retail financial investments while minimising disruptions to pensioners caused by frequent or minor changes to the deeming rates.

STRATEGIES FOR MAXIMISING YOUR PENSION

A longstanding and well-respected industry figure whom I have known for nearly twenty years is Harold Bodinnar. In his book, *More Money for Your Retirement*, he talks about the 'Means Test seesaw' and how most age-pension applicants have either high assets or high income, one of which either invalidates or reduces their claim to a full or part pension.

Bodinnar recommends evening out the pension seesaw to obtain a much higher income (by thousands of dollars annually in some cases) by reducing the assets counted and the income counted. A number of strategies are available which can result in investors becoming eligible for social security benefits, or in qualifying for higher benefits than they might otherwise. Just a word of warning. Social Security legislation is constantly changing, so ensure that your financial adviser has up-to-date knowledge of the rules that affect these strategies, so that you are able to maximise your income.

The keys to maximising your pension entitlements in retirement or semi-retirement are:
- gifting and deprivation
- funeral bonds
- life-expectancy annuities.

Gifting and deprivation

Under the assets test, the home you live in and own is excluded from the calculations until you sell it. Shares, bonds, investment property, managed funds, and the present value of any life insurance policy are all included in the assets test.

All assessable assets like cars and furniture are valued at their present market value rather than at the price that you paid for them. Additionally, if there is a loan outstanding on an asset, the current market value of the asset less the outstanding amount of the loan is assessable.

429

For those of you thinking that giving away some of your assets might be a way around the assets test, think again. Currently you can give away assets up to the value of $10,000 in any twelve-month period without affecting your entitlement to the age pension under the means test. The government doesn't care how much you give away to family and friends, but it's very important that you are aware of the consequences of doing this.

If you give away more than $10,000 worth of assets in any twelve-month period, the value of the 'gifted' assets in excess of $10,000 will be added on to the value of your other financial investments and be subject to evaluation under the 'deprivation' regulations.

Take the following example: Imran and Rose are on a full pension. They own a roomy three-bedroom house with a study and big garden that has become too hard to look after. Youssef, their son, lives in a townhouse that has become too small for him and his growing family. Imran, Rose and Youssef decide that the best solution for all concerned is to swap homes without any exchange of money. Imran and Rose's house is valued at $350,000: that is $110,000 more than Youssef's townhouse valued at $240,000.

If Imran and Rose had sold their house for $350,000 and purchased a townhouse or apartment unit for $240,000, they would have for argument's sake $110,000 (actually rather less due to the agent's commission) left to invest or spend. Exchanging houses valued at these amounts has meant that Imran and Rose have not received the true market value on the sale of their home. So, given the gifting limit is $10,000, this amount is taken off the $110,000 leaving $100,000 which will be treated as an additional financial asset and will be deemed to be earning interest.

Gifting amounts to relatives in the years prior to your retirement can be another way of enabling your eventual access to the age pension. But I recommend that if you are considering such a strategy, you should talk to a financial adviser to ensure you get maximum results.

Funeral bonds

Although many of us don't like thinking about it, putting some money away for our funeral can actually help us earn extra money from the age pension. Companies such as IOOF and Australian Unity offer investors managed investments known as 'funeral bonds' that are set up with this purpose in mind. Funeral bonds are investments that let us put aside some money for our funerals in advance. Research from IOOF indicates that the average policy expectancy of these bonds is about seven years (meaning that on average people die seven years after purchasing the funeral bonds).

To make this investment option attractive, the Federal Government lets us invest up to a maximum of $5,000 per person (or $10,000 per couple) which is exempted from the assets and income test. The Government has chosen a figure of $5,000 as being the average cost of a 'reasonable' funeral – whatever that may be. Emile Blazzetti from IOOF says that there is a proviso to this $5,000 limit. Some people may choose to hand over the complete responsibility for their funeral to a funeral director. Not only does this mean the organisation of a casket, flowers, church and cemetery are taken out of your hands and your family's, but moreover the funeral bond is transferred to the funeral director. If this service costs a bit more (say $7,500), then you can arrange a funeral bond for this amount. The funeral director can't touch the money until you die and your estate is duty bound to carry out the funeral at the prearranged cost or pay more for extras. The Department of Social Security will apply what they call the 'test of reasonableness' to see if your claim for an exemption on the income earned by the $7,500 invested in this funeral bond is justified. Much more than about $8,500 and the Department will probably reject your application.

According to Harold Bodinnar, a couple on a part pension investing $10,000 in funeral bonds – which is exempt from means testing – could earn about $780.00 per annum extra in age-pension payouts. This could go towards paying for a very nice annual holiday interstate or, if you are not a traveller, several cases of very nice red wine, meals out, clothes or whatever.

You can make an initial investment in funeral bonds for as little as $500 and additional lump sum investments of at least $500, or you can top up your investment with regular monthly contributions from as little as $50. As far as investments go, funeral bonds are quite secure. The fund manager invests the majority of your money in cash and government bonds – just be sure to choose large and reputable firms.

Generally funeral bonds don't pay interest on your investments but pay a bonus, which could be as much as 5%. Funeral bonds generally return in the range of 1.5% to 3% more than inflation. Because you can't touch these investments, any interest is delivered to you as an annual bonus that is reinvested each year. When the 'time' comes and there is money left over in the fund after paying for your funeral, any surplus money is paid back to your estate. So if you invested $5,000 in Year 1 by Year 7 your investment would have grown to about $7,050. If your funeral cost $6,050, then your estate would receive a $1,000 cheque for the balance. Your estate can spend this windfall any way it chooses, not necessarily at the funeral parlour!

Previously there was no tax on the bonuses, but since 1 July 2001, funeral bonds will be taxed at 30%. This new tax has been imposed on all policies dated after December

1999, which according to IOOF will leave you with around $700 less to spend on a funeral if the policy runs the average seven years. All policies dated before December 1999 will continue to be tax-exempt. This, of course, has no impact on the deeming exemptions enjoyed by funeral bonds.

There are some other fairly obvious reasons why funeral bonds can be a good idea. Funerals can be a stressful time for the people we leave behind and expenses run into thousands of dollars these days. Some funeral bonds link you up with a funeral director of your choice who can help you pre-plan your funeral to suit your personal, cultural or religious wishes. This reduces some of the impact that a family experiences at a difficult time.

Life-expectancy annuities

An annuity is a regular income paid to you by a financial institution (such as AMP, MLC or AXA) in exchange for a lump sum. The income stream received is a combination of return of capital and investment earnings. A life-expectancy annuity pays you a regular income just like a wage or salary for a fixed period (namely, the period of time you are expected to live based on your age at commencement).

Life-expectancy annuity policies can range from one to twenty years. So if you're 65 and female you might consider a 20-year policy, but of course it all depends on how good your health is. With healthier lifestyles, better medical knowledge and procedures, many 65-year-old females can today expect to live to between 80 and 85 years old.

You can invest as much money as you want and, apart from the tax benefits, life expectancy annuities are exempt under the assets and incomes mean test. Whilst life expectancy annuities offer retirees a regular and guaranteed income for a fixed period of time, this can be good if interest rates go down, but disastrous if they climb, because you are

433

Years of Life Expectancy

Age as at 31 December 1998	Male	Female
40	38.05	42.73
45	33.39	37.95
50	28.80	33.25
55	24.37	28.67
60	20.18	24.25
65	16.32	20.01
70	12.86	16.01
75	9.85	12.34
80	7.32	9.13
85	5.37	6.52
90	4.05	4.61
95	3.34	3.41

Source: ABS

locked in at an interest rate on the day you invest. Policy period (often ten years) is a major problem if you drop dead a short while after you buy an annuity, which is why they are not a terribly popular option. Death is a bit of a gamble!

Let's look at a case study from *More Money for Your Retirement* by Harold Bodinnar, Managing Director of Harold Bodinnar and Associates.

Case study 1

Bev and Tom are a retiree couple with their own home (say, $750,000 in Sydney, but could be of any value) aged 65 and 64 (i.e. both are eligible for the Age Pension provided the assets test is not over $407,000).

They have $500,000 in the bank, plus house contents of $10,000 and a car worth $20,000 (also wholesale price, not retail – car may have cost, for example, $27,000 new, but wholesale value would be closer to $20,000). Therefore, their total assets are $530,000.

If, they are self-funded with money in the bank, they will earn approximately $20,000 per annum at 4% or $25,000 at 5%, pay a small amount of tax and not receive any concession cards.

The following is a summary of suggested alternative investments for this retiree couple that would give them a much better result. (Note that consultation with a financial planner will be necessary as the actual income will usually vary from one client to another.)

Alternative Investments for a Retiree Couple

	Capital invested	Interest rate	Amount	Centrelink assessment income test	
Bank interest	40,000	5%	$2,000	3% deemed	$1,400
Funeral bonds	($10,000)	5%	($500)	Nil	Nil
Allocated pension	$200,000	6.16%#	$12,320	Nil	Nil
Life expectancy annuities (LEA)	$250,000	3%*	$7,500	3%*	$7,500
Investment income	$500,000		$21,820		$8,900
Plus age pension (couple)			$12,000 (estimate)	Asset test investments only $240,000 is counted after LEAs and funeral bonds are exempted	
Retirement income p.a.			$33,820	Tax nil	
Plus return of capital LEA p.a.			$16,666+		
			$50,486		

\# We generally recommend clients take minimum pension, unless there are special circumstances (e.g. where the preservation of capital is not so important) for an individual client.

* Whilst 6% is actual interest rate, Centrelink only takes 3% (i.e. lower than current deeming rates of 3.5% and 5.5% — this can represent a considerable increase in pension if you are being assessed under the Income Test) as average capital invested over fifteen years is $125,000. The fund manager actually prepares the necessary documents for Centrelink.

\+ Would need to spend on house and improvements, trips, gifting and more LEAs, i.e. like recycling your own capital and by doing so receive more pension and therefore more retirement money to live on.

Source: Harold Bodinnar, *More Money for Your Retirement*, Sydney, 2000

Therefore, after-tax income is now $33,820 p.a. plus con-cession card savings of say $1,500 p.a., making it the equivalent of $35,320 p.a. tax-free, compared to $20,000 p.a. and no concessions for self-funded retirees who have all their retirement capital in bank deposits.

In addition to the 6.16% income from allocated pension (first year $12,320 p.a. and then increases each year by a small percentage based on life expectancy), there is likely to be approximately 2% p.a. average growth, i.e. $4,000 annually which could be used for holidays or a new car in the future.

This second case study comes courtesy of the Kilkenny Rose and Associates accounting firm.

Case study 2

Bill is a 66-year old widower who owns his own home and has assets worth $300,000 and earns $18,611 in income from his investments. Despite the fact that he earns less than the income means test limit for the part pension of $28,000, he is not able to claim a part pension because his assets are worth more than the $264,250 assets limit. (If either your assets or your income are above either limit, you can't claim even a part pension.)

Let's look on the next page at a breakdown of his assets and the income that he is earning from these investments.

Being a widower, Bill is keen to leave some money to his two children, Frank and Mary, and therefore he has chosen to draw down the minimum amount he can from his allocated pension. He could draw down $21,519, but has decided that he only wants to draw down $11,111 to make sure that he can leave an inheritance for his children.

Scenario 1

Asset	Asset value	Income	Assessable
Bank account	$10,000	$300	Yes
Fixed interest	$10,000	$600	Yes
Australian share fund	$90,000	$3,600	Yes
Allocated pension	$170,000	$11,111*	Yes
Personal assets	$20,000	$0	Yes
Total	$300,000	$15,611	

* Minimum draw down of capital plus interest (maximum as at 30 June 2001 is $21,519)
Source: Kilkenny Rose and Associates

However Bill, a keen lawn bowler, has heard some of his team mates talking about their financial situation down at the Club and has been convinced that he can do a bit better with his money. So he has decided to seek the advice of a financial planner.

To his surprise, the financial planner helps him structure his investments in such a way that not only is he able to earn more money from his retirement nest egg, but he is also able to earn an extra $1,099 from a part pension.

The financial planner advises Bill that if he withdrew $50,000 from his allocated pension and invested it in a complying term certain annuity (that is exempted from means testing), he could earn as much as $2,677 extra a year. Because this $50,000 was exempt from the means test, he now had only $250,000 in assets that could be tested which also enables him to earn a part pension of $1,099.

Scenario 2

Asset	Asset value	Income	Assessable
Bank account	$10,000	$300	Yes
Fixed interest	$10,000	$600	Yes
Australian share fund	$90,000	$3,600	Yes
Allocated pension	$120,000	$7,843#	Yes
Complying term annuity	$50,000	$4,846*	No
Part pension		$1,099	
Personal assets	$20,000	0	Yes
Total	$300,000	$18,288	

\# Minimum draw down of capital plus interest (maximum as at 30 June 2001 is $15,190)

* Minimum draw down of capital plus interest

Source: Kilkenny Rose and Associates

NEWSTART ALLOWANCE

According to Government statistics from the ABS, most people retire before they qualify for the age pension and probably earlier than they had planned. Unemployed males under the age of 65 and females under the age of 60 (and eventually under the age of 65 by July 2013) may qualify for the Newstart Allowance.

Potential Newstart applicants are means-tested for both income and assets. The test, which gives the lowest benefit, applies. The principle place of residence is not included in the assets test, and there is no limit on its value unless the land is over two hectares. Applicants can earn $60 per fortnight without their entitlement being affected. Entitlements are reduced at varying rates if income above this amount is earned.

Newstart Allowance will not be available if your assets exceed the following amounts:

Single home owner	$133,250
Single non-home owner	$228,750
Married home owner (couple combined)	$189,500
Married non-home owner (couple combined)	$285,000

Source: Centrelink

The basic rates and method of payment are as follows:

Single, 21 or over, no children	$350.80 per fortnight
Single, 21 or over, with children	$379.30 per fortnight
Single, aged 60 or over, after 9 months	$379.30 per fortnight
Partnered (each)	$316.40 per fortnight

Source: Centrelink

MATURE AGE ALLOWANCE

For those experiencing difficulty finding a job and who want to keep working and are over 60 and obviously not yet old enough for the age pension, there is the Mature Age Allowance. There are a number of criteria that you must meet other than the age component. If you worked 20 hours or more for thirteen weeks or more during the past twelve months, you are not eligible. You must be an Australian resident living in Australia and registered for Newstart at the time of your claim. Alternatively, you could have received a Veterans' Affairs service pension, a widow, partner, sickness or parenting allowance at any time within the thirteen weeks immediately prior to claiming; or have previously received the Mature Age Allowance.

The Mature Age Allowance is not activity-tested, and

recipients are therefore not required to look for work or do training. Recipients will have access to labour market assistance to find work if they choose to register with Centrelink. Mature Age Allowance recipients may qualify for a $200 Education Entry Payment if undertaking an approved full-time course of education (or part-time from 1 July 1996).

You might be wondering what's the benefit of moving from Newstart to the Mature Age Allowance. One good reason could be the lump sum advance of up to $500 that Centrelink will pay you when you swap over. This loan is interest-free and is paid back over the next thirteen fortnightly payments. Though it's not a huge amount, it could alleviate some of the immediate financial pressure. Other reasons include getting access to some of the benefits that are available on the age pension – such as the pensioner concession card, the pharmaceutical allowance and possibly the telephone allowance.

chapter 15

EARNING EXTRA INCOME

One of the best things about going overseas on holidays for business or pleasure is knowing that I will be coming back. Don't get me wrong, I enjoy travelling, but I often just can't wait to get back home – especially after a business trip when I haven't been able to take my family with me. And why not? This is such a great country in which to grow up, work, raise a family, and eventually retire. Sometimes, I think it's very easy to take for granted what we have here in Australia: the best beaches; great sport and leisure options; an excellent climate pretty much all year around; and some of the best food and wine in the world.

While you don't need to be wealthy to enjoy some of the trappings of the millionaire's lifestyle when you do retire, an active retirement will cost a bit more. Whether it's an annual trip to one of Australia's multitude of spectacular tourist destinations or a weekly trip to your favourite restaurant or RSL club, you are going to need a bit of extra money to cover the cost of doing these things when you retire. But how much?

We considered this question in Chapter 3 'Planning to be

Free', but if you don't have enough money put aside, don't be deterred. One option is to earn more money. There are a number of ways to earn this extra money. What options you choose will largely depend on the standard of living that you expect to maintain in retirement.

Anecdotal evidence suggests that the baby boomers want to maintain the lifestyle that they have enjoyed through most of their working life. Some experts have estimated that boomers will require up to 80% of their pre-retirement income once they retire (personally, I think about 150% of final income would be ideal!). The pension, which ranges from between 20% and 25% of the average weekly wage, will not be enough for these boomers, and so they will need to consider other ways of earning extra income to fund their retirement. Some will prolong their working lives (which we looked at in Chapter 4 'Careers'), while others will consider starting a small business, working as sole traders or independent workers. So is this a good idea?

IS SMALL BUSINESS THE BEST OPTION?

While I was writing this book, the Federal Government released a report called 'Age Counts'. The report looked at the employment options of mature-age workers (workers over 45 years of age) who either retired or were retrenched. One of the major concerns outlined in the report was that many retrenched workers, some with very limited business skills, were starting up their own businesses. Many mature-age workers see a redundancy package as an opportunity to set up a small business to give them more freedom and let them be their own boss. While the report cautiously supported the small business option, it stated that it was important that people were informed about the risks involved in starting a small business.

Now, I don't need to tell you that going into business is an option for some, but not all, of us. The best thing about starting your own business is the freedom it gives you to do your own thing. This is obviously a great incentive for those of us planning to retire, or wanting a way out of the employment rat race or longing to try out a business idea in which you have confidence. But it's not a licence to print money. Far from it – to make a small business work you need considerable knowledge, skill, management experience, as well as a high level of commitment, plenty of hard work, access to finance, and some good luck. Department of Employment, Workplace Relations and Small Business (DEWRSB) research tells us that self-employed people work longer hours and face greater stress than employees – and the chances of losing a business are greater than losing a job.

My own business

I remember when I started up ipac securities with my four partners in 1983. I gave up a well-paid job, and earned next to nothing for five years, working incredible hours. We used to joke about our 35 hours of work: 35 hours on Monday, Tuesday and half of Wednesday; and then another 35 hours on the rest of Wednesday, Thursday and Friday. You could throw in most Saturdays as well. We tried our best to stay out of the office on Sundays and public holidays and any holiday leave was confined to a few days at Christmas.

Don't get me wrong, a successful business is a good way to create significant wealth, but not every business will grow into a News Corporation or a McDonalds. In fact according to research from the Employment Strategies Council, about 40% of small businesses operate on the brink of closure and only about 3% of small businesses will be hugely successful. But then how you measure success is very difficult and depends on what the individual is setting out to achieve.

Some people chase financial success, but others measure success by the lifestyle and freedom that they enjoy.

Whatever your ambitions are, I recommend that if you are considering setting up a small business that you consider the risks because, as we now know, the failure rate is high.

> Small businesses have increased in number by 56% to almost 900,000 for the period between 1983–84 and 1996–97.

Source: ABS, 'Small Business in Australia', (Cat. No. 1321.0)

REDUCING SMALL BUSINESS HAZARDS
Training

Some of the major obstacles that new businesses tend to encounter include: lack of business skills; lack of access to finance; and lack of relevant advice when the business is being planned. In Germany these issues are directly tackled by allowing only those who have undergone an accreditation process and some form of business management training to register as a business entity.

According to Department of Employment, Workplace Relations and Small Business, less than 50% of mature-age people starting a business have undergone a small-business management training course. This is pretty silly and I would urge more people to undertake training as part of the start-up process – and, no, we are not talking about taking two years to do an MBA at a university management school. There are a number of government-subsidised programs on offer.

In New South Wales for example, Business Enterprise Centres (BECs) run training seminars that begin at $45 for an introductory course. Courses cover topics such as: starting a business; choosing the right business; finance; market research; tax; insurance and business planning. They also offer one-on-one advice with counsellors.

To get more information on the training courses available, contact the Government organisation responsible for small business advice in your State.

Government contacts for small business

Australian Capital Territory
Business Support and Employment
Chief Minister's Department
PO Box 243
CIVIC SQUARE ACT 2608
Tel: 1800 244 650
E-mail: actbg@act.gov.au

New South Wales
Small Business Advisory Services
State and Regional Development NSW
Level 35, Governor Macquarie Tower
1 Farrer Place
SYDNEY NSW 2000
Hotline: 13 11 45
Fax: (02) 9228 3626

Northern Territory
Territory Business Centre
Department of Industry and Business
Ground Floor, Development House
76 The Esplanade
DARWIN NT 0800
Tel: (08) 8924 4280
Hotline: 1800 193 111
Fax: (08) 8924 4290

Queensland
SmartLicence
Department of State Development
Corner Boundary & Fortescue Streets
Spring Hill BRISBANE QLD 4000
Tel: (07) 32211620
Hotline: 1800 061 631
(outside Brisbane metropolitan area)
Fax: (07) 3234 0024
E-mail: Smart.Licence@sd.qld.gov.au

South Australia
The Business Centre
145 South Terrace
ADELAIDE SA 5001
Tel: (08) 8463 3800
Country callers: 1800 188 018
Fax: (08) 8231 1199
E-mail:
business.info@saugov.sa.gov.au

Tasmania
Business Tasmania
Department of State Development
5th Floor, ANZ Centre
22 Elizabeth Street
HOBART TAS 7000
Tel: (03) 6233 5858
Country callers: 1800 005 262
Fax: (03) 6233 5800

Victoria
Small Business Victoria
Level 5, 55 Collins Street
MELBOURNE VIC 3000
Tel: 13 22 15 (local call cost)
Fax: (03) 9651 9725
E-mail: sbv@sbv.vic.gov.au

Western Australia
Small Business Development
  Corporation
553 Hay Street
PERTH WA 6000
Tel: (08) 9220 0222
Country callers: 1800 199 125
Fax: (08) 9325 3981
E-mail: info@sbdc.com.au

A useful web site for finding out about Government support for small business is the Business Entry Point at www.business.gov.au. It provides information on starting up and operating a business, gives employment and taxation advice, outlines codes of practice and provides links to other business sites.

One paradoxical benefit of completing a small-business training course is that it deters some people from embarking on their business. Small business training may reveal that you aren't suited or that venture-market research indicates there really wasn't a good market for your product or service idea, after all.

Access to finance

Typically those who start a small business have only a limited amount of capital in the kitty. This more than anything else can cripple a business before it has time to get established. A 1997 industry report indicated that about 11% of bankruptcies were caused by business failure, whilst an earlier report indicated that 50% of all business bankruptcies occurred within the first two years.

Because of the large numbers of people who take the plunge into small business – according to the ABS, in 1999, there were 930,000 small businesses in Australia – it's almost impossible for governments (both State and Federal) to find the money to help all small businesses in the initial phase. As a compromise, the Federal and most State governments have focussed on providing non-financial support in terms of training programs and ongoing advice to help get small businesses off the ground.

But there are exceptions for those lucky enough to live in the ACT or South Australia, your governments actually offer limited financial assistance. The ACT government provides loans of up to $10,000 at concessional rates, while the South Australian Government provides a $3,000 grant payment for those people who have completed NEIS (New Enterprise Incentive Scheme) training and who are working on a business idea that is innovative and different. Regardless of whether you get government assistance or not, you will need a business plan.

Business planning

A business plan is an outline or road map that can set your business on the course to success. It explains what the business opportunity is, where it is and how it will operate. It includes information about your customers, your employees, and you. It explains something about the industry you will be a part of and briefly describes the market for your product or service. It expresses these things in both words and numbers.

Money Tip

Any business of excellence will have a budget. It is a key to running profitably.

Individuals and families would be significantly better off if they applied basic business principles to their own finances.

The numbers in a business plan are really important because they translate the anticipated activities of the business into a language that anybody involved in business will understand. For example, the numbers in your income statements, balance sheets and cash-flow statements will be of particular interest to your bank manager or other lender when they look at your business plan.

BUYING OR ESTABLISHING A BUSINESS

Let's assume you decide your business idea is viable and you are determined to forge ahead with it. Let's also assume your idea is fairly straightforward and that it could be realised either by establishing a new venture from scratch or by buying a similar existing business and adapting it to your particular vision. There are basically three ways to begin a business:

- purchase an existing business
- invest in a franchise operation, or
- start your own.

There are good reasons for each choice and each carries its own benefits and risks. Most of us, however, will start our own because of the (usually) small initial investment required. Purchasing an existing business or a franchise can require a significant capital investment.

Starting up my own business was one of the best decisions I've made, but you do need to take great care, and seek advice with any business you plan to start or to buy.

BUYING AN EXISTING BUSINESS

For many people buying an existing business sounds like a good way to get started. But this may not always be the best option. Let's talk briefly about some of the important issues involved in buying an existing business.

Good stuff

There are numerous good reasons for buying an existing business, and you can probably think of most of them yourself:

- existing customer base
- established supplier network

- all or most equipment will generally come with the business
- former owner may be willing to advise you (free or for a small fee) on how the business runs
- no need to hunt for business locations, haggle with agents or landlords over lease terms, and so on
- may inherit experienced employees
- business may be profitable sooner than if you were starting a new business
- easier to obtain finance from banks if you can produce records of a successful business
- most of the inventory for operation may come with the business, so you will be able to avoid the headache of ordering everything you need afresh.

Bad stuff

There are also some obvious negatives about buying an existing business, which you have probably thought of already:

- you might inherit a business with a bad reputation, which wasn't apparent at the time of purchase
- old or inefficient plant and equipment
- the former owner, who is now on a plane heading to Majorca, misrepresented the business and got a higher price than the business is worth – a major con!
- the location may not be ideal, forcing you into a costly move
- existing contractual agreements with suppliers and customers may be unfavourable and difficult to renegotiate
- you might inherit difficult employees.

Though this list is not exhaustive, it makes the point that buying a business is a pretty tough task that requires considerable thought and investigation by the potential buyer. You need to know every possible thing about a business before you buy it. You could also think about the following factors when you consider buying a business or not and how much you should pay for it.

Why are they selling?

A crucial issue is: why is the owner selling? An owner trying to unload an unprofitable business may say exactly the same things as one selling a profitable one: 'I'm selling it because I'm getting old', 'I want to explore other options', 'My health is failing'. Don't fall for it. It could be true, but it's very rare for business owners to sell a really successful business to a total stranger. The real reason is generally one that would make you think again about buying the business.

In many cases, the real reason they want to sell is because they are losing money, or think they might in the future. Reasons businesses lose money are numerous. Typical reasons include a change in market trends (a Westfield shopping centre gobbles up all the business from the local strip shops) or the introduction of a new technology (how many record-player technicians would be doing a roaring trade these days?), increased competition, changes in key personnel, or the business is no longer able to obtain the necessary finance to continue operations.

Future profitability

The most crucial component in evaluating the business's value is its future profitability. Of course, you can't always measure future profits exactly, but a rough gauge of what to expect is possible. I would recommend that you start by looking at the past profits of the business. To get a sense of past profits, ask for tax records of the business for the past five to seven years. Ask the seller if you can have a look at the bank statements and auditor's reports, if they are available.

Benchmarking

I try to compare the performance of the business against industry benchmarks. If the business you are interested in buying does not stack up against its competitors, it's important to find out the reasons why, as they'll determine whether you are successful, merely break even, or lose money depending on how well you can improve the business's performance.

Expenses

It's also useful to analyse the expenses (costs) and capital improvements simultaneously. The reason being: low expenses and/or meagre capital investment generally indicate that the owner has not been putting money back into the business, which can be a sign that the business was seen as a poor investment and so the owner was not prepared to invest money in it. On the other hand, if you discover high expenses, this may indicate poor management or that the business is costly to run.

Money in History

350 B.C.

According to the ancient Greek orator Demosthenes 10% was the normal lending rate for run-of-the-mill business in ancient Athens – amazingly close to today's rates. For risky business – such as lending for shipping – rates of between 20% and 30% were more common.

As when buying any other investment (such as shares, managed funds or bonds), financial information like this tells you what happened in the past. However, it is future profits that are your primary interest. Use the past as a reference point for developing your projections about how well the business could do in the future. On top of this, you need to work out what sort of impact your own new ideas can have on the way the business operates. The projection of future profitability will contribute significantly to your decision about whether to buy the business, and it will help you determine a reasonable price to offer.

It is also useful – in fact, I think essential – to get the assistance of an accountant with significant small business experience to have a look at the business, particularly if this is your first business venture. They may help you find flaws if any exist.

FRANCHISING

Franchising is another option for those seeking to earn some extra income in retirement, and is probably better suited to people with limited or no small-business experience or who feel uncomfortable about going into business on their own. If you feel like this, you're not alone: there are over 49,000 franchised outlets across Australia. In fact, we are the most franchised nation per head of population in the world, with at least three times as many franchise outlets per head of population as the USA, where franchising originated.

Supporting the notion that franchising provides the business person with a little more security than a traditional business, industry statistics from the Franchise Council of Australia indicate that franchising enjoys a success rate more than two and half times better than stand-alone small businesses. Each year, only 1% of franchisees shut their doors. The most visible franchises are McDonalds, KFC and Pizza Hut, but there are plenty of other successful franchised businesses (such as couriers, trade exchanges, lawn mowing, domestic home help, real estate, pet care and carpet cleaning). You can pay as little as $7,000 for a franchise that suits you.

Here's the story of Ron Brown, formerly an accountant, who bought a Jim's Mowing franchise in 1998 at the age of 50. We featured Ron on 'Money' and in *Money Magazine* in 2000.

Because Ron was well paid, the decision to leave the corporate world was difficult. However, when Ron sat down and weighed up the benefits of buying a franchise against the ridiculous demands of the corporate world with its long hours and interruptions to home life, the decision almost made itself.

'There's no doubt about it, it was a lifestyle decision,' Ron confirmed. 'I was sick of the long hours and the midnight calls from clients. I wanted some independence and the chance to be my own boss. I didn't want to retire and in reality probably couldn't.' Despite being well paid during his career, Ron hadn't put enough money away, so even though he was over the corporate squeeze, he still needed to earn some extra.

'I actually can't ever see myself retiring. I'm not one for sitting around doing nothing anyway. I work four days a week and mow between five and six lawns a day. That takes around six hours including travel to and from jobs. On the fifth day I go to TAFE and am studying a horticulturist course.' Ron has a keen interest in the environment and is an avid bushwalker. When he finishes the current course, he plans to start a brick-laying course because he wants to add a room to his house. He recently remodelled his kitchen.

Ron paid around $20,000 for his franchise of about 65 customers. Jim's Mowing guaranteed him $800 a week in work if he wanted it. Ron is happy if he earns $150 a day (that works out at around six lawns). He is quite happy working between 25 and 30 hours a week, which gives him the extra money he needs to fund his lifestyle. He is also putting some away for the future.

> *'Like I said, I can't ever see myself retiring completely.*
> *When I get sick of lawn mowing, I'll probably do some part-*
> *time bookkeeping. I really recommend the lifestyle. If I feel*
> *like going for a two-hour lunch I can. I don't answer to*
> *anyone.'*

Advantages of franchising

There are some definite advantages in buying a franchised business. Of course, there are all different kinds of franchises and you need to be aware that some are good and some are not. Some offer fair value for what you pay and others just don't perform – but as the statistics suggest these would appear to be in the minority.

A franchise can get you off to a running start. The franchisor (parent company) has done some of the market research and plenty of the start-up work for you. The main advantages of franchising are the access to the assistance and advice of the franchisor, cooperative marketing, bulk buying, and the use of an established name and image such as Bob Jane T-Marts, Fastway Couriers or 7 Eleven.

Disadvantages

But of course there is a catch. You will have to pay for these benefits. Evaluate whether the benefits are worth the costs to you. Also remember that a franchise is often an on-going relationship that is not always easy to break. You are not totally independent and cannot always do as you please. The franchisor usually has something to say about how you operate your business.

Research is the key. Investigate any franchise thoroughly. Talk with other franchisees. Study the franchise agreement and understand what it says. Get legal or business advice. Look hard before you leap. With more and more retailing being done through the franchise method in Australia, there must be something good about it. But take great care with any franchise, in particular those that are unproved. Even for proven franchises, competition can be intense. Do your research first!

Colonel Sanders

Colonel Sanders was born in 1890 but didn't begin franchising his chicken business until the age of 65. Now, the Kentucky Fried Chicken (KFC) business he started has grown to be one of the largest retail food service systems in the world. And Colonel Sanders, a quick-service restaurant pioneer, has become a symbol of entrepreneurial spirit.

Before he started his franchising business the Colonel had worked as a farm hand, tram conductor, soldier, railroad fireman, lawyer, petrol station owner and finally motel proprietor in the town of Corbin in Kentucky.

It was during his nine years running the motel that he perfected the basic cooking technique that is still used today. However, in the early 1950s a new interstate highway bypassed his shop, forcing him to close his business. After paying his bills, he was reduced to living on his $105 social security cheque.

However, this was just the beginning for Colonel Sanders. Confident of the quality of his fried chicken, he devoted himself to the chicken business and decided to travel across the USA introducing others to his 'secret' recipe by cooking batches of chicken for restaurant owners and their employees. If they liked his cooking, they entered into a handshake agreement with him, whereby they agreed to pay him a nickel for every chicken they sold. By 1964 when he sold his interest in the company for $2 million, Colonel Sanders had more than 600 franchised outlets in the USA and Canada. Not bad for a guy who started out on $105 social security payment from the government!

ESTABLISHING A BUSINESS

All types of people make it in small business and all types fail. There is no personality type or educational level that qualifies or disqualifies anyone from succeeding in small business. Hundreds of thousands of people embark on business ventures every year. It is an individual choice that should be made only after serious study, self-examination, and advice. Preparation is your key to success.

The first thing you need to do is to choose a business activity that you will enjoy. Look at your interests, hobbies, and aptitudes. Don't pick one that has an uncertain market. There are a lot of small business start-ups that are doomed from the beginning because there simply are not enough customers wanting that product or service. If you look in the back of some magazines, you will find many products and services with dubious market potential on offer as businesses.

Avoid overcrowded areas of business. Many localities in major cities for example have far more restaurants, retail stores, petrol stations, and so on than are viable given the population. The same can be true in smaller communities. One of the disadvantages of our free-enterprise system is that there are just too many businesses.

Study the businesses you think you might like. Satisfy yourself that they will suit your needs. There are so many alternatives available – don't be too quick to choose. Just about any business can fail and any can succeed.

Be sure to do a quick feasibility study on the business of your choice before making up your mind for certain. Remember that it needs to work for you, in your situation, in your locality, in your market, and given your special set of circumstances.

If you feel confident about your expertise in and knowledge of your chosen business, then establishing your own business is a real option. You should also have a strong drive to succeed even when the hours get long and the decisions difficult. And you should stop and take stock before getting your business under way.

- Begin with a feasibility study that answers these three questions:
  1 What business am I in?
  2 How much money and skill do I need to be successful?
  3 What will it give me in terms of money and satisfaction?
- Seek advice from the local government organisation responsible for small business in your State (see page 445) or some other organisation that regularly deals with business start-ups.
- Learn as much about your new business as you can: the market; who your customers are; the competition; pricing practices; profit margins; who your suppliers are; and anything else that will help you fully understand your new business.
- If you can, talk to business owners in similar businesses. Even better, work as an employee for a time in such a business, so you can get a better feel for its requirements.
- Talk to suppliers in the industry.
- Read trade publications and magazines dealing with your chosen business.
- Attend seminars and trade shows that deal with subjects important to your business.
- Talk to franchisors doing what you plan to do. Ask them to provide you with any written information that they might have.

After you have completed your research and are comfortable that you have found the right business, you now need to develop a business plan that details what business you are in, how you plan to fund it, and how you will plan to get it off the ground. Once you have a business plan, you

457

can then start to gather the money, equipment and people you need to start. When you have done all of this, you can begin – *but not before*!

10 tips for small business success

1 Learn as much as you can about your proposed business. Ask questions. Join industry associations. Is there a need for the product or service you are going to offer?

2 Accept the fact that starting a business always takes more money than you anticipate.

3 Study successful competitors carefully.

4 Don't go into business with the sole objective of making a lot of money. Chances are you won't. But if you put service, quality, and customer satisfaction first – the money will follow.

5 Be willing to work harder and longer than you have ever worked before. Forget about the 8-hour day and the 40-hour week.

6 Keep complete and accurate records for tax purposes, for your banking needs and, most importantly, for your own guidance.

7 Hire good, experienced employees.

8 Find a lawyer, accountant, banker, and insurance agent and confer with them as needed. Now is the time to develop these relationships.

9 Run it yourself. Beware of absentee ownership. No one will look after your money, your property, and your business like you will.

10 Be prepared for disappointment and frustration. Be persistent and bounce back even more determined to succeed.

Source: BizLink, an initiative of the Australian Federal Government

IS SMALL BUSINESS THE BEST OPTION FOR RETIREES?

According to the Employment Strategies Council a successful small business:

is an activity that meets the costs of sales, pays its taxes, pays its employees their entitlements, sets aside funds for new or updated equipment or software, pays the proprietor a salary or equivalent, provides for a reserve fund for contingency situations and provides a return on investment at least equivalent to the return that can be reliably received from a secure investment (say around 20% before tax).

If your small business can achieve all this, then you are on a winner. More than likely in order to have achieved this, there has been a lot of hard work – and even then you are not guaranteed to succeed.

I mentioned earlier in the chapter that the 'Age Counts' report suggested that many mature-age workers considered small business as a way of replacing lost employment. My position on this is pretty simple, making the decision to start a business solely because you can't find a job is not a great idea. There are other options that might be worth exploring which probably involve a lot less risk overall.

SOLE TRADER

If you conduct a business alone, without a partner, you are classified as a sole trader. Operating as a sole trader requires less business knowledge than running a small business, so if your primary concern is making some extra money to fund your retirement, then working as a sole trader is an option worth exploring.

The advantages of operating as a sole trader are:
- You are entirely your own boss.
- All business profits are yours.
- Any business losses can be offset against any other present and future income you may have.

- It's the cheapest and simplest business structure to establish and maintain.
- Government reporting requirements are less than for other structures.
  The disadvantages of operating as a sole trader are:
- Since you are fully liable for your business's debts, your other assets, including your home, can be put at risk.
- You pay tax on profits at your marginal tax rate – which may be higher than the company tax rate.
- You must pay PAYG tax.
- You are solely responsible for the business, which means there is no one to take over if you need a break.
- You are not paid for sick days or holidays.

INDEPENDENT WORKER – STRESS-FREE MONEY

If you would like to earn extra income up to around $20 an hour and work between three and thirty hours rather than seventy hours a week, you could consider working as an independent worker. The ATO classifies an independent worker as someone who provides specialised home or family-care assistance (such as gardening, cooking, shopping, ironing, chauffeuring, caretaking, pet care and child care) to a client for a fee rather than a wage or salary. Unlike wage and salary earners, independent workers are responsible for their own taxation. Their clients do not need to deduct income tax from the fees paid to them.

Unlike a small business owner, who has to find their own clients, independent workers are referred to clients by agencies. It's worth understanding the role of agencies. The agency puts workers in touch with clients, for which service the agency earns a fee. The agency plays no role in negotiating the details of a job, including payment, that is the responsibility of the client and the worker.

Take, for instance, Dial-an-Angel (a domestic and family-care specialist with offices in Australia and New Zealand that was established over thirty years ago by Dena Blackman, a young working mother who saw a need for home-care help for people like herself). The obvious benefits for an Angel worker are extra income (up to $20 an hour), not needing to set up an office, working when you want to for a nominated number of hours per week (usually between three and thirty, though the very keen can work up to fifty hours!) For example, an Angel could work on Monday and Tuesday and then have the rest of the week off. If you need more money, you can simply call the agency and let it know and it will find you extra work.

The only pre-requisites are past experience, a suitable personality and good communication skills: you need to be able to communicate adequately in English.

According to Dial-an-Angel, the reasons workers sign up include finding extra money to pay for everything from a meal at a restaurant to a holiday away.

While you don't have the same level of responsibilities as a small business owner, or even a sole trader for that matter, there are still a number of things of which you need to be aware. As I said earlier, you are responsible for paying your own tax. Your clients or the agencies will not deduct tax for you. You must therefore keep your books in good order to ensure that everything runs smoothly at tax time. An accountant can help you with this. You should also keep in mind that there's no holiday or sick leave, no workers' compensation or superannuation, but this is a small price to pay for what is effectively stress-free money.

CONCLUSION

As the adage says, 'We don't live to work, we work to live'. If you have worked hard all your life and saved well and invested wisely, then by the time you retire, you'll no doubt be in pretty good shape. However, if you still need to earn some extra income, then small business might be an option you could consider. On the other hand, if this doesn't take your fancy, you could become an independent worker without the stress of business and earn as much as you like as often as you like and when you want.

chapter 16

ESTATE PLANNING

Whether it be famous people like rock star Michael Hutchence or entrepreneur Lang Hancock, it appears that very few of us like to sit around thinking about that time in the future when we can't look after our financial affairs any more. But as the Hutchence and Hancock cases have shown us in recent years, the failure to have an 'estate plan' in place, can cause unnecessary anguish and embarrassment for the loved ones we leave behind.

So what do we mean by 'estate'? Depending on your circumstances, your 'estate' might include a family home, other real estate (like a vacation home), your personal assets (like your car, furniture and family heirlooms) and your intangible assets (such as your insurance, shares, bonds, bank accounts, and superannuation pensions).

An 'estate plan' provides an outline as to how you want your property managed if you are incapacitated by illness while you are still alive, and then how you want your affairs managed after you die. It not only involves the development of a will, but should also include a document called a 'power of attorney' that sets out how you would like your affairs managed should you be incapacitated by illness or dementia. But let's start with the will.

WHAT IS A WILL?

Generally speaking, a will is the last statement that an individual makes regarding the distribution of their assets and liabilities and is effective immediately following their death. The writer of the will is called the testator (male) or testatrix (female). The choices that you can make in deciding how to distribute your estate are virtually limitless.

A person can only make a will if they are eighteen or older (unless married) and are of sound mind at the time of signature of the will. An unmarried person younger than eighteen can make a valid will, however they must obtain the consent of the Supreme Court to do so.

STRUCTURE OF A WILL

The formal requirements for a will have evolved in English legal history since the Norman Conquest in the eleventh century.

Wills begin with the simple statement 'This is the will of . . .' Following such a phrase, it is usual that the 'executor' be named. (An executor is the person who ensures that the details in the will are carried out as the deceased intended. The role and responsibilities of the executor will be discussed later in this chapter.) Instructions then follow as to how any debts should be managed and who will benefit from the deceased's estate. Last but not least, the testator and the witnesses must sign the document to confirm the details outlined in the will.

Other issues that a will may address include: the appointment of a 'testamentary guardian' (a de facto parent) for any dependent children the testator or testatrix may have in their care; directions as to the disposal of the body; whether the body can be used for scientific or medical purposes; clauses expressing general 'wish statements', for example, 'in the administration of my estate I wish that my Executor seek financial advice from . . .'.

From a practical perspective, a will lasts only as long as is necessary. That is to say, if a person's circumstances change, then the will should reflect this. A person should not be burdened with making a will last for many years. If this can be achieved, then great, but generally this is not the case. The cornerstone of any will should be its 'formal requirements'. Without these, it's worth nothing more than the paper it's written on. The primary formal requirements for a valid will are:

- It must be in writing.
- It must be signed by the testator or testatrix at the end of the will.
- The signature of the testator or testatrix must be witnessed by two witnesses both of whom must be present at the time the testator or testatrix signs and each of whom must sign in the presence of the testator or testatrix.

If these requirements are not met an informal or 'invalid will' may still be recognised by the courts, but by following these formal requirements, you will save your family time and hassles getting your will validated. It is important that a witness isn't also a beneficiary or a spouse of any beneficiary named in the will.

As a general rule, I recommend that you update your will regularly. A good time to do this is just after tax time when you have a clearer picture of your financial affairs. This doesn't have to be a formal process, merely a re-evaluation of your current financial position and an assessment of any changes that have occurred. If you do this regularly, it will become habit and you can then be sure that if something happens to you, your will should reflect the current state of your finances.

Money Tip

You've worked too hard for what you've got not to have a will. The majority of Australians don't.

If you die without one, the pain and suffering it can cause is a poor legacy for those you love.

WHO SHOULD DRAFT A WILL?

You can draft your own will. Printed will forms are available from stationers and most newsagents. There is no legal requirement that a will be drafted by a lawyer. But if you choose the do-it-yourself approach and there are significant assets, children who need care, or other complexities, then I recommend that you get a solicitor to review it for you.

The court lists are littered with cases where homemade wills have simply been held to be unclear or invalid. Sadly, many end up in court, causing distress, unnecessary expense and financial hardship.

In general, solicitors do not charge a large fee for making a will. Standard prices for a will can range from $40 to $150. The cost of tax-effective and other specialised wills (which should only be drafted by an experienced solicitor) usually starts at around $1,000.

Your will is probably one of the most important legal documents that you'll ever write. When you consider the value of many 'deceased estates', the cost of having a will professionally drafted to responsibly manage and distribute your estate in a valid fashion is relatively cheap indeed. For example, a standard will costs $100 but can control a

$100,000 estate. This represents a cost to the estate of less than one-tenth of one per cent (0.1%) of its value.

THE EXECUTOR

Being an executor of a will involves administrative duties, important legal responsibilities on behalf of the testator or testatrix, and acting in the best interests of the beneficiaries. The role of the executor involves making sure that the will is valid, that there is only one will, and that the testator or testatrix was of sound mind when the will was written. As a rule, probate must be applied for within six months of the death, unless the estate is small. A probate is a legal document that certifies the validity of a will, and authorises the executor to manage the estate. More on probates follows below.

It is necessary to work out what the deceased's assets and liabilities were, who the beneficiaries are, and whether the deceased married or divorced after the will was made. Except under specific circumstances, marriage automatically cancels an existing will. If you divorce and remarry, this revokes your former spouse's claim to your estate. Once this is all completed and a notice of intention has been published in a newspaper (like the *Sydney Morning Herald* or the *Age*), the executor must distribute the assets according to the instructions in the will.

An executor must be careful, since any delay in carrying out these responsibilities, and which results in loss of income or investment opportunities can lead to legal action being taken by the beneficiaries of the will against the executor. The executor must also keep the beneficiaries informed and ensure that all legal and non-legal costs don't get out of hand.

The role also involves organising the funeral and determining what to do with the body. It is a role that you should not assume lightly and without careful consideration if a friend asks you to be their executor. A spouse should not be named as the executor for their partner since there is the remote likelihood that the couple might die together in an accident. In general, it is best to look for someone who is younger than you are and in good health (that is, pragmatically speaking, someone who is unlikely to pre-decease you).

AVOIDING POTENTIAL CHALLENGES TO A WILL

Challenges against a will are more common than people realise. Most are settled before they reach the courts and with very good reason. For example, the New South Wales Family Provision legislation stipulates that any action taken against the estate must be paid for out of the estate, including costly legal fees – so effectively you are reducing the size of the inheritance pie of which you are seeking a share.

PROBATE

Probate comes from the Latin word *provare* which means 'to prove'. A probate is a document issued by the courts to certify that a will has been validated, and that the executor named in it has the authority to administer the estate. It is quite common for an estate to be 'tied up' until such time as a probate has been obtained. No one has power to touch the assets of the deceased until the courts grant probate. As I said earlier, it's the job of the executor to promptly initiate the granting of a probate and thereby protect the estate from any loss through delay. The executor is personally liable for any losses caused by a delay.

The formalities regarding probate have been eased over the past years and can actually be dispensed with if the estate is less than $15,000. Under the terms of the *Life Insurance*

Act 1995, life insurance companies can pay out life insurance policies below $50,000 on the production of a death certificate. Many banks and building societies are prepared to release accounts under $15,000 if given certified copies of the will and the death certificate and an indemnity from the person to whom those monies are to be paid.

DYING WITHOUT A WILL

If you die without a will or have a will that has been invalidated through some event such as a divorce, you are said to have died intestate. If this happens, the Supreme Court will appoint an administrator to distribute your estate to your next of kin according to the relevant laws in the State in which you were resident.

According to Argyle Partners, if, for instance, you were resident in New South Wales and died intestate, your estate would be divided in the following way:

- Where there is a spouse and no children, the entire estate passes to your spouse.
- Where there is a spouse and children:
  1 If the estate is worth less than $150,000, the entire estate goes to the spouse.
  2 If the estate is worth more than $150,000 (including presumably half the value of the family home) the spouse gets the first $150,000 plus all household effects, and the remainder of the estate is split 50/50 between the spouse and the children.
- Where there is no spouse and only children, the estate is split equally amongst the children.
- Where there is no spouse and no children, the parents of the deceased share the estate equally. If there are no parents, then the estate passes to other relatives (there is a kinship order here too).

- If no relatives can be located, then the estate goes to the New South Wales Government.
- In all cases above, a de facto partner has the same rights as a spouse if the relationship has been in existence for two or more years.

If a married or de facto couple die at the same time and both are intestate, the older person is deemed for probate purposes to have died first. This means that, before the younger person's estate is passed on to any beneficiaries, the younger person's estate must first receive its lawful share of the older person's estate. This in itself can present a number of problems. Consider the following.

A married couple from Sydney, Fred (45 years) and Sue (44 years) are killed in a car accident and because neither of them have a will are considered to be intestate. They have no children. Under New South Wales law, Fred, because he is older than Sue, is deemed to have died first. Sue, because she is legally considered to be his next of kin, inherits all of Fred's estate: a three-bedroom house, plus around $100,000 tied up in various investment and insurance products.

Now here's the rub. Because the estate has been transferred to Sue's name and because the couple had no children, the whole of the estate passes to Sue's next of kin — her parents who, incidentally, Fred didn't get on that well with anyway. Fred's parents, with whom he'd had a good relationship, miss out completely. The intestacy laws don't take into account things like family relationships, so if this is not an incentive to make a will and ensure that your estate ends up in the right hands, I don't know what is. Had Fred made a will he could have stipulated that his estate pass to his parents should Sue die at the same time as he, or that a portion of his estate go to his parents and the remainder to Sue.

Contacts State by State

For more information on the intestacy laws and probates in your State, contact the following:

Australian Capital Territory	Supreme Court of ACT (02) 6267 2707
New South Wales	Supreme Court of New South Wales (02) 9230 8067
Northern Territory	Supreme Court of Northern Territory (08) 8999 7953
Queensland	Supreme Court of Queensland (07) 3247 4313
South Australia	Supreme Court of South Australia (08) 8204 0505
Tasmania	Supreme Court of Tasmania (03) 6233 3245
Victoria	Supreme Court of Victoria (03) 9603 6111
Western Australia	Supreme Court of Western Australia (08) 9261 7699

POWERS OF ATTORNEY

Now, you could be forgiven for thinking that estate planning is wholly and solely about the development and maintenance of a will. However, a will does absolutely nothing in respect to controlling your estate while you're still alive. As far as the law is concerned, a will does not even exist until after the testator or testatrix dies and is found by the court to have been properly written, witnessed and created without undue influence or other outside manipulation. Many people mistakenly believe that a will also applies before their death should they become incapacitated. It does not. What the courts do recognise is a document called a 'power of attorney'.

A power of attorney is a formal document, where one person (the grantor) empowers another (the grantee or attorney) to represent them, or act on their behalf if they are mentally or physically incapacitated. Generally a power of attorney gives a grantee the power to sell or buy assets (such as shares, property and other investments); take over the management of business interests; or sign important documents (such as cheques and contracts).

'Living probate'

One easy way of remembering the difference between a will and a power of attorney is that a will is sometimes called a 'death probate', whereas a power of attorney is also known as a 'living probate'. A power of attorney may be granted only by someone who is over eighteen years and who is of sound mind and fully capable of understanding the nature and purpose of the document that they are signing. The attorney must also be at least eighteen and of sound mind. Unless stipulated in the document, the attorney may not exercise their powers for their own benefit.

When doing your estate planning, I strongly recommend that you think about having a power of attorney. Remember that if you can't sign documents, your assets can't even be used to help you if you are sick and incapacitated. I should warn you though that a power of attorney can be a dangerous thing, but only if it falls into the hands of the wrong person. Ideally, you give power of attorney to someone you trust to act on your behalf and in your interests should you be incapable of looking after your own affairs.

Except in certain circumstances, the death of the grantor immediately cancels any grant of power of attorney. If you are cancelling a power of attorney, make sure you let your attorney know so as to avoid any confusion. This may be as simple as tearing the original power of attorney in half, however, it is also advisable to tell the original attorney that they no longer have power to act.

Groucho Marx

Remember Groucho Marx? He was probably the best known of America's famous Marx Brothers. Whilst Groucho is remembered as the cigar-smoking, wise-cracking rogue of the Marx Brothers' troupe, the sad story of his final years is a graphic reminder of the consequences that can arise when a person – no matter how famous and wealthy – ignores estate planning.

Unfortunately, the last three years of Groucho's life were hardly a laughing matter as he spent more time in court than out of it, while his 'live-in friend' Erin Fleming and Groucho's family fought over who would control his estate. The consequences of this battle were draining on both Groucho's health and finances.

Fleming, a constant companion of Groucho in his later years, decided that she was best placed to look after Groucho's affairs and began legal proceedings to take control in 1974, when she filed court papers in a Santa Monica court seeking to have Groucho declared incompetent. Her goal was to take control of both Groucho and his assets.

This is where the fun and games began. Groucho's advisers had already devised what they thought was a 'water-tight' will to help Groucho manage his estate. But, as we now know, and you would have thought his 'highly paid' advisers should have known, a will was of little use to Groucho while he was still alive. In fact, the US courts ruled that Groucho's will didn't even exist – until after Groucho died. Initially, the court appointed Fleming as Groucho's personal guardian and named the Bank of America as guardian of his finances. This lasted for three years, until Fleming decided she wanted to have control of everything, so she went back to court to try to have the bank removed from the picture.

The verdict was fought by both the bank and Groucho's family who claimed that Erin was less than nice to Groucho and was greedy. For months, Groucho's housekeeper, deliverymen, cooks and anyone else who had contact with him were brought into court to testify about Groucho's state of mind. The impact of this second court battle on Groucho's health was said to be enormous. At the end of this second go-around, Fleming was removed as Groucho's personal guardian and was replaced by Groucho's grandson; but Groucho was on his last legs. Less than five months later, Groucho was dead!

Unfortunately, Groucho's death wasn't the end of the saga, but signalled the start of a new fight for the control of his estate. There was still the death probate process to be completed in order to determine the validity of his will and who would inherit his estate. Thus, the battle began all over again with many of the same witnesses, duplicated costs and days in court – but this time, it was to determine Groucho's competency and freedom from duress at the time he created his will.

Though the court records show that Groucho's estate was fairly substantial compared to most people's, all of Groucho's money did not help him and his family avoid the circus of the probate courts. If better planning had been undertaken – for both Groucho's potential disability as well as his death – the wear and tear on his finances and health through the court battles could have been avoided.

Source: Robert E. Alderman, Loyola University School of Law

SPENDING YOUR INHERITANCE

'Thrift is a wonderful virtue, especially in an ancestor.' – Mark Twain

Australia's middle-aged generation stands to get a massive windfall of inherited wealth in the next decade. Some inheritances will turn thousands of already financially comfortable 40- to 55-year-olds into overnight millionaires. But trying to comprehend just how big the inheritance pie will be is a bit like measuring the impact tax cuts have on the economy – experts produce different figures, depending on the context. According to Peter Bobbin from Argyle Partners, the best-known estimate of the estate bonanza in Australia is said to be $140 billion between 1990 and 2010.

It's a family affair

However, there is another side to consider. We are all living longer and this includes Mum and Dad. And because they are living longer, they are slowly eating into their estates – what the baby boomers might have counted on as their inheritance – to pay for things like healthcare, extended homecare and retirement village accommodation.

Nonetheless, $140 billion is a lot of money. But you need to remember that this is going to be split among a large number of people – after all, the baby boomers are called 'boomers' because there are so many of them. Currently there are around 5 million Australians born between the boomer years of 1946 and 1964. Furthermore, much of the wealth that's expected to change hands is concentrated in a small number of portfolios. I haven't seen any local estimates, but, if we use some American research from Avery and Rendall at Cornell University as a benchmark, it's fair to expect that one-third of this $140 billion will go to the richest 1% of Australian boomers. Another third will pass to the next wealthiest 10%, and the remaining third will be shared amongst the rest of us.

But even with these statistics in mind, it's not all doom and gloom. The Cornell academics also estimate that the parents of baby boomers might leave as much as $US23,000 ($AUD40,000) for each of their children; while the December 1999 edition of *Money* in the USA has suggested that $90,000 ($AUD156,000) is closer to the mark.

Whichever way you look at it, whether it's $23,000 or $90,000, both figures are better than a poke in the eye. Maybe the reality is that you'll have to put the holiday home in the south of France on hold. But there's plenty of other things that you could use the money for, such as paying off the balance on your credit card; taking that much-talked-about overseas trip; much-needed home renovations; or to top up your own retirement nest egg. Of course, there is a catch: You and your parents need to sit down and divvy up their estate so that all parties are happy and this can sometimes be easier said than done.

Can we talk?

It's my experience that the sooner the topic of estate planning is raised (and it is best, and certainly more comfortable, if ageing parents approach their middle-aged kids rather than the other way round), and the more fully you explore it, the better. The subject of money was never taboo when I was growing up. We talked openly about all issues relating to money, and estate planning was no different.

But there's no denying that it's still a difficult subject to discuss. Estates are a sensitive issue and as complicated as the lives that created them. Estate planning is not just about probate laws and nominating executors, but also about confronting the emotional issues – the potential loss of loved ones and the distribution of their property. As we have seen earlier in this chapter, the failure to address these issues adequately can cause much heartache to those left behind.

But still, let's not forget that there is money involved. No amount of planning can fully prepare you for the loss of a family member, but if you're a baby boomer, an inheritance may bring about changes – some spectacular, some small – to your life that are going to make a big difference to the way you live your life. So, now is probably the best time to approach your parents and start the planning process.

If your parents are a bit bewildered by the task of developing an estate plan, that's to be expected.

- Suggest that they write down what they have saved, what they owe, and list their most significant purchases and investments.
- Then, they need to work out how and to whom they will distribute those assets in their will.
- Alternatively, they could consult a solicitor who can help them to prepare their estate plan.

WHAT DOES AN INHERITANCE MEAN FOR BOOMERS?

So what are you going to do with this extra money that eventually will come your way? Remember that an inheritance doesn't simply mean that you now have extra money to buy things or invest; it can also enable you to subsidise a change in your lifestyle. In some ways, this may be the greatest gift that your parents leave you.

Consider Joan Smith. The inheritance Joan's mother left her, allowed her to work part time, spend more time with her children and get more involved in their sporting and cultural interests and pursue her long-held dream of returning to university to complete a Bachelor of Arts degree. It also enabled her to pursue her ultimate ambition to work from home as a writer. So the inheritance helped Joan and her children – what better gift can one generation leave another?

But let me now focus on an important estate-planning concept.

THE TESTAMENTARY TRUST

Peter Bobbin of the Argyle Partnership first alerted me to testamentary trusts and they are part of my own personal estate planning.

A testamentary trust is established as part of your will and becomes effective after your death. A will that creates a testamentary trust allows you (as the creator) to place assets in trust, name someone to manage those assets (a trustee) and give instructions for distributing your assets for the benefit of one or more individuals (beneficiaries). A testamentary trust goes further than the typical will and provides a lot more detail, such as: how the creator would like their investments managed; what assets they would like their money invested in; and who they would like to manage their investments, whether it be a particular financial planner, stockbroker or fund manager.

Benefits

There are a number of good reasons for setting up a testamentary trust. Testamentary trusts can help protect your estate once you've died from legal action taken against your beneficiaries. If for some reason any of your beneficiaries are successfully sued, your estate won't be affected because the assets (shares, managed funds, bonds, property and cash) aren't in the beneficiary's name but in the name of a trustee.

Testamentary trusts also provide social security benefits. Take the example of Angelo and Maria who are both part pensioners on the age pension.

> *When Maria's brother Frank died, he left them a $250,000 home unit. On face value, this sounds like a nice little winner for Angelo and Maria, however the problem is that by inheriting this home unit, they may no longer be eligible for the age pension and all the benefits associated with the pension.*
>
> *Fortunately for Angelo and Maria, Frank was a shrewd investor and had set up a testamentary trust that put the home unit in the name of a trustee with Maria and Angelo and their children and grandchildren nominated as the beneficiaries of the trust. Consequently, the rental income from the property is available for the benefit of Maria and Angelo and their family, but because the property is not included as an asset in their name, they get to keep their part pension.*

Testamentary trusts can also set up tax breaks that you might like to consider. Let's look at an example.

> *Ian dies and leaves his $500,000 investment portfolio to his wife and children. Ian had been a fairly conservative investor with most of the $500,000 invested in cash and bonds that earned him around 5% a year or $25,000. But, because his wife Lee is a high-income earner, she pays tax at the highest marginal rate.*
>
> *On this extra investment income, she stands to lose around $12,500 in tax annually. However, Ian's solicitor had advised him to set up a testamentary trust to take advantage of Section 102AG, a little-known section of the Federal Tax Act. Section 102AG allows Lee to maintain*

control of the $500,000 investment portfolio, but as it is in a testamentary trust, it means that rather than receiving the income directly and then paying a large slab of it back to the Government as tax, the trust can pay the income in equal amounts to the other beneficiaries – Ian's three children.

This means that each child receives a payment of $8,333 annually – of which the first $6,000 is tax-free (the ATO calls this the 'tax-free threshold'). You see, beneficiaries of a testamentary trust are treated like adults for tax purposes, unlike a normal trust. The balance of $2,333 is taxed at 17%, which is the lowest marginal rate of tax. But according to Peter Bobbin, given the various Government rebates for low-income earners – the children could in fact end up paying no tax at all – which is a saving of around $12,500 to the estate. Ian can therefore 'rest in peace' in the knowledge that this inheritance, whilst providing support for his family, is also protected from future possible creditors of his wife and/or a future husband.

RIP

A sound estate plan will ensure that your family is taken care of if you are incapacitated or you die. It can also minimise the problem of squabbling heirs fighting over their inheritance; and, if done properly, can protect your investments from disappearing in taxes and litigation fees.

As the saying goes 'you can't take it with you', but with a bit of planning now you can make sure that your estate will be in pretty good shape for those you leave behind.

chapter 17

PROTECTING YOUR WEALTH

*'That the loss lighteth easily on many rather than heavilie on few.' –
Elizabeth I of England introducing the* Insurance Act, *over 400 years ago*

Insurance, the idea of compensating someone financially if
they experience loss of or damage to property, is not new. In
fact there is evidence that a form of insurance may have
existed 5,000 years ago in Babylon – which isn't surprising
given that the Babylonians were the original creators of
money. More than a century after Babylon was vanquished
by Cyrus and his fearsome Persians, the government of
ancient Rome introduced a form of life insurance in 400 B.C.
by offering to pay compensation to the families of all soldiers
killed in battle.

More recently, during the late 1500s, the entrepreneurs of
Elizabethan England – the merchants – developed an important form of business insurance. Then, as now, the British
economy depended largely upon trade with other nations.
The cornerstone of this trade was wooden sailing ships which
carried goods across the globe – there were no Boeing 767s or
Channel Tunnel!

The problem with shipping in those times was that so
much could go wrong. The ships could easily stray off course

and be smashed against rocks due to a combination of poor maps and treacherous currents. Then, even if nature worked in your favour, there was still the threat of pirates who lurked along most trading routes stealing cargo, murdering sailors, and sinking sailing ships.

In other words, trade was a tough and risky way to do business. While commercial shipping and trade could make a merchant very wealthy, it could just as easily send him broke as well. To solve this problem, the merchants developed a form of insurance that worked this way: if a merchant lost a ship, the other merchants would pay a certain amount of money to help compensate for the loss of the ship. While this money would not cover the cost of the ships, it would at least help the merchants to stay in business. If, on the other hand, the ships returned safely, the merchant would share a percentage of the profits with the other merchants. Some merchants thought this was such a good idea that they gave up their 'day jobs' and opened the first insurance companies.

Money Tip

Overinsuring your assets is silly, but underinsuring is downright stupid.

Since these early beginnings, insurance has evolved into a large and complex business. Insurance is all about protecting what you have now and what you would like to have in the future. But, as you go through life, the protection you need changes. What I'll look at in this chapter are the types of insurance relevant to protecting the wealth you have created by investing in stocks and managed funds. As such I will focus on:

- health insurance

- income insurance
- small business insurance
- home insurance
- life insurance.

HEALTH INSURANCE

Obviously our health is fundamental to achieving our goals, and we want to ensure we'll be able to afford medical care when the need arises. In the past, most Australians had private health insurance. Then, in 1984, the Federal Government introduced a public health insurance system called Medicare that meant you could now go to the doctor and to hospital and not have to pay a cent. Sure, you might not end up in five-star accommodation, but it was basically free – though you were still paying for it, indirectly, through your taxes.

Not surprisingly, this led to a mass exodus from private healthcare. In 1984, 63% of Australians were privately insured, but by the end of 1998 only 30% of Australians had private health insurance. As most of you are probably aware, a number of legislative and product initiatives, which I will discuss in more detail later in this chapter, have begun to reverse this decline over the past few years – the national level of coverage, according to the Federal Government, was 41% at the end of June 2000. The basic problem with private healthcare is that many people think they can do without it.

And in a sense they are right. Private health insurance is quite different from other types of insurance like property insurance or car insurance. You can get by without private health insurance. Not only that, you can happily do without some of its more annoying attributes, such as the relatively high costs involved and the dreaded 'gap'. The 'gap' refers to the amount not covered by your private health fund, such as the amount you must pay when you are in hospital. One of the great anomalies of the health insurance system is that if you end up in a public hospital in a bed next to an uninsured public patient who is having exactly the same treatment, the chances are the public patient will not pay an extra cent in hospital charges, but you will pay the gap.

So why take out health insurance? Well, it does have its benefits, including:

- medical treatment when you want it
- a doctor of your choice
- immediate access to a hospital of your choice
- avoiding queues in the public system, particularly for elective surgery
- better hospital accommodation, such as a private room
- cover for ancillary services (outside of a hospital) not covered by Medicare, such as physiotherapy, dental, chiropractic and acupuncture
- the possibility of claiming gym membership, sports shoes and tennis lessons
- in the case of some funds, taking coverage that eliminates the gap by using selected hospitals and doctors
- a tax rebate.

Legislative changes

The reasons for the increased popularity of health insurance is not hard to fathom. The first initiative that encouraged more people to sign up was the Medicare levy surcharge that was introduced on 1 July 1997. This is an additional 1% levy on the total taxable income of those higher-income earners (above $50,000 or $100,000 for couples or families) who do not take out health insurance. This is in addition to the current, universal Medicare levy of 1.5%.

But if you have private health insurance you are spared

this levy, which, depending on your taxable income, alone may make it an offer you can't refuse. For instance, a couple earning a combined income of $105,000 would pay $1,050 in Medicare surcharge levy if not privately insured, whereas they could get basic hospital insurance for much the same amount. For example, in South Australia they could get HCF Value Cover with an excess of $250 or $500 for $1,026.45 per annum, and not pay the $1,050 levy. All round the benefits are obvious – the surcharge encourages more people to get health insurance, and the more money that flows into health funds, the less pressure there is on the public purse.

30% rebate

The next major initiative to increase private health fund membership was the Federal Government's 30% rebate on private health insurance, introduced on 1 January 1999. This is available to all people with health insurance, regardless of how much they earn. It also benefits anyone taking out a policy now, not just those who were already insured on 1 January 1999. There are three ways you can receive the rebate: by having your premiums reduced by 30%; by claiming it at tax time; or by receiving a direct payment through a Medicare office.

Lifetime Health Cover

Finally, the Federal Government introduced 'Lifetime Health Cover' (LHC). Under this scheme, if you had taken up private hospital insurance by 15 July 2000, you locked in the lowest base-rate premiums offered by an insurer. If you missed the boat, you will pay an extra 2% loading on your base premium for every year you are aged over 30. The maximum loading a person can pay under this scheme is 70%, i.e. for people joining at age 65 (though those born before 1 July 1934 pay no loading).

If you're insured and you're over 30, there's no reason to worry. Regardless of your age, you will be treated under LHC as a 30-year-old and pay no loading. Age 30 becomes your 'certified age at entry', and you will be treated as 30 years old, while ever you stay insured. Similarly, if you joined a health fund on 16 July 2000 after the crucial deadline, and you're actually 44, then 44 becomes your 'certified age at entry', with its 28% loading – and you'll remain 44 forever with a 28% loading for as long as you remain insured.

For more details on Lifetime Health Cover call the Department of Health's private health insurance infoline on 1800 676 296, or visit their web site at www.health.gov.au/lhc.

Different types of cover

So, given all these incentives, what type of cover can you expect from private health insurance? As a 'private' patient (meaning, you are privately insured), all hospital accommodation charges, theatre fees (unless it's for a procedure excluded from the cover), medication, ancillary costs and the costs of surgically implanted prostheses should be covered by Medicare and your fund. Ancillary services include such treatments as physiotherapy, speech pathology and podiatry, which are provided by health professionals.

However, you will have to pay the gap between the Medicare Schedule fee and the doctors' bill (including anaesthetics, X-rays or pathology), as well as any excess and any co-payment (explained below). You will also have to pay for extras like TV rental, phone calls and newspapers. If you have paid for gap cover, the health fund should pay the difference between the Schedule fees and the doctor's fees. It's also worth knowing that if you go to a public hospital as a 'public' (uninsured) patient, Medicare covers the costs of accommodation and treatment by hospital-appointed doctors. This includes medication, pathology and X-rays.

However, as a public patient going to a private hospital, you would be up for some heavy fees. The only way you could manage would be if you had saved the equivalent of an average health insurance premium annually in a bank account just for this purpose. Otherwise you really wouldn't want to consider it.

A popular misconception about private health insurance is that it covers the cost of going to your doctor, at his or her surgery. Private health insurance is primarily about covering hospital or approved medical day centre accommodation and theatre costs, hence it should, more accurately, be known as 'hospital' insurance. You should also note that it does not cover the cost of your chemist bill for things like antibiotics or penicillin.

Choosing the cover that is right for you

Making the choice between private and public cover is the easy part. Making the choice of the cover that is right for you can be much more confusing. You have to choose to include or exclude cover for the same procedures, set different waiting periods, with or without ancillaries, gap or no gap cover, and so on. Then you have to consider the different premiums if you are single or if you are a couple or family. Don't forget that premiums can vary from State to State – and all this is within the one fund!

But there are almost 50 registered health funds nationwide and trying to compare them all is difficult for any consumer. Trying to work through the brochures of three or four funds and picking the one that is best for you is hard enough.

According to iSelect, a web-based company that provides advice and recommendations on certain policies, 48% of consumers without health insurance find the health insurance purchasing and decision-making process perplexing. I'm amazed it's not 100%. Anyway, all that said, private health insurance policies can generally be broken into four categories:

- **Those that cover all procedures in most hospitals (which may or may not charge an excess).**

  If you're considering health insurance, these provide the most comprehensive cover you can choose. While some medical conditions are relatively uncommon, particularly amongst the young, you never know when something might strike you down – it's good to be prepared. The catch with these policies is usually the cost; they're the most expensive option, unless you choose an excess. And you'd expect that the higher the excess, the lower your premium. The excess is an agreed amount that you must pay for your hospital treatment and/or ancillary services in exchange for lower premium costs.

  For example, at the time of writing, the rate for the GEHF (Government Employees Health Fund) hospital policy with a $1,000 excess costs $655.20 in New South Wales each year. Compare this with the cost of the same hospital cover with no excess at $1,951.00. If you go to hospital and have to pay the excess you are still in front. Note, however, that with some policies the excess may only be charged once, twice or three times per year, despite the fact you or your family are hospitalised more often than that. With other policies, the excess may apply every time someone goes to hospital. ·

- **Those that cover all procedures but may restrict the hospitals to which you can go (which may or may not charge excess).**

  This is similar to the option above, but check in which hospitals you are fully covered – ideally, good ones that are in your local area. Also find out how much you're going to pay if you go to a hospital that's not listed. The best thing about these products is that they offer cover in most private hospitals.

- **Those that cover most hospitals and may or may not charge an excess, but also charge a co-payment for each day you are in hospital.**

  The co-payment is payable on top of any excess that may apply. Be sure that you know from Day 1 what the co-payment is. If you don't, you may end up receiving a hospital bill that you weren't expecting and perhaps can't easily afford.

- **Those that exclude or pay lower benefits for some services (commonly called 'exclusion' products).**

  Most people are attracted to these products because they are cheaper. The reason that they are less costly is because there are lower benefits paid for the things that most people are likely to claim. Problems with these sorts of policies are noted in the January–March 2000 *Quarterly Bulletin of the Private Health Insurance Ombudsman*, available at www.phio.org.au and, according to many experts, these policies are not recommended.

One way to make choosing a health policy easier is to use a health insurance broker. They are free of charge and will suggest a number of policies for you to consider. Just make sure that they're not pushing a particular product or products because of more favourable commissions. I've mentioned iSelect (www.iselect.com.au), another one is Health Insurance Consultants Australia (www.hica.com.au).

INCOME INSURANCE

Try this quick quiz, giving the first answer that comes to mind. What is your most important asset? If you answered 'house' or 'car', you'd be with the majority of Australians.

However, the correct answer is 'your own ability to earn an income'. In the September 1999 edition of *Money Magazine*, my colleague Chris Walker looked at one of the least popular, yet one of the most important, kinds of insurance: income protection insurance.

It won't happen to me . . .

The common thought that 'it won't happen to me' is surely the only reason that there aren't more policy holders of income protection insurance. We don't think twice about insuring our home or our car, probably because we know something can happen to them. We take out life insurance because deep down we know that death is inevitable. And many people take out private health insurance, but few consider getting wealth insurance to protect on-going income.

Statistics tell us that a 25-year-old male has a 24% chance of becoming disabled for some period of his life before he reaches 65 and, if he is disabled for more than three months, then the average claim duration is 2.2 years. Two years out of work would place intolerable pressure on most of our finances.

Income insurance works like this. If accident, illness or injury prevents you from working, the insurer will pay you up to 75% or 80% of your gross income. The premiums are based on various factors including health, age, gender, occupation, previous medical history, out-of-work-hours activities, smoking habits, waiting period and benefit period. For instance, white-collar workers usually have lower premiums than manual labourers do because they are in less physically risky occupations.

It's difficult to generalise on annual premiums due to this range of factors, but here are two examples from Prudential Insurance in 2000:

- For a female nurse aged 30 (non-smoker) to be insured for

$2,500 gross income per month, after a 30-day waiting period, the annual premium was $835.

- For a male plumber aged 50 (smoker) to be insured for $3,437 gross income per month with a 30-day waiting period, the annual premium was $3,657.

The older you get, the more expensive it gets, but the premium is tax deductible.

Money Tip

Don't forget insurance to protect your income in case you have an accident or get ill.

It is called 'income protection' or 'disability' insurance and the premium you pay is tax deductible.

While workers' compensation provides cover for work-related injuries, most disabilities are caused by illness, not by injuries at work. Sick leave and holiday leave only provide limited cover and the benefits from social security will almost certainly be far less than the previous income. Also, an ever-growing number of Australians are self-employed contractors or run their own businesses. Unfortunately for them, with no employer-sponsored sick leave, their income stops immediately they stop working. But the bills don't.

Some time ago my TV program, 'Money', featured this pertinent story.

Andrew had his own plumbing business and was caught out. Like many of us, he thought workers' compensation would cover him if he was injured at work; third party would cover him in the event of a car accident; and, if he was injured while participating in his sport of surf-boat rowing, he'd be covered by the Surf Life Saving Association's insurance.

While Andrew was at work he felt a slight twinge in his back. A doctor told him it was just muscular and he continued his work and demanding sport. The pain got worse, physiotherapy didn't help, and eventually Andrew was forced to take two weeks off work. From there the nightmare really began. As a sub-contractor Andrew was only paid for the hours he worked and he wasn't prepared for what was coming. Soon after returning to work, he had to take another four weeks off: in traction and continuous physio, followed by an emergency operation as a result of a protruding disc.

All up, Andrew spent five and a half months off work without pay. As a result he had to cash in his life insurance policy, worth around $6,000, and eat into his savings of around $5,500. He also had to resort to Social Security Sickness Benefits for about three months. On top of this, he had to struggle with his car repayments, rent and mounting hospital bills.

Andrew estimates he lost around $17,000 in wages for the time he was off work. Apart from becoming aware of the financial burden of not having income protection insurance, he found the emotional and psychological trauma to be just as damaging. Now 38, Andrew is still a commercial drainer and is now insured for 75% of his average annual income in the event of an accident and $100,000 in the event of his death.

So, what are the important things to consider when taking out an income protection policy?
- Make sure the contract is in simple English so that you understand all the terms and conditions.
- Aim for the highest benefit amount, which is usually 75% of your gross income, but can be 80%.
- Carefully choose the waiting time for benefits to apply. This involves weighing up how long you can eat into

your savings before the payments begin. Terms vary from fourteen days to three months.

- Ensure that the policy has a clear definition of disablement that will pay a benefit if you're unable to perform one or more of your usual tasks at work. For example, if you're a dentist and were to break your arm, would you still receive the full benefit, even though you would be able to do some tasks that relate to your job?
- The benefits paid should be indexed to inflation.
- Insure to the age of 65 in case you suffer from a long-term disability.
- Check with your existing superannuation scheme to see if you already have cover.
- Don't confuse income insurance with total and permanent disability cover – they are not the same.

And finally, three things worth remembering – as I said earlier, income insurance premiums are tax deductible, it's worth organising insurance when you are still young and healthy to qualify for the standard rates and, most importantly shop around as criteria and premiums can vary enormously between insurers. The real questions for any self-employed person are 'Could it happen to me?' and 'Can I afford not to have income protection insurance?'.

Money Tip

One of the cheapest ways to buy personal insurance is through your employer's super fund.

SMALL BUSINESS INSURANCE

As we discussed in Chapter 15, 'Earning Extra Income', there are plenty of Australians who are going into or running a small business. As we saw, it takes plenty of courage to start up your own business, and even with the best planning things can still go wrong. You must be prepared to take risks, but you can manage some of this risk by taking out an insurance policy with a reasonable premium that can provide for emergencies and help you get through the more difficult times.

According to the New South Wales Department of State and Regional Development's Small Business web site at www.smallbiz.gov.au, there are many types of general insurance policies commonly used by small business. Few businesses will need all the policy types available and some will need more specialised policies. You should telephone at least three insurance agents and ask them to meet you at your place of business or your home and have them suggest the type of insurance you need.

You can find an insurance broker by contacting the National Insurance Brokers Association (NIBA) at www.niba.com.au or phoning 1800 333 172. They have access to insurance companies' products and can talk to you about the needs of small business. Any fees charged can easily be offset by the time and money saved in getting the right product.

Choosing the right small business insurance policy

Small business insurance products are usually developed for specific occupation groups (such as newsagents, motels, rural industries) and are invariably no more than a selective combination of what the insurance companies already offer, tailored for your specific small business needs. They will cover a selection of the following insurance products and it's up to you to work out with your insurance company or insurance broker which combination of products will best protect your business.

- *Fire insurance* – This is designed to cover the building, contents and stock of the business should fire, lightning, storms, a truck driving through the front wall, malicious damage and/or an explosion cause damage to your property. The standard fire insurance policy covers the depreciated value of items insured at the time of the loss. This means that your insurance policy provides cover only for the value of the existing stock and won't pay for the cost of new stock. If you plan to replace damaged stock with new stock, you'll have to pay the difference yourself between the cost of the new stock and the value of your old stock as agreed with the insurance company.
- *Business interruption or loss of profits insurance* – This provides cover similar to fire insurance, but covers more than the loss of property. It ensures that forecast profits are maintained, employees are paid and additional working costs are covered if you need to move to new premises. To claim business interruption insurance, you have to prove you are staying in business.
- *Burglary insurance* – This covers theft of property and damage caused by a break-in. It does not cover theft by shoplifters or staff and you can't claim for inconvenience caused or profits lost through theft. 'Fidelity Guarantee Insurance' will cover you for loss due to stealing or embezzlement by staff.
- *Workers' compensation* – This insurance is compulsory for all businesses employing staff. In New South Wales, the State government got serious about workers' compensation in 1996 with the introduction of stronger penalties for employers who failed to take out workers' compensation, including the introduction of imprisonment for up to six months. For more information on workers' compensation go to the Workcover New South Wales site at www.workcover.nsw.gov.au which will provide you

with all the relevant information, as well as links to similar sites in the other States and Territories.

- *Personal accident or sickness* – If you are self-employed or a subcontractor, you are not covered by workers' compensation insurance. It is particularly important for you to provide yourself with funds to compensate for loss of income due to illness or accident. Talk to your insurance company about this.
- *Money* – This covers money lost or stolen while being taken to and from the bank or while it is still on your premises. It also can cover money taken home overnight or deposited in a bank night safe.
- *Public risk* – This covers your legal liability for compensation if someone who is not an employee or a family member (third party) suffers injury, damage to property or death as a result of your business operations, should you be proven negligent.
- *Electronic equipment insurance for computers* – Computer insurance is designed to cover sudden and unforeseen loss or damage. It does not cover the cost of maintenance or general wear and tear.
- *Machinery breakdown* – This policy covers the breakdown of all mechanical and electrical equipment at the work site. It can also cover the costs of any food damaged by the breakdown.
- *Professional indemnity* – It is becoming increasingly common for consultants to take out this cover due to the growing trend for clients to take legal action against them for losses as a result of their advice. This insurance is not cheap, but could be critical for consultants and other experts.
- *Product liability* – This policy covers the damage caused to another business and/or personal injury due to failure of your product or someone else's product that you are

selling. That other product only has to be modified or assembled by you to be considered your responsibility. This is quite a common practice in the computer business where PCs are built from parts from various manufacturers. The damages claimed against you could be high if your product is a component in an expensive piece of equipment that failed because of your product.

This is only a sample of the insurance products available, so if you would like to know more I suggest you contact the Insurance Council of Australia on 02 9253 5100 (www.ica.com.au) or the Government organisations responsible for small business in your State, referred to in Chapter 15 'Earning Extra Income'.

HOME INSURANCE

There's a lot at stake, if you're an owner-occupier or an investor in residential property, but fortunately there are plenty of insurance companies that offer home and contents insurance that provides protection against unforeseen loss or damage to your property.

When you consider that your home is one of the biggest investments you'll ever make, not having enough home and content insurance can cost you a lot of money. Picture these scenarios:

1 A bush fire ravages your home, and your insurance doesn't completely cover everything that needs to be replaced (such as furniture, clothes, valuables and electrical goods).

2 A 'friend' trips on a step at your home, breaking her arm. A few weeks later you get a letter from her solicitor informing you that the only way she won't sue you is if you pay a sizeable amount to keep it out of the courts.

3 A semi-trailer loses control and smashes through the front

of your home and your property insurance only partially covers the repair costs.

Generally, home insurance covers a broad range of calamities and most types of losses. Home insurance policies offer three key types of protection: home building insurance, contents insurance, and public liability that relates to claims by others. Let's have a look at all three.

1 Home building insurance

Home building insurance protects your home in case of a fire, wind or hail or some other catastrophe, such as a tree crashing through your roof, but generally excludes flood. You should be aware that a number of insurers do provide flood cover but at a much higher premium.

2 Contents insurance

We tend to accumulate more and more 'things' every year. Therefore, many of your assets may be in the form of personal property, instead of financial assets. Your home is more than the structure itself: it also includes everything that is in it. Contents insurance can protect your personal property both at and away from home, including furniture, jewellery, boats and other collectibles. Don't forget to insure them for the replacement value.

3 Public liability

The third type of coverage is public liability coverage for you and your family generally up to a limit of $10 million. This covers you for the accidental death, personal injury or damage to property suffered by another party for which you might be held legally liable due to your negligence. Unfortunately, in today's litigious society, lawsuits aren't uncommon even among friends and acquaintances, so it's worth considering this protection.

Money Tip

Don't travel without travel insurance. Get sick in places like the USA without it and you may need to sell your house to pay the medical bills.

TIPS TO CONSIDER WHEN CHOOSING HOME AND CONTENTS INSURANCE

- As we have seen, household insurance policies come in different forms. You can insure your property and/or its contents on separate policies, or you can combine the two policies. Buying a combined policy is generally cheaper than buying separate policies.
- You can also choose between an indemnity policy and a replacement/reinstatement policy.
  - *An indemnity policy* allows you to insure your home and/or contents for their value less their depreciation based on the home or item's age and condition. The depreciation factor with indemnity policies means that money will have to come out of your pocket to restore your property to its original state – and this can be a killer in the case of a major claim.
  - *A replacement/reinstatement policy* (the more popular option) allows you to insure the property and/or contents for the cost of replacing them with new items. You need to be careful when considering such a policy because some insurers may not replace all the old items with new items. In terms of premiums, replacement/reinstatement policies are more expensive because the cost of replacing damaged items is more, but I would recommend them anyway.
- Above all, make sure you can prove what you own if you need to make a claim. Write down details of every piece

in every room. Include clothes and curtains. Take photos, or even better a video and keep a copy some place other than your home.

LIFE INSURANCE

Actually, 'life insurance' should probably be called 'death insurance' because it's death rather than life that you are insuring against. But even the best marketing guru might struggle to come up with a sales pitch for death insurance – so life insurance it is. There are two types of life insurance: whole-of-life insurance and term.

Life insurance was developed for anybody with a family, dependent relatives or debt. If you die, and you have life insurance, your dependents receive a lump sum payout. In the case of families, it's important that both parents are insured, even if only one is working. Often the cost of child rearing is underestimated and it therefore makes sense to insure the homecarer's life at a similar level to the bread-winner's. Experts suggest that you should insure your life for anywhere between three and fifteen times your annual salary, but the real issue is how much you and your family need. Only you can work this out.

Whole-of-life insurance

Whole-of-life insurance (WOL) is structured on the under-standing that you contribute to it for virtually all of your life. The premium stays the same for the term of the policy – your life – and is calculated based on the age at which you sign up. The idea is that you contribute to the policy until you die (obviously) or the policy matures when you turn 60 or 65.

A WOL provides an agreed payout to your beneficiaries when you die and it has an investment component towards which part of the premium goes. If you are still alive at the maturity date, you receive a lump-sum payment which is a return on the investment component of the premium.

You should be aware that you can cash your WOL in early, but you will only be able to recoup the full amount of annual premiums paid in after making contributions for around five to ten years. If you cash in (called 'surrendering') earlier than this, you will get back less than you invested. For this reason, WOL policies have gradually lost their popularity, and I have always thought they were a dog. My advice is to buy cheap term insurance and invest separately.

Term life insurance

Thankfully, WOL has gradually lost its allure and insurance companies have actively promoted a different type of life cover called 'term life insurance' which differs from WOL in that it insures against death only and offers no investment options. This has substantially reduced the cost of life insurance and is in fact one of the few financial products to come down in price over the past decade and half.

Term life insurance is calculated by looking at the age, sex and smoking habits of the policyholder. Through one major insurance company, a 30-year-old smoker will pay about 60% more ($1.25 per $1,000 of cover per year) than a non-smoker of the same sex and age ($0.75 per $1,000 of cover per year). The moral here is (if smokers didn't already know it) if smoking doesn't kill, its cost will.

If you shop around, you will find that most of the insurance companies offer similar premiums to these. While the cost of premiums are one way of choosing the right term life policy, you should also consider other features such as how easy it is to renew your policy regardless of changes to your health and whether the amount insured is linked to the Consumer Price Index. This is important in ensuring that the real value of your cover is not eaten away by inflation over time.

Whole-of-life versus term

'Should I take out whole-of-life or term life insurance?' is a question I am frequently asked by investors who are considering the best income protection options. Many have a preconceived idea that because a WOL policy provides a fixed price on their insurance (the premium doesn't go up as you get older) and that it has an investment component, then it's probably better. On first inspection, these features do look pretty good, but there are some hitches of which you should be aware. Consider the following.

> *Tim is a healthy 32-year-old, non-smoking male, who decides to take out life insurance with a death cover of $200,000 through one of the major life insurance companies. He will pay an annual WOL premium of around $4,200 on a policy that matures when he's 65. Over 33 years Tim will pay around $140,000 into the policy. If he does cash in the policy at 65, it would be worth around $290,000 (or about double his $140,000 investment).*
>
> *According to research from Expotential Pty Ltd, if Tim decides to take out term insurance cover of $200,000 until 65, his annual premiums will be cheaper than the WOL policy over the whole term of the policy. There is the assumption that because the premiums of WOLs are fixed they are relatively cheaper in later life. However, this theory is debunked by Expotential Pty Ltd, which suggests that at 60 years, Tim could pay around $1,880 for term cover. This is well short of the $4,200 he is paying annually for the WOL cover.*

My advice is simple, if you are considering life insurance, take out term insurance because it's cheaper, and then invest what you are saving (the difference between your term policy and a WOL policy) in other investments such as shares, property or super, which, as we know, will provide you with a much better long-term return – and the costs are far lower.

SHOP AROUND AND READ THE FINE PRINT

When you decide to buy insurance, you need to be aware of two important points. The first point is to shop around because there can be significant differences in the premiums offered by the various insurance companies. For example, in October 2000 (see the table on the next page) you could have paid $512.12 for home insurance from AMP on a three-bedroom home in Sydney, but only $363.21 from the NRMA.

This leads into my second point. Despite the fact that on the surface the deal from the NRMA looks better than AMP's, you need to be aware of how the policies differ and, in particular, what they do and don't cover. If this means asking questions and doing research, do it, because it's your possessions that have been covered.

BETTER SAFE THAN SORRY

Insurance is an essential component of wealth creation. It protects the assets you have built up, such as your home and your income. It's not really a luxury, it's a necessity that you can't afford to do without.

Don't take the risk and underinsure, because, believe me, what you have taken a lifetime to build up can be lost in a flash.

Insurance Quotes at 24 October 2000

Income cover	AMP	MLC	CBA
30-year-old male plumber (smoker)	$682.62	$776.56	$708.73
30-year-old female professional (non-smoker)	$606.48	$721.95	$898.84

Home insurance	AMP	NRMA	CBA
3-bedroom home Sydney ($250,000) – building insurance only	$512.12	$363.21	$366.34
3-bedroom home Sydney ($400,000) – building insurance only	$738.87	$503.98	$483.00
3-bedroom home Melbourne ($250,000) – building insurance only	$430.66	$290.80	$365.25
3-bedroom home Melbourne ($400,000) – building insurance only	$652.72	$411.79	$507.71
3-bedroom home Sydney ($250,000) – building insurance and $50,000 contents	$851.33	$508.38	$551.25
3-bedroom home Sydney ($400,000) – building insurance and $50,000 contents	$1,078.08	$642.10	$656.24
3-bedroom home Melbourne ($250,000) – building insurance and $50,000 contents	$752.91	$475.53	$571.53
3-bedroom home Melbourne ($400,000) – building insurance and $50,000 contents	$947.97	$592.88	$699.73
Contents only Sydney ($50,000)	$370.30	$171.92	$246.15
Contents only Melbourne ($50,000)	$352.82	$199.46	$269.77

Life insurance	AMP	MLC	CBA
30-year-old male non-smoker	$234.60	$118.05	$198.00
30-year-old male smoker	$419.60	$178.40	$310.00
30-year-old female non-smoker	$212.10	$112.10	$180.00
30-year-old female smoker	$372.10	$150.35	$254.00
45-year-old male non-smoker	$447.17	$203.90	$386.00
45-year-old male smoker	$934.67	$370.50	$796.00
45-year-old female non-smoker	$330.17	$165.65	$292.00
45-year-old female smoker	$790.85	$294.00	$522.00

chapter 18

SCAMS

You will have to forgive my occasionally flippant attitude towards investment scams. Yes, I am aware that the Australian Securities and Investment Commission (ASIC) believes that over 100,000 Australians have lost money to a scam in the last decade, but while I am always outraged when I hear about investors being ripped off, I have to admit that the ingenuity of some of the cons is pretty impressive. We are prone to fall for a whole range of scams in our search for quick wealth, but fortunately the great majority can be easily detected by applying the simple test: if it sounds too good to be true, it is.

Scams come in many guises. One of the more ingenious was put together by a conniving entrepreneur who purchased a mailing list of 10,000 high-income individuals. He produced two newsletters, one stating a certain volatile stock would rise, the other predicting the very same stock would fall. He mailed 5,000 people his 'rise' prediction, the other 5,000 his 'fall' prediction. He then waited to see what happened and repeated the process with another tip, but this was sent only to the 5,000 who had received the correct initial tip. A process of elimination and three different tips meant that eventually 1,250 people had received three accurate predictions.

He then mailed these people a dual proposal. After pointing out his proven accuracy, he offered a subscription to his monthly newsletter for $1,000 per annum ($3,000 for five years), plus the opportunity to join his investment syndicate for a minimum contribution of $50,000. No one knows how much he got away with, because many who handed over their money are too embarrassed to admit to being conned, but it is rumoured that he is living very well in Europe.

Less damaging because of the smaller amounts of money involved are pyramid schemes. Some of these take off in a big way. Pyramid schemes offering huge returns to investors caused a financial crisis not so long ago in Albania. In Australia, Joker 88 was the most well supported in recent times, delivering its originators hundreds of thousands of dollars. Those who jumped in early also made money, but thousands of late entrants were out of pocket.

JOKER 88

Channel 9 ran a story on Joker 88 on my 'Money' program back in 1998, but its conclusions are worth repeating. Joker 88 and similar pyramid schemes are a scam. For each of the Australian hopefuls who put $150 into the scheme, to receive the $109,000 promised, we estimated that another 540 million people had to sign up. And if those 540 million were to make $109,000 out of their $150 investment? Unfortunately, at this stage our financial calculator just didn't have a display board big enough to give us the answer, but clearly it was well in excess of the entire human population now or in about 500 years time!

This was no surprise to me. But I was amazed to receive

dozens of letters from outraged Joker 88 participants who were under the impression that it was a godsend to the average Australian battler. If Joker 88 was a godsend, then presumably some more notorious personal finance companies impoverishing Australians with 26% to 29% loans are a group of angels. But that's another story!

In this era of information, as our knowledge about money improves, you'd hope that we would be less likely to be conned. But I doubt it. Hope springs eternal and we may win lotto next week. And given that we've been chasing scams and schemes for thousands of years, a little knowledge is not likely to stop us.

TULIP MANIA

One of the classic speculative panics involved the humble tulip bulb. In the mid sixteenth century tulips arrived in Europe (particularly Holland) from Constantinople and rapidly became the symbol of good taste. Eighty years later in the 1630s, tulip bulbs became a fad with people speculating on the likely trendy colour for the next season. Every man, woman and dog jumped into the market. Sure enough, call options (a contract to buy tulips) based on a 20% deposit were introduced and between 1634 and 1638 people abandoned cash and property to acquire tulip bulbs. Prices got pretty hot and in the 1850s Charles Mackay reports in the aptly titled *Extraordinary Popular Delusions* (Volume 1) that a Haarlem species of bulb was swapped for twelve acres of prime building land. There was an instance where one wealthy gentleman was sold a bulb for '17 bushels of wheat, 4 fat oxen, 8 fat swain, 12 fat sheep, 2 hogshead of wine, 4 tons of beer, 2 tons of butter, 1,000 pounds of cheese, a complete bed, plus a silver drinking cup.' Don't ask me what that lot is worth, but it's a pretty penny. Had I been the seller, I would have parted with it just for the four tons of beer.

To even the most ardent bulb owner, this was all getting too silly, so the great sell-off began. Defying commonsense, government ministers of the day 'stated officially that there was no reason for tulip bulbs to fall in price'. In a way they were right. Prices didn't fall. They collapsed and the shock waves caused a prolonged depression in Holland.

SOUTH SEA BUBBLE

Another wonderful example of speculative madness was the South Sea Bubble. In the UK in 1711, the South Sea company took over a £10 million government IOU and in return was granted a monopoly over trade in the South Seas. The public was impressed. And even more so in 1719 when the company directors offered to fund the entire National Debt. In 1720 a Bill was introduced to that effect and the company's share price went from £130 to £300. The directors issued new shares at £400. By June 1720 they hit £890 and soon after £1,000. A wonderful range of new companies emerged to soak up the punters' money. These 'Bubble' companies (numbering over 100) were going to turn salt water into fresh water, turn lead into silver, develop a perpetual-motion wheel, and import jackasses from Spain. The prize, however, goes to the promoter of the company called 'A Company for Carrying On and Undertaking Business of Great Advantage, But Nobody Knows What It Is'. In the true tradition of a frenzied market, swamped by money the promoters departed post-haste for the Continent.

But when the directors of the South Sea Company, foreseeing the end, flogged their own shares, the price plummeted and the bubble burst.

The Parliamentary History of England summarises the sad

saga: It was 'seen in the space of eight months the rise progress and fall of that mighty fabric, which being wound up
by mysterious springs to a wonderful height, had fixed the
eyes and expectation of all Europe, but whose foundation
being fraud, illusion, credulity and infatuation, fell to the
ground as soon as the artful management of its directors was
discovered'.

One notable citizen of the time who blew a nice inheritance in the collapse was Sir Isaac Newton, reminding us that
even the intelligent can make woeful financial decisions.

CONTEMPORARY SCAMS: PROPERTY SCHEMES

While not as exotic as the South Sea Bubble nor promising
the vast returns of Joker 88, one of the most dangerous
schemes going on around Australia today is the sale of
grossly over-priced property, mainly in Queensland. As I
stated in the November 2000 issue of *Money Magazine*, these
property schemes have been in operation for over a decade
and, despite negative publicity in the media, people continue
to fly to Queensland on some sort of special deal which
involves paying far too much for a property.

Now don't get me wrong. I've got no problem with people
buying a property for lifestyle or investment in Queensland.
It's a terrific place, which is why its population is growing
so quickly. But you've got to buy at the right price and in
the right location and very few of the investment properties
being sold to interstate buyers are in the right place or sold
for the right price.

But let's start at the beginning and see what we can learn.
You don't need to be Albert Einstein (or Isaac Newton) to
work out that if you can sell a property for around $50,000
more than it's worth, you'll soon be rich. You also are very
unlikely to go to jail, because there is no law that says you

shouldn't maximise the price for which you sell a property. In fact, when selling a home you should make every effort to maximise its sale price. But to get really rich you'll need to sell many, many houses and this is not easy because most people buying a home look at the market carefully and will pay what it's worth, not $50,000 too much. So to sell many properties at an inflated price the key ingredient you need is uninformed buyers. And the best way to get buyers with no idea of what is going on, is to drag them in to you from interstate.

It sounds very simple, and this is exactly what a number of property-making companies have done. They set up a call centre and cold-call people to attend a free wealth creation seminar. At this seminar you'll get a very slick sales pitch on the benefits of negative gearing, historical information on property, and a very convincing pitch on why property is a terrific asset. What is so clever about this is that in general terms, it's true. Well-located property has been an excellent investment and negative gearing can really enhance your returns. The seminars, I am told by attendees, are very credible and well presented. But they are devised to lead to one thing: a free or discounted flight to Queensland.

Once you agree to go, you are already well on the hook. As you can imagine, the whole thing is rather surreal. You fly out of Sydney, Melbourne, Adelaide, or Perth and land in Brisbane or on the Gold Coast. Here you are met by an enthusiastic company representative and driven to inspect a number of properties. Typically, these are in the corridor between Brisbane and the Gold Coast and are two-bedroom townhouses, in attractive compounds with a tennis court and pool.

You drive around all day and see many properties. This gives you an impression of really looking at the market in depth, but of course you are only shown properties that the marketing company has to sell. You'll be taken to lunch and to the shops, but the sales pitch is relentless and the pressure is on because you'll be back at the airport for an evening flight home. Very few people escape without signing up for a property.

I know this all sounds quite bizarre, but to residents of our major capital cities the properties you are shown look good, and seem inexpensive. Back in 1996 on my first trip to look at a number of the properties being sold, I was quite impressed. Sure, they were small, but they were brand-new and the average sale price was around $130,000. Being used to big-city prices I thought this was good value, until I wandered around to a few local real-estate agents and discovered that you could buy a similar property for around $80,000.

As they say, the best trick is a simple trick, and the vast success enjoyed by the property marketing companies involved in these practices comes about because we've been taken for a ride out of our own locality and area of expertise. The chance of you paying $130,000 for an $80,000 property in your own area is nil, because you know local values. But fly for a day to an interstate location, after attending an impressive and credible seminar, and it is not too hard to be fleeced, even if you are in other regards a knowledgeable investor.

People such as Tammy and Graham Smith, who appeared on my 'Money' TV program, are just the tip of the iceberg.

Lure a couple away from their home base, family and friends, add a bit of surf and sun, stir with a friendly property salesperson or two, and keep them out late with their two young kids. They're ready to sign anything to escape and you've got the makings of a property deal.

That's basically what happened to Victorian couple Tammy and Graham Smith one fateful day in Queensland *when they signed on the dotted line to buy an investment property, a townhouse for $201,500, after being out for around 10 or 12 hours with the property agent.*

'We were going from, I think it was about 10 o'clock in the morning, till it turned out to be nearly 9 o'clock at night,' says Tammy.

They did the deal at a lawyer's office at night with their two young kids both aged under four to cope with too. The company marketing the property introduced them to the lawyer.

'It must have been about 8, 8:30 at night by now and so we were standing outside in the dark somewhere on the Gold Coast,' says Tammy. 'The kids were getting very tired and a bit cranky. We just wanted to get them home and at this point we said to the girl, 'Look, why don't we get them home, have some sleep and finish it off tomorrow'.'

But that didn't happen. The Smiths used their credit card to pay a $1,000 deposit on the property.

So why did they sign when they'd agreed they wouldn't buy anything on the day? 'It probably sounds silly, but she had been really nice to us and we appreciated her efforts and things, so I guess we didn't want to say no, look, forget it,' says Tammy.

The Smiths quickly wished they had waited, because the next day, when they made some real-estate inquiries of their own, the alarm bells started ringing.

'We were a bit concerned when we found freestanding houses on decent blocks of land we could get for the cost of that townhouse or less,' says Tammy.

The Smiths' fears were justified when the 'Money' show commissioned an independent valuation which found the property to be worth just $170,000. And bigger units with the same sort of facilities, but in better locations, were selling for $145,000 to $169,000. Units in the immediate *area were were for sale at prices below what the developers were asking.*

The Smiths' unfortunate situation came about after Graham responded to a phone invitation to attend an investment seminar which extolled the attractions of life in Queensland. 'We were going up to Queensland, so it fitted in quite well and we organised to make a time and meet with them up there.' Once there the salesperson 'looked after the kids for us for a little, while we were talking about paperwork and things', says Tammy. She even took them out for lunch at McDonald's.

It was a day which ended with them putting a deposit on a property which wasn't finished, let alone ready to rent out, even though the Smiths say the property developer told them it didn't sell off the plan.

Once the 'Money' program got involved, the property developer returned the Smiths' money and agreed to cancel the contract. The company's legal counsel said at the time: 'The saleswoman says to us that she didn't feel that she put them under pressure in that situation. When the allegations were brought to us by you ('Money') we were very distressed about it.'

The legal counsel did agree that the $1,600 solicitor's fee being charged for conveyancing seemed excessive. But he said the valuation that the property developer had received on the property was different to the one received by the 'Money' program. Now the property developer has decided to provide bank valuations of the properties it is marketing, as well as introducing a five-day cooling-off period.

The property developer says it'll also disclose to prospective buyers the commissions its sales team receives, as well as a break-down of costs for solicitors and loan application fees. People will know where the money is going.

Tammy and Graham are happy to have their $1,000

> *back, they're happy to be home and out of that property deal.*
> *Ironically, not long ago the Smiths got another phone call*
> *inviting them to an investment seminar conducted by the*
> *same property developer. They're not going.*

Tens of thousands of people like the Smiths have been sold a property for far more than it is worth. Many have written to me outlining these experiences. A typical letter came from Marie of North Queensland. She paid a little over $200,000 in 1998 for her property in Chevron Palm Waters on the Gold Coast. In June 2000, concerned about the price she had paid, she obtained an independent valuation. This valued the property at $74,900 less than she had paid. As Marie said to the company that sold her the property, 'You sold me this property at an unfair market price . . . it is a millstone around my neck, which will guarantee that I will remain in debt long after I should be retired'.

I have passed Marie's letter onto the ACCC and they are looking at this area with great interest. However, if selling to people with no local knowledge is one key ingredient, another is the role of the property valuer. Now this really is quite interesting, because clearly there are valuations and there are valuations. In the case of the property developer that dealt with the Smiths, it said in a letter to yet another concerned investor that, 'The property developer is the only investment property marketeer that obtains valuations from developers before it agrees to market the property. These valuations are closely scrutinised and the maximum variation the company will allow between Fair Market Value and the developer's listing price is five per cent (recently reduced from nine per cent)'.

This is very interesting. In the Smiths' case, the valuation provided to them was $183,700. But according to the property developer, that didn't include $12,859 of GST, giving a total valuation of $196,559. Based on the purchase price of $201,500, the variance was 2.45%, or well within the property developer's tolerance. But our 'Money' valuation by Eccleston and Fraser came in at $170,000 – including GST. So who is right and who is wrong?

Well, frankly I don't care what the developer or seller of the property thinks it is worth – accepting the developer's valuation is a pretty silly basis for pricing a property. You can just imagine the developer instructing the valuer, can't you: 'Make sure you put the lowest, toughest market value you can on the property'. As if!

It only stands to reason that the developer will want the highest possible valuation in order to obtain the best price. Making a decision to purchase based on a valuation supplied by the seller is about as bright as jumping in a tank of starving sharks. You'll get eaten alive.

If I'm considering the purchase of a property, I'm not interested in a sales pitch. I want facts. And the best facts are actual sales to knowledgeable buyers. Let's take a look at some of the information in our Eccleston and Fraser valuation of the Smiths' Queensland property:

Market comments

Premiums are currently being paid for new condition in the market place. These premiums may cease to exist as the unit ages and consequently initial purchase prices may not be achieveable in the short term.

The majority of units in this market, in this area, have apparently sold to non-local investors, via negative-gearing seminars promoting the tax benefits of owning an investment property.

Purchasers should be aware of the ongoing maintenance and management costs plus the cost of the on-site manager. These costs will reduce the return to investors.

SALES EVIDENCE

Palm Crest Heights
Palm Meadows Drive, Carrara
Four-year-old complex with similar facilities.

Unit 23   Under Contract $169,000
Three-bedroom villa unit with single garage. Larger in size. Superior location.

Unit 34   Under Contract $145,000
Three-bedroom townhouse unit of larger size with single garage. Superior location.

Somerset Park
Langport Parade, Reedy Creek
Two-year-old complex by same developer.

Unit 52   Sold February 2000 $161,000
Slightly larger detached villa unit with three bedrooms, double lock-up garage. Inferior location. Developer sale price $188,750, shows 14.7% reduction.

Unit 21   Under Contract $159,000
Slightly larger detached villa unit with three bedrooms and double lock-up garage. Inferior location. Developer sale price $189,900, shows 16.27% reduction.

So I am left struggling and failing to accept that the $201,500 is a genuine price that the property could be sold for to a knowledgeable buyer. Moreover, given the evidence of 'superior' properties being sold for $145,000 to $169,000, I suspect that the property the Smiths contracted to buy for $201,500 would be lucky to realise much above $150,000 were it to be resold.

Money Tip

Holiday homes are rarely a good investment. They cost heaps to run and tend not to increase in value. If you do buy one, treat it as a lifestyle item rather than as an investment.

KEY TIP

The point here is very simple. If you are buying a property from anyone, anywhere in Australia then dump their valuation in the bin. It is not in the seller's interest to get anything other than the highest possible valuation. Spend your own money and instruct your own valuer to value the property on what it would resell for in a normal six-week marketing campaign to a knowledgeable buyer. That will tell you what it is really worth. If you want to know the bad news, which is what the property is worth if you need to sell quickly, you can also ask for this.

Well, no doubt you are wondering how a professional valuer could overvalue a property, thereby helping the developer and marketing company to rip off investors. Well, the interesting thing here is that legally valuers are doing nothing wrong. If a developer says to a valuer 'what could this property be sold for', the valuer quite correctly asks how it will be sold. If the response is that it will be done via seminars to interstate investors, the valuer will find plenty of sales evidence to support the fact that an $80,000 property can be sold for $130,000 and a $150,000 property for $200,000.

VALUATION REPORTS

An astute reader will look carefully at the valuation report, look at the instructions to the valuer (which the valuer will refer to) and will very quickly realise that the valuation requested has got nothing to do with what an informed buyer would pay – rather it reflects what an uninformed buyer could be conned into paying.

The valuation report will also give many other hints, such as comments about seminar sales and will list sales of similar or 'superior' properties for much less. But let's get real here. Firstly, few people know how to read a valuation and secondly, the marketing company often will selectively quote from the report the bits that suit them.

So clearly, you can only trust a valuation when you instruct the valuer and you pay for it. But are valuers knowingly or unwittingly supporting the sale and financing of grossly overpriced property? I put this question to John McAuliffe, President of the Queensland Branch of the Australian Property Institute. His response was:

> Valuers are greatly concerned about the two/multi-tier market because of the marketing strategies being used and the high prices being paid. Valuer members of the Australian Property Institute are subject to the Code of Professional Practice which includes Practice Standards and Guidance notes.
>
> For mortgage security reports on real property for new homes, units and townhouses, the valuer should inquire as to whether sales prices in the housing estate are influenced by financial or other incentives being offered by the developer or any other party; and further to comment on any existence of a two/multi-tier market for that class or property in that marketplace.
>
> Where property is being purchased from the developer, re-sales or sales from other comparable developments should be provided and considered where available as a crosscheck.

When considering valuation advice never accept extracts from a valuation report; always ask for the full valuation. Carefully read the full report and note particularly the instruction to the valuer and the date of valuation – is it current? Fully understand what the report is telling you and, if in doubt, query the valuer and/or seek further professional advice.

This all makes sense to me, and the bottom line is to make sure you get your own valuation, where you instruct and pay the valuer. But from a consumer's perspective, the board of the Australian Property Institute would do us a great favour by issuing a large red 'warning' stamp to its members and have them stamp this prominently on valuations where the valuation given is not linked to the resale price to a knowledgable buyer.

So far we've looked at the sales process – which is very clever – and the role of the valuer. But let me tell you that there are plenty of other catches. The property marketing company will generally offer to do the finance application for you, and introduce you to a local solicitor. The finance application fees they charge can be outrageous. For a $200,000 loan, they often charge up to $4,000. A bank's application fees would cost you $300 to $500 at the most.

I also wondered why the local solicitor would in so many cases come out late at night to oversee contract signing. The answer is simple, as you no doubt guessed. For a very basic conveyancing job, the solicitor may charge a fee of around $1,500, which is several times more than the standard fee.

In case you need further convincing, here is another salutary story.

It all started with one of those investment seminars in Kerry Marrett's home town of Nowra where she was told all about the benefits of negative gearing. 'It was slick all right. They made it sound so easy and at the end of it you were all fired up to do something about it,' says Kerry.

She took the 'free flight' and climaxed a breathless day before she went home by signing up to buy a three-bedroom townhouse in Brisbane's southern suburbs for $120,000.

'It was Melbourne Cup Day and after we looked at various properties, the agent took me around to his place to watch the race and eat pizza and by that stage I felt completely obligated to sign on the dotted line,' she says.

But Kerry went home satisfied she'd made a good investment, until she found out the price of the townhouse had dropped dramatically – or at least that's what she thought.

'About three years ago I was told that it was worth about $95,000 and needless to say I was in shock, but I thought, we'll just keep paying the thing off and hopefully the market will pick up again. But earlier this year we asked local agents again what it might be worth and they told me it was now worth about $65,000.'

This was a real knock for Kerry, who had been trying to pay off the place with the help of her fiancé. She felt really taken for a chump when the 'Money' show found that the property was probably never worth the price she paid for it in the first place.

Kerry has been wondering for some time whether she should sell the property and take a loss, or keep beavering away in the hope that one day she'd get her money back. It's been a nightmare, with Kerry owing $73,000 on a property that's worth only about $65,000.

The one thing going in her favour when the 'Money' show caught up with her was that she'd been able to save $30,000 in an advantage saver account and $10,000 which she'd put into shares. My advice was to put the savings into an investment to build up her capital, such as a *balanced fund which would give her a better return on her money. I also suggested she put the new investment in her name only, so that when the time came to sell the property, which is in her name, there would be the possibility of offsetting the capital loss on the Queensland real estate against any capital gains.*

THE LESSONS

So you can see, thousands of people are being absolutely fleeced. The winners include the developers, solicitors and finance companies who earn very tasty fees and profits, but it is often the marketing companies who really are swimming in champagne. To date, market evidence is that the marketing group receives a fee of around $30,000 for every property sold. No wonder they have nice brochures, friendly salespeople and will fly you to Queensland for a nominal or even free airfare!

If you have already bought one of these properties, I fear you will have to hang on. Talk to a local real-estate agent and you'll soon get the sorry news about what your property is really worth. Thousands of them have been built and the market is in oversupply. But the word about this rip-off is spreading and many new projects will not get off the ground, as potential interstate buyers dry up. Over time, given that the population of Queensland is growing and once fewer new properties are built, this oversupply will dry up and prices will rally. The townhouse that Kerry Marrett paid $120,000 for is now unlikely to sell for much more than $70,000, which is below replacement cost, but sooner or later (probably later) it should improve in value somewhat.

If you are thinking about buying interstate, do your own research and visit many local agents. If you are considering buying from a marketing company, my advice is take great care and get your own valuation. I'd quite happily buy a Queensland property on a beach, or on a deepwater canal with ocean access that are near modern facilities. But I'd buy at a price based on a genuine market resale value after doing on my own intensive research.

Unfortunately, when it comes to your money it pays to be a cynic. Trust no one without double- and triple-checking all the facts and evidence. As for the principles of the property-marketing companies who are deliberately selling grossly overpriced properties, I'd like to see the whole lot of them locked up or at least forced to use their entire asset base to buy out interstate investors at the price they paid for their investment property. Now that would be justice – but unfortunately neither of these things are likely to happen.

Let me restate my earlier comments. When it comes to buying property do your own intensive research, seek many opinions, instruct and pay for your own valuer, and, if you are buying away from where you live, take great care.

It's pretty sad, isn't it? It seems that your best starting point is to trust no one. The reason we chase vast returns and fall for scams is that we recognise the need for financial independence (or we are just plain greedy). Since time immemorial we have desired eternal life and wealth. About the only clue I have got to the former is to eat more vegetables, rice and fish, and get regular exercise – but despite lectures from my exasperated doctor I have decided that, if this is the price of eternal life, I'll give it a miss.

Now the secret to wealth is something I should know a little bit more about. Since I left university in the late 1970s, apart from serving beers for a couple of years at the Regent Hotel near the University of NSW, my career has consisted of giving financial advice, either directly to my clients, through my 'Money' program on Channel 9, *Money Magazine*, newspaper columns, or on radio.

Over the last two decades I have worked with a wide variety of Australians, helping them either to accumulate wealth or to preserve their wealth in retirement. I've worked with people earning under $20,000 a year and people earning over $1 million. I always look for the common themes from all of these people in an attempt to isolate that elusive secret, how to get rich, preferably as quickly and easily as possible.

Forget gambling

Over the centuries much effort was spent trying to turn lead into gold. Modern physics has ruined this game, as even the most hopeful wealth seekers found some of the basic laws of our elements too tough to change. At least trying to turn lead into gold involved playing games in the garage, melting things and generally playing junior scientist, but today we have replaced the alchemist's search with the armchair activity of watching a red bouncing ball. Yes, after thousands of years of human development our search for easy wealth has turned to gambling games such as Lotto. On the one hand it is depressing, but at least someone wins Lotto on a regular basis, because as far as I know even King Midas didn't crack the lead-into-gold formula. Unfortunately, the reliability of Lotto-type games in bringing us instant wealth is not too hot. I very quickly ran out of fingers and toes to count on, but it seems to me that picking the numbers correctly is about a seven-million-to-one chance. Though I admit to having several clients who won over a million dollars in Lotto, gambling is not a reliable wealth-making strategy.

The high-income myth

So abandoning lead, gold and red bouncing balls we turn our investigation to things more mundane. Simple logic leads us to the conclusion that the secret to wealth lies in earning a high income. This seems compellingly logical, but again it is wrong. A reasonably consistent percentage of low-, medium- and high-income earners acquire wealth. And high-income earners have, in general, by far the worst financial habits. They are the least likely to do a budget (too boring, I'm too busy), have very expensive habits (I need a luxury car, house, holidays, etc.) and often carry quite an outrageous level of debt (don't worry, if I get a bonus this year, I'll be able to make the repayments).

What about inherited wealth? Well, yes, a small minority of my clients have inherited their wealth. But a huge majority (in excess of 90%) have made whatever wealth they have in their own lifetime. Maybe this is a good thing because in the great circle of life their children, or, historically it's more likely, the grandchildren will lose the lot, allowing the great-grandchildren the luxury of low expectations and the need to make their own way in life. If you don't believe me, cast your eye over the Australian business magazine *BRW*'s list of the 'Top 100 Wealthy Australians'. Many created their wealth from a very modest start and in some cases from a position of zero assets.

Picking the right investments

We are rapidly eliminating possibilities here. It seems the secret does not generally lie in lead, gold, red bouncing balls, high income or even an inheritance. So maybe it's the uncanny knack to pick the right investment. Without doubt property owners in Sydney, Melbourne (and even Noosa) have done very well. In particular, those who owned a home or negatively-geared property in the 'golden zones' – a circle approximately 20 minutes from the centre of Sydney or Melbourne – have done extremely well. But I've got a terrible feeling that this is an old secret. Sure, an ageing population combined with much smaller families means that property located for the demands of the next century (smaller, closer to new public transport, recreation, restaurants and entertainment should at least keep pace with inflation). But vast areas of Australia which don't have these facilities for the population of the future, or are areas with low job growth will be investment shockers. Just ask the people of Tasmania, South Australia and Canberra what happens to property values in a low-inflation climate when job growth slows or dries up completely.

So property was indeed one of the secrets, but a secret of the past. Sure, own a home and get it paid off, but for most parts of Australia this will not be the wealth secret of the future.

Get rich slow?

Shares? Well yes, since 1900 shares have averaged around 10% per annum based on the all accumulation index and international shares have returned over 17% per annum over the last decade and half, but the dream of picking the 'right' share to generate huge wealth is about as extreme as relying on Lotto! So I support the view that regular investments into shares is a definite get-rich-slow strategy, but it's no investment miracle.

THE SECRET TO WEALTH

Now I've been guilty of dragging out this tale, because after years of trying to find the financial equivalent of turning lead into gold, my very own clients and those who write to me at 'Money' have without doubt given me conclusive proof as to the secret of wealth. Now don't get too excited, because you already know it. For us mere mortals the secret is to spend less than you earn and to invest on a regular basis by paying off your mortgage, topping up your super, buying local and international shares, and if you must buy property, be sure to buy it where people will want to live in the 21st century.

It's that simple . . . and, of course, beware of any scheme that tells you that it can provide you with the key to instant wealth. In my experience, there is no such thing.

index